P9-AQI-024

"In *The Myth of the Lost Cause*, noted Civil War scholar and author Ed Bonekemper lays bare one of the most persistent and pernicious examples of revisionist history in the annals of America. The subject could hardly be more timely, as states' rights advocates deny the root causes of the Civil War, dismiss the ignominious legacy of slavery, and seek to sugarcoat one of the most difficult and tragic interludes in our national history as the romantic last stand of a gallant, noble culture. Important reading for all Americans and for all who wish to understand the Civil War and how its significance was misrepresented in the ensuing century and a half."

—DR. PEYTON R. HELM, president and professor of history, Muhlenberg College

"This is not a book that believers in the Lost Cause will find comforting. It thoroughly, effectively, and convincingly demolishes the long-held mythology—as only Bonekemper can. It is must-reading for all Civil War scholars and buffs—but be prepared to have long-held beliefs put to the test."

—JOHN F. MARSZALEK, professor emeritus of history and executive director, Ulysses S. Grant Presidential Library, Mississippi State University

"Ed Bonekemper has written a thought-provoking, even controversial, look at how ex-Confederates came to frame the Civil War's military history and how that history has shaped the reputations of Robert E. Lee and Ulysses S. Grant. This new work is well worth the read."

—JEFFRY D. WERT, author of *A Glorious Army* and eight other Civil War books

"It is remarkable that even 150 years after the Civil War's guns fell silent so many still believe and are influenced by the ideas of the Lost Cause—the most egregious of which is that slavery had absolutely nothing to do with the conflict. Bonekemper does an exemplary job of breaking down those myths and offering a better understanding of our nation's most tragic moment, what the conflict was really about, and why ultimately the Confederate nation collapsed."

"The myth of the Lost Cause continues to hold sway in many parts of American popular culture, from the belief that secession had little to do with slavery, to the contention that Ulysses S. Grant was a butcher. In this deeply researched book, Edward H. Bonekemper III draws on his wealth of knowledge about the Civil War and his skills as an attorney to provide a point-by-point refutation of the key tenets of the Lost Cause mythology."

"Winners do not always write the history books. For generations, legions of writers and historians perpetuated the myth of the Lost Cause, contending that the Civil War was not a struggle over slavery, but rather the hopeless effort of heroic leaders who defended local, home rule. In this vigorously argued book, Bonekemper refreshingly winnows fact from fiction, tackling the Lost Cause tenet by tenet. Clearly written and thoroughly documented, this welcome addition to the literature issues an indictment against the myth that is at once powerful, important, and timely."

# THE MYTH OF THE LOST CAUSE

# THE **MYTH** OF THE
# **LOST CAUSE**

## WHY THE SOUTH FOUGHT THE CIVIL WAR
## AND WHY THE NORTH WON

### EDWARD H. BONEKEMPER III

REGNERY
HISTORY

Regnery History™ is a trademark of Salem Communications Holding Corporation; Regnery® is a registered trademark of Salem Communications Holding Corporation

Cataloging-in-Publication Data on file with the Library of Congress

ISBN 978-1-62157-454-5

Published in the United States by
Regnery History
An imprint of Regnery Publishing
A Division of Salem Media Group
300 New Jersey Ave NW
Washington, DC 20001
www.RegneryHistory.com

Manufactured in the United States of America

10 9 8 7 6 5 4 3 2 1

Books are available in quantity for promotional or premium use. For information on discounts and terms, please visit our website: www.Regnery.com.

Distributed to the trade by
Perseus Distribution
250 West 57th Street
New York, NY 10107

## DEDICATION

*This book is dedicated to Susan and her Dad.*

# CONTENTS

# PROLOGUE

This is a book I have felt compelled to write for a number of years as I encountered too many people with mistaken impressions about the Civil War. Their viewpoints are an outgrowth of the Myth of the Lost Cause, which some Confederate leaders fostered to justify their causing and losing the Civil War. At the heart of the myth is the contention that the Civil War had nothing to do with slavery. It had everything to do with it.

Other facets of the Myth include the idealization of slavery, the adoration of Robert E. Lee and denigration of Ulysses S. Grant, the insistence that the South had no chance of winning the war, blaming James Longstreet (not Lee) for losing the Battle of Gettysburg, and condemning the North for waging "total war."

This book is intended to examine and refute each of these components of the Myth of the Lost Cause.

# CHAPTER ONE

# THE MYTH OF
# THE LOST CAUSE

W inners write the history of wars. So it is said. Confederate Major
General Patrick Cleburne agreed: "Surrender means that the history of this heroic struggle will be written by the enemy; that our
youth will be trained by Northern school teachers; will learn from
Northern school books their version of the War; will be impressed by all
the influences of history and education to regard our gallant dead as
traitors, and our maimed veterans as fit subjects for derision." It did not
work out quite that way.

   To the contrary, a coterie of disappointed Southerners, aided by
many other "conveniently forgetful" and "purposely misleading"[1]
comrades, spent three decades after the Civil War creating the Myth
of the Lost Cause.[2] They "nurtured a public memory of the Confederacy that placed their wartime sacrifice and shattering defeat in the
best possible light."[3] They formed the Southern Historical Society in
1868–1869 and published fifty-two volumes of papers dealing almost

1

exclusively with Civil War experiences and memories. The society—which some say should have been called the Confederate Historical Society—and its published papers became the chief means of propagating the Myth of the Lost Cause.[4] The Myth is a collection of fictions, lies, and component myths that purport to explain why much of the South seceded from the Union and why the Confederacy lost the Civil War. It is important to understand because that Myth came to dominate the historiography of the Civil War for most of the next 150 years. Alan Nolan commented that "the purpose of the legend was to hide the Southerners' tragic and self-destructive mistake.... The victim of the Lost Cause legend has been *history*, for which the legend has been substituted in the national memory."[5]

As early as 1871, the former slave Frederick Douglass expressed his concern about the revival of secessionism in the South, describing "the spirit of secession" as "a deeply rooted, devoutly cherished sentiment, inseparably identified with the 'lost cause,' which the half measures of the Government towards the traitors has helped to cultivate and strengthen."[6]

By 1880, the Myth had become apparent to Abraham Lincoln's former secretaries and official biographers:

> By the time [John] Nicolay and [John] Hay began their writing in earnest, roughly fifteen years after the collapse of the Confederacy, prominent Southerners had already begun crafting a new narrative—one that would afford their people a modicum of self-respect in the wake of devastating defeat and inspire Northerners to embrace a revisionist history in which everyone was right and no one was wrong. In these efforts, the progenitors of America's reunion romance achieved considerable success.[7]

Their view is supported by Gary Gallagher, who concludes that "because the Confederacy lost so unequivocally, its citizens probably devoted more energy to [creating a "suitable public memory"] than their Northern counterparts." Creators of the Myth "succeeded to a remarkable degree" in "shaping how Americans have assessed and understood the Civil War."[8]

The Myth was developed during Reconstruction as shell-shocked and impoverished Southerners tried to rationalize the institution of slavery and the heroic performance of Confederate leaders and soldiers. As W. J. Cash explains,

> [I]t is probably no exaggeration to say [Southerners] were to become in Reconstruction years the most sentimental people in history.... [The] Southern legend...moved, more powerfully even than it moved toward splendor and magnificence, toward *a sort of ecstatic, teary-eyed vision of the Old South as Happy-Happy Land.* This legend is most perfectly rendered in the tone of Thomas Nelson Page's Billy as he dreams of the old plantation. And of course the sentimentality waxed fat on the theme of the Confederate soldier and the cause for which he had fought and died.... And men (Western men, at least) have everywhere and eternally sentimentalized the causes of their wars and particularly the causes that were lost. All of them have bled for God and Womanhood and Holy Right; *no one has ever died for anything so crass and unbeautiful as the preservation of slavery.* But I doubt that the process has ever elsewhere been carried to the length to which it was carried in the South in this time....[9]

The Myth, writes Gallagher, "addressed the nature of antebellum Southern society and the institution of slavery, the constitutionality of secession, the causes of the Civil War, the characteristics of their wartime society, and the reasons for their defeat."[10] It originated with Generals Jubal Early and William Nelson Pendleton[11] and was promulgated in memoirs, veterans' reunion speeches, ceremonies at Confederate cemeteries and elsewhere, and Confederate-themed art.

In his analysis of myths surrounding Robert E. Lee, Alan Nolan sees a broader problem: "The distortions of fact that mark the Lee tradition are not unique in Civil War history; on the contrary, they are suggestive of a larger and more widespread problem. Fiction—in the form of misinterpretation or the form of outright misrepresentation—is endemic to the study of the history of the Civil War.... Touching on almost all aspects of the struggle, these fictions have ousted the facts and gained wide currency, so that what is treated as history of the Civil War is instead a legend, a folk epic told over and over again."[12]

What exactly are the primary components of the full-blown Myth of the Lost Cause? Broadly speaking, the Myth consists of the following contentions:

1. Slavery was a benevolent institution for all involved but was dying by 1861. There was therefore no need to abolish slavery suddenly, especially by war.
2. States' rights, not slavery, was the cause of secession and the establishment of the Confederacy and thus of the Civil War.
3. The Confederacy had no chance of winning the Civil War and did the best it could with the limited resources it had.
4. Robert E. Lee, who led the Confederates to a near-victory, was one of the greatest generals in history.
5. James Longstreet caused Lee to lose the Battle of Gettysburg and thus the Civil War.
6. Ulysses S. Grant was an incompetent "butcher" who won the war only by brute force and superior numbers.
7. The Union won the war by waging unprecedented and precedent-setting "total war."

Is the Lost Cause still important? David W. Blight observes,

The Lost Cause tradition—as both a version of history and as a racial ideology—is still certainly very much alive in neo-Confederate organizations, on numerous Web sites, among white supremacist groups, in staunch advocates of the Confederate battle flag, and even among some mainstream American politicians. Multitudes

still cannot bring themselves to confront the story of slavery as both
lived experience and the central cause of the Civil War.[13]

Another historian, Gordon Rhea, the great-grandson of a Confederate company commander, urges readers to ignore the myths about the
war and focus on contemporary evidence:

> Our ancestors were unapologetic about why they wanted to
> secede; it is up to us to take them at their word and dispas-
> sionately form our own judgments about their actions. This
> is a discussion we Southerners need to have. The Sesquicen-
> tennial affords us an opportunity to insist on a fact-based
> dialogue about the wellsprings of secession, a dialogue based
> on what the participants said at the time, not what they and
> their apologists said later to justify their actions to posterity.
> We are a diverse people with a wide array of opinions. I am
> very happy that the Confederacy lost the Civil War, and I
> believe that the Confederacy's stated goals and ideology
> should offend the sensibility of anyone living in our times. We
> ought to be able to look history squarely in the face and call
> it for what it was. Only by discarding the myths of the past
> can we move forward to an honest future.[14]

One of the most popular narrative histories of the Civil War continues to perpetuate the Myth of the Lost Cause, laments the historian
Michael Dyson: "Let's be honest: Shelby Foote's view that Lincoln
injected slavery as an issue into the Civil War to gain tactical advantage
over the South is just too close for comfort to the idea that all the bloodshed was more about states' rights than whether we should continue to
shackle black humanity. Foote's Civil War trilogy unabashedly tilted
toward the Confederacy and can be read as a monumental brief in behalf
of the Southern view of the Late Unpleasantness."[15]

Part and parcel of the Myth was a deliberate cover-up of the anti-
black evils of Reconstruction. One ex-Confederate soldier, the popular

Southern writer George Washington Cable, found himself blackballed because of his criticism of the new Jim Crow system and refusal to stick to picturing the supposed romance and harmony of antebellum plantation life.[16]

The primary focus, however, was on sanitizing the history of the Civil War itself. The well-known series of books *Battles and Leaders of the Civil War*, published in the 1880s, was deliberately not titled *Men and Events of the Civil War* because, as one of its editors told his staff, "'Events' might seem as if we were going into, say, the condition & action of the freedmen—the Emancipation Proclamation—& other events not connected with battles." His co-editor agreed to exclude all political issues. As Joshua Zeitz concludes, "Thus sanitized of race, ideology, or partisanship, the result was pleasing to all concerned [Northern and Southern readers]."[17]

In the first two decades of the 1900s, Charles Beard and other Progressive historians contended that the Civil War was an inevitable conflict between the industrial North and the agrarian South, a conflict in which slavery played only an ancillary role. In the following decades, Frank L. Owsley, Avery Craven, and James G. Randall denied the role of slavery in causing the war, blamed the war on radical politicians and editors, and painted an idealized picture of slavery. Randall wrote that slaves "adapted...to bondage with a minimum of resistance, doing cheerfully the manual work of the South." In his view, slave-owners probably erred in being too lenient.[18]

Zeitz asserts that these "revisionist strains in Civil War historiography cannot be understood outside the context of Jim Crow culture and politics"—"a new and elaborate system of enforced racial hierarchy that pervaded nearly every facet of American life until the mid-twentieth century." White Americans enforced their view of racial supremacy by demeaning blacks, imposing segregation, disenfranchising most black voters, and gruesomely lynching thousands of blacks.[19]

All of this provides some insight into why a false remembrance of the Civil War is important today. Alan Nolan ties together the Myth and the false memory:

The Lost Cause version of the war is a caricature, possible, among other reasons, because of the false treatment of slavery and the black people. This false treatment struck at the core of the truth of the war, unhinging cause and effect, depriving the United States of any high purpose, and removing African Americans from their true role as the issue of the war and participants in the war, and characterizing them as historically irrelevant. With slavery exorcised, it appeared that the North had conducted itself within the Union so as to provoke secession and then bloodily defeated the secessionists in war so as to compel them to stay in the Union against their will.[20]

We need to understand the Myth and its deleterious effect on our understanding of historical and social issues that are still important to all Americans.

CHAPTER TWO

# WHAT WAS THE NATURE OF SLAVERY IN 1861 AND WAS IT A DYING INSTITUTION?

## THE MYTH

By 1860 Southerners had convinced themselves that slavery, far from being an evil practice, benefitted both master and slave. This position was a far cry from the one that prevailed in the days of the American Revolution and its immediate aftermath, when abolition and manumission enjoyed popularity and resulted in the gradual abolishment of slavery in many Northern states. The myth holds that slavery was Bible-sanctioned, benevolent, and a boon to all involved in it.

This myth began long before the Civil War. Michael C. C. Adams observes, "even before the abolitionist attack from the North, Southerners began the defense of slavery as a social system that provided unique benefits, both for the slaves whom it placed under the fatherly care of a superior race and for the master who was given the freedom from toil necessary to the creation of a superior culture."[1]

When abolitionists, especially after 1830, began seriously attacking slavery, Southerners tried even harder to justify the institution. In the 1830s, "[p]rominent southern politicians, clergymen, and academics presented a more positive view of slavery, as something not only necessary but also good for African Americans and for the entire society." Justifications for it were found in the Bible and scientific studies. Masters were supposedly benevolent patriarchs.[2] In 1853, the Georgian Robert Toombs explained that "whenever the two races co-exist a state of slavery is best for [the African] and society. And under it in our country he is in a better condition than he has ever attained in any other age and country, either in bondage or freedom."[3]

As the Civil War drew to a close, the myth continued and seems to have been embellished. In 1865, an Atlanta editor wrote that slaves' position was "an enviable one" and contended that "they constitute a privileged class in the community." He mused, "how happy we should be were we the slave of some good and provident owner" because "simple daily toil would fill the measure of duty, and comfortable food and clothing would be the assured reward."[4]

Edward A. Pollard of Richmond, an editor and author, wrote this analysis in 1866: "The occasion of that conflict was what the Yankees called—by one of their convenient libels in political nomenclature—slavery; but what was in fact nothing more than a system of Negro servitude in the South…one of the mildest and most beneficent systems of servitude in the world."[5] Interestingly, in his haste to disclaim the term "slavery," Pollard conceded that it was the "occasion of that conflict"—contrary to the Myth's tenet that slavery was not the cause of the war.

A prominent Southern journalist, J. D. B. DeBow, writing in 1867, explained the alleged loyalty and contentment of blacks during the war. They had, he said, "adhered *in general* with great fidelity to the cause of their masters during the struggle.… They followed their masters to the field without desertion, and were proud of the service. They worked cheerfully upon the fortifications and earth-works in sight of the enemy, and without thought of desertion. They…maintained obedience, docility and respect." All of this supposed loyalty was "evidence of the mild, paternal and patriarchal nature of the institution of slavery as it existed at the South."[6] DeBow overlooked the nine hundred "contrabands" who fled in three months in mid-1861 to General Benjamin Butler's Union lines at Fort Monroe, Virginia,[7] the two hundred thousand blacks (about three quarters being defecting ex-slaves)[8] who served in the Union military, and the hundreds of thousands of slaves who fled to Union lines as Union armies moved deeper and deeper into the Confederacy.[9]

The mass exodus of slaves to Union lines exposed the myth of loyalty and contentment. As early as summer 1862, a Natchez provost marshal reported to Mississippi's governor, "There is a great disposition among the negroes to be insubordinate, and to run away to the federals. Within the last 12 months we have had to hang some 40 for plotting an insurrection, and there has been about that number put in irons." That fall, after the Battle of Corinth (Mississippi), Union chaplain John Eaton reported that as cotton planters fled, their slaves "flocked in vast numbers—an army in themselves—to the camps of the Yankees."[10]

Before, during, and after the war, promoters of the Myth used words like "happy," "content," "faithful," "amiable," and "cheerful" to describe slaves' attitudes about their condition. Opposing the Emancipation Proclamation, Jefferson Davis called the slaves "peaceful and contented laborers."[11]

Twenty years after war began, Davis continued to claim that slavery involved close relationships between masters and slaves: "[Slaves] were trained in the gentle arts of peace and order and civilization; they increased from a few unprofitable savages to millions of efficient Christian laborers. Their servile instincts rendered them *contented* with their lot.... Their strong local and personal attachment secured faithful service to those to whom their service or labor was due. A *strong mutual affection* was the natural result of this lifelong relation.... Never was there *happier dependence* of labor and capital on each other."[12] Davis was part of a Southern tradition: "It was the uniform contention of Southern spokesmen—the press, the clergy, and the politicians—that the slaves liked their status."[13]

Davis and his brother Joseph must have been shocked, therefore, when their families' slaves refused to accompany Joseph when he fled home, fleeing instead into the countryside. Perhaps the president himself was surprised when his personal servant and his wife's maid, both slaves, escaped from the executive mansion in Richmond in January 1864 and when, later that month, another slave tried to burn the mansion.[14]

W. J. Cash, in his brilliant *The Mind of the South*, noted that the vast majority of early abolition societies were Southern and that evangelical religions first denounced slavery before their Southern congregations changed their minds. He added, "And, worst of all, there was the fact that the South itself definitely shared in these moral notions—in its secret heart always carried a powerful and uneasy sense of the essential rightness of the nineteenth century's position on slavery.... The Old South...was a society beset by the specters of defeat, of shame, of guilt...[and] a large part—in a way, the very largest part—of its history from the day that [William Lloyd] Garrison began to thunder in Boston is the history of its efforts to [justify itself] and characteristically by means of romantic fictions."[15]

Ultimately, however, this myth was not confined to the South. Alan Nolan explains: "This revisionism in regard to the role of slavery and the character of the slaves could have remained an entirely Southern theme. The revision could not become part of the Civil War legend without Northern acceptance, and the North, including its academic historians, did accept the South's rewriting of the record. The North let the South substitute a war for liberty for the war for slavery, and the North ceased to think of slaves and freedmen as serious persons. Exported to the North, the happy darky stereotype was widely embraced, prevailing well into the twentieth century and pervading the popular imagination from novels and the press to Walt Disney movies."[16]

The myth concludes that, whatever the merits of slavery, the Civil War was unnecessary to end it because the institution was economically doomed and would have died a natural death within a reasonable time. The argument is essentially that the war was unnecessary or could not have been about slavery because slavery was on the cusp of extinction without a war.

One might ask how slavery could have been on the verge of extinction if it was of such great benefit to whites and blacks alike. How could it have been so successful yet so likely to have been terminated within a few years? I will ignore the apparent inconsistency of those two contentions and focus on each separately.

## REALITY OF THE INSTITUTION

Margaret Mitchell captured the "mint julep school" of antebellum Southern history—happy, indolent, and ignorant slaves protected by their kind and benevolent masters—in her novel *Gone with the Wind*, published in 1936, and the epic film version of 1939 engraved it on the popular imagination. This picture was first painted by antebellum Southerners: "Seeing the tide of history turning against them, Southerners went on the offensive. Their 'peculiar institution' morphed from a 'necessary evil' to a 'positive good,' a 'practical and moral necessity,' and the 'will of Almighty God.'"[17] The historian U. B. Phillips, a Georgian, promoted this benign view of slavery in the early twentieth century. "His portrayal of blacks as passive, inferior people, whose African origins made them uncivilized, seemed to provide historical evidence for the theories of racial inferiority that supported racial segregation. Drawing evidence exclusively from plantation records, letters, southern newspapers, and other sources reflecting the slaveholder's point of view, Phillips depicted slave masters who provided for the welfare of their slaves and contended that true affection existed between slave and master." Phillips's interpretation had a lasting effect and influenced Mitchell's novel.[18]

A different and likely more accurate view of slavery emerged in 1956 with Kenneth Stampp's *The Peculiar Institution: Slavery in the Ante-Bellum South*. Stampp used many of the same sources as Phillips but "relied more heavily on diaries, journals, newspaper runaway-slave ads, and even a few slave narratives."[19] Stampp found that non-slaveholding whites supported slavery as "a means of controlling the social and economic competition of Negroes, concrete evidence of membership in a superior caste, a chance perhaps to rise into the planter class."[20]

James and Lois Horton offer a matter-of-fact depiction of Revolution-
ary-era slavery:

> Planters required both men and women to engage in hard
> physical labor, and they worked in marshy rice fields, hot and
> humid tobacco fields, dusty wheat fields, and dangerous back-
> breaking lumbering camps. Workers on rice plantations spent
> days standing in the water of the rice field, prey to insects and
> disease, with a minimal diet to sustain them. Children were
> expected to work as soon as they were deemed old enough to
> be useful. Pregnant women worked, and after childbirth
> women returned to the fields quickly, with little time lost. All
> worked under the compulsion of the overseer's or slave driv-
> er's lash, and they were liable to be lashed for working too
> slowly.... [W]omen working in the owner's house were espe-
> cially vulnerable to sexual exploitation.[21]

Frederick Law Olmsted was dismayed by what he saw in Mississippi:
"[T]he stupid, plodding, machine-like manner in which they labor is
painful to witness. This was especially true with the hoe-gangs. One of
them numbered nearly two hundred hands...moving across the field in
parallel lines, with a considerable degree of precision. I repeatedly rode
through the lines at a canter, without producing the smallest change or
interruption in the dogged action of the laborers, or causing one of them,
so far as I could see, to lift an eye from the ground.... I think it told a
more painful story than any I have ever heard, of the cruelty of slavery."[22]

During harvesting season on sugar plantations, slaves worked six-
teen-to-eighteen-hour days, seven days a week. Sunstroke killed many
slaves overworked on all types of plantations.[23] Their harsh working
conditions, minimal food and clothing; abominable housing, lack of
freedom to move about, and vulnerability to sale and family dispersion
led many slaves, not surprisingly, to become what Stampp called "troublesome property." They tried to sabotage production, challenge overseers, fight back when provoked, flee for their freedom, or even (rarely)

kill their overseers or plan or participate in slave revolts.[24] Owners, aware that blacks were not natural-born slaves, tried to control them by a series of steps: "establish and maintain strict discipline," "implant a conscious-ness of personal inferiority," "awe them with a sense of the master's power," and persuade them to support the owner's enterprise and stan-dard of conduct."[25]

In a generally successful effort to maintain discipline among the supposedly satisfied slaves, each slave state had a slave code. Because the states copied each other's codes, their provisions were generally uniform throughout the South. Among many other restrictions, they required slaves to submit to masters and respect all whites, forbade them to travel without passes, limited their preaching and religious services, forbade anyone from teaching them to read or write, limited their independent economic activities, and forbade them to possess firearms or liquor.[26]

Slave-owners' ultimate weapon was virtually unlimited force. In Holly Springs, Mississippi, one planter punished his slaves by slashing the soles of their feet with a Bowie knife. In that state's Rankin County, Colonel Easterling threw a woman over a barrel and beat her, beat her "husband" to a pulp when he visited from another plantation, and killed a man by hitching him to a plow and "plowin [sic] him till one day he died." In nearby Jones County, Bryant Craft beat his slave Jessie so severely that his shirt was embedded in his back and left him to die; when a neighbor nursed Jessie back to health and brought him back to recon-cile with the master, a furious Craft killed the slave on the spot and told the "interfering" neighbor, "Let that be an example to you."[27]

W. J. Cash pointed out that slavery rested on force: the lash, chains and shackles, hounds and pistols to chase runaways, and mutilations and brandings (reflected in runaway slave advertisements). It was brutalizing to white men—releasing sadism and cruelty in masters and breeding in the "common whites" a savage hate for blacks in response to the "white trash" epithets they endured.[28]

Southern whites remained constantly in fear of revolts by their "happy and contented" slaves. "The panic of the slaveholders at the slightest hint of slave insurrection revealed what lay beneath their endless self-congratulation over the supposed docility, contentment, and loyalty of their slaves."[29] One of the few actual revolts was Nat Turner's 1831 rebellion in Southampton County, Virginia. He and his band of sixty insurgents roamed the countryside killing most whites they encountered—a total of sixty-one. In response, there was a frenzy of whites' killing blacks on sight—most of them uninvolved in the uprising. Whites from Richmond rode through the county killing all blacks they saw—one hundred and twenty in one day. Innocent slaves were "tortured, burned to death, shot or otherwise horribly murdered." Turner himself was hanged and his body skinned and dissected to create souvenirs of the event. Revenge spread to other states. From then until the Civil War, Southern whites did all they could to prevent similar uprisings by tightening legal restrictions on slaves and free blacks.[30] The massacre of blacks following this revolt discouraged further insurrections.[31]

The more one studies antebellum slavery, the clearer it becomes that "[h]olding millions of African people in bondage required a virtual police state, and southern society came to tolerate, and even honor, a military social climate that accepted violence as a necessity."[32] Southern slave patrols and militias provided the South with a head start on military preparation for the Civil War.

Two justice systems developed side by side in the South: a formal one and an extralegal system of plantation justice. Whips and switches were used on the spot in the Upper South while more formal weekly "settlements" were used in the Lower South. All of a plantation's slaves, "for their moral improvement," were gathered to watch their peers whipped while hung by the thumbs, have an ear nailed to a post before severing, or be "tomcatted" (having a tomcat dragged across their bare backs and thighs).[33] Those punishments were for minor offenses.

The most extreme punishments (all without benefit of judge, jury, or trial) were reserved for alleged sex-related offenses. A North Carolina slave who boasted that he preferred white women was castrated. Another there was burned alive for suspected rape. Such burnings occurred throughout the South; two thousand slaves were compelled to attend one in Mississippi, and another in Alabama was justified by an editor as consistent with "the law of self-protection.... The whole subject was disposed of with the coolest deliberation and with regard only to interest of the public."[34] In South Carolina two slaves suspected of kidnapping and rape were stripped, tied to forked poles, had their mouths bound, and were left to be eaten by crows and buzzards. The French traveler Hector St. John Crèvecoeur discovered a similar scene: a slave accused of slaying a white overseer was suspended in a cage to be devoured by birds and insects. The Frenchman's hosts explained that "the laws of self-preservation rendered such executions necessary."[35]

The reality was that slavery often involved beating, killing, and raping slaves, as well as breaking up slave families for economic or disciplinary reasons. Slave marriages were not recognized under state laws. If slaves were so happy, why do we see photographs of them with backs scarred from beatings? Owners' and overseers' beatings, rapes, and even murders of slaves rarely, if ever, resulted in legal prosecution, let alone conviction or meaningful punishment.

The best evidence of the frequency of masters' raping their female slaves was the widespread appearance of "mulattoes" or light-skinned blacks throughout the South—many of them with facial and physical characteristics similar to those of their masters. The masters' wives had to ignore the mixed-race children and dared not confront their husbands about the obvious sexual misconduct.[36] Masters seemed to compensate for their sexual relations with slaves by elevating their wives onto a high pedestal honoring Pure Southern Womanhood.

This elevation became a component of the myth. "[E]ven more brave and constant" than Southern soldiers, wrote Thomas Nelson Page, "were the women who stayed at home. Gentle and simple, they gave their husbands, their brothers and their sons to the cause of the South, sorrowing chiefly that they themselves were too feeble to stand at their side. Hungering in body and heart they bore with more than a soldier's courage, more than a soldier's hardship, and to the last, undaunted and dauntless, gave them a new courage as with tear-dimmed eyes they sustained them in the darkest hours of their despondency and defeat."[37]

Page's tribute was a perfect example of what W. J. Cash described as the cover-up for master-slave sexual relations:

> And the only really satisfactory escape here...would be fiction. On the one hand, the convention must be set up that the thing simply did not exist, and enforced under penalty of being shot; and on the other, the [white] woman must be compensated, the revolting suspicion in the male that he might be slipping into bestiality got rid of, by glorifying her; the Yankee must be answered by proclaiming from the housetops that Southern Virtue, so far from being inferior, was superior, not alone to the North's but to any on earth, and adducing Southern Womanhood in proof.[38]

The fugitive slave Harriet Jacobs reported that she was constantly sexually threatened by her master and added that white men preyed on female slaves so often that "if God has bestowed beauty upon her, it will prove her greatest curse."[39] The ex-slave Henry Bibb observed the sexual activities of slave-owners: "I have long thought from what has fallen under my own observation while a slave, that the strongest reason why southerners stick with such tenacity to their 'peculiar institution,' is because licentious white men could not carry out their wicked purposes among the defenceless colored population as they now do, without being exposed and punished by law, if slavery was abolished. Female virtue could not be trampled under foot with impunity, and marriage among the people of color kept in utter obscurity."[40]

Glorification of Southern women often took the form of harsh penalties for blacks who raped, tried to rape, or even ogled white women. The possibility of such actions by blacks became a favorite argument of those opposing emancipation, including the proposals to arm and free slaves to prevent loss of the Civil War. Southern critics contended that emancipation meant equality and that blacks with equality "would soon aspire to be the husbands of our daughters and sisters." A Virginian was more vivid: "The [black] conscript must be sometimes furloughed and I forbear to depict the state of things which will exist when the furloughed conscripts return to the home" and encounter young white women whose father is still in camp.[41]

Cash provides an example of the heights which the worship of Southern womanhood could reach: "'Woman!!! The center and circumference, diameter and periphery, sine, tangent and secant of all our affections!' Such was the toast which brought twenty great cheers from the audience at the celebration of Georgia's one-hundredth anniversary in the 1830's."[42]

Plantation and slave-trader records are replete with instances of family separations. Children were separated from their parents and grandparents, spouses were separated from each other, and numerous other relatives were separated from their kin. To facilitate perhaps a million of these heartless and usually economically motivated transactions, Southerners did not recognize slave "marriages" or encourage black family relationships. Slaves generally had no last names.

Eugene Genovese describes the psychological hardships imposed on slaves by the forced separation of family members: "But the pain remained, and the slaveholders knew as much. Is it possible that no slaveholder noticed the grief of the woman who [said] that she had had six children, three of whom had died and three of whom had been sold: 'When they took from me the last little girl, oh, I believed I never should have got over it! It almost broke my heart.' Could any white southerner pretend not to know from direct observation the meaning of Sojourner Truth's statement: 'I have borne thirteen chillun and seen em' mos' all sold off into slavery, and when I cried out with a mother's grief, none but Jesus heard.'...A black woman...recalled her first husband's being sold away from her: 'White folks got a heap to answer for the way they've done to colored folks! So much they won't ever pray it away.'"[43]

Southerners' violent opposition to criticism of slavery may have betrayed their fear that the true nature of the institution would be revealed. Cash stated that Southerners questioning the institution were hanged, tarred, horsewhipped, or assaulted in other ways. Newspaper editors were a favorite target; five editors of the *Vicksburg Journal* were killed in thirteen years.[44]

## SLAVERY'S PROSPECTS IN 1861

Some advocates of the Lost Cause have contended that Southerners, aware that slavery's disappearance was inevitable, would not have fought a war to save the dying institution. Yet Southern lawmakers and citizens had gone to great lengths to protect slavery from any criticism, denying freedom of speech, freedom of the press, freedom of the mails, and, in Virginia at least, the right to say that owners had no property rights in their slaves.[45] Why protect a dying institution?

Allan Nevins examined the late antebellum period and concluded, "The South, as a whole, in 1846–61 was not moving toward emancipation but away from it. It was not relaxing the laws which guarded the system, but reinforcing them. It was not ameliorating slavery, but making it harsher and more implacable. The South was further from a just solution of the slavery problem in 1830 than it had been in 1789. It was further from tenable solution in 1860 than it had been in 1830."[46]

There is much evidence that slavery was strong and thriving on the eve of the Civil War. James and Lois Horton conclude that "by the late 1850s, the South seemed stronger than ever. Its economic power had become so great that it could not be ignored." Its cotton exports were more valuable than all other U.S. exports combined. "The worth of slaves increased correspondingly, so that on the eve of the Civil War it was greater than the total dollar value of all the nation's banks, railroads, and manufacturing."[47]

Edward Ayers observes, "White Southerners hardly lashed out in desperation over a dying institution. If anything, they were too confident in the future of slavery, too certain that the nation's economy depended on the vast profits of the cotton and other goods produced by slavery, too sure that the industrialized world would stumble and fall without the bounty produced by the slave people of the South."[48] In fact, there was great interest in annexing the slavery-dominated island of Cuba.[49]

In 1860 Richmond had dozens of slave traders, about six major slave auction houses, and at least nineteen slave auctioneers. One auction house alone had more than $1,773,000 in sales in 1858. At that time, according to Charles Dew, the rental of slaves from their owners was "a very, very important part of the Virginia economy. Richmond's industry really depend[ed] on it. The tobacco factories hire[d] hundreds of slaves. Tredegar [Iron Works] hire[d] slaves every year."[50] Many Southerners envisioned the large-scale use of slaves in factories that could be built or expanded. "They believed that industrialization and slavery could proceed hand in hand."[51]

Slaves were so valuable that there was even talk about changing or overriding the 1807 congressional ban on the international slave trade. South Carolina's 1860–61 commissioner to Florida, Leonidas W. Spratt, was an advocate of reopening that trade. A Charleston lawyer, he defended the crew of the brig *Echo*, an American slaving vessel brought into Charleston harbor in 1858 after its capture off Cuba by the U.S. Navy, and as the editor of the *Charleston Southern Standard* after 1852 he argued in favor of resuming the importation of slaves from Africa.[52]

From 1853 to 1863, Britain's consul in Charleston, Robert Bunch, reported to his superiors on a continuing, high-level interest among influential South Carolinians in reviving the slave trade to the United States. In 1856, Governor James Hopkins Adams told the legislature, "To maintain our present position [of cotton dominance], we must have cheap labor also. This can be obtained in but one way—by re-opening the African slave trade." In March 1857, Bunch secretly wrote that increasing slave prices and cotton production would force the South to reopen the African slave trade: "Such is the evil which is rapidly developing." In fact, there were instances of slave importations with minimal, if any, legal repercussions. In 1861, Bunch encouraged the new Confederate government to abolish the slave trade. He and the British minister to the United States, Richard Lyons, advised London that the Confederate Constitution's ban on the slave trade was primarily to encourage Virginia and Maryland to secede and would not preclude African imports if economically beneficial. In late 1862, Confederate officials were reluctant to assure the British that the African slave trade would not be revived.[53] This continuing interest in reviving the slave trade suggested that slavery was not going away anytime soon.

The value of slaves to the Southern economy was reflected in the warning by the South Carolina planter John Townsend that Lincoln's election would mean "the annihilation and end of all Negro labor (agricultural especially) over the whole South. It means a loss to the planters of the South of, at least, FOUR BILLION dollars, by having this labor taken from them; and a loss, in addition, of FIVE BILLION dollars more, in lands, mills, machinery, and other great interests, which will be rendered valueless by the want of slave labor to cultivate the lands, and the loss of the crops which give to those interests life and prosperity."[54]

A sampling of antebellum slave prices reveals the economic health of slavery. The following table shows the estimated average prices of prime eighteen-to-twenty-year-old male and female field hands in Georgia between 1828 and 1860:

| Year | Price |
|------|-------|
| 1828 | $700 |
| 1835 | $900 |
| 1837 | $1,300 |
| 1839 | $1,000 |
| 1840 | $700 |
| 1844 | $600 |
| 1848 | $900 |
| 1851 | $1,050 |
| 1853 | $1,200 |
| 1859 | $1,650 |
| 1860 | $1,800[55] |

Other statistics shed light on the value of slaves throughout the South in 1859 and 1860. The following are the 1859–1860 price ranges for male and female slaves between the ages of eight and twenty-one in the states indicated:

| | |
|------|-------|
| Virginia | $1,275 to $1,425 |
| South Carolina | $1,283 to $1,325 |

| | |
|---|---|
| Georgia | $1,250 to $1,900 |
| Alabama | $1,193 to $1,635 |
| Mississippi | $1,450 to $1,625 |
| Texas | $1,403 to $2,015[56] |

Both sets of numbers become more meaningful when placed in the context of even longer-term slave values. The following are the New Orleans prices of prime field hands at five-year intervals throughout the nineteenth century:

| Year | Price |
|---|---|
| 1805 | $600 |
| 1810 | $900 |
| 1815 | $765 |
| 1820 | $970 |
| 1825 | $800 |
| 1830 | $810 |
| 1835 | $1,150 |
| 1840 | $1,020 |
| 1845 | $700 |
| 1850 | $1,100 |
| 1855 | $1,350 |
| 1860 | $1,800[57] |

All of these prices would have been affected by a wide variety of factors, including cotton and tobacco prices, financial crises, depressions, demand for slaves, the opening of lands in the old Southwest for cultivation, and general economic prosperity.[58] Nevertheless, the long-term trend of slave values seems to indicate a thriving institution.[59]

Charles Sydnor's study of slavery in Mississippi reveals that the value in 1860 of the state's 436,691 slaves, at eight hundred dollars each, was over $349 million, while the total cash value of its farmland, farming implements and livestock was only about $241 million.[60] Well-to-do Mississippians' financial stake in slavery as of 1860 is obvious.

More money could be made on female than male slaves because the children of female slaves became the property of the mothers' owners. This aspect of slavery was not publicized, however, because "[s]lave-breeding and slave-trading were not generally considered to be high or noble types of activity for a southern gentleman."[61]

In 1860, slaves were still a reasonable capital investment. In his extensive economic study of slavery, Harold Woodman concludes:

> [S]lavery was apparently about as remunerative as alternative employments to which slave capital might have been put.... This general sharing in the prosperity was more or less guaranteed, moreover, if proper market mechanisms existed so that slaves could be bred and reared on the poorest of land and then be sold to those owning the best. Slavery in the immediate ante bellum years was, therefore, an economically viable institution in virtually all areas of the South as long as slaves could be expeditiously and economically transferred from one sector to another.[62]

That qualification—regarding the economic importance of slaves' mobility—sheds light on Southerners' concerns about Republican opposition to slavery's expansion into U.S. territories. "With the natural increase in slave population," writes Sydnor, "the price must have declined unless a market for the surplus could be found.... [W]hen Texas and the rest of the new Southwest were supplied, slave prices would fall unless more territory suited to slave labor could be discovered. As there was little probability of finding this within the Union, economics demanded that the slave-owner be an expansionist, for without a market slave prices must soon have declined."[63]

Woodman's studies convinced him, however, that the slave market had room to grow within the existing slave states:

> The belief, however, that in 1860 slavery in the South was on the point of being "strangled for lack of room to expand"

is a wholly mistaken interpretation of actual conditions. The plantation system was not seriously limited by a scarcity of land. It had utilized only a small fraction of the available land area. The most fertile and easily accessible soils may have been occupied, but there was an extensive area remaining, a considerable part of which has been brought into cultivation since 1860. Before the Civil War railways were rapidly opening up new fertile areas to plantation agriculture. Far from being a decrepit institution, the economic motives for the continuance of slavery from the standpoint of the employer were never so strong as in the years just preceding the Civil War.[64]

A recent study of land usage, slavery, and other agricultural phenomena in the United States and Britain concludes that in fourteen slave states (all but small Delaware) in 1860 there were a total of 73.769 million developed acres and 170.644 million undeveloped acres on 755,209 farms.[65] The scope of undeveloped land on existing farms alone indicates that there was, as Woodman contends, room for expansion of slavery in the existing slave states. Actual experience confirms that analysis; the "land devoted to cotton nearly doubled between 1860 and 1890; it more than doubled between 1890 and 1925."[66]

U. B. Phillips, as Woodman explains, concluded that cotton prices had dropped in price, slavery had become unprofitable just prior to the Civil War, and that it was a dying institution. Phillips argued that speculation had raised slave prices to the point of unprofitability except in the most favorable circumstances. Woodman responds that slave prices, like cotton prices, varied over time and the cost of producing cotton had diminished considerably between 1794 and 1860. He concludes, "There is no apparent reason why high market values of slaves should be a permanent cause for unprofitable plantation economy.... [T]he active demand which tended to enhance the prices of slaves came from those planters who were making large profits and who sought to expand their slaveholdings on the basis of these profits." And, therefore:

It was the fact that slavery tended to be profitable in new regions, while unprofitable in regions in the wake of expansion, that resulted so generally in the mistaken conclusions that slavery can thrive only on the basis of geographical expansion and a migratory economy, that slavery is adapted only to extensive agriculture, that it inevitably results in soil exhaustion, and that it cannot be profitable in general farming; none of which conclusions...appears to be justified in the absolute sense in which it has been asserted.... If the prices of all Southern products had fallen so low that it was impossible in any industry or region to earn more than a few dollars a year as the net return for slave labor, it would still have been advantageous to employ it.[67]

Kenneth Stampp concurred in this analysis. After noting that slave hiring rates and sales prices in the 1850s had a solid economic foundation, he concluded that "the slave was earning for his owner a substantial, though varying, surplus above the cost of maintenance. For this reason, the critics of slavery who urged that the institution was an economic burden to the master were using the weakest weapon in their arsenal. There was no evidence in 1860 that bondage was a 'decrepit institution tottering toward a decline'—and, indeed, if the slave-holder's economic self-interest alone were to be consulted, the institution should have been preserved."[68]

Stampp's view is reinforced by Fogel and Engerman in a discussion they entitle "The Sanguinity of the Slaveholding Class on Economic Prospects." They use an index of sanguinity that compares the short-term value of slaves (based on current annual hire rates) with the long-term value of slaves (based on purchase prices). After examining the 1830–1860 data, they conclude that "[d]uring the decade of the fifties sanguinity was increasing quite rapidly, accounting for 40 percent of the rise in slave prices in the Old South and 75 percent of the rise in the New South. Slaveholders not only expected their social order to endure but foresaw an era of prosperity."[69]

The twentieth-century historian Charles W. Ramsdell made a different argument for the alleged impending doom of slavery. He contended that slave owners were being driven to an unhealthy overproduction of cotton that would soon lead to slavery's demise because of the inevitable decline in the price of cotton. Ramsdell claimed that "those who wished [slavery] destroyed had only to wait a little while—perhaps a generation, probably less." Robert William Fogel and Stanley L. Engerman contest that analysis by arguing that cotton production had become more efficient, that worldwide demand for it had increased, and that Southern planters actually had responded too slowly in increasing their 1850s cotton production in an effort to meet demands. They conclude, "the tale about the uncommercial planter who was gripped by an irresistible tendency to the overproduction of cotton is sheer fantasy."[70]

Although slavery was therefore proving to be of continuing economic benefit to those who engaged in it, it probably had a deleterious long-term effect on the Southern economy as a whole. Woodman cites the antislavery Kentucky politician Cassius Clay's analysis that because slaves could not participate as buyers of products in the marketplace, "A home market cannot exist in a slave state." Woodman himself then concludes, "Plantation slavery, then, so limited the purchasing power of the South that it could not sustain much industry.... Whatever other factors need to be considered in a complete analysis, the low level of demand in this plantation-based slave society was sufficient to retard the economic development of the South."[71] Despite slavery's harmful effects on the South generally, no change to it was imminent because gerrymandering of state legislative districts, property requirements for voting, and the traditional political power structure of the South kept crucial political and governmental decision-making in the hands of the slaveholding elite, who individually were reaping large financial benefits from the practice. The abolition of slavery or meaningful reform was therefore unlikely. In addition, the racial underpinning of slavery ensured its widespread support among whites who were not slave-owners. In summary, "There is simply no evidence tending to show that the South would have voluntarily abandoned slavery."[72]

## RACIAL UNDERPINNING OF SLAVERY

Aside from the huge economic value of black slaves, their subservience was critical to Southern culture. As the South Carolina planter and state senator John Townsend acknowledged in late 1864, "The color of the white man is now, in the South, a title of nobility in his relations as to the negro. He may be poor, it is true; but there is no point upon which he is so justly proud and sensitive as his privilege of caste; and there is nothing which he would resent with more fierce indignation than the attempt of the Abolitionist to emancipate the slaves and elevate the Negros [sic] to an equality with himself and his family."[73]

This fear of Negro equality had a long history. After the Revolution, Virginians, inspired by some Founding Fathers, considered some emancipation and colonization proposals. Winthrop Jordan concludes these had no realistic chance for adoption. They raised issues of social equality among blacks and whites, and there was pervasive and profound "thought and feeling about social intermixture." "As time went on in the nineteenth century," writes Jordan, "Virginians, realizing that colonization was utterly impractical and hating themselves as slaveowners, turned more and more to the self-solacing thought that realities of 'prejudice' were inevitable, innate and right. Indeed they came to think that their opinions about Negroes were not prejudices at all but merely objective assessments of the realities of Negro inferiority." Prospects for ending slavery in Virginia were increasingly bleak.[74]

Racism of this sort would have kept the institution of slavery alive and well for a long time if not for the Civil War. It is clear, therefore, that the "benefits" of slavery extended far beyond the slave-owning minority of white Southerners. Describing antebellum Southern society, Dew says, "The average Southern farmer is a yeoman who owns his own land and works it with the help of his family; he might own a slave. But [the yeoman and the 25 percent of whites who were slave-owners] have something in common, which is white skin. If you are white in the antebellum South, there is a floor below which you cannot go. You have a whole population of four million people whom you consider, and your society considers, inferior to you. You don't have to be actively involved in the system to derive at least the psychological benefits of the system."[75]

Confirmation of this situation was provided in Hinton Rowan Helper's *The Impending Crisis of the South*, a critical analysis of slavery written on the cusp of the Civil War. Helper explained:

> Every white man who is under the necessity of earning his bread, by the sweat of his brow, or by manual labor, in any capacity, no matter how unassuming in deportment, or exemplary in morals, is treated as if he was a loathsome beast, and shunned with the utmost disdain. His soul may be the very seat of honor and integrity, yet without slaves—himself a slave—he is accounted as nobody.... It is expected that the stupid and sequacious masses, the white victims of slavery, will believe, and as a general thing, they do believe, whatever the slaveholders tell them; and thus it is that they are cajoled into the notion that they are the freest, happiest and most intelligent people in the world....[76]

In *The Mind of the South*, W. J. Cash provided an even more forthright analysis of the role of non-slaveholding whites ("common whites") in the institution of slavery: "And in this loyalty [to slavery] the common white participated as fully as any other Southerner. If he had no worthwhile interest at stake in slavery, if his real interest ran the other way about, he did nevertheless have that, to him, dear treasure of his superiority as a white man, which had been conferred on him by slavery; and so was as determined to keep the black man in chains, saw in the offensive of the Yankee [abolitionism] as great a danger to himself, as the angriest planter."[77]

Southern repression of black economic, civil, voting, and other rights during the hundred years following the Civil War further demonstrated the lack of motivation to terminate the slavery or subordination of African Americans.

In summary, antebellum slavery in America was not a benevolent institution benefitting whites and blacks alike. It benefitted whites economically and socially and did the reverse for African Americans. Only by using as much force as was necessary did whites compel blacks to remain in a sub-human condition. The profits slavery provided to white slave-owners and the social superiority it provided to non-slaveholding whites gave the peculiar institution a firm hold on the South. One of the cruelest ramifications of slavery was its destruction of the black family unit; slaves could not legally marry, and their families were subject to permanent dissolution at the whim of the slave-owner or his estate.

An institution that was so profitable and accounted for such a huge portion of Southern wealth was unlikely to disappear without some outside compulsion. There was room for slavery to expand in Texas and in many bypassed sections of the South, and slavery would have provided a ready workforce in the industries that the South needed to develop. As the following chapter demonstrates, Southern opposition to the possible end of slavery was so violent that voluntary abolition was simply unforeseeable.

CHAPTER THREE

# WAS SLAVERY THE PRIMARY CAUSE OF SECESSION AND THE CIVIL WAR?

## THE MYTH

At the heart of the Myth of the Lost Cause is the insistence that secession, the Confederacy, and the Civil War were all about states' rights, not slavery.[1] This myth began almost as soon as the war ended. The newspaperman-turned-historian Edward A. Pollard in his immediate postwar histories described slavery as "an inferior object of the contest." His flimsy evidence included the rebels' supposed program of "Negro enlistments and consequent emancipation," which is discussed in detail below.[2] Robert E. Lee disavowed slavery's role in the war: "So far from engaging in a war to perpetuate slavery, I am rejoiced that slavery is abolished."[3]

More significantly, Confederate President Jefferson Davis explained in his postwar memoirs, "The truth remains intact and incontrovertible, that the existence of African servitude was in no wise the cause of the conflict, but only an incident." He argued that North-South hostility was "not the consequence of any difference on the abstract question of slavery.... It would have manifested itself just as certainly if slavery had existed in all the states, or if there had not been a negro in America."[4]

His vice president, Alexander Stephens, claimed after the war that the strife was between federalism and centralism: "Slavery, so called, was but *the question* on which these antagonistic principles...were finally brought into actual and active collision with each other on the field of battle." He also asserted that the war "was not a contest between the advocates or opponents of that Particular Institution, but a contest...between the supporters of a strictly Federative Government...and a thoroughly national one...."[5]

In the first three postwar decades, Pollard, Davis, Stephens, Jubal Early, William Nelson Pendleton, the Reverend J. William Jones, and others made and developed the proposition that slavery was not the cause for secession or the formation of the Confederacy. Their position became a "cardinal element of the Southern apologia," and postwar Southerners manifested "a nearly universal denial to escape the ignominy attached to slavery."[6]

In the North, where white racism and a desire for national reconciliation made slavery an issue no one wanted to discuss, the idea that slavery was not the cause of secession and the war found acceptance. According to Alan Nolan, "This belief was advanced by such prominent twentieth-century historians as Charles and Mary Beard, Avery Craven, and James G. Randall, influenced surely in part by their own racism. Others set slavery aside as the critical concern of the Confederacy and critical issue of the war."[7]

Non-slavery rationales for the Civil War certainly are not dead. For example, in his 1988 foreword to a republished edition of Pollard's *The Lost Cause*, Stefan R. Dziemianowicz writes, "If one were to look for a common denominator that linked all of the many reasons given for the Civil War—the slavery issue, the secession of the southern states and the formation of the Confederacy, the growing disaffection between the North and South as they evolved into separate political entities—the search would end on a difference in interpretation of the United States

Constitution." He proceeds to compare the Hamiltonian and Jeffersonian interpretations of the Constitution.[8]

There is, however, much evidence that contradicts the myth that slavery was not the cause of secession and the war.

## THE SETTING

Because the war resulted from the secession of seven Southern states and their formation of the Confederate States of America after Abraham Lincoln's election as president on November 6, 1860, and his inauguration on March 4, 1861, whatever caused those states to secede is the primary cause of the Civil War. The distinguishing feature of Lincoln's and the Republicans' campaign was opposition to the extension of slavery into the Western territories. That was, in fact, almost the only issue in the four-way presidential race. Did that question or others related to slavery affect those seven states' decision to secede and form the Confederacy?

But before examining why South Carolina, Mississippi, Florida, Alabama, Georgia, Louisiana, and Texas seceded from the United States and founded the Confederacy, we must distinguish between the motives of the secessionists and the motives of individual soldiers. Even if slavery was the catalyst, it does not follow that all rebel soldiers believed they were fighting for that cause. They may have been fighting for any number of other reasons. The Civil War, however, "was certainly not the first time in history...that good people fought valiantly for disgraceful causes.... But by joining the Confederate war machine, all of them, irrespective of their personal motivations, advanced their nation's political agenda—the perpetuation and territorial expansion of human bondage and the misery that it entailed."[9]

## BACKGROUND

The Founding Fathers generally sidestepped the awkward issue of slavery but did provide it with a constitutional foundation. Despite their declaration in 1776 that "all men are created equal," they affirmed the continuation of slavery in the U.S. Constitution of 1787. Each slave was to count as three-fifths of a person for purposes of determining a state's representation in the lower house of Congress, and the importation of slaves was to continue until at least 1808. The Constitution also provided that fugitive slaves who escaped across state lines were to be returned to their masters, a provision that would be a source of controversy for the next seventy-four years.

Slavery became a serious point of contention between the North and South in 1820 with the proposed admission of Missouri to the Union as a slave state. In the face of national turmoil over this issue, Congress reached the Missouri Compromise. Missouri was admitted as a slave state, Maine was admitted as a free state, slavery was prohibited north of Missouri's southern border except in Missouri itself, and a fugitive-slave provision was applied to those slavery-free territories. Thus slavery was prohibited in all new states north of the latitude thirty-six degrees, thirty minutes.

Over the next two decades, a Northern abolitionist movement, the Nat Turner Revolt of 1831, and Southern reaction to both revived the national contention over slavery. The issue was so divisive that it split America's major religious denominations into Northern and Southern wings. Of course, both sides claimed that God and the Bible were on their sides and had numerous biblical quotations to support their positions.[10]

# ANTI-STATES' RIGHTS: THE ROLE OF THE FEDERAL GOVERNMENT IN PRESERVING SLAVERY

The interplay between slavery and states' rights was always complex. David Blight observed, "The relationship of states' rights to slavery in all discussions of Civil War causation appears to be an eternal riddle in American public memory."[11]

According to the Myth, Southerners were moved by the principle of states' rights to secede. As their secession resolutions demonstrated (see below), Southerners were disappointed that some Northern states were exercising state power to obstruct federal enforcement of slave-owners' rights. Gary Gallagher explains the situation in late 1860 from a contemporary perspective:

> The best friend of the slaveholding South in that regard is the federal government. Increasingly the states and slaveholders of the South look to the United States government to ensure their hold on their property. They expect the entire nation to follow through with the legislation that came out of the Compromise of 1850 that said escaping slaves will be returned. State rights have been a problem from the Southern perspective in that many of the Northern states have passed laws that make it difficult to enforce federal law.[12]

Looking back on the growing national controversy over slavery, Lincoln's secretaries and biographers John Hay and John Nicolay wrote: "It is now universally understood, if not conceded, that the Rebellion of 1861 was begun for the sole purpose of defending and preserving to the seceding States the institution of African slavery and making them the nucleus of a great slave empire...."[13]

Perhaps surprisingly, Edward Pollard of Richmond, who had his finger on the Confederate pulse, explained in 1866 that Lincoln's 1860 election, with its power shift to the North, caused the South to leave the Union, "which no longer afforded any guaranty for her rights or any permanent sense of security" and which intended to "destroy her institutions, and even involve the lives of her people." His analysis continued: "Power in the hands of the North affected the safety and happiness of every individual in the South." The code words for slavery protection were the substance of his conclusions.[14] In fact, the seceding states themselves complained that the federal government was not doing enough to protect slavery and that non-slave states were exercising their own rights in a manner disagreeable to the slave states (for example, by passing "liberty laws" to hinder efforts to retrieve runaway slaves). They were upset that the Underground Railroad had helped between one thousand and five thousand slaves to escape each year between 1830 and 1860.[15]

At the root of these anti–states' rights complaints was the return of fugitive slaves. As the price for their signing the Declaration of Independence and ratifying the U.S. Constitution, the Southern states had demanded that anti-slavery statements in the Declaration be deleted and that certain concessions to slavery be made in the Constitution. In between, the Northwest Ordinance of 1787, governing what is now the upper Midwest, forbade slavery there but provided that any slave who escaped to the Northwest Territories "may be lawfully reclaimed and conveyed to the person claiming his or her labor or service."[16]

The federal Fugitive Slave Act of 1793 required state and local governments to return runaway slaves to their owners and penalized those who assisted the runaways. Northern opposition to that law led to conflicts about its enforcement and Southern anger about its non-enforcement in the North. The result was a strengthened Fugitive Slave Act of 1850, part of the Compromise of 1850, authorizing federal officials to compel the return of runaways slaves, requiring state officials and the public at large to aid in their capture and return, providing a modicum of non-judicial due process for alleged runaways, and setting magistrate fees of five dollars when an alleged runaway was released and ten dollars when that person was ordered to be transported to the slave state from which he or she allegedly had fled.

This tougher law provoked even more opposition in Northern states—including riots and fatal shootings. Clearly, many in the North disagreed with returning fugitive slaves to their owners and especially to the shipping south of innocent free blacks as alleged runaways under the new procedures. Northern Democrats, led by President Franklin Pierce, aggressively enforced the new Fugitive Slave Act, and the fear of being kidnapped and sold into slavery led some fifteen to twenty thousand free Northern blacks to migrate to Canada between 1850 and 1860.[17]

The efforts by congressional Democrats and Presidents Pierce and Buchanan to appease Southerners on the fugitive slave issue failed to satisfy them. The essence of the slave-states' complaints was not that their rights were being violated but rather that the federal government and the non-slave states were insufficiently helpful in defending slavery. As the *New York Times* pointed out in 1859, the South had made "the doctrine of state rights, so long slavery's friend,... its foe."[18]

Michael C. C. Adams agrees with this analysis: "Appeals to state sovereignty usually masked other, more pragmatic, interests. Southerners embraced states' rights when convenient but insisted that national authorities return fugitive slaves, overriding the states' rights protest of Northern local officials."[19]

The Democratic conventions of 1860 demonstrate Southerners' interest in greater federal government protection of slavery. At two conventions (Charleston and Baltimore) in mid-1860 Southern Democrats bolted because of the majority's unwillingness to approve a platform plank calling for a federal slave code for the territories. Their walkouts, which split the party and led to two separate party candidates for president, demonstrated the Southerners' concern for greater protection of slavery by the federal government—far from a states' rights position. Their desire for explicit central government protection of slavery in the territories came in the Confederate Constitution of 1861.

Dwight Pitcaithley sheds light on this ironic twist: "The use of the term 'states rights' in modern discussions of the causes of the Civil War almost exclusively connotes a cause separate from that of slavery[;] indeed it is used largely in opposition to the idea of slavery as a cause. Yet, when the South's political leaders discussed the subject of denied rights during the secession crisis they spoke almost exclusively with reference to federal rights not states' rights."[20]

Slavery, in Edward L. Ayers's formulation, is the "one-word" answer to the question of what caused the Civil War, but slavery per se was not the cause of the war. Ayers identifies slavery as "the key catalytic agent in a volatile new mix of democratic politics and accelerated communication, a process chemical in its complexity and subtlety." Specifically, "People on both sides were playing out future scenarios even as they responded to immediate threats. They recognized how deeply contingency could run and how quickly things could shift; a Supreme Court decision or a presidential election could change the evolution of vast structures of slavery and economic development."[21]

## SLAVERY-RELATED DEMOGRAPHICS

Did the extent of slave ownership in a state or the size of its slave population have anything to do with how likely a state was to secede? The demographics of slavery reveal a strong correlation. The higher the percentage of slaves and the higher the percentage of slaveholding families, the likelier a state was to secede.

Each of the first six states to secede had a slave population between 44 and 57 percent of the total population. Each of the last five states to secede had a slave population between 25 and 33 percent of the total, while the non-seceding slave states had slave populations between 2 and 20 percent. The average percentage of families that held slaves in the first seven seceding states was 37. That figure was 25 in the next four seceding states, and it was 16 in the four non-seceding slave states.[22]

Whatever part states' rights allegedly played in secession, concern for those rights corresponded to a state's interest in maintaining or protecting the institution of slavery.

One other set of numbers sheds some light on the connection between slavery and secession. Slave-owning soldiers' higher casualty rates and lower desertion rates suggest that they may have been more enthusiastic about participating in the war. Joseph Glatthaar's statistical study of the soldiers in Lee's army finds that soldier slave-owners had a 56.5 percent casualty rate, while that for non-slave-owner soldiers was 48.5 percent. Slave-owning soldiers, moreover, deserted at a "low" rate of 8.4 percent, while 18.1 percent of non-slave-owners deserted. Glatthaar concludes:

> As various Confederate states clearly explained in their justification of secession, they left the Union to preserve the institution of slavery. Although attempts by the Northern states to restore the Union required an invasion of those seceding states and Confederates rushed to arms to protect their home and homeland, among the issues central in their thoughts was

## SECESSION, SLAVES, AND SLAVE OWNERSHIP

| Seceding states (in chronological order) | Number of slaves & slaves' percent of state population (1860) | % Slaveholding families (1860) |
|---|---|---|
| South Carolina | 402,406 slaves, 57% | 46% |
| Mississippi | 436,631 slaves, 55% | 49% |
| Florida | 61,745 slaves, 44% | 34% |
| Alabama | 435,080 slaves, 45% | 35% |
| Georgia | 462,198 slaves, 44% | 37% |
| Louisiana | 331,726 slaves, 47% | 29% |
| Texas | 182,566 slaves, 30% | 28% |
| *States Seceding Before Lincoln's Inauguration* | 2,312,352 slaves, 47% | 37% |
| Virginia | 490,865 slaves, 31% | 26% |
| Arkansas | 111,115 slaves, 26% | 20% |
| Tennessee | 275,719 slaves, 25% | 25% |
| North Carolina | 331,059 slaves, 33% | 28% |
| *States Seceding After Fort Sumter* | 1,208,758 slaves, 29% | 25% |
| *All Seceding States* | 3,521,110 slaves, 39% | 31% |
| Non-seceding slave states | Number of slaves & slaves' percent of state population (1860) | % Slaveholding families (1860) |
| Delaware | 1,798 slaves, 2% | 3% |
| Kentucky | 225,483 slaves, 20% | 23% |
| Maryland | 87,189 slaves, 13% | 12% |
| Missouri | 114,931 slaves, 10% | 13% |
| *Non-seceding Slaves States* | 429,401 slaves, 14% | 16% |
| *All the Slave States* | 3,950,511 slaves, 32% | 26% |

the mission of safeguarding their right to own bondsmen and bondswomen. Soldiers who owned slaves—or lived with family members who did—turned out in great numbers to fight on behalf of their newly created nation. They incurred higher casualties, deserted less frequently, and suffered more for their slaveholding Confederacy than the troops who did not own slaves and were otherwise unconnected to the peculiar institution.[23]

## STATE SECESSION CONVENTIONS, RESOLUTIONS, AND DECLARATIONS

Indisputable evidence of the seceding states' reasons for secession comes from their own secession resolutions and declarations. What could tell us more accurately why states seceded than their own contemporaneous statements, explanations, and justifications?[24]

South Carolina, of course, went first. Its "Declaration of the Immediate Causes which Induce and Justify the Secession of South Carolina from the Federal Union," issued on December 24, 1860, complained of Northern states' and federal failure to return fugitive slaves in accordance with the Constitution and federal law: "But an increasing hostility on the part of the non-slaveholding States to the institution of slavery, has led to a disregard of their obligations, and the laws of the General Government have ceased to effect the objects of the Constitution." It complained that Northern states had condemned slavery as sinful and that Northerners had elected as president a man who had said, "Government cannot endure permanently half slave, half free." The South Carolinians even criticized Northern states for allowing free blacks (non-citizens under the notorious 1857 Supreme Court decision in *Dred Scott v. Sandford*) to vote. Far from respecting individual states' rights, they wanted to compel the federal and other state governments to enforce slaveholders' rights.[25]

Mississippi was simultaneously moving toward secession. On November 26, 1860, Governor John Pettus urged the legislature to convene a secession convention, declaring, "The existence or the abolition of African slavery in the Southern States is now up for a final settlement." He accused Northerners of regarding slavery as a sin and urging its destruction. The North, he said, was ordering the South to decide "whether it shall be a peaceable and gradual abolition or speedy and violent."[26]

On November 30, 1860, the Mississippi legislature called for a secession convention with delegates elected by voters and authorized the governor to appoint delegates to other slave states. The North, they complained, had defied the Constitution's fugitive slave provision, interfered with slavery, enticed slaves to flee, agitated against slavery, sought to exclude slavery from the territories, and opposed the admission of more slave states. Abolitionists, moreover, sought to amend the Constitution to prohibit slavery and to punish slaveholders. They had encouraged John Brown's raid and had elected a president and vice president hostile to the South and its system of labor. In convoking a secession convention, the Mississippi legislature left no doubt that slavery was the main reason for a withdrawal from the Union.[27]

With its legislature already having determined that secession was the proper remedy for all the slavery-related grievances, Mississippi's January 9, 1861, secession ordinance,[28] passed by the convention without a further vote by the people,[29] surprised no one.

The convention's declaration of the causes of secession got right to the point:

> Our position is thoroughly identified with the institution of slavery—the greatest material interest of the world. Its labor supplies the product which constitutes by far the largest and most important portions of commerce of the earth. These products are peculiar to the climate verging on the tropical regions, and by an imperious law of nature, none but the black race can bear exposure to the tropical sun. These products have become necessities of the world, and a blow at slavery is a blow at commerce and civilization. That blow has

been long aimed at the institution, and was at the point of reaching its consummation. There was no choice left us but submission to the mandates of abolition, or a dissolution of the Union, whose principles had been subverted to work out our ruin.[30]

After a long list of sixteen slavery-related grievances (many the same as those in the November 30 legislative resolutions), the declaration concluded, "We must either submit to degradation, and to the loss of property worth four billions of money, or we must secede from the Union framed by our fathers, to secure this as well as every other species of property."[31]

The convention's declaration was consistent with the fact that their debates had been dominated by slavery-related issues, including the Atlantic slave trade and taxation of slaves. As one leading delegate, Alexander M. Clayton, stated, "We are in the midst of a great work. This movement was inaugurated to protect the institution of slavery, and to preserve it from destruction." Timothy Smith concludes: "Still, despite some long-held and erroneous modern arguments about slavery's minuscule role in secession, the delegates obviously had slavery on their minds in almost every decision that they made, and it was on their tongues more than most Mississippians realize today.... [T]he commissioners' speeches leave no doubt that slavery was the key issue in the secession of Mississippi."[32]

On January 10, 1861, Florida seceded.[33] Its convention's January 7 "Cause for Secession" explained why: "All hope of the preservation of the Federal Union, upon terms consistent with the safety and honor of the slave-holding States, has finally dissipated by the recent indications of the strength of the anti-slavery sentiment of the free states."

A day later Alabama seceded by adopting a Secession Ordinance that gave only one reason: "Whereas, the election of Abraham Lincoln and Hannibal Hamlin to the offices of President and Vice-President of the United States of America by a sectional party avowedly hostile to the domestic institutions [slavery] and to the peace and security of the State of Alabama, preceded by many and dangerous infractions of the Constitution of the United States [the fugitive slave provision] by many of the States and people of the Northern section, is a political wrong of so insulting and menacing a character as to justify the people of the State of Alabama in the adoption of prompt and decided measures for their future peace and security."[34] So here was another state disappointed that the federal government and Northern states were no longer likely to protect slaveholders' interests.[35]

Georgia seceded eight days later.[36] Ten days thereafter, the State published its reasons for seceding. Its January 29 Declaration of Causes solely addressed "numerous and serious causes of complaint against our non-slave-holding confederate States with reference to the subject of African slavery." Georgia's declaration went on for pages about the Northern challenges to slavery that had culminated in the rise of the "anti-slavery" Republican Party and the election of Lincoln. It complained that "The prohibition of slavery in the Territories is the cardinal principle of [the Republicans]," and that "by their declared principles and policy they have outlawed $3,000,000,000 of our property in the common territories of the Union; put it under the ban of the Republic in the States where it exists and out of the protection of the Federal law everywhere."[37]

Louisiana seceded on January 26 but did not expressly state its reasons for secession.[38] Although Louisiana simply seceded without a written explanation, its commissioners to other slave states left no doubt that slavery was the driving force. See discussion below of their activities.

On February 2, Texas seceded. Its secession convention provided a laundry-list of slavery-related reasons for its withdrawal from the Union. In the midst of pages of almost exclusively slavery-related complaints, they criticized Republicans' "unnatural feeling of hostility to these Southern States and their beneficent and patriarchal system of African slavery, proclaiming the debasing doctrine of equality of all men, irrespective of race or color...." After complaining about abolitionists, Northern states' violations of the Constitution's fugitive-slave clause, and Republicans who threatened "the ruin of the slave-holding States," the

Texas Declaration stated, "We hold as undeniable truths that the governments of the various States, and of the confederacy itself, were established exclusively by the white race, for themselves and their posterity; that the African race had no agency in their establishment; that they were rightfully held and regarded as an inferior and dependent race, and in that condition only could their existence in this country be rendered beneficial and tolerable."[39]

The Texans continued: "That in this free government all white men are and of right ought to be entitled to equal civil and political rights; that the servitude of the African race, as existing in these States, is mutually beneficial to both bond and free, and is abundantly authorized and justified by the experience of mankind, and the revealed will of the Almighty Creator, as recognized by all Christian nations; while the destruction of the existing relations between the two races, as advocated by our sectional enemies, would bring inevitable calamities upon both and desolation upon the fifteen slave-holding states."[40]

Thus, six of the first seven seceding states (one remaining silent) left no doubt in their secession declarations that they were leaving the Union because of slavery and slavery-related issues. They announced that they were dissatisfied, not about insufficient states' rights, but about Northern states' exercise of states' rights and their failure to follow federal fugitive slave provisions in the U.S. Constitution and federal laws. Accompanied by anti-black harangues, the seceders' other primary concerns were the potential prohibition of slavery in the territories, threats to the institution of slavery, possible loss of the property value of their slaves, and the threat that abolition posed to the Southern economy and white-controlled society.

## SETTLEMENT EFFORTS ATTEMPTING TO STOP SECESSION AND AVOID CIVIL WAR

Many politicians, especially those from Border States, attempted to settle the festering 1860–61 dispute in order to avoid additional state secessions and civil war. An examination of those efforts should shed light on what issues were thought to be causing secession and threatening civil war.

Probably the first significant attempt to peacefully resolve secession-related issues came from Democratic and Southern sympathizing President James Buchanan, who thought secession was unconstitutional but that the Union was powerless to stop it. In his December 1860 annual message to Congress, Buchanan first blamed the North for the secession crisis: "The long-continued and intemperate interference of the northern people with the question of slavery in the southern States has at length produced its natural effects."[41]

The president proceeded to outline constitutional amendments to resolve "agitation of the slavery question." He proposed a Thirteenth Amendment, which would recognize the "right of property in slaves," the federal government's obligation to protect slavery in the Western territories, and the "right of the master to have his [runaway] slave... 'delivered up' to him."[42] Buchanan's focus on resolving slavery issues reinforced his statement about the secession crisis's slavery-related causes.

The best-known of the settlement efforts resulted in the Crittenden Compromise, named for Senator John J. Crittenden of Kentucky. He made his famous compromise proposal on the Senate floor on December 18, 1860.[43]

In introducing his compromise Constitutional amendments, Crittenden explained their context and thereby provided insights into the cause of the national crisis: "The questions of an alarming character are those which have grown out of the controversy between the northern and southern sections of our country in relation to the rights of the slaveholding States in the Territories of the United States, and in relation to the rights of the citizens of the latter in their slaves. I have endeavored by these resolutions to meet all these questions and causes of discontent...."[44]

That compromise proposal reveals what issues were generating widespread threats of secession by Southern states. The Crittenden

Compromise consisted of a series of proposed constitutional amend-ments. They would have extended the Missouri Compromise slave/free line to the Pacific Ocean, recognized and protected slavery both where it then existed and in territories "now held or hereafter acquired," and prohibited Congress from interfering with the interstate slave trade, abolishing slavery in the District of Columbia unless many conditions were met, freeing slaves of federal officials or members of Congress who brought them into Washington, prohibiting or hindering interstate trans-portation of slaves, or passing any future constitutional amendments allowing any of the above or authorizing congressional abolishment of, or interference with, slavery.[45] In addition, Crittenden proposed four congressional resolutions dealing with the fugitive slave laws and the slave trade.[46]

It is enlightening to see that all of these compromise proposals related to one issue: slavery. In fact, they were all aimed at enhancing protections for slavery and alleviating slave states' fears about threats to it. That fact sheds a great deal of light on what was causing secession and driving the nation toward war. On January 16, 1861, the Senate defeated the Crit-tenden Compromise. All Republicans voted against the proposal.[47]

Some compromise efforts continued thereafter—primarily led on the Northern side by William Seward, first as a senator and then as Lincoln's out-of-control secretary of state. In early March "[Confederate] Secretary of State Robert Toombs had sent [three commissioners] to buy time, spy on the Lincoln administration, and seek recognition for the South."[48] Without Lincoln's knowledge, Seward kept sending peace signals, like the likelihood of Fort Sumter's evacuation, to the South and even engaged the *Dred Scott*-tainted Supreme Court justice John A. Campbell as an intermediary.[49]

Seward was being played for a fool since the seceding states had no desire to compromise. A good example is found in a speech to the Texas secession convention by Louisiana commissioner George Williamson. On February 11, 1861, he stated, "I am authorized to say to your honor-able body that Louisiana does not expect any beneficial result from the peace conference now assembled in Washington. She is unwilling that her action should depend on the border states.... [I]n his own good time God will awaken the people of the border States to the vanity of asking for, or depending upon, guarantees or compromises wrung from a people whose consciences are too sublimated to be bound by that sacred compact, the constitution of the late United States."[50]

## SECEDING STATES' OUTREACH TO OTHER SLAVE STATES

After Lincoln's election and even before any state had actually seceded, the radical secessionists, sometimes called Fire-eaters, began planning for a large multiple-state confederacy that would not leave South Carolina or any other early-seceding states hanging out to dry. So Alabama, Mississippi, South Carolina, Georgia, and Louisiana named pro-secession commissioners to reach out to other slave states to urge their immediate secession. Charles B. Dew has explored their activities, speeches and letters in a revealing little book, *Apostles of Disunion*.[51]

Dew also synthesized his findings in a concurrent article. There he stressed the importance of these commissioners' presentations to other slave states: "The explanations the commissioners offered and the arguments the commissioners made, in short, provide us with extraordinary insight into the secession of the lower South in 1860–61. And by helping us to understand the 'why' of secession, these apostles of disunion have gone a long way toward answering that all-important question, 'The Civil War was fought over what important issue?'"[52]

In fact, between December 1860 and April 1861, five of the early-seceding states (South Carolina, Alabama, Mississippi, Georgia, and Louisiana) ultimately appointed a total of fifty-two commissioners (mini-ambassadors) to convince other Southern states to join them in the Confederacy. They were named by governors or secession conventions as official state representatives and usually sent to states that had announced they were convening secession conventions to consider whether to secede. Most of the commissioners were sent to the states in which they had been born, and a large majority of them were lawyers.[53]

Their outreach to other slave states provides "a remarkably clear window into the secessionist mind that has been largely ignored by students of this era."[54]

Fire-eater Robert Barnwell Rhett, through South Carolina's secession convention and his *Charleston Mercury*, urged the Palmetto State to send commissioners elsewhere. Demonstrating that state's concern about being isolated, its delegates were instructed to encourage secession *and* to propose a multi-state constitutional convention. South Carolina alone sent commissioners to nine other slave states.

In all, the fifty-two missionaries of the secessionist cause were sent by individual states to Alabama, Louisiana, Mississippi, Georgia, Florida, Texas, Arkansas, South Carolina, North Carolina, Kentucky, Maryland, Delaware, Missouri, and especially the huge and crucial state of Virginia. Several states both sent and received commissioners as Southerners reinforced each other's intent to secede and rationales for doing so.[55]

What were the compelling arguments these commissioners made to convince other states to secede and form the Confederacy? Their frank and revealing arguments, made by rabid secessionists to other or potential secessionists, provide real insight into the cause of secession. Their documents, letters and speeches are often-overlooked diamonds in the rough. In his exhaustive study, Dew concluded that the slavery and racial/racist content of their pleas to other states demonstrated the significant role of slavery in secession.[56] An examination of them is in order.

## SECEDING STATES' OUTREACH TO OTHER DEEP SOUTH STATES

Much of the earliest lobbying to encourage immediate secession was outreach to other Deep South states. Advocates of secession wanted to ensure that enough states seceded to quickly form a united confederacy before Lincoln took office. Presentations by these commissioners, a form of preaching to the converted, tended to stress the calamitous threat posed by Lincoln's election to the institution of slavery and white supremacy. Appeals to non-slave-owners reinforced appeals to the dominant slaveholding politicians. Michael C. C. Adams explains the connection: "The only aspect of Southern Agrarianism distinct enough to provoke a war remained plantation slavery. It lay at the base of the Southern way of life. Even though a majority of white people in Dixie might not own slaves, they subscribed to the caste system and could not conceive of a state of society in which blacks were free, let alone equal."[57]

## MISSISSIPPI'S OUTREACH TO OTHER DEEP SOUTH STATES

Mississippi was an early mover in this area. On November 26, 1860, its governor, John J. Pettus, asked his legislature, "Can the lives, liberty and property of the people of Mississippi be safely entrusted to the keeping of that sectional minority which must hereafter administer the Federal Government?" He answered with a resounding *no* and urged secession as necessary to avoid the blight of "Black Republican politics and free negro morals," which would transform the state into a "cess pool of vice, crime and infamy." He successfully urged lawmakers to convene a secession convention and authorize him to send commissioners to other slave states. Within days, he designated Whig and Democratic commissioners to every other slave state.[58]

The first significant presentation by a Southern commissioner was made by Judge William L. Harris, a member of Mississippi's highest court and that state's commissioner to Georgia. On December 17, 1860, he addressed a joint session of the Georgia General Assembly. His speech was important because there were in Georgia many Unionists who were not eager for secession. Therefore, he had to be convincing and expound upon issues that would promote secession.

His primary issues were slavery and race relations. He began with a recital of Northern "outrages," including the North's 1850s failure "to yield to us our constitutional rights in relation to slave property." The recently victorious Republicans, he said, "have demanded, and now demand, equality between the white and negro races, under our Constitution; equality in representation, equality in the right of suffrage, equality in the honors and emoluments of office, equality in the social circle, equality in the rights of matrimony." The new administration promised "freedom to the slave, but eternal degradation for you and for us."

In a somewhat biased interpretation of America's founding, Harris argued: "Our fathers made this a government for the white man, rejecting the negro, as an ignorant, inferior, barbarian race, incapable of self-government, and not, therefore, entitled to be associated with the white man upon terms of civil, political, or social equality." He warned that the Lincoln administration would "overturn and strike down this great feature of our Union, without which it never would have been formed, and to substitute in its stead their new theory of the universal equality of the black and white races."[59]

After complaining extensively about Northern failure to enforce fugitive slave requirements, Harris laid out the choice for the Georgia legislators: "This *new union* with Lincoln Black Republicans and free negroes, *without slavery*; or, slavery under our old constitutional bond of union, *without* Lincoln Black Republicans, or free negroes either, to molest us." This choice, he proclaimed, was no choice at all: to avoid "submission to negro equality... *secession* is inevitable."[60]

To be sure his listeners understood his major, virtually only, point, the judge finished with the words, "Sink or swim, live or die, survive or perish, the part of Mississippi is chosen, *she will never submit* to the principles and policy of this Black Republican Administration. She had rather see the last of her race, men, women and children, immolated in one common funeral pile [pyre], than see them subjected to the degradation of civil, political and social equality with the negro race."[61]

After Harris's speech, the Georgia Legislature adopted a resolution condemning Northerners for supporting a political party "organized ... for the avowed purpose of destroying the institution of slavery, and consequently spreading ruin and desolation among the people in every portion of the states where it exists." The legislature ordered a thousand copies of Harris's speech printed, and the *Athens Southern Banner* called the day of his speech "the greatest day of the session."[62]

These words and actions left no doubt that Mississippi and Georgia shared a common interest in secession in order to preserve slavery and white supremacy.

## SOUTH CAROLINA'S OUTREACH TO OTHER DEEP SOUTH STATES

South Carolina sent commissioners only to the nine states that had called secession conventions.[63] Son of John C. Calhoun, Andrew Pickens Calhoun was South Carolina's commissioner to Alabama. Just after Lincoln's election, Calhoun revealed his thoughts in a home-state address. He attacked the North for electing an abolitionist president and threatening the South with "political and social destruction." He warned of a Republican "depraved Government" that would seek "to seduce the poor, ignorant and stupid nature of the negro in the midst of his home and happiness." To avoid a Haitian-type slave uprising, he urged a "complete, thorough and radical" "Disentanglement from the North."[64]

On January 8, 1861, Calhoun carried his gospel to Alabama's secession convention: A "Black Republican" threatened the "degradation and annihilation" of South Carolina. He disingenuously claimed that South Carolina had no desire to take the secession lead but did so because of "accidental causes" and overwhelming public demands. Alabama seceded three days later and invited other slave states to a February 4 convention in Montgomery.[65]

South Carolina's delegate to Florida, Leonidas W. Spratt, an advocate of reopening the international slave trade, was fervently in favor of immediate secession. On January 7, he told the Florida secession convention that he welcomed the open break in American society along racial lines:

The one is the society of one race, the other of two races. The one is based on free labor, the other slave labor. The one is braced together by but the two great relations of life—the relations of husband and wife, and parent and child; the other by the three relations of husband and wife, parent and child, and master and slave. The one embodies the social principle that equality is the right of man; the other, the social principle that equality is not the right of man, but the right of equals only.[66]

Spratt justified South Carolina's secession because free men, unlike slaves, did not have to actually suffer "the repetition of the lash"; they could assume the lash was going to be used [by Republicans] and preempt its use. He urged Florida to join South Carolina, which had "erected at least one nationality under the authority of which the powers of slavery may stand in that fearful contest for existence which at some time or other was bound to come."[67] Every argument and statement made by Spratt left no doubt that South Carolina had seceded over the slavery issue and that Florida should join it for the same reason.

South Carolina's commissioner to Mississippi, Armistead Burt, explained to the Mississippi convention that the Palmetto State had seceded because Republicans intended "to uproot our institutions, and desolate the Southern country." Its commissioners to Georgia and Louisiana, James L. Orr and John L. Manning respectively, successfully carried similar messages to their assigned states. Orr had previously spoken against the specter of racial equality and announced that he *"would never submit* to such equality." He warned Georgia's convention about "Southern degradation and dishonor" if "the Black-Republican party had its way." Likewise, Manning warned Louisianans about the imminent threats from the South's "avowed enemies"—"the Black Republicans." Orr and Manning both successfully urged their assigned states to quickly secede and attend the Montgomery convention.[68]

The radical congressman John McQueen was South Carolina's commissioner to Texas, but he reached out to Virginia along the way. He first signed the Southern Manifesto of December 13, 1860, urging immediate secession of all slave states. Then, in declining an invitation to speak in Virginia, he nevertheless urged Virginians in writing to reject the domination of Lincoln, who had been chosen "upon the single idea that the African is equal to the Anglo-Saxon, and with the purpose of placing our slaves on [a position of] equality with ourselves and our friends of every condition." Next, on February 1, 1861, he told the Texas convention, "Lincoln was elected by a sectional vote, whose platform was that of the Black Republican party and whose policy was to be the abolition of slavery upon this continent and the elevation of our own slaves to an equality with ourselves and our children." After Texas seceded that day, McQueen praised their rejection of three distinct enemy classes, Indians, Mexicans, and Abolitionists, and predicted "that state would never be reunited with a non-slaveholding or fanatical people."[69]

McQueen's racist comments were a fitting and typical conclusion to South Carolina's lobbying of other early-seceding, Deep South states. Its commissioners attacked "Black Republicans" who supported racial equality and supposedly posed the immediate threat of abolition.

## ALABAMA'S OUTREACH TO OTHER DEEP SOUTH STATES

Alabama was another early leader in interstate outreach to encourage secession. Its Governor Andrew B. Moore decided on his own to appoint a total of sixteen commissioners to almost every slave state. He appointed the commissioners to consult with other slaveholding states "as to what is best to be done to protect the rights, interests, and honor" of those states in the impending crisis. He believed this consultative action with other slave-holding states was necessary because the Black Republicans intended to destroy slavery and thereby would "endanger the peace, interests, security, and honor of the slave-holding States." Those redundant statements were in his documents appointing the state's commissioners.[70] Elsewhere he justified his pre–state convention appointment of commissioners to other states: "the slave-holding States have a common interest in the institution of slavery, and must be common sufferers in its overthrow."[71]

On January 2, 1861, Alabama's commissioner to Louisiana, John A. Winston, reported to his Governor Moore on his mission to Louisiana concerning states' relations with the federal government "and the duty of the slave-holding States in the matter of their rights and honor, so menacingly involved in matters connected with the institution of African slavery." He said that he had consulted with Louisiana Governor T. O. Moore and legislators and found that "the legislative mind appeared fully alive to the importance and the absolute necessity of the action of the Southern States in resistance of that settled purpose of aggression on our constitutional and inherent natural rights by the majority of the people of the non-slaveholding States," which "has culminated in the election of a man to the Presidency of the United States whose opinions and constructions of constitutional duty are wholly incompatible with our safety in a longer union with them."[72]

The next day Alabama commissioner John Gill Shorter wrote a letter to Georgia Governor Joseph E. Brown. It was more circumspect than many commissioners' communications, but it is not difficult to find the code words:

> I have…authority to consult and advise…as to what is best to be done to protect the *rights, interests, and honor of the slave-holding States*.… The unnatural warfare which, in violation of the Federal compact and for a long series of years, has been unceasingly waged by the anti-slavery States upon the *institutions, rights and domestic tranquility of the slave-holding States*, has finally culminated in the election of an open and avowed enemy to our section of the Union.… [Republicans] will usurp the machinery of the Federal Government and madly attempt *to rule, if not to subjugate, and ruin the South*. Alabama will stand by and make common cause with [South Carolina] and every other State which shall assert her *independence of an abolitionized Government*.

> Having *similar institutions*, kindred sympathies, and honor alike imperiled, will not Georgia unite with Alabama and sister States in throwing off the insolent despotism of the North, and in the establishment of a Southern confederacy, *a government of homogeneous people*, which shall endure through all coming time...?[73]

Although the words "slavery" and "white supremacy" do not appear in Shorter's letter, he left little doubt concerning what he was talking about. Governor Brown certainly caught his meaning. Brown replied in a letter using the phrase "pro-slavery States" three times, made the usual Southern reference to "the Black republican party," and confirmed: "the people of the *pro-slavery States have common institutions*, common interests, common sympathies, and a common destiny."[74]

On January 5, J. A. Elmore reported to Governor Moore of Alabama on his activities as commissioner to South Carolina. He described how he and Charles E. Hooker, Mississippi's commissioner, had coordinated their activities and addressed the South Carolina convention on December 17. Both assured the convention that their own states would join the secession parade. Elmore assured Moore that South Carolinians were prepared for the horrors of war before they "would submit to subjugation by the Federal Government of the forces of the abolitionist States."[75]

## LOUISIANA'S OUTREACH TO TEXAS

The sixth seceding state was Louisiana, which held a convention in January 1861 that left no record of its reasons for seceding. It appointed a commissioner, George Williamson, to spread the gospel of secession to Texas, however. On February 11, speaking to the Texas secession convention, which had already voted to secede[76] but was still conducting other business, he explained Louisiana's secession rationale: "Louisiana looks to the formation of a Southern confederacy to preserve the blessings of African slavery.... Louisiana and Texas...are both so deeply interested in African slavery that it may be said to be absolutely necessary to

their existence, and is the keystone to the arch of their prosperity."[77]
Williamson continued,

> The people of Louisiana would consider it a most fatal blow to
> African slavery, if Texas either did not secede or having seceded
> should not join her destinies to theirs in a Southern Confed-
> eracy.... The people of the slave-holding States are bound
> together by the same necessity and determination to preserve
> African slavery.... [The U.S. Constitution] the Southern
> States have never violated, and taking it as the basis for our
> new government we hope to form a slave-holding confed-
> eracy that will secure to us and our remotest posterity the
> great blessings it authors designed in the Federal union. With
> the social balance wheel of slavery to regulate its machinery,
> we may fondly indulge the hope that our Southern govern-
> ment will be perpetual.[78]

In summary, the Deep South commissioners to other Deep South
states reinforced their counterparts' desire to immediately secede and
also convinced each other to convene a Confederate Constitutional
Convention in Montgomery, Alabama, in early 1861. The driving force
behind their efforts, as they made abundantly clear, was to preserve
slavery and exclude blacks from social, economic, or political equality
with whites.

## DEEP SOUTH STATES' OUTREACH TO UPPER SOUTH STATES

More significant, and sometimes desperate, pleas were made to the
Upper South States (North Carolina, Virginia, Tennessee, and Arkansas)
and Border States (Maryland, Kentucky, Delaware, and Missouri), whose
willingness to secede was much more in doubt. These two categories of
states deserve separate and detailed consideration.

One of the more remarkable commissioners was President James Buchanan's Secretary of the Interior Jacob Thompson, who served as a commissioner from Mississippi to North Carolina. His December 20 letter to Governor John W. Ellis again played the race card. He stated that the South faced "common humiliation and ruin," Northerners who hated Southern institutions were coming to power, and they would overthrow slavery in the name of freedom. He warned that our "Common Government will be revolutionized" and "it will be perverted into an engine for the destruction of our domestic institutions, and the subjugation of our people." Therefore, he ended, "all questions arising out of the institution of slavery, should be settled now and settled forever."[79]

On December 20, the day South Carolina seceded, two Alabama commissioners, Isham W. Garrott and Robert Hardy Smith, both North Carolina natives, addressed a joint session of the North Carolina legislature. They began with the usual warning that slavery would be banned in territories, no new slave states would be admitted, and the South would be emasculated. Further, they said, the North "proposes to impair the value of slave property in the States by unfriendly legislation" that would "render the institution dangerous to us, and compel us, as slaves increase, to abandon it, or be doomed to a servile war."[80]

The two commissioners spoke of the likely need for white Alabamians to ultimately flee their state because of its increasing slave population, denied any intent to revive the international slave trade, and tried to reassure the Tarheel audience that Alabamians would look to other Southern states for any more slaves they needed. Then they turned to the race issue. They urged an end to twenty years of rancorous conflict over slavery by means of secession. "Submission would but invite new and greater aggressions." It was time for a united South—for North Carolinians to join Alabamians in protecting the South and slavery from the "desecrating touch" of Northern fanaticism.[81]

An early report on the situation in Arkansas was a January 3, 1861, letter from Alabama commissioner David Hubbard to his governor, Andrew B. Moore. He found Unionist sentiments still in the majority among Arkansas legislators but nevertheless had told them that "no state which had seceded would ever go back without full power being given to protect themselves against anti-slavery projects and schemes of every kind." He had argued that whether Northerners sincerely thought slavery was a sin or were being hypocritical on that issue there was no way the South could live with them.[82] It was all about slavery.

The large and critical state of Virginia was the focus of considerable activity by Deep South commissioners. By the February 13 opening of Virginia's convention, three states' commissioners already were in Richmond. They were Mississippi's Fulton Anderson, Georgia's Henry Lewis Benning and South Carolina's John Smith Preston. To their consternation, they found overwhelming Unionist support at that time. But they did their best to present the case for secession in addresses to the convention.[83]

Mississippi's Anderson began with the usual anti-Republican rhetoric: that party was "founded upon the idea of unrelenting and eternal hostility to the institution of slavery" and planned "the ultimate extinction of slavery, and the degradation of the Southern people." He said Republicans intended to abolish slavery in the territories and then in Washington, D.C., corrupt federal judges, admit more free states, and then use a constitutional majority to outlaw slavery. He warned that Northerners were committed to a holy crusade to destroy "the institution which...lies at the very foundation of our social and political fabric." The solution: formation of a great Southern Confederacy.[84]

The reason for Georgia's secession was made clear to Virginians by Commissioner Benning (owner of ninety slaves): "It was a conviction, a deep conviction on the part of Georgia, that a separation from the North was the only thing that could prevent the abolition of her slavery." He said slavery was doomed because of Black Republicans' extreme hatred of slavery, their permanent majority in the North, the North's record of using all its power against slavery, and the danger that Border States like Delaware and Maryland would abolish slavery. When slavery was confined to the "Cotton South," it would be abolished, and "if a master refuses to yield to this policy, he will doubtless be hung for his disobedience."[85]

Having predicted slavery's demise within the Union, Benning then explained abolition's significance in a racist tirade: "By the time the North shall have attained the power [to end slavery], the black race will be in a large majority, and then we will have black governors, black legislatures, black juries, black everything [laughter]." He foresaw a Northern invasion of the South to enforce abolition—with dire consequences: "We will be overpowered and our men will be compelled to wander like vagabonds all over the earth, and, as for our women, the horrors of their state we cannot contemplate in imagination.... We will be completely exterminated and the land will be left in the possession of the blacks, and then it will go back to a wilderness and become another Africa or St. Domingo."[86] Benning had played the classic race cards of black revolution and black rapes of the South's exalted white women.

The final commissioner addressing the Virginia convention was famed orator, South Carolina's John Smith Preston. Like the other two commissioners, he focused on slavery and abolition. He planted the seed of fear: "For fully thirty years or more, the people of the Northern States have assailed the institution of African slavery.... [They embraced] the most fearful [route to emancipation]: the subject race rising...and murdering their masters." He added that there was no doubt "that the conflict between slavery and non-slavery is a conflict for life and death."[87]

Preston stressed the irrevocability of secession over the slavery issue. The North and South, he said, were two distinct nations and civilizations: "The South cannot exist without African slavery. None but an equal race can labor at the North; none but a subject race will labor at the South." The "fermenting millions" of the North were "canting fanatics, festering in the licentiousness of abolition and amalgamation."[88] In Preston's mind, secession was all about protecting slavery against the perils of abolition and racial equality.

Separately, an Alabama commissioner also focused on Virginia. Judge Francis Hopkins predicted that Republican-dominated federal courts, corrupted by the Republican "higher law" doctrine, would discharge every slave brought before them "and establish them as free-men and equals in our land."[89]

## DEEP SOUTH STATES' OUTREACH TO BORDER STATES

Although the border slave states of Delaware, Maryland, Kentucky, and Missouri never seceded, it was not because Deep South commissioners did not try to convert them. In fact, their appeals to these less likely allies in secession reflected a high level of desperation.

For example, Alabama's commissioner to Kentucky, Stephen Fowler Hale, had earned his appointment by attacking Lincoln and his party's purported goal: "extinction of slavery" by "arming their emissaries to cut the throats of Southern men, women, and children." These comments to an Alabama political meeting were followed a few days later by his appointment.[90]

Since the legislature was not in session when he arrived in the state, Kentucky native Hale wrote to Kentucky Governor Beriah Magoffin a long and revealing letter urging secession and paralleling similar, but generally shorter, pleas made by his fellow commissioners. He began by asking "what rights have been denied, what wrongs have been done, or threatened to be done, of which the Southern States or the people of the Southern States can complain?"[91]

To this question (essentially, why secession?), Hale had a long answer that boiled down to preservation of slavery and racial supremacy. He explained that the Constitution protected African slavery, that the North had abandoned it, and that it "has not only become one of the fixed domestic institutions of the Southern States, but forms an important element of their political power, and constitutes the most valuable species of their property, worth ... not less than $4,000,000,000; forming, in fact, the basis upon which rests the prosperity and wealth of most of those States...."[92]

He complained of the "unrelenting and fanatical war" against slavery for the prior twenty-five years and especially of the failure to enforce rendition of fugitive slaves. He launched a diatribe against Northern liberty laws, "Bleeding Kansas," John Brown's Raid, William Seward's "higher law" doctrine, U.S. naval vessels patrolling off Africa, defiance of the Supreme Court's *Dred Scott* decision, and other anti-slavery actions of the North.[93]

For Hale, however, the "crowning act of insult and outrage" had been the overwhelming Northern support for the election of Abraham Lincoln. He asserted that Lincoln's election was "nothing less than an open declaration of war, for the triumph of this new theory of government destroys the property of the South, lays waste her fields, and inaugurates all the horrors of a Santo Domingo servile insurrection, consigning her citizens to assassinations and her wives and daughters to pollution and violation to gratify the lust of half-civilized Africans"— especially in the cotton states, where blacks often outnumbered whites ten to one.[94]

The judge foresaw Southern degradation and ruin. He exclaimed, "What Southern man, be he slave-holder or non-slave-holder, can without indignation and horror contemplate the triumph of negro equality, and see his own sons and daughters in the not distant future associating with free negroes upon terms of political and social equality, and the white man stripped by the heaven-daring hand of fanaticism of that title to superiority over the black race which God himself has bestowed?" He said Southern white men could not submit to the "degradation and ruin" that would result from "amalgamation or...extermination" under the Republican program.[95]

Hale advocated the positive good of slavery and painted the horrors of any alternative:

> We can...preserve an institution that has done more to civilize and Christianize the heathen than all human agencies besides—an institution alike beneficial to both races, ameliorating the moral, physical, and intellectual condition of the one and giving wealth and happiness to the other. If we fail, the light of our civilization goes down in blood, our wives and our little ones will be driven from their homes...the dark pall of barbarism must soon gather over our sunny land, and the scenes of West India emancipation, with its attendant horrors and crimes...be re-enacted in their own land upon a more gigantic scale.[96]

As he brought his epistle to a close, the apostle Hale surmised that the South's ability to preserve slavery under the Constitution would only grow weaker by admission to the Union of the free states of Kansas, Nebraska, Washington, Jefferson, Nevada, Idaho, Chippewa, and Arizona—which "high sources" warned would occur within four years. All the more reason to secede now.[97]

And secession would come, he concluded, because there was an irrevocable divide between the North and South. First, the North: "Will the people of the North cease to make war upon the institution of slavery and award to it the protection guaranteed by the Constitution? The accumulated wrongs of many years, the late action of their members in Congress refusing every measure of justice to the South, as well as the experience of all the past, answers, No, never!"[98]

As to the South, he concluded: "Will the South give up the institution of slavery and consent that her citizens be stripped of their property, her civilization destroyed, the whole land laid waste by fire and sword? It is impossible. She cannot; she will not. Then why attempt to hold together hostile States under the stipulations of a violated Constitution? It is impossible. Disunion is inevitable."[99]

Judge Hale's letter, said Charles Dew, "touched on almost every major point in the secession persuasion...in language that left no room for doubt or ambiguity. His letter is as passionate, as powerful, and as revealing as any" delivered by any of the Southern commissioners.[100] Hale's approach was replicated by other Deep South commissioners. Although they were not as long-winded, they tried, without success, to convert the Border States to secession.

For example, another unsuccessful Alabama commissioner, Jabez Lamar Monroe Curry, wrote to Maryland's Governor Thomas Hicks on December 28, 1860, expressing Alabama's concerns about "the growth, power, and encroachments of anti-slaveryism" and the "common interests and destiny of all the States holding property in the labor of Africans." He believed Republicans were intent on diminishing and ultimately making slavery extinct. He added,

They refuse to recognize our rights of property in slaves, to make a division of the territory, to deprive themselves of their assumed constitutional power to abolish slavery in the Territories or the District of Columbia, to increase the efficiency of the fugitive slave law, or make provision for the compensation of the owners of runaway or stolen slaves, or place in the hands of the South any protection against the rapacity of an unscrupulous majority.

The sentiment of the sinfulness of slavery seems to be embedded in the Northern conscience.... Under an abolition Government the slave-holding States will be placed under a common ban of proscription, and an institution, interwoven in the very frame-work of their social and political being, must perish gradually or speedily with the Government in active hostility to it. Instead of the culture and development of the boundless capacities and productive resources of their social system, it is to be assaulted, humbled, dwarfed, degraded, and finally crushed out.[101]

In his final plea for Maryland's secession, Curry slipped in an economic threat that Marylanders might no longer be permitted to sell their surplus slaves to the Deep South: "To refuse union with the seceding States is to accept inferiority, to be deprived of an outlet for surplus slaves, and to remain in a hostile Government in a hopeless minority and remediless dependence."[102]

On January 8, Curry sent a copy of this letter to his own Governor Moore, informing him that Hicks, who had been absent when he went to Annapolis, had not acted on the requests of a Mississippi commissioner and others to convene the Maryland legislature. But Curry assured his governor that "Maryland will not long hesitate to make common cause with her sister States which have resolutely and wisely determined not to submit to Abolition domination."[103] Maryland did not secede.

When Maryland's governor refused to convene a special session of his legislature, Mississippi's commissioner, Alexander Hamilton Handy, decided to go around him and appeal directly to the people of Maryland. Addressing a raucous gathering of 1,500 people in Baltimore's Maryland Institute Hall on December 19, he began by explaining the Lincoln administration's threat to "the rights of the South"—specifically the right "by which one man can own property in his fellow man." "Slavery was ordained by God," he asserted, and Southerners would not relinquish their slaves because their cotton fields then would become "barren wastes."[104]

Handy was just getting warmed up. He argued that Republicans would abolish slavery wherever they could in "recognition that slavery is a sin." And "[t]he moment that slavery is pronounced a moral evil—a sin—by the general government, that moment the safety of the rights of the South will be entirely gone." He further warned that Lincoln's minions would repeal laws that "prohibit circulation of incendiary documents" in order to incite slaves against their masters, and they would "excite the slave to cut the throat of his master." The answer, he said, was immediate secession, an amputation to bring the patient "to a healthy position."[105]

Meanwhile, William Cooper, Alabama's commissioner to Missouri, consulted with Missouri's Governor R. M. Stewart about his secession mission. A sympathetic Stewart responded to Alabama's Governor Moore that, "we have a lively appreciation of the practical injuries suffered from the interference and depredations of Northern fanatics. Owing to the peculiarity of our geographical position, being bounded by nearly 1,000 miles of free territory, our State probably suffers more from the loss and abduction of slaves than any of her sisters, and our people are determined to seek redress for their wrongs and full security and indemnity for their rights."[106]

Shortly thereafter, Cooper told the Missouri legislature that "Under the policy of the Republican party, the time would arrive when the scenes of San Domingo and Hayti [where bloody slave revolts had occurred], with all their attendant horrors, would be enacted in the slaveholding States."[107]

On January 1, 1861, Alabama's commissioner to Delaware, Congressman David Clopton, warned Delaware's Governor William Burton that Northern Republicans intended to dominate the South and that party's "animus, its single bond of union, is hostility to the institution of slavery as it exists in the Southern States.... It had been molded into a compact mass of enmity to this particular institution." After quoting an 1859 anti-slavery address by Lincoln, Clopton warned that a Republican government would "circulate insurrectionary documents and disseminate insurrectionary sentiments among a hitherto contented servile population" and would seek "the establishment of an equality of races in our midst."[108]

Arguing for early secession and the hopelessness of compromise efforts, Clopton wrote, "But even if new guaranties could be obtained, they can bring no sense of security to the Southern mind; they would prove a temporary and delusive truce.... New guaranties will be utterly valueless without a revolution in the public temper, prejudices, opinions, sentiments, and education of the people of the non-slave-holding States. Laws passed in compliance with such new guaranties for the security and protection of property in slaves will avail nothing where their execution depends upon the Republican appointees of a Republican President."[109] It all came down to "protection of property in slaves."

As of January 8, Clopton had received no reply from Burton. Nevertheless, he reported optimistically to his own Governor Moore that there was popular sympathy in Delaware for Alabama, that the legislature was unlikely to "give expression by a majority vote to this sympathy," and that if the Union dissolved, "a majority of the people of Delaware will defend the South."[110]

Alabama's commissioners approached their assignments with enthusiasm and fear-mongering. As Dew observes, "Over and over again, the Alabamians described the same nightmare world...a South humbled, abolitionized, degraded, and threatened with destruction by a brutal Republican majority. Emancipation, race war, miscegenation—one apocalyptic vision after another. The death throes of white supremacy would be so horrific that no self-respecting southerner could fail to rally to the secessionist cause, they argued. Only through disunion could the South preserve the purity and insure the survival of the white race."[111]

## SUMMARY OF DEEP SOUTH OUTREACH EFFORTS

There were, according to Dew, shared issues in the presentations made by Deep South commissioners in their attempts to persuade other states to join them in seceding. The first of these was the threat of racial equality—a violation of the white supremacy they deemed to be a key element in the founding of the United States. The second common issue was the threat of a race war that they argued would inevitably follow from the Northern attempts to create racial equality. The common capstone of their arguments was the one most likely to stir Southern whites' fears: the threat of racial amalgamation that would result from racial equality, race war, or both. The latter issue opened the door for commissioners to argue that the purity of Southern white wives and daughters was at stake in the secession movement.[112] Words like "lust," "horrors," "pollution," "gratify the lust," "licentiousness," "purity," "wives," "daughters," and "women" peppered their speeches as they hit the hottest of the hot-buttons of Southern politics.

Given the racial and racist nature of the numerous pro-secession arguments made by official representatives of early-seceding states, it is not difficult to see why Dew concludes:

> In setting out to explain secession to their fellow southerners, the commissioners have explained a very great deal to us as well. By illuminating so clearly the racial content of the secession persuasion, the commissioners would seem to have laid to rest, once and for all, any notion that slavery had nothing to do with the coming of the Civil War. To put it quite simply, slavery and race were absolutely critical elements in the coming of the war. Present-day Americans need only read the speeches and letters of the secession commissioners to learn what was really driving the Deep South to the brink of war in 1860–1861.[113]

In summary, the commissioners designated by Deep South seceding states to convince other states to join them in seceding from the Union were sent only to slave states and made arguments to those other states that reveal their motivations for secession. They carried a message of disgust with Northern threats to and actions against slavery, followed by fear-mongering warnings about racial equality, a race war, and racial amalgamation. Their own words make it clear that the only states' right they were interested in was the right to maintain slavery.

## PRONOUNCEMENTS OF CONFEDERATE LEADERS ON REASONS FOR SECESSION AND THE CONFEDERACY

In his February 18, 1861, inaugural address, Jefferson Davis spoke in generalities and never used the word "slavery." But he did briefly provide a justification for secession: "Through many years of controversy with our late associates, the Northern States, we have vainly endeavored to secure tranquility, and to obtain respect for the rights to which we were entitled."[114] What were those rights?

Confederate Vice President Alexander Stephens provided an early explanation. On March 21, 1861, in Savannah, Georgia, he delivered his famous "Cornerstone Speech" explaining the Confederacy's basic foundations, especially slavery. He told a large crowd:

> The new [Confederate] constitution has put at rest, *forever*, all the agitating questions relating to our peculiar institution—African slavery as it exists amongst us—the proper *status* of the negro in our form of civilization. This was the immediate cause of the late rupture and present revolution. Jefferson in his forecast, had anticipated this, as the "rock upon which the old Union would split." He was right. What was conjecture with him, is now a realized fact. But whether he fully comprehended the great truth upon which that rock *stood* and *stands*, may be doubted. The prevailing ideas entertained by him and most of the leading statesmen at the time

of the formation of the old constitution, were that the enslave-
ment of the African was in violation of the laws of nature;
that it was wrong in *principle*, socially, morally, and politi-
cally. It was an evil they knew not well how to deal with, but
the general opinion of the men of that day was that, somehow
or other, in the order of Providence, the institution would be
evanescent and pass away. This idea, though not incorporated
in the constitution, was the prevailing idea at that time.... 
Those ideas, however, were fundamentally wrong. They
rested upon the assumption of the equality of the races. This
was an error. It was a sandy foundation, and the government
built upon it fell when the "storm came and the wind blew."

Stephens continued by explaining the Confederacy was different:
"Our new government is founded upon exactly the opposite idea; its
foundations are laid, its corner-stone rests upon the great truth, that the
negro is not equal to the white man; that slavery—subordination to the
superior race—is his natural and normal condition. [Applause] This, our
new government, is the first, in the history of the world, based upon this
great physical, philosophical and moral truth." He explained further:

Many governments have been founded upon the principle
of the subordination and serfdom of certain classes of the
same race; such were and are in violation of the laws of
nature. Our system commits no such violation of nature's
laws. With us, all of the white race, however high or low,
rich or poor, are equal in the eye of the law. Not so with the
negro. Subordination is his place. He, by nature, or by the
curse against Canaan, is fitted for that condition which he
occupies in our system. The architect, in the construction of
buildings, lays the foundation with the proper material—the
granite; then comes the brick or the marble. The substratum
of our society is made of the material fitted by nature for it,

and by experience we know that it is best, not only for the superior, but for the inferior race, that it should be so. It is, indeed, in conformity with the ordinance of the Creator. It is not for us to inquire into the wisdom of his ordinances, or to question them. For his own purposes, he has made one race to differ from another, as he has made "one star to differ from another."

On this point, Stephens concluded, "The great objects of humanity are best attained when there is conformity to his laws and decrees, in the formation of governments as well as in all things else. Our confederacy is founded upon principles in strict conformity with these laws. This stone which was rejected by the first builders 'is become the chief of the corner'—the real 'corner-stone'—in our new edifice. [Applause]" Thus, Stephens left no doubt that the Confederacy represented a rejection of the "all men are created equal" philosophy of the Founding Fathers and instead was built on the foundation of Negro subordination and slavery.[115] In light of the depth and specificity of Stephens's equating slavery and white supremacy with the Confederacy's founding, his later denials of such statements seem laughable.

A little more than a month later, on April 29, Davis addressed a special session of the Confederate Congress. After asserting states' right to secede from the Union, Davis explained why they had chosen to do so. He discussed the widespread existence of slavery in 1787 and the Constitution's recognition and protection of it. He recited how Northern states had sold their slaves, prohibited slavery and then "inaugurated and gradually extended" "a persistent and organized system of hostile measures against the rights of the owners of slaves in the Southern States."[116]

Davis continued his description of Northern anti-slavery activities: "A continuous series of measures was devised and prosecuted for the purpose of rendering insecure the tenure of property in slaves…. Senators and representatives were sent…to awaken the bitterest hatred against the citizens of sister States, by violent denunciation of their institutions;

the transaction of public affairs was impeded by repeated efforts to usurp
powers not delegated by the Constitution, for the purpose of impairing
the security of property in slaves, and reducing those States which held
slaves to a condition of inferiority."[117]

The Confederate President then expressed his displeasure with the
young Republican Party and its potential destruction of slave property
worth billions: "Finally a great party was organized for the purpose of
obtaining the administration of the Government, with the avowed object
of using its power for the total exclusion of the slave States from all par-
ticipation in the benefits of the public domain acquired by all the States
in common, whether by conquest or purchase; of surrounding them
entirely by States in which slavery should be prohibited; of...rendering
the property in slaves so insecure as to be comparatively worthless, and
thereby annihilating in effect property worth thousands of millions of
dollars."[118]

Davis continued by explaining how four million slaves had been
converted from "brutal savages into docile, intelligent, and civilized
agricultural laborers," their labors "[u]nder the supervision of a superior
race" had converted wilderness into cultivated lands, and "the productions in the South of cotton, rice, sugar, and tobacco, for the full development of which the labor of African slaves was and is indispensable, had
swollen to an amount which formed nearly three-fourths of the exports
of the whole United States and had become absolutely necessary to the
wants of civilized man."[119]

Finally, he concluded that the Northern threats to slavery had left
no choice but secession: "With interests of such overwhelming magnitude
imperiled, the people of the Southern States were driven by the conduct
of the North to the adoption of some course of action to avert the danger
with which they were openly menaced. With this view the Legislatures
of the several states invited the people to select delegates to conventions
to be held for the purpose of determining for themselves what measures
were best adapted to meet so alarming a crisis in their history."[120]

Even Lee at mid-war defended the institution of slavery and not so
subtly hinted at the danger to Southern women. He complained to Secretary

of War Seddon on January 10, 1863, about the Final Emancipation Proclamation: "In view of the vast increase of the forces of the enemy, of the
savage and brutal policy he has proclaimed, which leaves us no alternative
but success or *degradation worse than death, if we would save the honor
of our families from pollution, our social system from destruction*, let
every effort be made, every means be employed, to fill and maintain the
ranks of our armies...."[121]

Postwar backing and filling by Stephens and Davis attempted to
cover their slavery tracks. Stephens got off to an early start in a summer
1865 journal entry claiming that his Cornerstone Speech had been
misquoted by a Savannah reporter. The length and depth of such a
"misquote" would have been astounding. Stephens failed to address
similar "misquotes" by an Atlanta reporter of a contemporaneous
speech in which he said Confederate Constitution framers "solemnly
discarded the pestilent heresy of fancy politicians, that all men, of all
races, were equal, and we had made African *inequality* and subordination, and the *equality* of white men, the chief corner stone of the Southern
Republic."[122]

The former Confederate vice president's amnesia continued in a more
formal setting: his *A Constitutional View of the Late War between the
States*. In his first volume (1868), he insisted the struggle was between
federation and centralism [states' rights] and that slavery simply was the
question that brought these principles into conflict. It did violence to
history, he contended, to call Southern politicians a "Pro-Slavery Party."
He concluded that the war was a struggle between "the friends of Constitutional Liberty" and the "Demon of Centralism, Absolutism, [and]
Despotism!"[123] The states' rights rationale was off and running!

Jefferson Davis did some revisionism of his own after the war. In his
1881 *The Rise and Fall of the Confederate Government*, he followed the
lead of Stephens and created a non-slavery rationale for the war. Sectional
equilibrium and equality among the states were the Southern goals, he
contended—in contrast to the North's desire to acquire an empire. The
Confederacy, according to Davis, was all about constitutional government, supremacy of law, and the natural rights of man.

Most significantly, he argued that the Confederacy was *not* about slavery. His rationale: "The sectional hostility...was not the consequence of any difference on the abstract question of slavery. It would have manifested itself just as certainly if slavery had existed in all the States, or if there had not been a negro in America.... The truth remains intact and incontrovertible, that the existence of African servitude was in no wise the cause of the conflict, but only an incident.... [T]o whatever extent the question of slavery may have served as an *occasion*, it was far from being the cause."[124] Here were amnesia and selective memory at their finest.

Within a few years, John Nicolay and John Hay, in their ten-volume study of Lincoln, were having no part of Davis' assertions. Instead, they firmly and presciently warned, "The generation which fought the war needs no proof of the incorrectness of [Davis's] declaration; but the historian of the future, without such contemporary knowledge, may think this claim, so gravely put forth by the leader of the South, possesses some critical value." As Gary Gallagher has stated, "Anyone dealing honestly with testimony from the secession crisis and the war, as opposed to postwar efforts by ex-Confederates to rewrite the history of the conflict, must accept the absolute centrality of slavery."[125]

## THE CONFEDERACY'S CONSTITUTION

On February 8, 1861, representatives of South Carolina, Georgia, Florida, Alabama, Mississippi, and Louisiana, meeting in Birmingham, Alabama, agreed upon a Provisional Constitution of the Confederate States of America.[126] It paralleled most provisions of the U.S. Constitution but had special slavery provisions that reflected their priorities.

In order to entice surplus-slave states farther north into the Confederacy, these representatives proposed forbidding "the importation of African negroes from any foreign country other than the slaveholding States of the United States" and requiring the Confederate Congress to pass implementing laws. The provisional constitution gave Congress the power "to prohibit the introduction of slaves from any State not a member of this Confederacy." That provision appears to have been intended to encourage Virginia and other Upper South and Border States, with surpluses of slaves, to consider joining the Confederacy.

Finally, that provisional constitution contained a strong fugitive slave section: "A slave in one State, escaping to another, shall be delivered up on claim of the party to whom said slave may belong by the executive authority of the State in which such slave shall be found, and in case of any abduction or forcible rescue, full compensation, including the value of the slave and all costs and expenses, shall be made to the party, by the State in which such abduction or rescue shall take place." This language provided more rights to alleged slave-owners than to any state.

Interestingly, this early draft document also contained a Supremacy Clause, similar to that of the U.S. Constitution, declaring it and the laws of the Confederacy the supreme law of the land binding on judges in every state, "anything in the Constitution or laws of any State to the contrary notwithstanding." So much for states' rights!

The provisional constitution was converted to a permanent one through the work of a committee headed by South Carolina fire-eater Robert Barnwell Rhett. On March 11, 1861, the Confederate Congress, expanded by the addition of Texas, adopted the final Constitution of the Confederate States, which contained the above Supremacy Clause and a fugitive slave clause similar to that in the U.S. Constitution. Even more significantly, the final Confederate Constitution stated, "No...law impairing the right of property in negro slaves shall be passed."[127] Rhett, however, was disappointed that the constitution did not absolutely bar free states from joining the Confederacy.[128]

That final constitution contained the same prohibition on foreign slave imports into the Confederacy as the provisional constitution, much to Rhett's consternation, and expanded the non-Confederate state slave import provision to include territories: "Congress shall also have power to prohibit the introduction of slaves from any State not a member of, or Territory not belonging to, this Confederacy."[129]

Finally, that constitution addressed the issue that had been at stake in the 1860 presidential election, extension of slavery to territories. It provided that the Confederacy could acquire new territories and its Congress could regulate them and permit them to become Confederate states. It concluded: "In all such territory, the institution of negro slavery, as it now exists in the Confederate States, shall be recognized and protected by Congress and by the territorial government; and the inhabitants of the several Confederate States and Territories shall have the right to take to such territory any slaves lawfully held by them in any of the States or Territories of the Confederate States."[130] So much for popular sovereignty!

It is noteworthy that the Confederate Constitution differed from the U.S. Constitution primarily in ensuring the existence of slavery in its states and territories—but that it was virtually identical, with certain minor exceptions, on the issue of states' rights, as evidenced by its central government-oriented Supremacy Clause.[131] This clause is another piece of evidence that slavery, not states' rights, was the moving force in establishing the Confederacy.

Gordon Rhea has provided a pithy summary of the draft and final constitutional steps taken by the new Confederacy: "And so, seven score and ten years ago,[132] our Confederate forefathers brought forth on this continent a new nation dedicated to the principle that all men are not created equal; that some people have the right to own other people, that the owners deserve unfettered discretion to buy and sell the owned, to separate husbands from wives, children from mothers, and to administer beatings, whippings, and other punishments at will; and that the proper role of government is to protect and nourish this social arrangement."[133]

## MOTIVATION OF UPPER SOUTH STATES

Particularly in the Upper South there were significant blocs of antisecession, pro-Union supporters. One noteworthy area was northwestern Virginia, where there were few slaves and even fewer large slave-holders. The anti-secession opposition to the "Slave Power" was so strong that the *Wellsburg Herald* presciently predicted "a breakup of the state if

Virginia adopted an ordinance of secession." It said the area's non-slave-holders "had no more real interest in the institution of slavery in any part of Virginia than they had with slavery in Brazil."[134]

After Confederates fired on Fort Sumter on April 12, 1861, Lincoln called for 75,000 volunteers to put down the rebellion. That action placed the remaining slave states in a difficult position. Ultimately, four Upper South States (Virginia, North Carolina, Tennessee, and Arkansas) seceded and four Border States (Delaware, Maryland, Kentucky, and Missouri) chose to remain in the Union.

What motivated the four late-seceding states? They had to decide whether to take up arms against the seceded states on behalf of the Union or to decline to do so and most likely take up arms against the Union.

Dwight Pitcaithley discusses this question in a thoughtful and compelling manner.[135] Here is his conclusion:

> The answer to the question, then, of whether the secession of the upper South revolved around "slavery" or "states' rights" can only be answered by stating, "secession had everything to do with slavery and states rights.["] The South's secession arguments connected "securing our just rights" with the institution of slavery so completely they cannot be separated. The Southern political elite, especially those from the upper South, demanded explicit federal and constitutional protections for the right to expand slavery, protection the new Republican party was unable to afford. The events at Fort Sumter and Lincoln's call for troops simply became the "tipping point" that pushed the upper South into the ultimate act of dissolving their "Union" with the United States. After attempting to protect their "right" of property in slaves through amendments to the Constitution, the upper South resorted to the ultimate right of secession.[136]

He makes it clear that the states' rights at issue were the right to protection of slavery and the right to secede if that right was not protected.

He supplies dozens of contemporary quotes of Southerners to support that position.

Three of the four Upper South states, Arkansas, Tennessee, and Virginia, proposed Crittenden-like constitutional amendments. Arkansas's representative Thomas Hindman did so to settle "the agitation of the slavery question on a just and fair basis." Arkansas's Governor Henry M. Rector opened his state's secession convention by saying, "The extension of slavery is the vital point of the whole controversy between the North and the South.... [Northerners] believe slavery a sin, we do not, and there lies the problem." Arkansas delegate Hugh French Thomason agreed that hostility to slavery was the national issue and introduced Crittenden-style constitutional amendments.[137]

Tennessee's Governor Isham G. Harris introduced a slew of slavery-protecting constitutional amendments to address the "systematic, wanton, and long continued agitation of the slavery question." In response, that state's legislature approved a set of amendments and sent them to Congress.[138]

North Carolina's Senator Thomas Clingman decried the election of Lincoln, known, he said, to be a dangerous man. He charged Republicans with declaring slavery a crime and favoring its abolishment. Also, he claimed the North's position was "your institutions are not equal to ours, and you must accept an inferior position under the Government." But, "The sagacious men of the South see the danger, and...with the prospect in the future of the abolition of slavery and the utter destruction of their section, they are coming resolutely into the struggle."[139] After examining the causation of North Carolina's secession, Jay Gillispie concludes:

> In the final analysis it is clear that when North Carolinians officially seceded on May 20, 1861 to become the eleventh and final state to officially join the Confederacy they did so to protect and perpetuate slavery. Contemporary North Carolinians...understood and never denied during the years

leading up to the secession crisis that their society rested firmly upon the institution and that whites benefited from it in a variety of ways whether they owned slaves or not. When North Carolinians left the Union they often said they were doing so to preserve their "institutions" and their "rights." These were euphemisms for slavery—what other "institution" or "right" existed in North Carolina and the South that did not also exist in the North?[140]

The fourth Upper South state was Virginia, which proposed eleven constitutional amendments and called the February 1861 Washington Peace Conference seeking national consensus in favor of Crittenden-type proposals. "Before Congress, in the Virginia legislature, at the Washington Peace Conference, and in its own secession convention, a number of Virginia's leaders hoped that 'civil war' might be avoided by protecting slavery through the amendment process." In fact, its Governor John Letcher proposed six pro-slavery actions for the North to take after he complained, "Is it not monstrous to see a Government like ours destroyed merely because men cannot agree about a domestic institution, which existed at the formation of the Government, and which is now recognized by 15 out of the 33 States composing the Union?"[141]

Excerpts from delegates' secessionist speeches in the long-running Virginia convention provide some valuable insights. On February 28, 1861, Jeremiah Morton disclaimed, "Men in every branch of the business of life do not know how to shape their contracts because of the agitation every four years of this never-dying question of African slavery—I say, I want to see this question put to rest...." On March 16, George Wythe Randolph, Thomas Jefferson's grandson, complained of Northern power-grabs and tariff policies but then revealed his decisive concern: "The greatest of all wrongs, one which in my judgment would require separation from the north if they had never otherwise injured us, is the translation of anti-slaveryism to power, the change from passive sentiment to energetic action. While the anti-slavery sentiment was merely speculative we had no right to complain; but now that it has become an efficient agent in the government, it is no longer safe for a slave State to remain under that government."[142]

The culmination of a speech by Virginia delegate George Richardson, delivered on the eve of the firing on Fort Sumter, made it clear that Northerners' alleged opposition to slavery was his primary concern:

> Sir, let us say to these oppressors of the South... "Thus far shalt thou go and no farther." We demand stern, full and exact justice. Cease your assaults on our institutions; ... bow to the [Dred Scott] decision of the Supreme Court; sweep from the statues [sic] of your states every enactment warring on our property [slaves]; cease your attacks on the laws which have established slavery in places under jurisdiction of the Federal Government [e.g., the District of Columbia]; confess that...wherever in the common territories our flag floats, our property has the same right to protection as yours has.... [Then] the seceded South may return. The Union may again stretch its grand proportions from Maine to California, from the Atlantic to the Pacific. Deny us these, our right, and our separation from you is eternal."[143]

The record is clear that leaders in Arkansas, North Carolina, Tennessee, and Virginia saw a Northern threat to slavery as the cause of the secession crisis and sought to avoid the need for secession through proslavery constitutional amendments. Their hopes were dashed when Fort Sumter was attacked and Lincoln called for 75,000 volunteer troops.

## REJECTION OF USING SLAVES AS SOLDIERS

Part of the Myth has been that many, perhaps thousands, of blacks, fought for the Confederacy. The underlying themes here are that blacks supported life under a system of slavery and Confederate use of black soldiers demonstrated that the Civil War was not about slavery.

An early postwar example was the following synopsis by Southern journalist J. D. B. DeBow: "So firmly fixed did our people remain in the faith that the negro would be true to his master that it was finally proposed to receive him into the ranks of the army as a soldier.... [S]o popular was the idea, that enlistments began to take place, and had the war continued the negro must have formed a large element of our military strength." He concluded that three or four hundred thousand black troops could have been "thrown into field."[144] DeBow did not explain why the Confederacy waited until the war was essentially lost before enlisting any blacks, that there was violent opposition to arming blacks, and that at most a paltry handful may have been enlisted.

Even today, claims are made that regiments consisting of thousands of blacks fought for the Confederacy and that slaves who fought for the Confederacy received their freedom.[145]

Although blacks had compiled an impressive military record fighting in the Revolutionary War and the War of 1812, that history generally was ignored by both Southern and Northern decision-makers as they considered arming blacks in the Civil War. South Carolina's opposition to arming blacks appeared even in Revolutionary days. After the British captured Savannah and threatened South Carolina, the latter state rejected a congressional suggestion and a proposal by a South Carolina planter to arm their slaves. The slaveholder-dominated legislature rejected the concept and declared, "We are much disgusted here at the Congress recommending us to arm our Slaves, it was received with great resentment, as a very dangerous and impolitic Step." They considered arming slaves more dangerous than a British invasion. That same thinking prevailed in the Civil War as well.[146]

There is no credible evidence to support the claims about armed black Confederate soldiers or emancipation of them. The Confederacy forbid the use of black soldiers until the last month of Lee's army's existence—when it did so in such a conditional and tardy manner that it produced no black combat troops.

Most of the purported thousands of soldiers were nothing more than slaves who were compelled to accompany their masters or masters' sons to war; their role was not that of soldiers, but of slaves performing menial tasks. They were whipped or otherwise punished for misbehavior—not exactly a court-martial procedure. Although postwar Southerners' accounts mentioned their slaves' battlefield exploits, "[T]he vast majority of these stories of servants braving the battlefield to fight Yankees or rescue wounded masters litter postwar accounts...tell us much about how whites chose to remember their former slaves during the postwar period, but very little about what motivated camp servants during these moments of intense danger."[147]

White soldiers' wartime correspondence referred to their slaves merely as negro, boy, uncle, or other unsoldierly terms. When a slave named Luke asked for a parole so he could accompany his master home after their military incarceration, his master told him he did not need a parole because "You have never been a soldier."[148]

In summary, "Following the war the relationships between Confederate officers and their black camp servants were transformed into stories of loyal slaves and used as a pillar of the Lost Cause narrative ... [The stories and other postwar developments] made it easier to distance the Confederates' experiment in independence from their 'peculiar institution.'"

Just after the mid-1861 Confederate victory at the First Battle of Bull Run (Manassas), Brigadier General Richard Ewell suggested to an exuberant President Davis the necessity to emancipate and arm slaves to ensure Southern independence. Davis rejected this private plea as "stark madness that would revolt and disgust the whole South." Ewell rejoined that this step "will paralyze the North." Davis said the scheme was impossible and asked who would command a brigade of Negroes. When Ewell said he would, the president again rejected the proposal as simply impossible. Ewell's simple recommendation of arming and emancipating slaves would never be implemented by the Confederate government.[149]

From late 1863 through March 1865, other Southerners, seeing the Confederacy in serious jeopardy, proposed that slaves be armed as Confederate soldiers and possibly be granted their freedom for doing so. In December 1863, Major General Thomas Hindman, an Arkansan, anonymously made such a suggestion in an open letter to a Tennessee newspaper then being published in Georgia.[150]

The stage was set for the most serious and thoughtful proposal on this subject by another Arkansan, a former law partner of Hindman. The most famous proponent of this idea was perhaps the rebels' best Western Theater general, Major General Patrick Cleburne, who ended his prospects for promotion by making such a proposal.

Cleburne, along with thirteen subordinate officers, made his proposal on January 2, 1864, after the rebels had incurred high casualties at Chickamauga and Chattanooga while being driven out of Tennessee in late 1863. Cleburne's rear-guard action at Ringgold Gap had saved the Army of Tennessee and, by February, earned him the official thanks of the Confederate Congress.[151] But his sterling record did not protect him once he made his proposal to arm and free slaves.

A native of Ireland, Cleburne had a broader perspective than most Southerners. His proposal was designed to address Confederate manpower shortages and the lack of foreign recognition. He read his written proposal at a meeting with Army of Tennessee commander General Joseph Johnston and almost all his corps and division commanders.

Cleburne first described the Confederacy's dire straits, which he said were due to rebel armies' inferior numbers, inferior supply of potential soldiers, and "the fact that slavery, from being one of our chief sources of strength at the commencement of the war, has now become, in a military point of view, one of our chief sources of weakness." Although recognizing that the slavery issue "may rouse prejudice and passion," he said with understatement, "it would be madness" not to probe all relevant possibilities.[152]

He next described President Davis's recent proposals to increase rebel army manpower by a series of actions involving white men, including "placing in the ranks such of the able-bodied men now employed as wagoners [sic], nurses, cooks and other employés [sic], as are doing service for which the negroes may be found competent." Cleburne somewhat brazenly concluded that the Davis proposals would not provide adequate manpower and then daringly said:

[W]e propose...that we immediately commence training a
large reserve of the most courageous of our slaves, and further
that we guarantee freedom within a reasonable time to every
slave in the South who shall remain true to the Confederacy
in this war. As between the loss of independence and the loss
of slavery, we assume that every patriot will freely give up the
latter—give up the negro slave rather than be a slave himself.[153]

In no uncertain terms, Cleburne was advocating the abolition of
slavery and the recruitment of blacks to fight for the Confederacy. Among
the benefits of these actions, he said, were the attraction of foreign support for the Confederacy and the destruction of the purpose for which
Northern abolitionists and black Union troops were fighting. He also
answered the question "Will slaves fight?" by citing numerous historical
examples, including ex-slaves in Jamaica and, reluctantly, Union blacks
("... the experience of this war has been so far that half-trained negroes
have fought as bravely as half-trained Yankees...").[154]

In explaining his long and thoughtful proposal, Cleburne made some
justifying observations that obviously upset supporters of slavery. For
example, he said that his proposal "would instantly remove all the vulnerability, embarrassment and inherent weakness which result from
slavery. The approach of the enemy would no longer find every household
surrounded by spies; the fear that sealed the master's lips and the avarice
that has, in so many cases, tempted him practically to desert us would
alike be removed. There would be no recruits awaiting the enemy with
open arms, no complete history of every neighborhood with ready guides,
no fear of insurrection in the rear, or anxieties for the fate of loved ones
when our armies moved forward.... *It would remove forever all selfish
taint from our cause and place independence above every question of
property.*"[155]

Cleburne not only had to justify arming slaves, but he also had to
explain the reasons for freeing them—and their families and all "loyal"
slaves. His arguments included the following:

If we arm and train [the Negro] and make him fight for the country in her hour of dire distress, every consideration of principle and policy demand [sic] that we should set him and his whole race who side with us free. It is a first principle with mankind that he who offers his life in defense of the State should receive from her in return his freedom and his happiness, and we believe in acknowledgment of this principle.... The slaves are dangerous now, but armed, trained and collected in an army they would be a thousand fold more dangerous; therefore when we make soldiers of them we must make free men of them beyond all question, and thus enlist their sympathies also. We can do this more effectually than the North can now do, for we can give the negro not only his own freedom, but that of his wife and child, and can secure it to him in his old home. To do this, we must immediately make his marriage and parental relations sacred in the eyes of the law and forbid their sale.[156]

The proposal concluded, "It is said that slavery is all we are fighting for, and if we give it up we give up all. Even if this were true, which we deny, slavery is not all our enemies are fighting for.... We have now briefly proposed a plan which we believe will save our country.... No objection ought to outweigh it which is not weightier than independence."[157]

The major general from Ireland had carefully and thoroughly thought through his startling proposal. This was not just a flippant, off-the-top-of-his-head verbal recommendation. His was a serious "white-paper." He saw that the Confederates desperately needed more manpower, a large pool of people already existed in the South's slave population, huge numbers of soldiers could be "drafted" from that pool, blacks had historically and were concurrently showing for the North[158] an ability to fight, freedom for black soldiers was a necessity, freedom for their families also would be required, and the Southern practice of not recognizing slave marriages and family units would have to end.

But Cleburne had not reckoned with the deep-seated underlying beliefs in, and perceived economic necessity of, the institution of slavery. The well-to-do, whose wealth primarily consisted of slaves, would be reluctant to give up their valuable "property." After two centuries of fearing slave revolts, whites would perceive armed slaves as a threat to white society.

After more than two hundred years of justifying slavery partially on the grounds that Negroes were incapable of performing skilled functions, the shock of their being allowed to act as armed soldiers was too astounding to absorb. As Benjamin Quarles notes, "[Southerners] were enslaved by a system of values which stamped the blacks as inferiors, and to make the Negro a soldier would be to call into question the very foundation of their mythology, or compel them to invent new myths."[159] These foes of Cleburne's proposal ignored the success of black soldiers in the Revolutionary War, the War of 1812, the current Civil War (fighting for the Union), and even the astounding May 1862 feat of slave Robert Smalls, who commandeered the rebel vessel *Planter* and sailed it through and out of Charleston harbor with valuable supplies and his and his crew's families.[160]

Even if there could have been support for awarding freedom to black soldiers, extending that concept to their wives and children would undermine any remaining economic viability of slavery because those women and children no longer would be marketable economic commodities. Cleburne was not just recommending the arming of slaves; he was suggesting the end of slavery itself as the price for Southern victory. Not least, white supremacy was being challenged—despite assurances from Cleburne that it was not.

For many Southerners, slavery "had been so long and so thoroughly interwoven with the domestic economy, the comfort, and the traditions of Southern society, that the common thought revolted at any suggestion which contemplated its eradication either proximate or remote."[161]

The reaction to Cleburne's proposal reveals much about Southern priorities. In a nutshell, slavery trumped independence. All officers at the meeting with Johnston, except Hindman and the silent Johnston, condemned the proposal. There an "awe[-]struck horror apparently grew in the minds of several of the assembled generals as they were faced with this moment: they must choose either slavery or independence *but could not have both*. For the majority at the meeting the choice was an impossible one; they chose instead to make no decision at all and condemned both the conundrum itself and its proponent."[162]

The hostile reaction was just beginning. Major General W. H. T. Walker called the proposal "incendiary," and Major General A. P. Stewart wrote that arming and emancipating slaves was "at war with my social, moral and political principles." They were joined by Major General James Patton Anderson, who called the idea "monstrous" and wrote that he would not "attempt to describe my feelings on being confronted with a project so startling in its character—may I say *so revolting to southern sentiment, southern pride, and southern honor?*"[163]

Although Cleburne had hoped his written proposal would be forwarded to Richmond for high-level consideration, Johnston temporarily stymied that hope by sitting on it. For better or worse, Walker took matters into his own hands and, completely outside the chain of command, sent the paper to Jefferson Davis. Johnston had denied Walker's request to forward the document to the War Department. But Walker sent it directly to President Davis because, in his dramatic and self-serving words, "The gravity of the subject, the magnitude of the issues involved, my strong convictions that the further agitation of such sentiments and propositions would ruin the efficacy of our Army and involve our cause in ruin and disgrace constitute my reasons for bringing the document before the Executive."[164]

When the proposal reached Davis, he responded to Walker that it was "injurious to the public service [and] that the best policy under the circumstances will be to avoid all publicity... it should be kept private. If it be kept out of the public journals its ill effect will be much lessened."[165] Davis had Secretary of War James Seddon tell army commander Johnston, "the dissemination or even promulgation of such opinions under the present circumstances of the Confederacy, whether in the Army or among the people can be productive only of discouragement, distraction, and dissension."

He instructed Johnston to tell the meeting attendees of the president's disapproval and "urge on them the suppression, not only of the memorial itself, but likewise of all discussion and controversy respecting or growing out of it."[166] Johnston did so in a communication to his division commanders in which he simply reproduced the letter from Seddon. He added a note on Cleburne's copy requesting him to pass this information to his divisional officers.[167]

Suppression of the proposal, embarrassing to many ex-Confederates, lasted thirty years until its publication in the *Official Records*.[168] The significant point is that, as of January 1864, Cleburne's idea was viewed by Jefferson Davis himself as inconsistent with the Confederacy's *raison d'être*.

General Braxton Bragg, now military advisor to Jefferson Davis,[169] called Cleburne and his allies "abolitionist men" who "should be watched." He described the proposal as "treasonous" and stated, "I should like to know as a matter of safety the names of the traitors."[170] Bragg had no love for Cleburne, who had been one of many subordinate officers who had urged his removal from command of the Army of Tennessee the prior year.

Consistent with Bragg's warning, "We must mark the men," the more-than-deserving Cleburne never received a promotion to lieutenant general or corps command. This occurred despite the fact that there were three corps command openings in the first eleven months of 1864 before Cleburne's death in the Franklin, Tennessee, suicidal attack that November. As one officer much later described the situation,

> [T]he entire army recognized the gallantry, devotion, and military prowess of Cleburne, and for a year prior, and up to the day of his death, officers and men were anxiously expecting his promotion to the grade of lieutenant general, and few, very few knew why he was not so commissioned.... [His proposal] cost him promotion, yea, ever after kept him from attaining his just and well merited deserts—a lieutenant generalship.[171]

Bruce Levine summarizes the Confederate position on arming black soldiers that prevailed for most of the war: "[D]uring the war's first three and a half years, Richmond refused to consider this policy because it seemed to threaten both slavery and white supremacy, the twin pillars of southern economy, social relations, culture, and ideology. Having seceded from the Union and gone to war to protect those institutions, few southern political and community leaders were ready to seek military victory through a policy that apparently abandoned the original purpose of the struggle."[172]

But calamity caused some reconsideration of this position. Confederate losses mounted and their prospects declined in 1864 as Lee lost 33,000 irreplaceable soldiers opposing Grant's Overland Campaign movement to Richmond and then disaster struck with the September 1 loss of crucial Atlanta. Lincoln's November 1864 reelection dashed Southern hopes for a political victory and convinced Davis, Secretary of State Judah Benjamin, and eventually Robert E. Lee to urge the military use of slaves. None of them favored general emancipation—just military use of slaves in return for their freedom. Lee's support was conditioned on approval of the slaves' owners.[173] Although a critical Lee letter is missing, it appears that he became a convert to arming slaves in late October or early November 1864.[174]

To make such recommendations, Davis had to backtrack from the previous statement, made on his behalf by Secretary of War Seddon, that the Cleburne proposals "in their scope pass beyond the bounds of Confederate action, and could under our constitutional system neither be recommended by the Executive to Congress nor be entertained by that body."[175] Lee, on January 11, 1865, just over a year after Cleburne's spurned proposal, had to explain that military necessity drove his proposal for arming slaves, although he still agreed that "the relation of master and slave, controlled by humane laws and influenced by Christianity and enlightened public sentiment [was] the best that can exist between the white and black races while intermingled as at present in this country." He stressed that, "I would deprecate any sudden disturbance of that relation unless it be necessary to avert a greater calamity...."[176]

Even Lee, therefore, concluded, "Whatever may be the effect of our employing negro troops, it cannot be as mischievous as [Union use of those blacks]. If it end in subverting slavery it will be accomplished by ourselves, and we devise the means of alleviating the evil consequences to both races. I think, therefore, we must decide whether slavery shall be extinguished by our enemies and the slaves be used against us, or use them ourselves at the risk of the effects which may be produced upon our social institutions. My own opinion is that we should employ them without delay."[177] In a letter published late the next month, Lee wrote that arming slaves was "not only expedient but necessary" and "those who are employed should be freed."[178]

Even in those desperate final months of the war, the idea of some form of emancipation, supported by Davis and Lee, was widely opposed in the Southern press—often on grounds of inconsistency with the reasons for the Confederacy's existence. The *Macon* [Georgia] *Telegraph and Confederate* said, "This terrible war and extreme peril of our country" were "occasioned ... more by the institution of negro slavery" than "by any other subject of quarrel." "For it and its perpetuation, we commenced and have kept at war," said the *Memphis Appeal*. The *Richmond Examiner* succinctly concluded that the proposal was "opposite to all the sentiments and principles which have heretofore governed the Southern people."[179]

Robert Barnwell Rhett Jr.'s *Charleston Mercury* said, "the mere agitation in the Northern States to effect the emancipation of our slaves largely contributed to our separation from them.... [But incredibly] before a Confederacy which we established to put at rest forever all such agitation is four years old, we find the proposition gravely submitted that the Confederate Government should emancipate slaves in the States."[180]

The *Richmond Whig* launched a broad attack on the enlist-and-emancipate proposals. It stated its long-standing position that "servitude is a divinely appointed condition for the highest good of the slave, is that condition in which the negro race especially may attain the highest moral and intellectual advancement of which they are capable." Therefore, it concluded that emancipation, far from being an act of kindness, would "be an act of cruelty to deprive the slave of the care and guardianship of a master."[181]

Abolition was opposed by most Southern politicians. Former Confederate Secretary of State Robert M. T. Hunter urged the rejection of European pressure for emancipation. He argued, "What did we go to war for, if not to protect our property?" Tennessee Congressman Henry S. Foote asked, "If this government is to destroy slavery, why fight for it?"[182]

Even more heated opposition arose from the proposal to arm slaves, which had been a Southern nightmare for about 200 years. On January 8, 1865, Major General Howell Cobb of Georgia (first speaker of the Provisional Confederate Congress) wrote to Secretary of War James Seddon about the idea. He said, "I think that the proposition to make soldiers of our slaves is the most pernicious idea that has been suggested since the war began. It is to me a source of deep mortification and regret to see the name of that good and great man and soldier, General R. E. Lee, given as authority for such a policy.... You cannot make soldiers of slaves, nor slaves of soldiers.... The day you make soldiers of [Negroes] is the beginning of the end of the revolution. If slaves will make good soldiers our whole theory of slavery is wrong—but they won't make soldiers." Ignoring the successful Union experience with black soldiers,[183] Cobb added, "As a class they are wanting in every qualification of a soldier." He said it was better to abolish slavery to win British and French support than to pursue "the suicidal policy of arming our slaves."[184] Numerous sources reported widespread opposition from Confederate soldiers, who had little desire to fight alongside blacks.[185]

Georgia Governor Joseph E. Brown, the Richmond Whig, and R. M. T. Hunter contended that the proposed limited abolishment of slavery would violate the Confederate Constitution. Hunter said, "the Government had no power under the Constitution to arm and emancipate the slaves, and the Constitution granted no such great powers by implication."[186]

The debate of late 1864 and early 1865 about possibly arming slaves or other blacks stands as a sharp rebuke to those who argue that blacks were fighting for the Confederacy all along. Confederate soldiers in the field never reported that blacks were fighting alongside them or what such experience demonstrated. The problem with arming blacks was that it undercut the South's rationale for secession—opposition to abolition. For example, the *Richmond Examiner* opined in November 1864: "If a negro is fit to be a soldier he is not fit to be a slave. The employment of negroes as soldiers in our armies, either with or without prospective emancipation, would be the first step, but a step which would involve all the rest, to universal abolition." As historian Kevin Levin concluded, "The evidence is overwhelming that Confederate plans to arm slaves were considered a radical and dangerous step, not a continuation of the slave impressment policies that accepted slaves in camps as servants."[187]

In a chapter entitled "What Did We Go to War For?" Bruce Levine, in his *Confederate Emancipation*, detailed the widespread opposition throughout the South to arming and freeing slaves. He concluded that "opponents of the Davis administration's last-minute plan…agreed on one central and fundamental point, one that they considered nearly self-evident—that the South had withdrawn from and made war upon the old Union primarily to safeguard its "peculiar institution."[188]

Because similar views on emancipation and arming blacks prevailed among the Southern people, politicians, and press, the Confederate Congress never approved the military use of slaves in return for their freedom. On March 8, 1865, it barely approved (by a vote of forty-seven to thirty-eight in the House and nine to eight in the Senate) a watered-down program for use of slaves with their owners' permission and without manumission. The law specified "that nothing in this act shall be construed to authorize a change in the relation which the said slaves shall bear toward their owners except by consent of the owners and of the States in which they may reside."[189] Even advocacy from Robert E. Lee, the Confederacy's national hero, had been insufficient to convince the Confederate Congress to simply authorize arming and freeing slaves—let alone approve general manumission. In 1866, the Richmond editor and author E. A. Pollard confirmed the ludicrous nature of con-gressional inaction on arming slaves: "The actual results of the legislation of Congress on the subject were ridiculously small...—a pretence of doing something, yet so far below the necessities of the case, as to be to the last degree puerile, absurd, and contemptible."[190]

A disappointed Davis signed the weak legislation into law on March 13. After deliberation, he decided to go beyond the new law and implement some form of emancipation incentive. Thus, he issued a March 23 general order declining to accept any slaves as soldiers without their own consent and their owners' consent to their freedom (a still unlikely prospect).[191] Davis' action came two and a half weeks before Lee's surrender—too late for meaningful implementation.

The long-overdue Confederate implementation of the concept of black soldiers became something of a joke. Two companies of mixed free blacks and slaves (apparently medics) were assembled and put on exhibition in Richmond. A week before Richmond fell, these blacks paraded and went through the manual of arms, without arms, before thousands of onlookers.[192] At least one such review was canceled because black soldiers had not been issued uniforms, equipment, or arms.[193]

Bruce Levine explains the significance of this desperate end-of-war effort to arm blacks: "The whole sorry episode provides a fitting coda for our examination of modern claims that thousands and thousands of black troops loyally fought in Confederate armies. This strikingly unsuccessful last-ditch effort constituted the sole exception to the Confederacy's steadfast refusal to employ African American soldiers. As General Ewell's long-term aide-de-camp, Major George Campbell Brown, later affirmed, the handful of black soldiers mustered in the southern capital in March of 1865 constituted 'the *first and only* black troops used on our side.'"[194] Black soldiery in the Confederacy began late and ended with a whimper.[195]

In contrast, the Union used 180,000 black soldiers and 20,000 black sailors to achieve victory. Black Union soldiers fought in forty major engagements and about four hundred and fifty other firefights. Sixteen blacks received medals of honor.[196]

No black units fought for the Confederacy. The proposal to arm and liberate slaves failed "because of opposition by both blinkered masters and clear-eyed slaves—slaves who had their eyes on a much bigger prize than the one that Jefferson Davis was belatedly and grudgingly offering."[197] Protection of slavery had trumped the military needs of the Confederacy and demonstrated the extent to which slavery and white supremacy were the primary foundations of that would-be nation.

## CONFEDERATE DIPLOMACY

Unlike the American colonists during the American Revolution, the Confederates failed to obtain critical European recognition or intervention.[198] This failure was surprising to some, such as the Russian minister to Washington, Edouard de Stoeckl, who in April 1861 advised his superiors that "England will take advantage of the first opportunity to recognize the seceded States and that the French will follow her."[199] Although foreign recognition was critical to possible Confederate success, its diplomats were hindered by government pro-slavery policies and their own pro-slavery beliefs. Attempts to secure British, French, and even papal recognition faltered because Confederate leaders valued slavery more than diplomatic recognition—even at the cost of the Confederacy's destruction.[200]

"The main obstacle to their diplomatic success, Confederates grudgingly admitted, was the stubborn prejudice abroad that human slavery was morally reprehensible and their own admission that slavery lay at the very cornerstone of the national edifice they were trying to build.... It was the unspeakable dilemma: in order to win independence, they would have to renounce the main reason they had sought independence in the first place."[201]

The slavery issue was a diplomatic problem for the Confederacy just before and throughout the war. It was especially critical in the fall of 1862, when Great Britain was considering the possibility of mediation or an armistice. Conservative Lord Donoughmore warned Confederate envoy James Mason that Britain would require a "clause stipulating against the African slave trade" as a condition of any treaty of "amity and commerce." Mason's response that the Confederate Constitution banned the African slave trade was rejected because Britain's diplomats in the United States had warned London that the guarantee was legally ephemeral and unenforceable. "If South Carolina or Louisiana or any other state wanted to reopen the gruesome trade with Congo, there would be very little that the Confederate government could or would do about it. So the British would accept nothing less than an explicit commitment to the Crown that no slaves would be imported, and even that might not be enough." The Confederate secretary of state, Judah Benjamin, would not yield on either slavery or the slave trade.[202]

By the middle of the war, rebel diplomats Mason and John Slidell had given up on winning over England and France, respectively, and, in desperation, Confederate envoy Ambrose Dudley Mann unsuccessfully sought recognition from the ultra-conservative Pope Pius IX. But even the pope's letters to American Catholics urging an end to the "destructive *civil war*" undercut the rebel position that two countries were fighting each other.[203]

On July 6, 1864, Lee complained to Davis about Europeans' misunderstanding of the "true" nature of the war: "As far as I have been able to judge, this war presents to the European World but two aspects. A Contest in which one party is contending for abstract slavery & the other against it. The existence of vital rights involved does not seem to be understood or appreciated. As long as this lasts, we can expect neither sympathy or aid."[204] Michael Fellman analyzes Lee's statement: "Here Lee asserted what many Confederates wished to believe late in the war and what many Southern apologists have contended ever since the war ended, that independence and not slavery was the 'vital right' for which the Confederacy fought. Such a position refused to posit the inescapable next issue—that had slavery not existed there would have been no need for secession and war and that therefore the central point of independence was the freedom to continue slavery." Because of Europeans' accurate impression that slavery was at the root of the conflict, their intervention was unlikely.[205]

In late 1864 Secretary of State Judah Benjamin convinced Davis to authorize secret diplomacy in which emancipation would be exchanged for British and French recognition. He argued that Davis could take this step as a matter of military necessity—especially since the Confederacy's de facto, not de jure, status allowed the president to act outside the Confederate Constitution! Those two then sent the Louisianan Duncan F. Kenner on a secret and belated mission to exchange emancipation for British and French recognition. Kenner made the mistake of deferring to veteran diplomats Mason and Slidell, who opposed the exchange and sabotaged the proposal. Despite the president's directive, they could not bring themselves to support emancipation.[206]

Don Doyle puts an exclamation point on the issue of Confederate diplomacy and emancipation:

> Years later, Robert Toombs lamented that the South had not promised an end to slavery earlier in the war, for both France and Britain would have rushed to its support. John Bigelow was not about to let that rest. If the South had been willing to end slavery, he replied to Toombs in a popular magazine, "there would have been no war, and the Confederate maggot would never have been hatched."[207]

In summary, foreign diplomacy was another area in which Confederate leaders demonstrated that slavery was more important than independence.

## PRISONER-OF-WAR POLICIES

Confederate prisoner-of-war exchange policies reflected their attitudes toward blacks. Despite the fact that one-for-one prisoner exchanges would have benefitted the manpower-short Confederacy, its leaders, after blacks began fighting for the Union, declined to undertake such exchanges if black soldiers were included in the trades.

After the Confederates' loss of eighteen thousand troops in the fighting at Chickamauga in September 1864, the next month Lee proposed to Grant that prisoner exchanges be resumed. Grant responded that exchanges could be resumed if Lee agreed that black prisoners would be exchanged "the same as white soldiers." Lee, in turn, replied that "negroes belonging to our citizens are not considered subjects of exchange and were not included in my proposition." Grant, therefore, declined resumption of exchanges, in accordance with Lincoln's policy on the matter—a policy that cost Lincoln votes in the November election because of well-founded concerns about the health and welfare of Union POWs.[208]

Davis and Lee, therefore, made it much easier for Union forces to maintain the magnitude of their numerical superiority by refusing to treat captured black soldiers as normal prisoners of war. Again, slavery and race won over Confederate military needs.

## SUMMARY OF SLAVERY AS THE CAUSE OF SECESSION AND THE CONFEDERACY

In summary, contrary to the Myth of the Lost Cause, preservation of slavery was the primary cause of Southern states' secession and their creation of the Confederacy. Evidence of this connection is found in the slavery-related demographics of the South, the dedication of slave-owners to the war, the official secession resolutions and declarations of the seceding states, prewar settlement efforts, lobbying and diplomatic activities by early-seceding states, contemporaneous pronouncements of the Confederacy's military and political leaders, the Confederate Constitution, Confederate diplomacy, Confederate refusal to arm and liberate slaves, and Confederate prisoner-of-war exchange policies.

Southern secessionist leaders' own words made clear their economic dependence upon slavery, the interconnection between slavery and white supremacy, and their violent reactions to perceived threats to the peculiar institution—reactions that led them to secede. As the British historian D. W. Brogan concludes, Southerners "seceded over one thing and fought over one thing: slavery."[209]

CHAPTER FOUR

# COULD THE SOUTH HAVE WON THE CIVIL WAR?

## THE MYTH

Propagators of the Myth contend that the South did the best it could with the resources it had and that it never had a chance to win the Civil War. The North's superior industrial strength and its 3.5-to-1 manpower advantage, they contend, made it unbeatable.

Robert E. Lee originated this myth at Appomattox in his famous farewell to his troops, whom he consoled with the assurance, "After four years of arduous service, marked by unsurpassed courage and fortitude, the Army of Northern Virginia has been compelled to yield to over-whelming numbers and resources."[1] A rebel soldier repeated this theme: "They never whipped us, sir, unless they were four to one. If we had anything like a fair chance, or less disparity of numbers, we should have won our cause and established our independence."[2] A century later, Civil War historian Richard Current echoes Lee's assessment: "Surely, in view of the disparity in resources, it would have taken a miracle, a direct intervention of the Lord on the other side, to enable the South to win. As usual, God was on the side of the heaviest battalions."[3]

The theory, as Alan Nolan summarizes it, was that "the Confederates had not really been defeated, they had instead been overwhelmed by massive Northern manpower and materiel.... Furthermore, the South's loss was said to be inevitable from the beginning; the fact of loss was somehow mitigated in the myth because it was said that winning had been impossible. If the Confederacy could not have won, it somehow did not lose."[4] Or as the Southerner Shelby Foote put it in Ken Burns's influential 1990 documentary *The Civil War*, "The North fought the war with one hand behind its back.... [T]he North [could] have brought the other arm out from behind its back.... I don't think that the South ever had a chance to win the war."[5]

## HOW THE SOUTH COULD HAVE WON THE WAR

Yet as James McPherson has noted, "There was nothing inevitable about Northern victory in the Civil War."[6] Shortly after Confederates had fired on Fort Sumter, there was an eleven-state confederacy—a self-declared nation state—that asserted its independence. It also drew strength from military volunteers from the non-seceding slave states of Maryland, Kentucky, Missouri, and Delaware. All the Confederacy needed was a stalemate, which would confirm its existence as a separate country. The burden was on the North to defeat the Confederacy and compel the return of the eleven wayward states to the Union. "The South could 'win' the war by not losing," writes McPherson, but "the North could win only by winning."[7]

Although outnumbered and lacking the industrial resources of the North, the Confederacy was not without advantages of its own. It was vast—750,000 square miles the Federals would have to invade and conquer.[8] "Thus space was all in favour of the South; even should the enemy overrun her border, her principal cities, few in number, were far removed from the hostile bases, and the important railway junctions were perfectly secure from sudden attack. And space, especially when means of communication are scanty, and the country affords few supplies, is the greatest of all obstacles."[9] Southern troops, moreover, had to cover shorter distances than the invaders and could do so over a complex of well-placed railroads (if controlled and maintained properly).

A contemporary analysis of the American Civil War published in the *Times* of London recognized the Confederates' huge strategic advantage: "No war of independence ever terminated unsuccessfully except where the disparity of force was far greater than it is in this case. Just as England during the [American] revolution had to give up conquering the colonies, so the North will have to give up conquering the South."[10] The Confederate secretary of war, George W. Randolph, shared this optimism about the South's prospects early in the war: "[T]here is no instance in history of a people as numerous as we are inhabiting a country so extensive as ours being subjected if true to themselves."[11]

Other Southerners agreed. James Barbour, a delegate to the Virginia secession convention, quoted Confederate Vice President Alexander Stephens's assessment of Southern strength when the Confederacy consisted of only seven states: "With such an area of territory—with such an amount of population—with a climate and soil unsurpassed by any on the face of the earth—with such resources already at our command—with productions which control the commerce of the world—who can entertain any apprehensions as to our success, whether others join us or not?" Barbour himself voiced the hope that England and France, although they found slavery distasteful, would "deal with and make money out of the most lucrative customer on the face of the globe."[12]

After the war, various Confederate generals expressed their views that the war had been winnable. In 1874, Joseph E. Johnston insisted that the South had not been "guilty of the high crime of undertaking a war without the means of waging it successfully."[13] Pierre G. T. Beauregard added, "No people ever warred for independence with more relative advantages than the Confederates."[14] E. Porter Alexander's retrospective assessment was more modest than Beauregard's, but he too thought the South could have won:

When the South entered upon war with a power so immensely
her superior in men & money, & all the wealth of modern
resources in machinery and transportation appliances by land
& sea, she could entertain but one single hope of final success.
That was, that the desperation of her resistance would finally
exact from her adversary such a price in blood & treasure as
to exhaust the enthusiasm of its population for the objects of
the war. We could not hope to *conquer* her. Our one chance
was to wear her out.[15]

Much of Europe expected (and desired) a Confederate victory. The
downfall of "the American colossus," opined the *Times*, would be good
"riddance of a nightmare.... Excepting a few gentlemen of republican
tendencies, we all expect, we nearly all wish, success to the Confederate
cause." Joining in was the Earl of Shrewsbury, who cheerfully predicted
"that the dissolution of the Union is inevitable, and that men before [sic]
me will live to see an aristocracy established in America." As late as 1863,
Russia's minister to the United States declared, "The republican form of
government, so much talked about by the Europeans and so much praised
by the Americans, is breaking down. What can be expected from a country where men of humble origin are elevated to the highest positions?"[16]

A Southern victory was not out of the question.[17] After all, it had
been only eighty years since the supposedly inferior American revolu-
tionaries had vanquished the mighty Redcoats of King George III[18] and
less than fifty years since the outgunned Russians had repelled and
destroyed the powerful invading army of Napoleon.

John Cook has identified four specific Confederate advantages: the
psychological edge of fighting for independence and to protect their
homes and way of life; interior lines and geography, including rivers,
mountains, and swamps that were the equivalent of successive lines of
fortifications; higher per-capita production of corn, livestock, and other
necessities of life; and cotton, which, properly utilized, could provide
economic and diplomatic benefits.[19]

By declining to use slaves as soldiers, moreover, the heavily outnumbered Confederacy failed to exploit fully its available manpower. Some Southerners were counting on the manpower their slaves could provide in the war effort. In late February 1861, for example, Jeremiah Morton, a pro-secession delegate to Virginia's convention, explained that "if the tug of war ever comes, I would rather have the four millions of slaves and the eight millions of free men, than to have sixteen millions of free men and no slaves.... Give us four millions of slaves under the management and discipline of Southern planters and Southern men, and they will give you more sinews of war, than ten millions of free men, agitated with the cares of families and the harassments of military duties."[20] Morton did not foresee that slaves, under-utilized by the Confederacy, would become Union assets and that rebel soldiers, facing the invading Union armies, would soon enough concern themselves with "the cares of families."

The prompt use of black soldiers by the Confederacy could have been quite effective. "Early in the war, when Lincoln was still defining the Union cause narrowly (for reunion alone and not for emancipation) and when Union officers were still refusing sanctuary to runaway slaves," writes Bruce Levine, "... significant numbers of such slaves might have accepted an offer of emancipation in exchange for performing Confederate military service."[21] Instead the rebels ignored the encouraging precedents of black soldiers in the American Revolution (over George Washington's initial objections)[22] and the War of 1812 and allowed their support of slavery and white supremacy to rule out this option.

The war was winnable if Southern resources were husbanded carefully. But Lee's strategy and tactics dissipated irreplaceable manpower. His losses at Mechanicsville, Malvern Hill, Antietam, and Gettysburg and his costly "victories" at Gaines's Mill, Second Bull Run, and Chancellorsville—all in 1862 and 1863—made possible Grant's and Sherman's successful campaigns against Richmond and Atlanta in 1864 and produced a sense of the inevitability of Confederate defeat that contributed to Lincoln's reelection.

It did not help the South that Davis and Lee disagreed on strategy. The "fundamental flaw" of the Confederate strategy, writes Robert Tanner, was the lack of "consensus between Jefferson Davis and his senior commanders as to how they were going to use the military force they had created to achieve their political goals." As Steven Woodworth puts it, "Whereas Davis believed the South could win by not losing, Lee believed the South could lose by not winning."[23] Woodworth concludes that by 1864 the Confederacy's best hope to win the war "lay in convincing the North to abandon the struggle. This could be accomplished by running up northern casualty lists and denying the North the kind of morale-boosting victories that would convince its citizens and soldiers that the war was in fact being won.... In short, the South's easiest way to independence in 1864 would seem to have been to hold Atlanta and Richmond and bleed the blue-clad armies white."[24] The same strategy also would have been more successful in 1862 and 1863 than the offensive one that Lee pursued. "The weaker side can win; the South almost did."[25]

In *Why the South Lost the Civil War*, four historians analyze the South's defensive advantages:

> ... the Confederate Army suffered no crippling deficiency in weapons or supplies. Their principal handicap would be numerical inferiority. But to offset this lack Confederates fought the first major war in which both sides armed themselves with rifles and had the advantage of a temporary but very significant surge in the power of the tactical defensive. In addition, the problem of supply in a very large but thinly settled region was a powerful aid to the strategic defensive. Other things being equal, Confederate military leadership were confident that if the Union did not display Napoleonic genius, the tactical and strategic power of the defensive could offset the Northern superiority.... In short, the task of the North was literally gigantic. It was the task of organizing and harnessing its superior resources and committing them to

warfare on a financial scale that was historically unprecedented.... [I]nertia was on the South's side and would have
been fatal to the North. The North had the necessity to conquer. The South could have won simply by not being conquered. It did not have to occupy a foot of ground outside its
borders.[26]

The South's best hope for success was outlasting Lincoln, and deep
schisms among Northerners throughout the war kept that hope alive.
Northerners violently disagreed on slavery, the draft, civil liberties, and
the war itself. To exploit these divisions and prevail, the Confederates
needed to preserve their manpower, sap the strength of the North, make
continuation of the war intolerable, and compel recognition of the Confederacy's independence. Robert E. Lee's deliberate disregard of this
reality may have been his greatest failure.

A Confederate victory through Lincoln's defeat at the ballot box in
November 1864 was entirely plausible.[27] "Even [at the end of 1863] defeat
was not yet inevitable," explains Richard McMurry. "If the Confederates
could hold on, they might convince the northern public that victory was
not worth what it would cost. Northern voters might then turn the Lincoln administration out of office in the 1864 elections and replace it with
a government that would be willing to accept Confederate independence."[28]

Contemporary support for that proposition came from Pollard's
1866 work. In early 1864, he noted, Northern Democrats were beginning
work on a peace platform for the November election, Northerners were
impatient about the war's prolongation, and Southern maintenance of
the *status quo* through another military campaign would enable the
Democrats to win and to negotiate terms. Pollard concluded, "It was
said, with reason, in Richmond, that such was Northern impatience that
the question of the war had simply become one of *endurance* on the part
of the South; that even without positive victories in the field, and merely
by securing *negative results* in the ensuing campaign, the Democratic
party would be able to overthrow the Administration at Washington,

and to open negotiations with Richmond as between government and government."[29]

Morale in the North hit rock bottom in July and August 1864. Grant and Sherman had taken heavy casualties in advancing to Richmond and Atlanta, but their foes were still vigorous and those cities remained in Southern hands. By August 23, Lincoln was so sure of his defeat that he wrote a note to that effect and had his cabinet members sign the outside of the note without reading it. All informed and influential Republican politicians and newspaper editors urged him to allow someone else— perhaps Grant—to run in his stead.[30]

The importance of Lincoln's reelection for Union victory was not lost on contemporaries. President Davis and Generals Lee, Longstreet, and Josiah Gorgas, among others, wrote in 1863 and 1864 that the South could prevail if Lincoln lost his reelection battle. In fact, as early as his 1862 Antietam campaign, "Lee well realized that the only way for the Confederacy to win was by persuading the Union to lose."[31] Soon Lee was contemplating Lincoln's possible defeat for reelection. In April 1863 he wrote to his wife, "If successful this year, next fall [1864] there will be a great change in public opinion at the North. The Republicans will be destroyed & I think the friends of peace will become so strong as that the next administration will go in on that basis."[32]

Those Southerners realized that Lincoln was the steel backbone of the Union war effort and that his replacement, especially by a less than committed George B. McClellan,[33] would open up opportunities for the Confederacy. Southerners' confidence in McClellan's malleability was demonstrated by Pollard's early postwar analysis:

> Gen. McClellan's letter of acceptance [of his nomination]...
> by its pacific tone and conciliatory terms, removed much of
> the objection which the extreme peace men of his party had
> felt to his nomination. Affirming the necessity of preserving
> the Union entire in the most cogent terms, he declared, that
> its preservation "was the sole avowed object for which the
> war was commenced;" that "it should have been conducted

for that object only: "that it should have been conducted on the principles of conciliation and compromise; that the reestablishment of the Union must be the indispensable condition in any settlement; and that "they should exhaust all the resources of statesmanship to secure such a peace, to reestablish the Union, and to secure for the future the constitutional rights of every State.[34]

Certainly someone who stated that war should be conducted on principles of conciliation and compromise would be an ideal negotiating "adversary."

In fact, Lee's gambling offensive actions had been intended to win an overwhelming victory or two, thus deflating Northern morale and ensuring that Lincoln would be voted out of office. If he had wisely preserved his manpower by remaining on the strategic and tactical defensive, the South would have appeared to have a respectable chance of winning (if only by stalemate) as the crucial election approached. Instead, by late 1864, Lee had drained the South of too many men, and the fall of Atlanta, the loss of the Shenandoah Valley, the partial siege of his army at Richmond and Petersburg, and the fall of Mobile Harbor made Southern prospects look bleak. Pollard said that McClellan's election, which had some probability in midsummer 1864, "became impossible, in view of the rapid military successes of the North" and was stymied by the fact that the election occurred at the most propitious time possible for Lincoln.[35]

Could Lincoln have been defeated? A glance at the 1864 election returns might suggest that his reelection was assured. Riding a wave of military victories, Lincoln convincingly won reelection. Out of slightly more than four million votes cast, Lincoln received 2,218,388 (55 percent), while McClellan garnered 1,812,807 (45 percent). These votes resulted in an impressive 212-to-21 electoral-vote victory for Lincoln. Although these statistics seem to reflect a landslide, the election was much closer than it appeared. The switch of a mere .75 percent of the votes (29,935 out of 4,031,195) in specific states would have given

McClellan the ninety-seven additional electoral votes he needed. He could have picked up the huge states of Pennsylvania and New York— and their fifty-nine electoral votes—with a swing of fewer than thirteen thousand votes. The additional thirty-eight electoral votes he would have then needed could have been found in any number of smaller states where he won substantial percentages of the vote.[36] Lincoln was right to have been concerned about his reelection prospects[37] and would not have won without the military victories that preceded the election.

In the twelve states where military ballots were counted separately, Lincoln received 78 percent of them (119,754 to 34,291)—compared with his 53 percent of the civilian vote in those states.[38] The soldiers' decision may have been a striking endorsement of Lincoln's and Grant's approach to war, which contrasted sharply with that of McClellan, under whose command many of them had served.[39] Chester Hearn has found that the military vote was decisive in Connecticut, New York, and Maryland (where that vote also was responsible for passage of a new state constitution that banned slavery).[40]

On November 10, Grant sent his congratulations to Lincoln by way of the secretary of war, Edwin M. Stanton: "Enough now seems to be known to say who is to hold the reins of Government for the next four years. Congratulate the President for me for the double victory. The election having passed off quietly, no bloodshed or rioit [sic] throughout the land, is a victory worth more to the country than a battle won. Rebeldom and Europe will so construe it."[41] A few days later, Grant told John Hay that he was impressed most by "the quiet and orderly character of the whole affair."[42]

Defeating Lincoln in 1864 had been the Confederacy's best opportunity for victory. McClellan's well-documented respect for Southern "property rights" in their slaves could have led to some sort of settlement short of total Union victory and the abolition of slavery—perhaps even to a ceasefire and de facto Southern independence while the peace terms were being negotiated. Although some have contended that McClellan would not have allowed the South to remain independent,[43] he had demonstrated his reluctance to engage in the offensive warfare necessary for the Union to prevail.[44] David Donald, Jean Baker, and Michael Holt conclude that "Lincoln's reelection ensured that the conflict would not be interrupted by a cease-fire followed by negotiations, and in that sense was as important a Union victory as any on the battlefield...."[45] The closeness of the election of 1864 confirmed the importance of Grant's aggressive offensive beginning in May, only two months after becoming the Union general in chief.

Instead of adopting the gambling offensive strategy and tactics of Lee, the Confederacy would have been well advised to follow the more conservative approach favored by Jefferson Davis. Lee deviated from Davis's approach by launching major strategic offensives, either without Davis's advance knowledge or approval (e.g., the Antietam campaign) or with Davis's acquiescence in the face of Lee's forceful advocacy (e.g., the Gettysburg campaign). Of course, Lee himself was responsible for all the tactical offensives that proved so devastating to his troops and ultimately to Confederate hopes for victory. The details of Lee's aggressiveness are analyzed in the next two chapters.

Could the South have won the Civil War? Unquestionably. It foolishly withheld cotton from the world market at the war's beginning in an attempt to blackmail England and France into supporting it (compelling those countries to develop alternative sources of cotton), recklessly sacrificed its limited manpower in unnecessary and unwise strategic and tactical offensives although it needed only to achieve a stalemate to win, and was so concerned about preserving slavery that it acted against its own military interests in such areas as foreign diplomacy, prisoner-of war policies, and, most critically, the deployment of slaves as soldiers. The South could have won, but its counter-productive military and political policies ensured its defeat.

# WAS ROBERT E. LEE ONE OF THE GREATEST GENERALS IN HISTORY?

## THE MYTH

Robert E. Lee has been the flawless god of the Myth of the Lost Cause since shortly after his death in 1870. A primary tenet of the Myth is that Lee fought extremely well while Grant's armies were butchered by Grant's own aggressiveness. The approach has been to emphasize Lee's 1862–1863 victories, cast Antietam as a victory, blame his Gettysburg defeat on others, and stress the heavy casualties he imposed on Grant's army in the 1864 Overland Campaign.

Michael Fellman says that Lee's final general order to his army, praising their "unsurpassed courage and fortitude" and asserting they had been forced to "yield to overwhelming numbers and resources," was the beginning of the Lost Cause. He adds:

At the McLean House, suffering the physical death of military surrender, the Confederacy became immortal.

Exactly here can one find the essential moment of origin
of the "lost cause," of which Robert E. Lee was the effective first father.... Southern white nationalism arose from
the ashes of the lost cause to a considerable extent because
of the prideful spirit Lee both articulated and embodied.
He was the sacrificial lamb, the Confederate Christ on the
cross at Appomattox who then was resurrected by others
in the spirit and the body politic. Before he died, he also
became the soft-spoken but implacable foe of submission
and conciliation.[1]

The success of this pro-Lee propaganda campaign, notes John
Keegan, is curious: "[T]he only cult general in the English-speaking
world—Robert E. Lee—was the paladin of its only component community to suffer military catastrophe, the Confederacy."[2]

In the immediate aftermath of the Civil War, historians dealt with
Lee as with most other participants in the war, treating him positively
for the most part but discussing his faults. This treatment was consistent with newspapers' treatment of Lee during the war itself, when
Stonewall Jackson rivaled or surpassed him as the most adored Confederate general.[3] Both men were venerated in death as martyrs for the
Confederacy.

The first postwar historians praised Lee but found fault with his
actions at Gettysburg and Malvern Hill and sometimes at Antietam,
Fredericksburg, and the Seven Days' Battles.[4] While Jackson, Longstreet,
Joseph E. Johnston, Albert Sidney Johnston, and others received gener-
ally favorable treatment, Richard Ewell and Jubal Early were universally
criticized for their timidity on the first day at Gettysburg.[5] In *The Lost
Cause* (1866), Edward A. Pollard concluded that Lee's influence on the
Confederacy's fortunes was on the whole negative.[6]

After his death on October 12, 1870, however, Lee became a Southern and then a national deity. The groundwork for this transformation
was being laid as early as 1868, when a Southern publication said he was
"bathed in the white light that falls directly upon him from the smile of

an approving and sustaining God." By 1880, John W. Daniel, one of Early's former staff officers, would write, "The Divinity in [Lee's] bosom shone translucent through the man and his spirit rose up to the Godlike." Christ-like images of Lee continued well into the twentieth century in the writings of, among others, Douglas Southall Freeman, Gamaliel Bradford, and Clifford Dowdey.[7]

A wonderful example of this deification is found at the very end of Freeman's four-volume paean to Lee, published in 1935:

> And, if one, only one, of all the myriad incidents of his stirring life had to be selected to typify his message, as a man, to the young Americans who stood in hushed awe that rainy October morning [after his death] as their parents wept at the passing of the *Southern Arthur*, who would hesitate in selecting that incident? It occurred in Northern Virginia, probably on his last visit there. *A young mother brought her baby to him to be blessed.* He took the infant in his arms and looked at it and then at her and slowly said, "Teach him he must deny himself."[8]

Presenting Lee as a combination of King Arthur and Jesus, Freeman built upon the early Lost Causers' myth of the perfect Lee and passed it on to later generations.

Perpetuating the myth of Lee, the *Encyclopedia of American Biography* (1974) calls him *"a rare example of a man who looked like a perfect soldier, and was....* He fought with the Confederacy not because he loved warfare but for Virginia and the abstract principle of states' rights.... [H]e was always outnumbered by the enemy, and usually short of food, equipment and ammunition.... He was able without strain to equate the effort for the Confederacy with the effort for Virginia.... In sum he was *a marvelous soldier*—cool, quick, decisive, resourceful, amazingly tactful in dealing with Jefferson Davis, and, when defeat eventually faced him, *a beautiful loser."*[9] The one source provided for this analysis is Freeman's *R. E. Lee.*

The myth was alive and well a quarter-century later when the *Oxford Companion to American Military History* (1999) praised him as "a man of high personal character and intelligence, charismatic and charming, a natural leader. *As a leading actor in the Civil War legend of martial glory, he has become a legendary figure, an American hero of exceptional nobility.* The legend rationalizes or rejects characteristics of the man that might lessen his appeal." After a brief discussion of his critics' and defenders' contentions, the entry on Lee concludes, "Whatever his shortcomings, Lee became the white South's greatest hero, and many northern and foreign commentators have praised both the man and the general."[10] Freeman's *R. E. Lee* is the first source cited.

After his death, no criticism of Lee went unchallenged, while any Confederate general who was seen as a threat to Lee's reputation became fair game for censure and condemnation. One of the major reasons for Lee's apotheosis was that former Confederate officers associated with him could promote themselves through idolization of Lee. Generals Jubal Early and William Nelson Pendleton, whose war records were undistinguished, were among the leaders of the effort to elevate Lee by disparaging J. E. B. Stuart and James Longstreet.[11]

Early, who had faltered at Gettysburg, lost the Shenandoah Valley and his corps, been relieved of command by Lee, and fled the country for a few years after the war, was an early critic of Longstreet and others who could be blamed for Lee's shortcomings. Early was a better propagandist than general. As an author and as president of the Lee Monument Association, the Association of the Army of Northern Virginia, and the Southern Historical Society, he acted as Lee's chief votary for three decades.[12]

Pendleton, a minister and Lee's incompetent and nominal chief of artillery,[13] served as executive director of the Lee Monument Association and developed in his speeches, sermons, and writings the parallels between the perfect Jesus Christ and the faultless Robert E. Lee. He joined Early in falsely alleging that Lee had issued attack orders to Longstreet at Gettysburg at dawn on July 2, 1863. Another minister, J. William Jones, published his idolizing *Personal Reminiscences of General*

*Robert E. Lee*[14] in 1874, gained control (with Early) of the Southern Historical Society, and used its periodic *Papers* to extol Lee and damn his critics from 1876 through 1887.[15]

Praise for Lee continued unabated in hundreds of books and articles published in the late nineteenth and early twentieth centuries. In *The Rise and Fall of the Confederate Government* (1881), Jefferson Davis referred to the *Southern Historical Society Papers* as resolving the issue of responsibility for Gettysburg, implying that Longstreet was to blame. Among the other influential books in this period were Robert E. Lee Jr.'s *Recollections and Letters of General Robert E. Lee* (1904); Jones's sequel to his *Personal Reminiscences, Life and Letters of Robert Edward Lee, Soldier and Man* (1906); Thomas Nelson Page's *Robert E. Lee: The Southerner* (1909); and Page's nationalist revision, *Robert E. Lee: Man and Soldier* (1911).[16]

Praise for Lee knew no bounds in this period. His nephew and biographer, Fitzhugh Lee, quoted Senator Benjamin Hill of Georgia's oration at the Lee memorial service:

> [Lee] was a foe without hate, a friend without treachery, a soldier without cruelty, and a victim without murmuring. He was a public officer without vices, a private citizen without wrong, a neighbor without reproach, a Christian without hypocrisy, and a man without guilt. He was Caesar without his ambition, Frederick without his tyranny, Napoleon without his selfishness, and Washington without his reward. He was as obedient to authority as a servant and royal in authority as a king. He was as gentle as a woman in life, pure and modest as a virgin in thought, watchful as a Roman vestal, submissive to law as Socrates, and grand in battle as Achilles.[17]

The preeminent literary monument to Lee is the classic seven volumes written by Douglas Southall Freeman—the four-volume, Pulitzer Prize–winning *R. E. Lee: A Biography* (1934–35)[18] and the three-volume *Lee's*

*Lieutenants: A Study in Command* (1942–44).[19] During his twenty-five years of work on these authoritative studies, Freeman, the editor of the *Richmond News Leader*, saluted Lee's statue each day as he went to work.[20] As early as 1914, in an introduction to *Lee's Dispatches*, Freeman had revealed his view of Lee: "He entered upon the year 1863 with a series of victories unbroken from the time he had taken command [ignoring Malvern Hill and Antietam].[21] ... He ended the year with the greatest opportunity of his career lost through the blunders and worse of his subordinates.... Lee seemed then the very incarnation of knighthood."[22]

In his seven volumes of flowing prose and detailed documentation, Freeman depicted Lee as flawless in nearly every way. In Lee's veins flowed the blood of the finest families of Virginia, the finest society America ever had produced. Lee was brilliant, prescient, humane, intelligent, and virtually unerring. What imperfections he did have only seemed to make him greater. For example, he was so tolerant of the faults of others (his lieutenants, for example) that sometimes their mistakes would result in defeats for which Lee would be held responsible. Like some of his nineteenth-century predecessors, Freeman cited Lee's failure to criticize Longstreet's conduct at Gettysburg as proof of Lee's magnanimity instead of evidence that Lee had in fact found little or no fault with Longstreet's performance. As did many of his predecessors, Freeman lauded Lee by criticizing Longstreet and deftly denigrating the accomplishments of Stonewall Jackson, whom he regarded as a threat to the supremacy of Lee's reputation. In a nutshell, *R. E. Lee* demonstrated how great Lee was, and *Lee's Lieutenants* described how all his subordinates had let him down.[23]

Freeman's work affected that of later writers, such as Clifford Dowdey, who wrote a series of worshipful books about Lee in the 1950s and 1960s.[24] One of his chapter titles says it all: "The God Emerges."[25] Freeman's influence also is present but muted in Emory M. Thomas's excellent *Robert E. Lee: A Biography* (1995),[26] which contains some criticism of Lee but adopts some of Freeman's strong pro-Lee positions, such as solely blaming Longstreet for the delays on Day Two at Gettysburg.

Thomas Nelson Page's early twentieth-century works[27] were typical in their portrait of a godlike Lee. Page shares Freeman's admiration of Lee's bloodlines: "No drop of blood alien to Virginia coursed in his veins; his rearing was wholly within her borders and according to the principles of her life."[28] He added, "In his veins flowed the best blood of the gentry of the Old Dominion and, for that matter, of England...."[29] Like other propagators of the Myth, Page was eager to connect Lee with George Washington: "As Washington was the consummate flower of the life of Colonial Virginia, so Lee, clinging close to 'his precious example,' became the perfect fruit of her later civilization."[30]

Page justified Lee's defection to the Confederacy: "All that we know is that, sacrificing place and honors and emoluments; leaving his home to the sack of the enemy preparing to seize it, he decided in the sight of God, under the all-compelling sense of duty, and this is enough for us to know."[31] His description of Lee at Appomattox, laden with biblical images, is a classic example of how the Myth turned almost into a religion:

> If [signing the instrument of surrender] was the very Geth-semane of his trials, yet he must have had then one moment of supreme, if chastened, joy. [He rode through his men.] Then occurred one of the most notable scenes in the history of war. In an instant they were about him, bare-headed, with tear-wet faces; thronging him, kissing his hand, his boots, his saddle; weeping; cheering him amid their tears; shouting his name to the very skies. He said, "Men, we have fought through the war together; I have done my best for you; my heart is too full to say more." Thus, with kindly words, as of a father, and a heart that must have felt some solace in such devotion, he bade them farewell, and left them like the devoted band that wept for the great Apostle to the gentiles, weeping most of all that they should see his face no more.[32]

The idolization did not stop there. In 1909, while president of Princeton University, Woodrow Wilson, a Virginian, declared that Lee was "unapproachable in the history of our country." In an early work (1914), Freeman said that "noble he was; nobler he became." In 1964 and 1965, Dowdey described Lee's Seven Days' Campaign as "The Early Work of a Master" and Lee's emergence as "a people's god." For Dowdey, writes William Garrett Piston, "the Civil War was a passion play, with Lee as Christ."[33]

More recently, Lee has been described as "one of the truly gifted commanders of all time" in the *Encyclopedia Americana* (1989),[34] while Mark Boatner's *Civil War Dictionary* (1959, 1988) proclaims Lee the "[g]reat leader of the lost Confederate cause, in which capacity he earned rank with history's most distinguished generals."[35] Perhaps the most influential popular work, Time-Life's Civil War series, describes Lee as "the greatest soldier of the Civil War."[36]

## REACTIONS TO THE LEE MYTH

It was inevitable that the discrepancy between the myth of the flawless Lee and the reality of the devastating defeat of his Confederate army would attract more critical historical analysis. One of the first breakthroughs, even though it was heavily edited to remove many passages critical of Lee and others, came in 1907 with the publication of Confederate Brigadier General E. Porter Alexander's classic and balanced *Military Memoirs of a Confederate: A Critical Narrative.*[37] Aware of but ignoring the legions of Lee-worshippers, Alexander offered his frank assessments of all the leading Civil War generals. All of them, including Lee, received both plaudits and criticism. Even more valuable is the 1989 printing of the original, unexpurgated version of Alexander's work, *Fighting for the Confederacy: The Personal Recollections of General Edward Porter Alexander,* which was retrieved and edited by Gary W. Gallagher.[38] Among Alexander's many valuable insights are his criticisms of Lee's decision to fight a battle he could not win at Antietam, many of Lee's tactical decisions at Gettysburg, and Lee's failure to coordinate his activities with those of Confederate forces unsuccessfully defending Vicksburg and Tennessee in 1863 and Atlanta in 1864.

Another critical evaluation of Lee came from the British major general J. F. C. Fuller. In *Grant and Lee: A Study in Personality and Generalship* (1933), Fuller described Lee as "in several respects...one of the most incapable Generals-in-Chief in history."[39] He deemed Grant the superior commander because of his broad strategic outlook, which he contrasted to Lee's narrow Eastern Theater perspective.[40] He also criticized Lee for his over-aggressiveness during the Peninsula, Gettysburg, and 1864 Virginia campaigns. Fuller summed up his comparison of the two generals in an earlier work, *The Generalship of Ulysses S. Grant* (1929): "Unlike Grant, [Lee] did not create a strategy in spite of his Government; instead, by his restless audacity, he ruined such strategy as his Government created."[41] While Davis, especially early in the war, preferred a strategically defensive approach to the war, Lee instead went on the offensive, covertly in his Antietam campaign and overtly in his Gettysburg campaign.

In the mid-1930s, another British military historian, Basil Liddell Hart, wrote two devastating articles about Lee in *The Saturday Review of Literature*. In "Lee: A Psychological Problem," he found Lee to be mediocre, overly concerned about Virginia (instead of the entire Confederacy), and guilty of bleeding the South to death with his suicidally aggressive tactics.[42] In "Why Lee Lost Gettysburg," Lidell Hart criticized Lee as a strategist for failing to recognize the Confederacy's limited manpower.[43]

A pioneer analyst was T. Harry Williams, who in 1955 began questioning the myths surrounding Lee in a short and shocking *Journal of Southern History* article criticizing Freeman's analysis of Lee. The general's biographer, wrote Williams, "came close to arguing that whatever Lee did was right because he was Lee" and "was more like the little girl in Richmond who came home from Sunday School and said 'Mama, I can never remember. Was General Lee in the Old Testament or the New Testament?'" Williams thought the problem was that Freeman was "a Virginia gentleman writing about a Virginia gentleman":

The emotion that impelled Lee into the war also influenced the way he fought. He fought for Virginia. Freeman did not recognize Lee's limitation because to him too the war is in Virginia. It did not occur to him to examine the effect of Lee's preoccupation with Virginia on total Confederate strategy. Nor did he see the tragic result of Lee's limitation. In the end, all the brilliance and fortitude of the greatest Confederate general availed little to save his country. It fell to pieces behind his back, and most of his efforts in Virginia went for nothing.[44]

Thomas L. Connelly followed up on Williams's work in 1969 with an article in *Civil War History* criticizing Lee's ignorance of the Western Theater, his obsession with defending Virginia, and his persistent uninformed demands for reinforcements from the West and Deep South.[45] In 1973, in the same publication, Connelly argued that historians had made Lee "a symbol of victory in a defeated region," citing articles from the 1880s in *Southern Historical Society Papers* contending that Lee had never lost (Antietam and Gettysburg being strategic withdrawals).[46] Connelly then teamed with Archer Jones in *The Politics of Command: Factions and Ideas in Confederate Strategy (1973)*, arguing that Lee's close relationship with Jefferson Davis enabled him to get attention for the Virginia front and special treatment for the Army of Northern Virginia at the expense of Confederate forces in the West.[47] Finally, in his remarkable *The Marble Man: Robert E. Lee and His Image in American Society* (1977), Connelly traced the idealized historiography about Lee, beginning with the former Confederate officers who established the Myth of the Lost Cause.[48]

The work of historical revision continued with William Garrett Piston's *Lee's Tarnished Lieutenant: James Longstreet and His Place in Southern History* (1987)[49] and Alan T. Nolan's *Lee Considered: General Robert E. Lee and Civil War History* (1991).[50] Douglas Savage followed with a semi-fictional examination of Lee's mistakes in his creative historical novel, *The Court Martial of Robert E. Lee* (1993).[51] A later criticism of Lee's overly aggressive approach was John D. McKenzie's *Uncertain Glory: Lee's Generalship Re-Examined* (1997).[52]

Grady McWhiney's and Perry D. Jamieson's *Attack and Die: Civil War Military Tactics and the Southern Heritage* (1982)[53] provided valuable insight into the Confederacy's unnecessary and self-defeating aggressiveness during the Civil War. They described the devastating losses suffered by attacking armies and demonstrated that Lee's troops suffered and imposed far more casualties than those of any other general on either side.

Despite the corrective efforts of these historians, the myth of Robert E. Lee and the corresponding deprecation of James Longstreet and Ulysses S. Grant are deeply ingrained in the American imagination. As J. F. C. Fuller wrote in his study of Grant, "The truth is, the more we inquire into the generalship of *Lee*, the more we discover that *Lee*, or rather the popular conception of him, is a myth...."[54]

## LEE'S CIVIL WAR RECORD

Lee's Civil War record was considerably less impressive than the Myth of the Lost Cause portrays it.[55] After declining command of the Union army because he would not lift his sword against his beloved Commonwealth of Virginia (as distinguished from the Confederacy), Lee did an excellent job organizing the Virginia militia and defending that state in the early months of the war. As its militia became part of the Confederacy's army, Lee became President Jefferson Davis's military advisor.

Disappointed that he was not on the field for the Confederate victory at First Bull Run (Manassas), Lee continued to lobby for a field command. His wish was granted when he was sent to northwestern Virginia in late 1861, but there he demonstrated some of the weaknesses that would plague him throughout the war. At Cheat Mountain, he issued long, complicated orders and failed to exercise hands-on control. While in that small theater, he failed to deal with squabbling subordinates whose disputes were undermining Confederate efforts to regain control of northwestern Virginia, and he returned to Richmond a failure.

Davis then gave Lee a chance for redemption by assigning him to command the South Carolina, Georgia, and Florida coasts. First, Davis had to write letters to affected governors ensuring them that Lee was indeed a highly competent general (contrary to what they may have heard about his western Virginia experience). Lee did an excellent job building defensive coastal fortifications and withdrawing most of the rebel defenses to waters beyond the reach of Union gunboats.

Apparently because Davis was becoming disenchanted with independent, uncooperative, and personally despised generals such as Joseph Johnston and P. G. T. Beauregard, he recalled Lee to Richmond as his primary military advisor once again. There Lee helped Davis to pressure Johnston into more aggressive defensive actions, especially after George B. McClellan started slowly moving up the Virginia peninsula from the Norfolk area toward Richmond.

After two months of dalliance, McClellan finally reached the vicinity of Richmond and split his army on both sides of the Chickahominy River. On May 31, 1862, with prodding, Johnston attacked an isolated portion of Little Mac's army on the south side of the river. In what became the two-day Battle of Seven Pines (Fair Oaks), Longstreet bungled his attack, and reinforcements from north of the river were able to avert a Union disaster.

The most important result of the battle was that Johnston was badly wounded and on June 1, 1862, Lee succeeded to command of the major Confederate army in the east, which he promptly dubbed the Army of Northern Virginia. His record as its commander requires deep examination before judgment can be rendered about the quality of his Civil War performance.

Lee enhanced his early-war reputation as the "King of Spades" by ordering his army to dig fortifications south of the Chickahominy between Richmond and McClellan's Army of the Potomac. Contrary to many people's expectation that he would be a cautious general, he was preparing the first of many offensives against his foes. His strategic and tactical aggressiveness would soon be apparent to all.

The Seven Days' Battle, ending McClellan's disastrous Peninsula Campaign, began in late June and was Lee's first as army commander. Correctly predicting that McClellan would not have the moral courage to attack Lee's lines and Richmond while Lee moved his army to the north side of the Chickahominy, Lee took two-thirds of his army above the river and attacked Little Mac's largest corps, which was alone there.

In a sign of things to come, Lee had his army attack the enemy for most of one week and pushed them away from Richmond and back to the James River. Although Lee knew that he had achieved his strategic objective of saving Richmond after two days of fighting, he continued his attacks for days more, taking substantial casualties. His army suffered twenty thousand casualties (dead, wounded, missing, or captured), while McClellan's army suffered "only" sixteen thousand. Most of Lee's casualties were "hard" ones—killed or wounded. Only ten thousand of Little Mac's men were killed or wounded.

That week of fighting was marked by McClellan's constant retreats (under his usual misapprehension that he was outnumbered two to one) and Lee's over-aggressiveness and mismanagement of his army. He generally issued a battle order for the day and then simply let things unfold without close battlefield control by him or his deliberately small staff. Virtually every daily order called for Stonewall Jackson to come in on Lee's left flank after the rest of Lee's army diverted the Yankees' attention with frontal assaults. While those assaults resulted in horrendous casualties, Jackson was either a no-show or late-show on almost every occasion. Lee took no corrective action.

The final battle of the week was Malvern Hill, where a disorganized and disastrous rebel assault against a strong, elevated Union position resulted in such slaughter that D. H. Hill, one of Lee's generals, described it as "not war, but murder." By then, Lee had so decimated and disorganized his army that McClellan's subordinates recommended an immediate counterattack to destroy Lee's army or capture Richmond. McClellan, of course, declined and retreated farther downriver.

Lee's strategic victory made him an instant hero in the South, which was losing battles on most other fronts. He had, however, demonstrated a proclivity for complicated and ambiguous orders, lack of battlefield control, and relentless offensive action that resulted in irreplaceable casualties for the manpower-starved Confederacy.

While McClellan, pouting at Harrison's Landing on the James River, kept requesting more reinforcements, Lee determined that the Army of the Potomac was no threat to Richmond and decided to go on the offensive. He moved into central and northern Virginia to challenge John Pope's new Army of Virginia. With help from McClellan, who delayed sending reinforcements to Pope and kept twenty-five thousand Union troops away from the battlefield, Lee won perhaps his greatest victory at Second Manassas. With Jackson on the defensive and Longstreet then overwhelming Pope's left flank, Lee suffered only 9,500 casualties to the Union army's 14,400. With Lee present, Jackson inexplicably failed to leave his position and join Longstreet's attack.

After a minor victory at Chantilly, Lee took unilateral action, approved neither by Davis nor the Confederate Congress or cabinet, that proved devastating to rebel prospects—he crossed the Potomac and invaded the North in hopes of reaching Pennsylvania. In that Maryland (Antietam) campaign, he hoped to feed his army, gather thousands of recruits, and win a great victory that would dismay the Northern people and convince England and France to recognize the Confederacy. For about three weeks, Lee's army lived on non-Virginia soil, but he failed to gain recruits. He was in the western part of Maryland, where pro-slavery sentiment was weak, and those Marylanders interested in joining his army had already done so.

More importantly, he squandered what had been a grand opportunity for European recognition. England and France had been poised to recognize the Confederacy until Lee's invasion, but they decided to wait for the outcome of his campaign. That campaign started well for Lee as he took advantage of McClellan's slow response to the discovery of Lee's "lost order" and captured more than eleven thousand Union soldiers at Harpers Ferry. Instead of declaring the campaign a success after the capture of Harpers Ferry and its garrison, however, Lee put his pitifully small and exhausted army in a trap at Sharpsburg, Maryland. In the Battle of Antietam (Sharpsburg) on September 17, he suffered severe losses and would have been destroyed by almost any general other than McClellan. Lee's and Jackson's counterattacks at Miller's Cornfield in the early hours of the battle were acts of tactical suicide, not genius. Although McClellan allowed Lee's army to escape, the Confederates had suffered a crushing strategic defeat that opened the door for Lincoln's preliminary Emancipation Proclamation on September 22 and virtually ended all hopes of European intervention. Lee's net casualties at Harpers Ferry had been a plus-11,500, but his army suffered 11,500 casualties in the rest of the Antietam campaign (to the attacking Union army's 12,400).[56]

After retreating to Virginia, Lee was the beneficiary of foolhardy Union assaults ordered by Ambrose Burnside at Marye's Heights at Fredericksburg in December 1862. Lee's army, fighting from entrenched positions most of the day, inflicted almost thirteen thousand casualties on the Union attackers while incurring a few more than five thousand themselves. Although Lee was not satisfied with the defensive nature of the victory, it was sufficient to bolster Southern morale for many months.

The lesson of Fredericksburg was that a frontal assault on the enemy, if not absolutely necessary, was unwise, but Lee failed to learn it. After Stonewall Jackson's famous flanking maneuver at Chancellorsville in early May 1863, Lee spent the next couple of days frontally assaulting Joseph Hooker's Union lines. As a result, his army suffered almost thirteen thousand casualties while inflicting over seventeen thousand on the weakly led enemy. But Lee's army paid too high a price, including the loss of Jackson,[57] for the Chancellorsville victory. Its butcher bill would have been even higher had Lee been able to launch a planned final assault on another strong Union position. Lee was angry, but his subordinates were relieved, when Hooker retreated across the Rapidan River before Lee could attack.

Gettysburg proved even more disastrous to the Confederacy and the Army of Northern Virginia. By invading Pennsylvania, Lee deprived rebel armies in other theaters of desperately needed reinforcements. Had Longstreet's troops reinforced the badly outnumbered Bragg against George Thomas's Tullahoma campaign, Thomas might have been prevented from crossing the Tennessee River and seizing Chattanooga and more rebel troops might have been sent to oppose Grant's Vicksburg campaign.

On the first day of the three-day battle at Gettysburg, Lee missed a grand opportunity to occupy the high ground, a failure that proved costly over the next forty-eight hours. Longstreet, his senior general, opposed Lee's plan for frontal assaults on the second and third days against Union troops in strong defensive positions. That campaign cost Lee an intolerable twenty-eight thousand casualties, while the Union lost twenty-three thousand. As a result, Lee no longer had the strength to initiate strategic offensives (which had been a bad idea anyway) and, more importantly, he lacked the manpower to counterpunch effectively when attacked.

Some regard Gettysburg as a turning point of the war. Lost Cause adherents have attempted to make it *the* turning point and have expended considerable effort attempting to relieve Lee of responsibility for that major tactical and strategic defeat. Their position is that Longstreet lost Gettysburg and thus the war, while Lee was blameless. Although Douglas Southall Freeman recited a litany of guilty parties (Longstreet, Ewell, A. P. Hill, Jeb Stuart), most of Lee's apologists found the only scapegoat they needed in James Longstreet. Because the Lee-Longstreet saga has become such a fundamental part of the Myth, I have devoted the next chapter to a thorough examination of the Gettysburg campaign and the allegations against Longstreet. Readers can determine for themselves whether Lee or Longstreet was primarily responsible for that disaster.

The cumulative casualties of 1862 and 1863 had taken a severe toll on Lee's army—both in the number and the quality of the men lost. It was a toll the Confederacy, outnumbered almost four to one at the war's outset, could not afford. With an army that was a mere shadow of the one he had inherited, Lee was finally forced to fight truly defensively in opposing Grant's Overland Campaign of 1864.[58] Staying generally on the defensive at the Wilderness, Spotsylvania Court House, the North Anna River, and Cold Harbor enabled Lee to post the kinds of numbers he had needed in prior years. Before Grant had reached the James River, Lee lost "only" thirty-three thousand men while inflicting fifty-five thousand casualties on the Army of the Potomac.[59] But it was too little, too late, for Lee. He had so weakened his army with his offensive strategy and tactics in 1862 and 1863 that he could not prevent Grant from forcing him into a partial siege situation at Richmond and Petersburg in which Lee's army was doomed. Thereafter, he continued to focus solely on his own army as the rest of the Confederacy was collapsing.

Ironically, the Overland Campaign of 1864, in which Grant, according to his critics, took too many casualties, shows what Lee could have accomplished had he stayed on the strategic and tactical defensive in 1862 and 1863. As Alan Nolan concludes, "The truth is that in 1864, Lee himself demonstrated the alternative to his earlier offensive strategy and tactics."[60] Grady McWhiney reaches the same conclusion: "Though Lee was at his best on defense, he adopted a defensive strategy only after attrition had deprived him of the power to attack. His brilliant defensive campaign against Grant in 1864 made the Union pay in manpower as it had never paid before. But the Confederates adopted defensive tactics too late; Lee started the campaign with too few men, nor could he replace his losses as could Grant."[61]

## A COMPARISON OF LEE'S AND GRANT'S CASUALTIES

Before drawing conclusions about Lee's Civil War performance, it is helpful to compare the casualty statistics of Lee and Grant in order to emphasize the sharply contrasting losses and accomplishments of the two generals.

Lee's strategic and tactical aggression while commanding a single army in a single theater cost him 209,000 casualties (see the table of Lee's casualties below)—a loss the South could not afford. Almost incomprehensibly, Lee's single army suffered fifty-five thousand more casualties than the five armies commanded (victoriously) by Grant in three theaters. Lee's willingness to incur such devastating casualties might be explained, in part, by his religious faith. Richard Rollins speculates, "Perhaps, most importantly, Lee believed the results would be best for all concerned, and if a man died he would be in a better place. It was this faith that allowed him to pray that 'our merciful Father in Heaven may protect & direct us,' and then to add, 'In that case I fear no odds & no numbers.'"[62] In any case, if a single statistic explains the outcome of the war, it is those 209,000 casualties. On the other side of the ledger, Lee did impose 240,000 casualties on his foes, for an advantage of thirty-one thousand.[63] But the South could not afford or compensate for Lee's overly aggressive and offensive style of fighting.

Grant, on the other hand, was able to capture Fort Henry, Fort Donelson, and Vicksburg (along with their defending armies); save a trapped Union army at Chattanooga and drive the Confederate Army of Tennessee into Georgia; and come east to defeat Lee and finish the war in less than a year—all while incurring a reasonable 154,000 casualties (see the table of Grant's casualties below). By inflicting 191,000 casualties on his opponents, Grant achieved a favorable margin of thirty-seven thousand. Considering the breadth and depth of Grant's successes in a necessarily offensive mode, even a negative balance of casualties would have been militarily acceptable. In Gordon C. Rhea's judgment, "[t]he very nature of Grant's [offensive] assignment guaranteed severe casualties." What he achieved with his tolerable losses was amazing. (Grant's achievements are analyzed further in chapter 7.)

Grady McWhiney and Perry D. Jamieson shed light on Grant's and Lee's casualties in *Attack and Die: Civil War Military Tactics and the Southern Heritage*. Their analysis reveals that an average of "only" 15 percent of Grant's Federal troops were killed or wounded in his major campaigns over the course of the war—a total of slightly more than ninety-four thousand men. In contrast, Lee had higher "hard" casualties, both in absolute numbers and as a percentage of his force. An average of 20 percent of his troops were killed or wounded in his major campaigns—a total of more than 121,000 (far more than any other Civil

War general). Eighty thousand of Lee's men were killed or wounded in his first fourteen months in command (about the same number he started with). By focusing only on killed and wounded, *Attack and Die* necessarily understates Grant's and Lee's total casualties, which also include missing and captured troops. It also does not purport to reflect all their battles, just selected major ones. As these numbers and those below demonstrate, Lee's soldiers had higher absolute casualties and percentage of casualties—both in total and in killed and wounded—than did Grant's.

Both Grant and Lee were aggressive generals who liked to seize the offensive, but only Grant's aggressiveness was consistent with the strategic aims of his government. Although the Confederacy needed only to avoid conquest, Lee acted as though he had to conquer the North. The burden of conquest was on the Union, and Grant appropriately went on the offensive throughout the war. He won in the Western, Middle, and Eastern theaters and won the war. Although we cannot judge either Lee or Grant on numbers alone, their casualty statistics are quite enlightening. The performance of Lee's army during the strategically and tactically defensive (for Lee) Overland Campaign of 1864 (including its imposition of massive casualties on the enemy) was achieved by an army that was a shadow of the one Lee had inherited on June 1, 1862. That success was due primarily to Grant's having no choice but to go on the offensive and to Lee's finally being forced to fight on the defensive, and it suggests how successful (and with fewer casualties) Lee might have been in 1862 and 1863 if he had avoided the frontal assaults at Seven Days' (especially Mechanicsville and Malvern Hill), the latter days at Chancellorsville, and the final two days at Gettysburg.

Lee's strategic offensive into Maryland in 1862 ended in a strategic defeat, irreplaceable losses of men and officers, Lincoln's preliminary Emancipation Proclamation, and dashed Confederate hopes for European intervention. Similarly, his 1863 strategic offensive into Pennsylvania resulted in about twenty-eight thousand casualties, a major demoralizing defeat, and the virtual end of economic support from abroad. In summary, Lee's overly aggressive strategy and tactics in 1862 and 1863 seriously weakened his army and, together with his undermining of rebel efforts in other theaters, doomed the Confederacy. If Grant had fought less aggressively, the Union would not have won. If Lee had fought less aggressively, the Confederacy's prospects for success would have been enhanced. Their respective casualty numbers follow.

## SUMMARY OF CASUALTIES INCURRED BY BOTH SIDES IN CAMPAIGNS AND BATTLES OF ROBERT E. LEE[64]

| Campaign/Battle | Total Confederate Casualties | Total Union Casualties |
|---|---|---|
| Seven Days' | 20,000 | 16,000 |
| Cedar Mountain | 1,300 | 2,400 |
| Second Manassas | 9,500 | 14,400 |
| Chantilly | 800 | 1,300 |
| Harpers Ferry | 286 | 11,783 |
| Crampton's Gap & South Mountain | 3,434 | 2,346 |
| Antietam/Sharpsburg | 11,500 | 12,400 |
| Fredericksburg | 4,201 | 12,653 |
| Kelly's Ford | 133 | 78 |
| Chancellorsville | 12,764 | 17,287 |
| Brandy Station | 523 | 866 |
| Winchester (June 1863) | 269 | 4,443 |
| Aldie, Middleburg, Upperville | 510 | 613 |
| Hanover | 150 | 200 |
| Gettysburg | 28,000 | 23,000 |
| Retreat from Gettysburg | 5,000 | 1,000 |
| Bristoe Station | 1,378 | 546 |
| Kelly's Ford & Rappahannock Stn. | 2,000 | 400 |

| | | |
|---|---|---|
| Mine Run | 601 | 1,653 |
| Wilderness | 11,125 | 17,666 |
| Spotsylvania Court House | 13,421 | 18,399 |
| North Anna River, etc. | 3,766 | 3,986 |
| Cold Harbor | 4,595 | 12,737 |
| Petersburg Assaults | 4,000 | 11,386 |
| Petersburg Siege/Campaign | 28,000 | 42,000 |
| Appomattox Campaign | 41,666 | 10,780 |
| TOTALS (killed, wounded, missing, captured) | **208,922** | 240,322 |
| NET DIFFERENCE  +31,400 | | |

## SUMMARY OF CASUALTIES INCURRED BY BOTH SIDES IN CAMPAIGNS AND BATTLES OF ULYSSES S. GRANT[65]

| Campaign/Battle | Total Confederate Casualties | Total Union Casualties |
|---|---|---|
| Belmont | 641 | 501 |
| Fort Donelson | 16,000 | 2,832 |
| Shiloh | 10,694 | 13,147 |
| Iuka | 1,600 | 790 |
| Corinth/Hatchie River | 6,527 | 3,120 |
| Vicksburg Campaign | 40,718 | 9,362 |
| Return to Jackson | 1,340 | 1,122 |
| Chattanooga | 6,667 | 5,814 |
| WESTERN AND MIDDLE THEATERS TOTALS | 84,187 | 36,688 |
| Wilderness | 11,125 | 17,666 |

| | | |
|---|---|---|
| Spotsylvania Court House | 13,421 | 18,399 |
| North Anna River, etc. | 3,766 | 3,986 |
| Cold Harbor | 4,595 | 12,737 |
| Petersburg Assaults | 4,000 | 11,386 |
| Petersburg Siege/Campaign | 28,000 | 42,000 |
| Appomattox Campaign | 41,666 | 10,780 |
| EASTERN THEATER TOTALS | 106,573 | 116,954 |
| GRAND TOTALS (killed, wounded, missing/captured) | 190,760 | 153,642 |
| NET DIFFERENCE +37,118 | | |

# LEE'S SHORTCOMINGS AS A CIVIL WAR GENERAL

## OVER-AGGRESSIVENESS

As the foregoing figures indicate, Lee fought the war even more aggressively than Grant. "Lee, [like John Bell Hood], liked to attack. He often suggested offensives to the President and urged other generals to be aggressive."[66] Yet the new weaponry deployed in the Civil War rendered Napoleonic concepts of a grand victory obsolete. Fuller's judgment is that Lee's audacity more than once assisted the Union in achieving its strategic goal of conquering the South.[67] Bevin Alexander adds that Lee's obsession with seeking battle and his limited strategic vision lost the war.[68] Elsewhere he writes:

> Even some generals who enjoy high reputations or fame have actually been predominantly direct soldiers who brought disaster to their side. One such general was Robert E. Lee, the *beau ideal* of the Southern Confederacy, who possessed integrity, honor, and loyalty in the highest degree and who also possessed skills as a commander far in excess of those of the Union generals arrayed against him. But Lee was not, himself,

a great general. Lee generally and in decisively critical situa-
tions always chose the direct over the indirect approach.[69]

That is a judgment shared by many military historians. Assessing
Lee's strategy, Russell Weigley writes, "Like Napoleon himself, with his
passion for the strategy of annihilation and the climactic, decisive battle
as its expression, he destroyed in the end not the enemy armies, but his
own."[70]

Lee's aggressiveness was on display throughout the Seven Days'
Battle, his first major campaign. In his after-battle report, he complained
that "under ordinary circumstances the Federal Army should have been
destroyed." As Michael Fellman observes, "Lee ignored the fact that
Malvern Hill had been a poorly organized and bloody Confederate
defeat.... Indeed the notion of a total victory that would vaporize the
enemy army in one battle remained Lee's unrealistic goal right through
Gettysburg.... Lee was remarkable in the tenacity with which he held
this belief, which both grew out of his 'audacity' and reinforced it."[71]

Lee's counter-productive aggressiveness was particularly unwise for
at least three additional reasons. First, the heavily outnumbered South
could not afford the casualties Lee was running up. Second, weaponry
had changed since the Mexican War, and the widespread use of rifles
(instead of muskets), Minié balls, rifled artillery, breech-loading (instead
of muzzle-loading) firearms, and repeating weapons provided an advantage to defenders in the Civil War.[72] Third, Lee's aggressiveness in the
East drained resources from the rest of the Confederacy, improving the
Union's prospects in the Western and Middle theaters, where many
contend the war was lost. The Confederacy had probably lost the war in
the West before Grant came east, and Grant trusted Sherman to finish
the job.

In Lee's defense, Gary Gallagher argues that Lee was correct in seeing Virginia as the critical battleground, was successful on several occasions, and had a chance for success at Antietam and Gettysburg. He adds
that Lee's propensity for the offensive was consistent with the hopes and
needs of the Southern people.[73] Lee's focus on Virginia is discussed below.

It is unlikely that he would have enjoyed the successes that Gallagher cites had he been facing Grant instead of a series of incompetent Union generals in the East. And Antietam and Gettysburg not only were huge strategic losses, they came close to eliminating Lee's army as well. The Southern people seemed perfectly satisfied with their soldiers' defensive victories at First Bull Run, Ball's Bluff, and Fredericksburg. It was the victories, not the tactics, that won their support.

Recently William C. Davis has maintained that "Lee's audacity was stunning, though not unduly reckless." Interestingly enough, he explains that Lee's boldness was a result, in part, of his religious faith. "[H]is fatalistic providentialism gave him strength in making a decision. If man achieved nothing God did not will, then in a way there was no risk. The Almighty guided his hand in making the effort, win or lose. If he suffered defeat, he was only a divine instrument. That gave him the freedom to gamble boldly."[74] But Lee's faith, writes Davis, was erroneous: "Lee persisted in the belief in the battle of annihilation, and the old Napoleonic notion of one great army winning a war. The size, organization, and weaponry of Civil War armies, plus the heavy casualties even to victors in major engagements, made the former virtually impossible."[75]

Lee's strategic offensives into the North, both Antietam and Gettysburg, were almost certain to end in his retreat to Virginia as he exhausted his men, horses, ammunition, and other critical materiel, deflating his army's morale, seriously diminishing rebel prospects for victory, and thus contributing to Lincoln's reelection in 1864.

Lee's tactical aggressiveness complemented and aggravated his strategic aggressiveness. Although seven of eight Civil War frontal assaults failed, Lee kept attacking.[76] At the Seven Days' Battle (particularly at Mechanicsville and Malvern Hill), Chantilly, Antietam, Chancellorsville, Gettysburg, Rappahannock Station, the Wilderness, and Fort Stedman, Lee's overly aggressive tactics damaged his army. Citing Malvern Hill, Chantilly, the end of Chancellorsville, and Pickett's Charge, Archer Jones points to Lee's refusal to "quit while he was ahead."[77]

Lee was not the only commander who failed to compensate for the enhanced defensive firepower in the war, but with his numerically inferior army, it was a mistake he could not afford to make. He lost 20.2 percent of his soldiers in battle while inflicting only 15.4 percent losses on his opponents. This negative differential (4.8 percent) was exceeded among major Confederate generals only by Lee's protégé John Bell Hood (19.2 percent of his men lost, with a negative differential of 13.7 percent) and John Pemberton, who surrendered his army at Vicksburg and lost 50.3 percent of his men, with a negative differential of 44.1 percent). Other rebel generals' casualty and casualty differential numbers were: Joseph Johnston (10.5 percent, negative 1.7 percent), Bragg (19.5 percent, negative 4.1 percent) and Beauregard (16.1 percent, negative 3.3 percent). No other Confederate general except Hood sacrificed a greater percentage of his troops in frontal assaults than Lee.[78] In contrast to Lee, Grant incurred 18.1 percent casualties while imposing 31.0 percent on his foes for a positive differential of 12.9 percent.

## LOSS OF BATTLEFIELD CONTROL

Lee's own explanation of his battlefield management sheds a great deal of light on his all-too-frequent loss of control on the battlefield. He tried to make his "plans as good as my human skill allows." But their implementation suffered: "I plan and work with all my might to bring the troops to the right place at the right time; with that I have done my duty. As soon as I order the troops forward into battle, I lay the fate of my army at the hands of God." Then, he said, "it is my Generals' turn to perform their duty."[79] He issued scarcely any orders once a battle had started.

Hard as it is to conceive, Lee appeared to absolve himself of responsibility for a battle's outcome, considering it his subordinates' responsibility to adjust to changing conditions and win the battle. If his army did not win the battle, moreover, it must have been because God did not want it to.[80]

At Seven Days' and Gettysburg, for example, Lee again and again issued morning orders and then watched the battles progress without making any real attempt to steer the outcomes. There were more than a dozen instances at Gettysburg when his orders were not obeyed—and he did not send anyone to investigate. William Davis explains Pickett's Charge: "It was his most hazardous battlefield expedient yet, but then his men could do anything. Moreover, when he made any decision, success or failure lay not in his hands, but in His. If God meant for the assault to succeed, it would. If not, it did not. Lee and his staff sat their horses on Seminary Ridge and watched the mile-wide ranks of 12,000 men go forward, but from that moment he made no effort to coordinate or direct the assault."[81] Thirty years later, Confederate General Lafayette McLaws, remarked, "The Battle of Gettysburg has not yet been analyzed to make the combination of movements comprehensible. The disjointed assaults which could not under any circumstances have produced favorable results, have not yet been explained."[82]

Lee's failure to take control on many battlefields may have been caused in part by the inadequately small staff he deliberately retained, an issue that is addressed below.

## ONE-THEATER MYOPIA

Lee was first, foremost, and almost only a Virginian. His focus on Virginia throughout the war came at the expense of the Confederacy. Although conceding that Lee's preoccupation with Virginia was a product of the times, T. Harry Williams concludes that "it must be recognized that his restricted view constituted a tragic command limitation in a modern war."[83]

Lee's strategy concentrated all the resources he could obtain and retain almost exclusively in the Eastern theater of operations, while fatal events were occurring in the West (primarily in Tennessee, Mississippi, and Georgia). Archer Jones notes how this failure combined disastrously with Lee's over-aggressiveness: "if the Virginia armies were strong enough for an offensive they were too strong for the good of the Confederacy. They would have done better to spare some of their strength to bolster the sagging West where the war was being lost."[84]

Many historians have criticized his undue concentration on Virginia. Thomas Connelly points out that Lee operated in an area of twenty-two thousand square miles, while the Western theater covered 225,000 square miles in seven states.[85] While Lee "managed to defend Richmond for almost three years," writes Philip Katcher, "he allowed the rest of the Confederacy to be slowly eaten away."[86] General Fuller likewise complained that Lee's "thoughts were always concentrated on Virginia, consequently he never fully realized the importance of Tennessee, or the strategic power which resided in the size of the Confederacy."[87] Although defenders of Lee contend that he was merely an Eastern army commander for most of the war and thus not responsible for the situation elsewhere, he frequently advised President Davis on national issues, including military strategy.[88] He was Davis's primary military advisor throughout the war. It is also telling that he at least twice declined offers to command in other theaters.

Perhaps Lee's greatest damage to other theaters occurred in late 1863 when the critical Battle of Chattanooga resulted in Union rather than Confederate control in the Southeast. Davis rejected a plan for rebel reinforcements there because Lee refused to provide more troops. Then, based on a Lee recommendation, Davis encouraged the transfer of Longstreet and his troops away from Chattanooga to attack Knoxville. Lee wrote to Davis twice about this movement, which would result in Longstreet's earliest possible return to Lee, who stressed his urgent need for them. The Lee-recommended transfer was made, Bragg's strength at Chattanooga was reduced to 36,000, and Grant's 80,000 troops swept Bragg's army back into Georgia after a breakthrough at Missionary Ridge.[89] Not knowing Lee's role in the "astounding" Longstreet transfer, Pollard in 1866 criticized Davis for ordering it: "This extraordinary military movement was the work of President Davis, who seems, indeed, to have had a singular fondness for erratic campaigns.... He planned the expedition against Knoxville. He was in love with the extraordinary design..."[90] Davis actually was implementing the "extraordinary design" of Robert E. Lee.

As Sherman marched from Atlanta to Savannah in late 1864, Grant wrote to him about Lee's options: "If you capture the garrison of Savannah it certainly will compel Lee to detach from Richmond or give us nearly the whole South. My own opinion is that Lee is averse to going out of Virginia, and if the cause of the South is lost he wants Richmond to be the last place surrendered. If he has such views it may be well to indulge him until everything else is in our hands."[91]

Before undertaking his early 1865 trek through the Carolinas, Sherman was still concerned about the possibility of Lee's shifting troops to oppose his advance: "[T]he only serious question that occurred to me was, would General Lee sit down in Richmond (besieged by General Grant), and permit us, almost unopposed, to pass through the States of South and North Carolina, cutting off and consuming the very supplies on which he depended to feed his army in Virginia, or would he make an effort to escape from General Grant, and endeavor to catch us inland somewhere between Columbia and Raleigh?"[92]

His concerns proved to be unfounded. On January 19, 1865, Lee wrote to South Carolina congressman William P. Miles that he would not send a blocking force to the south, offering the implausible suggestion, "If the people in South Carolina & Georgia would turn out in all their strength, aided by the troops now in the department, the advance of Sherman ought to be checked."[93] T. Harry Williams points out Lee's failure to even comprehend the threat Sherman posed: "[Lee's] mastery of logistics did not extend beyond departmental limits. In February, 1865, he said that he could not believe Sherman would be able to move into North Carolina. The evidence of Sherman's great march was before him, and yet he was not quite sure it had really happened."[94]

On March 1, as Sherman marched through the Carolinas toward Lee's army, Confederate Carolinas commander Joseph Johnston proposed that Lee bring a large number of his troops to North Carolina to join Johnston in defeating Sherman. Grant and Sherman had been concerned about such a merger even before they began their simultaneous campaigns in May 1864. Sherman said that "if Lee is a soldier of genius, he will seek to transfer his army from Richmond to Raleigh or Columbia; if he is a man simply of detail, he will remain where he is, and his speedy defeat is sure." Lee declined to move against Sherman until the Federals had crossed the Roanoke River, a mere fifty-five miles south of Petersburg. At the time of his proposal, Johnston had about twenty-one thousand troops to oppose Sherman's ninety thousand. Lee's and Johnston's armies would lose separately.[95]

McPherson concludes, "Lee's strategic vision was limited to the Virginia theater, where his influence concentrated Confederate resources at the expense of the western theaters…where [the Confederacy] really lost the war."[96] Surprising agreement with that view came from E. A. Pollard in 1866. Pollard, who started many elements of the Myth of the Lost Cause, was writing a few years before Early, Pendleton, and others decided to deify Lee. Pollard's analysis was that Lee took a narrow, unselfish view of his authority and thus: "The fact was that, although many of Gen. Lee's views were sound, yet, outside of the limits of the Army of Northern Virginia, and with reference to the general affairs of the Confederacy, his influence was negative and accomplished absolutely nothing."[97]

## INADEQUATE STAFF

Lee's staff was too small and inexperienced for the responsibilities Lee bore. "Outsiders complained that he should have more seasoned men, but Lee preferred not to take such men away from field assignments."[98] He should have realized what a powerful effect a few such men would have had as members of his staff.

T. Harry Williams notes the significance of Lee's inadequate staff: "In many respects Lee was not a modern-minded general. He probably did not understand the real function of a staff and certainly failed to put together an adequate staff for his army."[99] While Lee's small staff was headed by a colonel or lieutenant colonel, the Army of the Potomac's large staff was headed by a major general and included several brigadier generals.[100] Staffing problems and the poor coordination that resulted had a greater effect on offensive than defensive tactics and thus were particularly troublesome for Lee.[101]

Even the admiring Freeman questioned the size of Lee's small staff: "No general ever had more devoted service than he received from his personal assistants, but surely no officer of like rank ever fought a campaign comparable to that of 1864 with only three men on his staff, and not one of the three a professional soldier."[102] Allen Guelzo agrees: "Lee's staff was inadequate, and much of its inadequacy was due to the Confederate Congress's parsimony in limiting its size, and to the lack of staff training before the war in the Old Army.... Staffers were still, [as in] the Napoleonic Wars, drawn from friends or relations with no particular qualifications."[103]

"It would not be accurate to say that Lee's general staff were glorified clerks," comments T. Harry Williams, "but the statement would not be too wide of the mark. Certainly, his staff was not, in the modern sense, a planning staff, which was why Lee was often a tired general."[104]

Lee made poor use of his staff and inadequately delegated authority, a failing that William Davis attributes to the general's own character. "From youth his instinct was to do things himself to see them done well.... No doubt his concept of duty influenced him too."[105] Twice during the Overland Campaign, Lee tried to lead some of his troops into the heart of battle—perhaps because he did not trust subordinates to do the job—and had to be sent to the rear by his worried troops. From Seven Days' to Gettysburg to the North Anna River, his failure to delegate impaired Lee's performance and cost his army dearly. He could not rely on others to do what had to be done because he had not built and trained a capable staff.

## COMPLEX AND UNCOORDINATED BATTLE PLANS

Beginning with his late 1861 foray into northwestern Virginia, Lee tended to issue complicated pre-battle orders that led to Confederate failure. There, at the so-called Battle of Cheat Mountain, his complex orders resulted in a failed attack. He often devised battle plans that required impossible coordination and timing or dissipated his limited strength though consecutive instead of concurrent attacks. At the Seven Days' Battle, for example, Lee ordered a series of frontal and flanking assaults that were plagued by poor coordination and timing. Although the battle was a strategic victory, the rebels suffered tactical failures and huge losses. Day after day Lee's orders depended upon flanking movements by an exhausted Jackson and his weary troops, all transferred to the Richmond area immediately after two months of continuous fighting in the Shenandoah. Unsurprisingly, Jackson was a no-show or late-show as Lee's other troops were being slaughtered in their frontal assaults.

At Gettysburg, for about thirty consecutive hours, Lee "oversaw" three separate, uncoordinated assaults on the left, then the right, and then on the center of the strong Union line. In each instance, about one-third of his army attacked while the other two-thirds watched. These disjointed attacks allowed Meade to transfer his defending troops from one unattacked front to another requiring assistance.

## POOR ORDERS

Not only were Lee's plans overly complex, but he complicated things further with inadequate orders. On numerous occasions they were too vague or discretionary, flaws that were often magnified by the orders' verbal transmission.[106]

Lee issued confused and discretionary orders at Malvern Hill and to Stuart as Lee's army moved north to Pennsylvania prior to the Battle of Gettysburg. On the first day of Gettysburg he ordered Ewell to take the high ground "if practicable." Emory Thomas maintains that Gettysburg was lost "principally because of who Lee was. He was a soldier who preferred to suggest rather than order, a general who attempted to lead from consensus and shrank from confrontation. He insisted upon making possible for others the freedom of thought and action he sought for himself."[107]

There are times for discretionary orders, but Lee overused them without adequate consideration of who was receiving them.

## SENSELESS CONTINUATION OF THE WAR

After the fall of Atlanta, Mobile, and Savannah and the reelection of Lincoln, Lee must have realized that the Confederacy had no hope of winning. His troops were deserting by the thousands—often because of the suffering the war inflicted on their distant families—and he was unable to properly feed, clothe, or shelter the ones who remained with him. By late 1864 and early 1865, Lee had more credibility than any

Confederate, including President Davis. Over the opposition of Davis, who always wanted to be the unchallenged military decision-maker, the Confederate Congress elevated Lee to general in chief in early 1865. Lee's resignation would have effectively ended the war. His men and those elsewhere would have returned to their homes in droves.

But his sense of duty apparently overcame everything, even his sympathy for his officers and men and their families.[108] So he fought on. As Dowdey says, "Actually, the most practical move Lee could make was to arrange terms to end the suffering of his dwindling band of followers."[109]

Dowdey and Louis Manarin, who admire Lee, provide some telling insight on this issue:

> [In early February 1865] Lee held a private conversation with Virginia's Senator R. M. T. Hunter.... Lee urged him to offer a resolution in the [Confederate] Senate that would obtain better terms than, as Hunter reported Lee as saying, "we're likely to be given after a surrender." Hunter claimed that Davis had already impugned his motives for seeking peace terms, and told Lee, "if he thought the chances of success desperate, I thought he ought to say so to the President." Though Lee held frequent conversations with Davis during February, it is unlikely that he ever brought himself to introduce a subject which would be so distasteful to the president.... [T]he crux of the matter was that men in a position to know recognized that the South was defeated, but no one was willing to assume the responsibility of trying to convince Davis of this.[110]

Lee's reticence definitely was a major part of the problem. T. Harry Williams places it in context: "It has been suggested that Lee did not try to impose his will on the government because of his humility of character, and this may well be true. But it would also seem to be true that he did not know that a commander had any political responsibility."[111]

Lee, who had the power but not the resolve, should at least have recommended in writing to Davis that the war be concluded because its outcome was certain and further suffering was unnecessary. For five months after Lincoln's reelection, which clinched the war, until the last hours at Appomattox, Lee and Davis continued the futile struggle. The result was continued death and destruction throughout the South. This senseless continuation of the war was Lee's final failure because he had made no real effort to preclude it.

## SUMMARY

Robert E. Lee was not one of the great generals of history—certainly not the greatest of the Civil War. His performance was flawed by overly aggressive strategy and tactics, a myopic focus on Virginia, loss of battle-field control, a deliberately inadequate staff, complex and uncoordinated battle plans, poor orders, and a senseless continuation of the war after its outcome was certain. Lee actually is one of the most overrated generals in military history thanks primarily to the power of the Myth of the Lost Cause, which went unchallenged all too long.

# CHAPTER SIX

# DID JAMES LONGSTREET LOSE THE BATTLE OF GETTYSBURG AND THUS THE WAR?

## THE MYTH

Blaming James Longstreet for the Confederate disaster at Gettysburg is a crucial part of the myth of Robert E. Lee's greatness. The defeat at Gettysburg was supposedly fatal to the Southern cause. Since Lee could not be held accountable for such a defeat, scapegoats had to be found. Lee himself placed some blame upon Jeb Stuart because of his absence and on Longstreet, Ewell, and A. P. Hill for their failure to initiate coordinated attacks.[1] The theory that Longstreet lost Gettysburg and thus the war is inconsistent, by the way, with the myth that the South never had a chance of winning the war.

Some argue that Lee did not blame anyone for the Gettysburg defeat. He initially accepted the blame for Pickett's Charge, and he offered to resign because of the loss. But in the years that followed, Lee defended his record at Gettysburg by blaming the defeat on, among others, Stuart, Ewell, and even his own soldiers (for falling short of his expectations).[2] On other occasions he blamed Longstreet and either William Nelson Pendleton or Edward Porter Alexander, his two artillery commanders.[3]

Other defenders of Lee are content to blame his subordinates in general for the defeat. Page, for example, explains that "Lee's plan of battle failed here, but the student of war knows how it failed and why. It failed because his lieutenants failed, and his orders were not carried out—possibly because he called upon his intrepid army for more than human strength was able to achieve."[4]

Why, then, have others singled out Longstreet?[5] Stewart Sifakis offers a simple answer: "He argued with Lee, he was right, and he became a Republican."[6] According to the *Oxford Companion to American Military History*,

> During Reconstruction, Longstreet settled in New Orleans and joined the Republican Party. He held a variety of political patronage positions until his death in 1904. Viewing him as a traitor to the white South, many former comrades turned against him and attacked his military record. His enemies' lies and fabrications, particularly in relation to the Battle of Gettysburg, where he was unfairly accused of deliberately delaying the attack on the second day, were accepted uncritically by later historians, such as Douglas Southall Freeman, who misrepresented both Longstreet's personality and his record.[7]

Freeman's effort to exonerate Lee is typical. After contending in the three volumes of *R. E. Lee* that the general almost walked on water, Freeman took four volumes to exculpate him for the rebel loss of the war in *Lee's Lieutenants*—which may as well have been titled *Lee's Scapegoats*.[8]

Jubal Early became the power and brains behind the anti-Longstreet movement with his famous Lee Birthday speech at Washington and Lee University on January 19, 1872.[9] In that speech, which was widely distributed as a "Lost Cause" pamphlet, Early, an old adversary of Longstreet, asserted that Lee had ordered Longstreet to attack at dawn on the second day at Gettysburg and that Longstreet's failure to do so had lost the battle.[10]

Pendleton, Lee's incompetent chief of artillery, followed Early's lead. In his own Lee Birthday speech the following year, Pendleton repeated the story that Lee had ordered Longstreet to attack at dawn on the second day at Gettysburg, contradicting his own report to Lee after the battle.[11] Jefferson Davis joined the chorus in 1881 with his saga of the Confederacy. After questioning and distorting Longstreet's advice early on Day Two to move around the Union left flank, Davis proceeded with the tired "attack-at-dawn" criticism: "Had there been a concentrated attack at sunrise on the second day, with the same gallantry and skill which were exhibited in the partial assaults, it may reasonably be assumed that the enemy would have been routed."[12]

Early made the purported "order at dawn" the centerpiece of the lectures in which for years he promoted the Myth of the Lost Cause. But Mark Perry notes, "There was only one problem in all of this, of course, and that was that Lee did not issue a 'sunrise attack order' on July 2." There is no record of such an order, and key members of Lee's staff denied it ever occurred. Lee's aide Charles Venable said Pendleton, whom Lee did not take seriously, was in no position to know of any such order, and his ludicrous claim may have been due to "an absolute loss of memory." Another Lee aide, Walter Taylor, perceptively wrote to Longstreet, "I regard it as a great mistake on the part of those who, perhaps because of political differences, now undertake to criticize & attack your war record."[13]

Thomas L. Connelly offers a similar explanation for Pendleton's allegation:

> [It] was pure fabrication, even embarrassing to some members
> of Lee's staff. Charles Venable admitted the statement was
> due to Pendleton's obvious emotional illness, "to an absolute
> loss of memory said to be brought on by frequent attacks

resembling paralysis." Other Lee staff members—A. L. Long, Walter Taylor, and Charles Marshall—however much they hated Longstreet, denied that any sunrise order had been given. Venable even lamented, "It is a pity, it ever got into print."[14]

Nevertheless, Early, Pendleton, and their allies, through misleading speeches and articles in the *Southern Historical Society Papers*, quickly convinced most Southerners in the 1870s that the infallible Lee had been undercut by Longstreet at Gettysburg. They solicited anti-Longstreet papers from Confederate officers who had old scores to settle or wanted to protect themselves from Early's vicious campaign.[15] One of the last of the major Lost Cause myth-makers to join the attack on Longstreet was the Reverend J. William Jones, who wrote in 1884 that the South would have "won Gettysburg and Independence, but for the failure of *one man*"—Longstreet.[16]

Some of the old Confederates who turned on Longstreet, however, could not ignore Lee's part in the defeat at Gettysburg. William Oates, a former subordinate who did not like Longstreet, submitted an article to the *Southern Historical Society Papers* that criticized Longstreet's alleged tardiness, his disagreement with Lee at Gettysburg, and his failure to honor Lee's sacred memory. But, remarkably, he slipped in some criticisms of Lee: "It may have been best for Lee to have flanked Meade out of his strong position and have forced him to attack and thus to have acted on the defensive [as Longstreet had recommended].... Lee, with all his robust daring and adventurous spirit, should not have ordered the impossible, as was apparent to a skilled observer." Oates's criticisms of Lee's impossible frontal assaults and failure to go on the defensive—all contrary to Longstreet's advice—may have been over-looked by Early in his eagerness to publish Oates's generally anti-Longstreet article.[17]

Lee's aides' denial of the sunrise attack order and Oates's criticism of Lee's tactics, however, were lost in a tidal wave of pro-Lee and anti-Longstreet commentary and publications that indelibly established the myth of the sunrise attack order and Longstreet's responsibility for the loss of Gettysburg. "For three generations and more—until the centennial anniversary of the war in 1960—Lee's sunrise attack order remained an unquestioned pillar of southern faith."[18]

Like some of his nineteenth-century predecessors, Douglas Southall Freeman made Longstreet a major scapegoat for Gettysburg. After stating that Longstreet was "disgruntled" because Lee did not accept his advice, Freeman launched a searing personal attack on Longstreet premised on the imaginary plan for an early-morning attack: "Determined, apparently, to force a situation in which his plan would have to be adopted in spite of Lee, he delayed the attack on the right until Cemetery Ridge was crowded with men, whereas if he had attacked early in the morning, as Lee intended, he probably could have stormed that position and assuredly could have taken Round Top. Longstreet's slow and stubborn mind rendered him incapable of the quick daring and loyal obedience that had characterized Jackson. . . . It was Lee's misfortune at Gettysburg that he had to employ in offensive operations a man whose whole inclination was toward the defensive."[19]

Freeman acknowledged that part of the blame for the "late" attack rested with Lee, but Longstreet is very much the villain of the piece:

> [Lee's] greatest weakness as a soldier was displayed along with Longstreet's for when Longstreet sulked, Lee's temperament was such that he could not bring himself to either shake Longstreet out of his bad humor by a sharp order, or to take direction of the field when Longstreet delayed. No candid critic of the battle can follow the events of that fateful morning and not have a feeling that Lee virtually surrendered to Longstreet, who obeyed only when he could no longer find an excuse for delay. Lee's one positive order was that delivered at about 11 o'clock for Longstreet to attack. Having done this much, Lee permitted Longstreet to waste the time until after 4 o'clock. It is scarcely too much to say that on July 2 the Army of Northern Virginia was without a commander.[20]

Freeman first criticizes Longstreet for failing to attack "early in the morning, as Lee intended" but then concedes that Lee's only attack order to Longstreet came at 11 a.m. In other words, Freeman did not allow the lateness of the order to deter him from continuing, in the Jubal Early tradition, the myth of the supposed "early morning" attack order.

Freeman's influence is present in Emory M. Thomas's *Robert E. Lee: A Biography* (1995),[21] which blames Longstreet for the delays on Day Two at Gettysburg: "Longstreet acted out his prolonged pout on July 2 and attacked Meade's flank only after giving the Federals enough time to accumulate and implant ample defenders."[22]

More recently, William Davis has implied that Longstreet unduly delayed his attack: "Unfortunately, [Lee] seems merely to have waited for Longstreet's attack to commence rather than sending an officer to regain control."[23] He does not explain how Longstreet erred or how any such error affected the outcome on Day Two—especially in light of Lee's failure to send in all of A .P. Hill's troops when the Longstreet/Hill attack reached its climax and was repelled.[24]

Emory Thomas adds a different charge: Longstreet did not adequately support Pickett's Charge on July 3.[25] Yet Pickett's Charge happened right in front of Lee, who was standing on Seminary Ridge. If he wanted Longstreet's divisions on the rebel right to join the attack, all he had to do was issue the order and enforce it.

Thomas Connelly describes how Early and Jones had falsified documents and cut deals with other authors in their effort to praise Lee and Early and to damn Longstreet. For example, when they published Jeb Stuart's report on Gettysburg, they deleted a paragraph in which Stuart had criticized Early for failing to watch for Stuart's cavalry. When Stuart's former adjutant caught them, they reached an agreement with him in which neither Stuart nor Early would be criticized while all the blame for Gettysburg was apportioned to Longstreet.[26]

It was for a variety of reasons, then, that the propagators of the Myth focused more and more on Longstreet, finally agreeing that he had single-handedly lost Gettysburg. Their version of Gettysburg became so embedded in Civil War historiography that even the noted British military historian John Keegan, echoing Freeman, concluded that Lee was too much the Virginia gentleman to hurt his subordinates' feelings. The result, said Keegan, was that "[Lee's] defeat at Gettysburg stemmed largely from his failure to give direct orders to General James Longstreet and to insist on those orders being carried out."[27]

The tenacity of this myth is reflected in the account of Longstreet's role at Gettysburg in the *Oxford Encyclopedia of the Civil War* (2011):

> Doubting the wisdom of the campaign into Pennsylvania, Longstreet particularly opposed Lee's decision to take the offensive at Gettysburg on July 2 and 3. "If he is there," Longstreet told Lee in reference to the Union position on Cemetery Hill, "it will be because he is anxious that we should attack him: a good reason, in my judgment, for not doing so." Lee went ahead with his plan, and postwar critics insisted that Longstreet's reluctance to carry out those attacks cost the Confederacy a priceless victory.... He was an active Republican and a supporter of Reconstruction, political stands that further embittered Southern whites led by Jubal A. Early, who now made him the scapegoat for the Confederate defeat at Gettysburg. In his memoirs, published in 1896, Longstreet responded to his critics in an effort to salvage his military reputation.[28]

There is nothing here to question the contention that Longstreet was reluctant to obey Lee's orders and that that reluctance "cost the Confederacy a priceless victory."

# DID LONGSTREET REALLY CAUSE THE CONFEDERATES TO LOSE GETTYSBURG AND THE WAR?

The first problem with the "Longstreet Lost Gettysburg and the War" theory is that the Battle of Gettysburg, fought at the mid-point of the war, did not in itself cost the Confederacy the war. Earlier critical

turning points were Forts Henry and Donelson, as well as the Battle of
Antietam. Alan Nolan points out that the Union won significant victories simultaneously with Gettysburg (Vicksburg) and later (Missionary Ridge (Chattanooga), Nashville, and Sherman's March to the
Sea).[29] Rebel defeats at Franklin (Tennessee), Mobile, the Shenandoah
Valley, Sherman's 1865 March through the Carolinas, and Fort Fisher
(North Carolina) could be added to that list. And there was Lincoln's
come-from-behind reelection in November 1864. The loss at Gettysburg did not guarantee Confederate defeat in the war, and a win would
not have guaranteed a victory in the war.

Lost Cause proponents, nevertheless, have been fond of focusing on
Gettysburg, and the battle soon became one of the great legends of
American history in both the North and the South. Gettysburg, writes
Kenneth Nivison, "lent itself to an almost Homeric retelling of acts of
heroism, bravery, and leadership." He continues:

> Equally as critical, though, was the fact that no black soldiers
> played a role in the three days of combat at Gettysburg. This
> permitted those who shaped Gettysburg's story to ignore
> slavery and race as a part of the conflict as they reconstructed
> the place and its memory for its middle-class consumer pub-
> lic.... In the end, the Gettysburg myth was created as a unique
> moment of American greatness: a Union victory with Con-
> federate valor. In the telling and re-telling of the events, the
> efforts of both Union and Confederate soldiers were thus
> gradually Americanized; combatants were hailed for their
> common honor, bravery, and manliness, while the distinct
> causes for which they fought escaped the narrative and, in
> large measure, the national memory.[30]

Someone besides Lee had to be blamed—preferably a non-Virginian
and certainly no one involved in the creation of the Myth. Among the
reasons that Longstreet was singled out was that he had the temerity to
criticize Lee after the war, became a Republican, publicly urged white

Southerners to join the Republican Party, and even held a political position (surveyor of customs in New Orleans) in the Grant administration.
"But," argues Mark Perry, "the importance of the Longstreet controversy
has less to do with Gettysburg than with the rewriting of the war's history by southerners that was necessary given the Confederacy's belief
that God had blessed their cause."[31]

A careful analysis of the preparation and execution of the Gettysburg
campaign, including the Battle of Gettysburg itself, will allow the reader
to determine for himself the roles of Lee and Longstreet in this venture
that proved so damaging to the Confederacy. The story begins with Lee's
plans and preparations for a Northern invasion, his supposedly great
victory at Chancellorsville in the first few days of May 1863, and the
consequences of that battle.

In early 1863, Lee's aggressive strategy and tactics in the Virginia
Theater substantially affected Grant's prospects for success in the Mississippi Valley. Apparently emboldened by his actual and apparent victories in mid- to late-1862, Lee resisted suggestions in April 1863 that he
transfer troops elsewhere, and in early May he went on the tactical
offensive at Chancellorsville, which became a costly strategic victory.

Capitalizing on his acclaim from Chancellorsville, Lee in mid-May
pushed Jefferson Davis into making a crucial mistake that led to major
Confederate defeats in the three primary theaters of the war (Eastern,
Middle, and Western). Lee strongly opposed the transfer of Longstreet
and any of his First Corps outside the Virginia Theater, and he convinced
Davis and most of his cabinet to leave Longstreet with him for an offensive into the North. The Gettysburg campaign was Lee's idea; Davis and
the cabinet approved his strong recommendation.[32]

After the Union fiasco at Fredericksburg in December 1862, Lincoln
named "Fighting Joe" Hooker to replace Ambrose Burnside as commander of the Army of the Potomac. Lincoln and Halleck had decided
that the best strategy in the East was to go after Lee's army, not Richmond.[33] Because of Lee's heavy casualties in 1862, Hooker outnumbered
him 130,000 to 56,000 during the Chancellorsville campaign that
Hooker initiated in early May.[34] Lee was also hampered by the absence

of Longstreet's corps, which was resupplying in southeastern Virginia and northeastern North Carolina.

At this critical juncture in April 1863, Lee demonstrated his one-theater mindset and stoutly resisted the use of any of his army to help in the West. Union leaders in March had moved Burnside's Ninth Corps to the Middle Theater from the vicinity of Longstreet in southeastern Virginia,[35] and Lee was content to leave Longstreet far away from Lee's Fredericksburg position. Lee had received a report of Burnside's movement on March 28 and was convinced of the report's validity by April 1.[36] Nevertheless, Lee resisted requests and suggestions by western Confederates, President Davis, Secretary of War James Seddon, and Longstreet that Longstreet's corps be sent westward to counter the increased Union strength there.[37]

In early April, two Confederate generals in the West, John C. Pemberton and the recovered Joseph E. Johnston, mistakenly advised Richmond that Grant apparently was moving troops from Mississippi to Tennessee to join Burnside and Rosecrans. Confederate leaders responded by sending eight thousand troops from Alabama and Mississippi to Bragg in Tennessee and requesting reinforcements from Lee.

On April 6, ironically the same day that Lee himself observed that the Union apparently "had a general plan to deceive us while reinforcing the western armies,"[38] Seddon asked him to acquiesce in the transfer westward of two or three of Longstreet's brigades. Lee strongly opposed the request and argued, contrary to his usual advocacy of concentration of forces,[39] that separate Confederate forces should launch separate offensives from Mississippi to Maryland—reminiscent of the failed offensives of the prior autumn.[40] Minimizing the threat to Vicksburg, he wrote, "If the statements which I see in the papers are true, Genl Grant is withdrawing from Vicksburg, and will hardly return to his former position there this summer."[41] Lee wanted to launch a major campaign into the North in his Eastern Theater and did not want to give up any of his troops. Weeks before he had ordered the preparation of maps from the Shenandoah through Harrisburg to Philadelphia.[42]

When Seddon came back with a renewed and expanded request for some of Longstreet's forces, Lee raised a new set of objections. Longstreet's foraging, he insisted, was critical to his own imminent move north to test Hooker's strength, ascertain the distribution of Union troops between the East and West, and attempt to drive Hooker north of the Potomac. He suggested that Tennessee be strengthened by moving troops from Charleston, Savannah, Mobile, and Vicksburg—anywhere but Virginia![43] Learning that Grant actually had not moved forces to Tennessee and yielding to Lee, Davis and Seddon sent reinforcements to Bragg in Tennessee only from Beauregard in the southeast.

As soon as he was assured that he was not going to lose any troops, Lee dropped his plans for an early Northern offensive and left Longstreet where he was. Lee remained concerned about his supplies but optimistic that the Northern will to win could be destroyed:

I do not think our enemies are so confident of success as they used to be. If we can baffle them in their various designs this year & our people are true to our cause & not so devoted to themselves and their own aggrandisement, I think our success will be certain. But it will all come right. This year I hope will establish our supplies on a firm basis. On every other point we are strong. If successful this year, next fall [1864] will be a great change in public opinion in the North. The Republicans will be destroyed & I think the friends of peace will become so strong as that the next administration will go in on that basis. We have only therefore to resist manfully.[44]

Lee wanted to do more than resist in the East, and his refusal to part with any of his men left the Confederates in the West shorthanded in two areas. Johnston and Pemberton would be unable to deal with Grant's imminent movement on Vicksburg, and the fall of that Mississippi River citadel within three months would be an ill omen for Confederate hopes about the 1864 presidential election. Just as ominously, Bragg's army in

Tennessee also went unreinforced against a stronger opponent. It ran out of meat and was short on rations while occupying an area from which all crops and livestock were being shipped to Lee.[45]

Back on the Eastern front, Hooker launched a major offensive west of Fredericksburg on April 26. Three entire Union corps crossed the Rappahannock and Rapidan rivers and converged on the key Chancellorsville crossroads on Lee's left flank.[46]

Hooker was now in a position to march south out of the Wilderness and interpose the bulk of his army between Lee and Richmond—unless Lee hastily retreated south, which is what Hooker expected. At worst, Hooker presumed, Lee would attack the Union forces in a way that Hooker could fight with superior numbers from a strong defensive position.

When Lee sent Jackson and others out of Fredericksburg to challenge Hooker, however, "Fighting Joe" flinched. He halted his offensive and yielded the initiative to Lee, who sent Jackson on a famous sweep around Hooker's "hanging" right flank and pushed the surprised and panicked Yankees back about two miles.

Then things went downhill for the Confederates. Jackson was accidentally shot by North Carolina troops. The next morning Lee and Jeb Stuart (replacing Jackson) had to go on the offensive to reunite the Confederate troops who had been separated by Jackson's flanking attack. After that costly offensive, Lee received word that his rear was threatened by Union troops coming from Fredericksburg. Lee wasted a whole day trapping and frontally assaulting the outnumbered troops of John Sedgwick instead of going after them immediately.[47] This delay gave Sedgwick time to entrench and ultimately to escape.

Never one to pass up an opportunity to attack, Lee hurried back to Chancellorsville on May 5 after Sedgwick's nighttime retreat in an effort to assault Hooker's forces before they too could retreat across the Rappahannock. General Winfield Scott Hancock was overseeing an orderly and well-defended retreat, and Lee was fortunate not to have had the opportunity to attack. In fact, according to Porter Alexander, Lee was saved from disaster by Hooker's May 5–6 retreat back across the river:

There was still another occasion when I recalled ruefully Ives's prophecy that I would see all the audacity [on Lee's part] I wanted to see, & felt that it was already overfulfilled: but when, to my intense delight, the enemy crossed the river in retreat during the night, & thus saved us from what would have been probably the bloodiest defeat of the war. It was on the 6th of May 1863 at the end of Chancellorsville.... Hooker's entire army, some 90,000 infantry, were in the Wilderness, backed against the Rapidan [and the Rappahannock], & had had nearly three days to fortify a short front, from the river above to the river below. And, in that dense forest of small wood, a timber slashing in front of a line of breastworks could in a few hours make a position absolutely impregnable to assault. But on the afternoon of the 5th Gen. Lee gave orders for a grand assault the next morning by his whole force of about 40,000 infantry, & I was all night getting my artillery in position for it. And how I did thank God when in the morning the enemy were gone![48]

Bitterly disappointed at the failure to launch the ill-conceived offensive[49] that he had hoped would bring a grand victory, Lee erupted when told that the Federal entrenchments had been abandoned overnight.[50]

Chancellorsville, Jackson's last battle, also proved to be Lee's last major "victory." Jackson's classic flanking maneuver was not to be repeated.[51] After Jackson's death there was no one forceful enough (and apparently only Longstreet tried) to convince Lee of the necessity to preserve his most precious resource, his army, by remaining on the defensive whenever possible and by flanking, rather than frontally assaulting, superior enemy forces. There also was no one left capable of converting Lee's discretionary orders into daring success on the battlefield.[52]

Although often regarded as Lee's greatest victory, Chancellorsville was a tribute to Hooker's incompetence under fire. It was, in fact, a disaster for the South.[53] After the success of Jackson's flanking maneuver, the Confederates were decimated in a series of frontal attacks on Union defenders. While killing or wounding 10,700 Northern soldiers (an 11 percent casualty rate), the rebels suffered casualties of their own of almost 11,100 (a 19 percent rate). The number killed or wounded was close to equal on both sides, though a few more Confederates were killed.[54] Outnumbered at the outset of the war and devastated by their losses from 1862, the Confederates could not afford many more battles with such unbalanced casualty rates.

Lee's numerical losses were serious enough for him to change his army's manner of counting casualties by eliminating "slight injuries,"[55] to complain of his numerical inferiority, and to make one of his periodic appeals to President Davis for reinforcements from elsewhere. Vicksburg and Chattanooga were both threatened, but on May 10 Lee opposed sending one of Longstreet's divisions to the West and warned Seddon that unless he was reinforced he would have "to withdraw into the defences around Richmond.... The strength of this army has been reduced by the casualties in the late battles."[56] The next day Lee wrote Davis: "It would seem therefore that Virginia is to be the theater of action, and this army, if possible, ought to be strengthened.... I think that you will agree with me that every effort should be made to reinforce this army in order to oppose the large force which the enemy seems to be concentrating against it."[57]

Chancellorsville demonstrated Lee's propensity for an offensive strategy and his Virginia-first focus as he refused to part with Long-street beforehand and sought reinforcements afterward. While his focus on Virginia had serious consequences elsewhere, Lee's aggressive strategy and tactics again resulted in irreplaceable losses to his own army.

Perhaps as damaging as those losses was the over-confidence that Chancellorsville inspired in Confederate minds—particularly in the mind of Robert E. Lee.[58] On May 21, Lee wrote to Hood about the men in the Army of Northern Virginia: "I agree with you in believing that our army would be invincible if it could be properly organized and officered. There never were such men in an army before. They will go anywhere and do anything if properly led."[59] Lee had great confidence in his soldiers although tempered by a concern about his officers.

Every tactical gamble Lee had taken appeared to have been success-ful, the enemy had been driven from the field and across the Rappahan-nock, and no task seemed beyond the capability of his brave army. Lee's actions in the succeeding weeks reflected a fatal confidence that the Army of Northern Virginia was invincible,[60] a confidence reciprocated, accord-ing to Porter Alexander, by his men:

> But, like the rest of the army generally, nothing gave me much concern so long as I knew that Gen. Lee was in command. I am sure there can never have been an army with more supreme confidence in its commander than that army had in Gen. Lee. We looked forward to victory under him as confidently as to successive sunrises.[61]

Lee's over-confident army, however, had seen its last major strategic "victory."

With Jackson no longer at his side, Lee finalized his fateful decision to invade the North. In doing so, he rejected pleas to send part of his army to rescue the thirty thousand troops bottled up near Vicksburg, Mississippi, by Ulysses S. Grant. Seddon and Longstreet initially recom-mended to President Davis either that course of action or a reinforcement of Bragg for an assault on middle Tennessee. They could have argued that Chancellorsville demonstrated that Lee could survive and even win without Longstreet.[62]

Between May 14 and 17, while Grant took Jackson, Mississippi, and moved toward Vicksburg, the Confederacy's leadership met in Richmond to debate sending some of Lee's troops to trap Grant between Jackson and John Pemberton's thirty-thousand-man army in Vicksburg. Drawing on the political capital he had earned with his Chancellorsville "victory," Lee convinced Davis that Richmond would be threatened if Lee's army was reduced in strength and that the best defense of Richmond would be an offensive campaign into the North. Lee demonstrated his biased and flawed national strategic vision by arguing that this was a "question between Virginia and the Mississippi." He also argued that the oppressive Mississippi climate would cause Grant to withdraw from the Vicksburg area in June.[63]

On May 26 the Confederate cabinet, with one dissent, approved his recommendation and authorized him to launch a Northern offensive in the East. As Lee moved north, he unrealistically wrote to Davis that his Eastern offensive might even result in the Union's recalling some of its troops from the West, though he hedged his bet by requesting that troops be transferred to Virginia from the Carolinas to protect Richmond, threaten Washington, and aid his advance.[64] Although Longstreet acquiesced in Lee's strategic offensive, he spent a great deal of time trying to convince Lee to go on the tactical defensive once in the North in an effort to repeat the defensive victory at Fredericksburg. Confederate General Wade Hampton later complained that while he thought the Pennsylvania campaign would enable the Confederates to choose a battlefield, "we let Meade choose his position & we then attacked."[65]

Lee's correspondence reveals mixed intentions as he headed north. In the first of two letters of June 25 to Davis, he wrote, "I think I can throw Genl Hooker's army across the Potomac and draw troops from the south, embarrassing their plan of campaign in a measure, if I can do nothing more and have to return."[66] Writing later in the day, Lee appeared to share Longstreet's view: "It seems to me that we cannot afford to keep our troops awaiting possible movements of the enemy, but that our true policy is, as far as we can, so to employ our own forces as to give occupation to his at points of our own selection."[67]

Alexander later stated that sending troops to the West would have been a better use of them and would have taken advantage of the South's interior lines; indeed, such a move was successful that autumn (at Chickamauga) under less favorable circumstances.[68] Lee's refusal to send troops to either Vicksburg or middle Tennessee contributed to the fall of Vicksburg and the loss of the Mississippi Valley to Union control. A weakened Bragg, who sent some of his own troops to aid Vicksburg, had to retreat through southeastern Tennessee and Chattanooga. As Archer Jones explains, "This opening of the Mississippi had a profound effect by spreading hope in the North for an early victory and in the South widespread pessimism."[69]

Bragg's Army of Tennessee had been considerably weakened that spring and summer because the Confederate commissary in Atlanta shipped massive amounts of foodstuffs to Lee and virtually nothing to Bragg.[70] Not only did Lee refuse to send troops to the West, but he implored Bragg to invade Ohio to complement Lee's planned incursion into Pennsylvania.[71] At the time, Bragg had only fifty thousand troops either to hold Tennessee or to send assistance to Vicksburg. Union strength in the West was 214,000.[72]

Gettysburg, which extinguished any prospects for Confederate victory in the East, showed Lee at his worst. As when he went north in 1862, the numbers made an embarrassing retreat and perceived defeat inevitable.[73] General Alexander later expressed his concern that Lee's nearest ammunition supply railhead was at Staunton, Virginia, 150 wagon-miles from Gettysburg.[74] Just as in 1862, Lee was moving north with a badly weakened army but was blinded by its tactical success earlier in the year.[75] In addition, Lee spread his forces all around south-central Pennsylvania without knowing the location of the Army of the Potomac.

In going north again, Lee acted on his flawed philosophy that the best defense is a good offense.[76] He hoped to draw Hooker's army out of Virginia and live off the Pennsylvania countryside throughout the summer and early fall. He succeeded in taking everyone north, but his stay was shorter than he had hoped, and his eventual retreat to the Rappahannock line looked like a defeat to those not mesmerized by the myth of Lee's invincibility. His losses ensured that Gettysburg was his final major strategic offensive campaign.[77]

Following Chancellorsville and Jackson's death, Lee reorganized his seventy-five-thousand-man army. From two infantry corps of four divisions each, he assembled three corps, each having three divisions. The First Corps was commanded by Longstreet, the Second by Ewell, and the Third by A. P. Hill. Neither Ewell nor Hill had worked directly under Lee's command, and neither officer was a Stonewall Jackson. Lee's offensive strategy and tactics had weakened the entire command structure of his army.[78] Lee's failure to adjust his style, expectations, and orders to the poorer and less experienced generals in his army after Chancellorsville would prove to be troublesome and even disastrous.

The swashbuckling style of Jeb Stuart, in command of the cavalry division, caused problems from the beginning. On the eve of their departure on a major invasion of the North, Stuart's cavalrymen had seemed less interested than usual. One Confederate captain later explained that the troops were "worried out by the military foppery and display (which was Stuart's greatest weakness)."[79]

Lee's lax oversight of Stuart and the cavalry arm of his army led to one near-disaster and to one actual disaster. Stuart's cavalry was supposed to protect Lee's right flank and hide his northward movement from Yankee eyes. On June 5, the third day of the invasion campaign, Stuart's approximately 9,500 officers and men held a grand parade at Brandy Station near the Orange and Alexandria Railroad—to the delight of the local ladies and the disgust of the Confederate infantry.[80] Lee was not present, but Stuart received another opportunity to strut his forces when Lee arrived on the seventh and requested another review the next day. Thus the cavalry's spectacle was repeated on June 8[81]—the day they were to move across the Rappahannock to cover the continuing northward march of Ewell and Longstreet. A pleased Lee wrote to his wife, "I reviewed the cavalry in this section yesterday. It was a splendid sight. The men & horses looked well. They had recuperated since last fall. Stuart was in all his glory."[82] Lee relished Stuart's showmanship. "People do not often see what deleterious effects resulted from Lee's tendency to play favorites; on the other hand, that was how he had advanced in his own career, by serving as a protégé, first of [Charles] Gratiot, then [Joseph] Totten, and finally [Winfield] Scott."[83]

Early the next morning, June 9, an attack by Brigadier General Alfred Pleasonton's Union cavalry caught the Confederates off guard. Eleven thousand Union troops crossed the Rappahannock and launched attacks on Stuart's scattered forces. They got all the way to Brandy Station and Stuart's headquarters at nearby Fleetwood House before being repulsed by superior numbers of Confederate cavalry under Brigadier Generals Rooney Lee (Robert E. Lee's son) and William E. "Grumble" Jones, their horse artillery, and eventually rebel infantry. Stuart almost lost his artillery in the all-day battle that swirled around Fleetwood Hill. Union losses were about nine hundred to the rebels' five hundred, but the Northern horsemen achieved their goal of determining the probable location of the bulk of the Army of Northern Virginia while demonstrating, for the first time, their ability to initiate and sustain a credible offensive.

Embarrassed by his lack of preparedness and near-defeat at Brandy Station, Stuart sought to redeem himself later in June by setting off on another grand swing around the Union army. Instead of reining in the flamboyant Stuart, Lee provided him with such ambiguous orders that Lee carried out the invasion of Pennsylvania and most of the battle at Gettysburg without precise knowledge of where his adversaries were and without adequate screening forces. Lee allowed Stuart to depart with half his cavalry and take along his best subordinate commanders, Major General Wade Hampton and Brigadier General Fitzhugh Lee, while leaving the weak Brigadier General Beverly Robertson to screen and scout for the army commander.

How could this have happened? Stuart had a series of orders to choose from and decided upon the most exciting and glorious opportunity offered to him. Taking advantage of the confusing discretion Lee had provided to him, Stuart crossed the Potomac east of the Blue Ridge Mountains and engaged in a meaningless frolic and detour behind the Union army. Beginning on June 24, he swung east of the northward-moving Federals and thus separated his troopers from the rest of Lee's army. Although he entered Pennsylvania only a few miles east of Gettysburg, Stuart had no idea where Lee was and therefore headed farther, north to Carlisle instead of west to Gettysburg. All the while Stuart was slowed down by a captured wagon train that he regarded as precious booty.

Because of this eight-day jaunt, Stuart did not join Lee at Gettysburg until the evening of July 2—too late to be of any real assistance. Lee had to learn, on June 28, from a spy of Longstreet's about George Meade's appointment to succeed Hooker and of Meade's army's northward movement across the Potomac. When Lee then concentrated his army in the Cashtown-Gettysburg area, he needed Stuart's missing cavalry, which would have screened the convergence of the scattered units of Lee's army—an often overlooked consequence of Stuart's absence.[84]

Lee had no idea which Union corps were going to arrive at Gettysburg or when, and on the critical second day of July he had to base his plan of battle on skimpy and incorrect information concerning Union strength in the area of the Round Tops south of Gettysburg. Lee had only himself to blame for letting his strong-willed cavalry commander get away from his army.[85]

Lee's vague orders to Stuart presaged a series of such orders that plagued the Confederates throughout the Gettysburg campaign. Some defenders of Lee have attempted to justify the ambiguity of his orders as a consequence of his aggressive tactics and strategy. If so, dangerously vague orders were another disadvantage of the offensive style of warfare that lost the war.

While Stuart campaigned east of the Blue Ridge, Lee was having success to the west. Ewell's Second Corps led the northward sweep and routed nine thousand Yankee defenders at Winchester, Virginia, on June 14 and 15. Word of the rout reached Richmond the next day, when the Confederate chief of ordnance, Josiah Gorgas, ominously noted Lee's movement in his journal: "What the movement means it is difficult to divine. I trust we are not to have the Maryland [Antietam] campaign over again."[86] After Winchester, Ewell, A. P. Hill, and Longstreet moved their respective corps, in that order, through Sharpsburg and Hagerstown, Maryland, and across the Mason-Dixon Line into the Cumberland Valley of Pennsylvania. Ewell moved his leading corps through Chambersburg and then eastward through the mountains to Gettysburg, York, and Carlisle.

In the midst of this movement, Lee finally revealed to Davis the scope of his planned offensive by belatedly requesting back-up diversionary reinforcements. On June 23 and twice on June 25, he wrote to Davis that

an army should be raised in the southeast under Beauregard and moved
to Culpeper Court House to threaten Washington.[87] In one of the June
25 letters, he explained that his own northward movement "has aroused
the Federal Government and people to great exertions and it is incumbent
upon us to call forth all our energies."[88] Lee's unrealistic but typical suggestion to reinforce Virginia overlooked the facts that Grant by then had
Pemberton trapped in Vicksburg and that Beauregard already had sent
reinforcements to Tennessee.

By June 28 Ewell was in position to move on the Pennsylvania
capital of Harrisburg. Meanwhile Lee, unaware of the precise whereabouts of the Union army, was with Hill and Longstreet back at Chambersburg. That night Lee learned from Thomas Harrison, one of
Longstreet's spies, that Meade had replaced Hooker as commander of
the ninety-five-thousand-man Army of the Potomac and had moved
north to Frederick, Maryland. Lee decided to meet them east of the
mountains. Recognizing the necessity of concentrating his numerically
inferior force but not sure where the enemy was or how fast he could
move, Lee sent discretionary orders to Ewell to head back toward either
Cashtown or Gettysburg.[89]

July 1, 1863—Day One of the Battle of Gettysburg—brought Lee's
army a stiff rebuff, a fortuitous success, and finally a missed opportunity
for victory.[90] The previous day the Confederates had discovered a division
of Federal cavalry under Brigadier General John Buford at Gettysburg.
So a stronger Confederate force, the divisions of major generals Henry
Heth and Dorsey Pender of Hill's Corps, headed east from Cashtown
toward Gettysburg the next day to deal with Buford.

Because of Stuart's absence and Lee's ignorance of the timing of the
approaches of Meade's corps to Gettysburg, Heth's and Pender's infantry
divisions found more than they had bargained for. Initially they were
handicapped because two-thirds of Lee's army was going to have to use
a single route, the Chambersburg Pike or Cashtown Road, to get to Gettysburg. Heth pushed ahead with two brigades. Why did A. P. Hill send
Heth against a position known to be held by Union forces if he was not
to bring on a general engagement? Was he to stand in place when he

encountered resistance, backing up at least two-thirds of Lee's army on a single road?

On June 30 Buford had astutely recognized the tactical value of the high ground south and east of Gettysburg and decided to save it for the main Union army once it arrived. Instead of putting his own cavalrymen on those hills, therefore, he deployed them during the night west and north of the town so they could delay the Confederates until Union infantry arrived. He sent word to his superior, Pleasonton, that A. P. Hill's corps were massed back of Cashtown, nine miles west, and that Hill's pickets, composed of infantry and artillery, were in sight. He also passed along accurate rumors that Ewell was coming south over the mountains from Carlisle.[91]

In a fierce struggle that began around 7:30 a.m. on July 1, Buford's cavalry stubbornly resisted the 7,500-man advance of two of Heth's brigades. With the firing of the first shot, Buford had sent word of the fighting to Major General John F. Reynolds, commander of the Union First Corps. Reynolds, then eight miles away at Moritz Tavern, just inside Pennsylvania north of Emmitsburg, Maryland, ordered his 9,500 men to shed their baggage and speedily march to Gettysburg.

The evening before, Buford had posted videttes, in the usual three-tier line of outposts, on the Chambersburg Pike to Herr Ridge and Belmont Schoolhouse Ridge west of his main camp between the Lutheran Theological Seminary and Gettysburg College. Their determined resistance forced the Confederates to spend more than a precious hour deploying into a battle line. Meanwhile, Reynolds arrived and conferred with Buford about the critical situation. Reynolds then went back to hasten his infantry to the front, sent word to Oliver O. Howard to speed his Eleventh Corps to Gettysburg, and sent a message to Meade advising him that Gettysburg was to be the collision point of the East's two armies.

Heth, enjoying momentary superiority, ordered his two brigades forward. Buford's skirmishers grudgingly gave up the forward ridges and a small stream called Willoughby Run. They gradually fell back to McPherson's Farm on McPherson's Ridge, only a mile west of Gettysburg. Buford sent a message to Pleasonton describing the battle, stating that A. P. Hill's entire corps was moving on Gettysburg, and advising that Confederate troops had been discovered approaching Gettysburg from the north.[92]

The nature of the battle changed shortly after 10 a.m. when Reynolds's men, led by Cutler's brigade, began to arrive, joined by the "Iron Brigade"—the First Brigade of the First Division of the First Corps of the Army of the Potomac—composed of proud black-hatted troops from the upper Midwest. A rebel bullet killed Reynolds while he was directing his troops in an assault on Archer's brigade. Nevertheless, the devastating Union counterattack drove the Confederates back toward Herr Ridge. Buford's brilliant delaying tactics had saved the day and perhaps the entire battle, and Reynolds had arrived in the nick of time to repel the first serious Confederate assault.

Back at Cashtown, Lee had heard the sounds of battle and started toward Gettysburg. His distress at Stuart's absence was evident in a comment attributed to him as he headed toward the fateful battlefield: "I cannot think what has become of Stuart; I ought to have heard from him long before now.... In the absence of reports from him, I am in ignorance of what we have in front of us here. It may be the whole Federal army, or it may be only a detachment. If it is the whole Federal force, we must fight a battle here...."[93]

As the Union forces gained strength, so did Lee's. Down Mummasburg Road and over Oak Hill from the northwest came Robert E. Rodes's eight-thousand-man division of Ewell's Second Corps, which had wandered as far north as Carlisle, arriving about 11 a.m., just as advance elements of Howard's Eleventh Corps arrived to impede their advance. Howard assumed overall command of the Union forces after Reynolds's death, and Major General Carl Schurz took command of the Eleventh Corps. About noon Rodes's artillery began shelling the Union lines, and by 2 p.m. his infantry launched an assault on Schurz's troops north of town. At about the same time, Meade learned of Reynolds's death and dispatched Winfield Hancock to Gettysburg to take command (even though Howard was senior to Hancock).

Rodes's five-brigade attack from the northwest was uncoordinated and ineffective. Brigadier General Alfred Iverson Jr.'s brigade was slaughtered and then pinned down by Union troops, who may have fired a hundred thousand shots at them from behind a stone wall. Iverson lost more than nine hundred of his 1,400 men.[94] Rodes failed to break through the Eleventh Corps' lines, and the Confederate situation looked bleak. Good fortune for the Confederates, however, arrived around 3 p.m. in the person of Jubal Early and his 5,500-man division (also of Ewell's Corps), who had heard the battle and headed for Gettysburg. Early's approach from the north brought him in on Schurz's right and, more importantly, east of Schurz's exposed right flank.

Although the arrival of Rodes's and Early's divisions of Ewell's Second Corps prevented a disastrous defeat of Hill's men marching east on the bottlenecked Chambersburg Pike, their earlier arrival would have been even better for the rebels. Because of his ignorance of the Union army's precise whereabouts, Lee had ordered Ewell to march from Carlisle to either Cashtown or Gettysburg. Ewell's initial choice of Cashtown delayed his corps' arrival at Gettysburg by several hours. At Arendtsville, Ewell learned about the Gettysburg fighting and sent Rodes's division in that direction. But Major General Edward "Allegheny" Johnson's division had gone farther west toward Cashtown with Ewell's trains. Had Ewell been ordered to march directly to Gettysburg, his men should have been able to drive out Buford's and Reynolds's troops, reduce Hill's and their own casualties, and occupy the high ground above the town before the arrival of Union reinforcements. Lee could not have known this, but he had to know that giving Ewell discretion to go to Cashtown risked a logjam on the limited roads in that area.

But this was not the end of the problems that resulted from Lee's ignorance of the Union army's whereabouts. A messenger from Ewell advised Lee, still at Cashtown as the morning fighting erupted in Gettysburg, that Ewell was heading south toward the sounds of battle. Lee asked about Stuart, ordered Ewell to send scouting parties to look for Stuart, and then, remarkably, told the messenger that he did not want a major engagement brought on that day.[95]

Even worse, Lee then sent Ewell's third division (under Johnson) and Ewell's entire wagon train east toward Gettysburg on the critical Chambersburg Pike, the same road that Hill's and Longstreet's corps were using. Filling that road for ten hours with Ewell's fourteen-mile-long wagon train[96] compounded the bottleneck. Meade, on the other hand, had his army marching full-bore for Gettysburg on several roads with their trains behind. Lee's action delayed the arrival near Gettysburg of Longstreet's leading divisions, those of McLaws and Hood, until midnight and later.[97] Not expecting a major engagement until July 2, Lee had bottlenecked seven of his nine divisions on a single road[98] and thereby retarded their arrival for both the first and second days of battle at Gettysburg.

Nevertheless, thanks to Early's fortuitous afternoon arrival on the field, Lee arrived on Herr Ridge from Cashtown in time to see the Eleventh Corps' line crumbling and its troops starting to retreat. He hastily sent Heth's badly beaten-up division and Abner Perrin's fresh brigade into the fray west of town around 3:30. Taking advantage of their momentary advantage in numbers and position, Lee's army destroyed two Union corps before Meade had even a majority of his army on the battlefield.

Between three and five o'clock in the afternoon on Day One, it looked like Gettysburg was going to be a great victory for Lee. Ewell's two-division attack from the north forced the outflanked Eleventh Corps to flee south in disarray into Gettysburg and through the town to Cemetery Hill. Uncovered by that retreat, the Union's exhausted First Corps, which had been defending the Chambersburg Pike approach west of town for many hours, had no choice but to retreat to Seminary Ridge by four o'clock and ultimately to Cemetery Hill.

Arriving at Cemetery Hill before four o'clock, in time to see the massive retreat of two Union corps, Hancock sent some troops to unoccupied Culp's Hill and started the men entrenching. Although Hancock later would take credit, Howard already had laid out the Union defensive line. Between 6 and 6:30, Slocum began arriving with his 8,500-man Twelfth Corps but deployed along Cemetery Ridge, south of the high ground. An immediate attack by all of Lee's forces, therefore, would have had an excellent chance of dislodging the minimal Union forces from their position on the heights. Indeed, Ewell nearly succeeded on those same hills twenty-four hours later against greater odds. Some argue that Lee was unlikely to have captured the high ground late on July 1, but this was his best opportunity to do so. Instead, he attacked against stronger, reinforced Union lines for the next two days. Unaware of the enemy army's proximity, Lee apparently thought he could wait until the next morning to take the high ground, underestimating the speed with which Meade's soldiers would reach Gettysburg.

Lee persisted in issuing ambiguous orders that only Stonewall Jackson could have turned into victories. With an edge in manpower through the late afternoon and evening of at least thirty-five thousand to twenty-one thousand, Lee did not aggressively take charge of the field or order any of Hill's troops to join or support an attack by Ewell on the two hills. Ewell and Early were on their own. At this point, Ewell should have had over ten thousand men still able to attack—including five thousand relatively fresh men in four brigades of Early's division. Early's men were pursuing the Union troops through the town and could have tried moving ahead to higher ground. Disruption in the town hindered the Confederates' movements, however, and Early halted the pursuit, sending two brigades off to the east because of a report of Union troops coming in from that direction.[99] Receiving Early's report and conflicting information concerning Union strength on Culp's Hill, Ewell decided not to attack.

With Union troops in chaotic retreat through the town, Lee committed two egregious errors. First, he failed to concentrate his troop strength in an attack on the eighty-foot-high Cemetery Hill or the hundred-foot-high Culp's Hill, the dominant heights in the immediate vicinity of the town. Ignoring all troops other than Ewell's—particularly Hill's—he failed to take advantage of his numerical superiority.

Second, at 4:30 he issued a verbal order, by way of Major Walter Taylor, to the stalled Ewell to take the high ground "if he found it practicable, but to avoid a general engagement until the arrival of the other divisions of the army,"[100] which were being hurried to Gettysburg. Under the circumstances, this order is nearly inexplicable. There had been a general engagement since about dawn that day,[101] the awaited Confederate forces were caught in a traffic jam on Chambersburg Pike, and the Union presence would inevitably increase. Left to his own discretion, Ewell not surprisingly failed to move on Culp's Hill or Cemetery Hill before the outnumbered and disorganized Union forces there had dug in and been reinforced.

Even the arrival at dusk of Ewell's third division, that of Edward "Allegheny" Johnson, was insufficient to encourage the reluctant Ewell, unmoved by Lee's weak order, to take the high ground—at the very least the dominant heights of Culp's Hill. Virtually all of Ewell's generals urged an assault on the high ground, including Early, who had passed up the opportunity to do so himself when he alone would have been responsible.[102] Major General Isaac R. Trimble asked for a single regiment to take the two hills and stalked away in disgust when Ewell declined to attack.[103] At this same time, Lee deliberately held in reserve the nearby unbloodied troops of Major General Richard H. Anderson's division in Hill's corps and two brigades of Dorsey Pender, apparently because Lee's whole army was not yet concentrated and he lacked information on the enemy's strength.[104] "Responsibility for the failure of the Confederates to make an all-out assault on Cemetery Hill on July 1 must rest with Lee," concludes Edwin B. Coddington.[105] This was the only time on July 1 that either side did not immediately use (usually successfully) all the forces it had available at Gettysburg.

As for Lee's responsibility for Hill's failure to get involved late that day, Allen Guelzo concludes, "Perhaps, in the end, it was the great mistake of Robert E. Lee at Gettysburg that, having had to reach past his corps commanders to direct operations that afternoon, he did not keep reaching past them. Whatever blame attaches to Ambrose Powell Hill in the twilight of July 1st also attached to Robert E. Lee for not overriding him."[106]

Lee's, Ewell's, and Early's hesitation proved disastrous. By failing to take full advantage of his temporary superiority and to issue definitive orders to Ewell, Lee left his enemy in control of the high ground for the final two days of the battle and allowed reinforcements to arrive. Union forces retained the commanding heights that Buford, Reynolds, Howard, and Hancock had successively determined to protect and hold because they were the key to battlefield control at Gettysburg.

After the war, Early and his allies laid the blame for the failure to capture any of the dominating high ground late on July 1 entirely on Ewell. Dispelling this myth, Chris Mackowski and Kristopher White show that after it was discovered that Culp's Hill initially was unoccupied, Ewell suggested that Early occupy it, but Early declined, recommending that the assignment be given to Edward Johnson. Ewell followed his advice, but by the time Johnson arrived, Culp's Hill was occupied. "The chance to take the ground without a fight slipped away," and Confederates took 2,500 casualties trying to take Culp's Hill over the next two days. "After the war, Early contended that he had vigorously supported an assault on Cemetery Hill, yet on the evening of the battle he claimed his men were too tired and disorganized to occupy unoccupied Culp's Hill. If his men were in no condition to move unopposed to an empty hilltop, how could they have led an attack against a heavily fortified enemy position?"[107]

On the morning of July 2, Lee apparently expressed his disappointment concerning the events of the prior afternoon: "We did not or could not pursue our advantage of yesterday and now the enemy are in a good position."[108] This amounted to a rebuke of Ewell, but Lee must have known that he bore at least as much responsibility as Ewell for the failure to seize the commanding heights on the first day. With Confederate casualties at 6,500 to the Union's 9,000, Lee had won an engagement but missed an opportunity to win the Battle of Gettysburg.

The situation had radically changed by the next morning. Hancock's thirteen-thousand-man Second Corps and Major General Dan Sickles's twelve-thousand-man Third Corps had arrived by early morning. Instead of three corps with twenty-one thousand men on the battlefield, the Union now had five corps and forty-six thousand men. Two more corps (the Fifth and Sixth) with twenty-eight thousand more men were on forced marches that would get them there that day. Instead of scrambling for any position as they had done the previous day, the Northerners had established a strong line running from near Little Round Top (two miles south of town) north along Taneytown Road and Cemetery Ridge to Cemetery Hill and then curving east to Culp's Hill and southeast parallel to the Baltimore Pike. They had superior numbers, an imposing defensive position, and the advantage of interior lines, which permitted them to move soldiers quickly to threatened points in their lines. Meade had twenty-seven thousand men per mile along a three-mile inverted-fishhook line, while Lee had ten thousand men per mile along a five-mile semi-circle.[109] That disparity augured ill for Lee's army.

On July 2 Lee erred again—in several ways.[110] Without Stuart's cavalry to apprise him of the enemy's positions and movements, Lee sent a small reconnaissance expedition under his staff engineer, Captain Samuel Johnston, to scout out the Union left. The scouts somehow failed to detect Federal forces on the south end of Cemetery Ridge and at the Round Tops, so Lee erroneously believed that the prominent hills, Little Round Top and the more southerly Big Round Top, and the areas around them were not occupied by Union troops.[111] Johnston reported that he had ascended Little Round Top, that there were no Union troops south of Cemetery Hill, and that there was a clear route to the areas west of the Round Tops from which Lee wanted to attack. Guelzo speculates that Johnston, in the morning fog, may have climbed the wrong hill.[112]

Contrary to Longstreet's advice, Lee ordered him with his two delayed and exhausted divisions to march several miles and attack the Union's left flank. Late the previous afternoon, Longstreet and Lee had watched the retreat of the Yankee forces to the high ground immediately south of Gettysburg and discussed what to do the following day. Longstreet wanted to turn the Union left flank, establish a strong position and await an attack.[113] At about that same hour, Hancock was sending a message to Meade that the Union's strong position would be difficult to take but could be turned.[114] Longstreet argued that the Union forces would be compelled to attack any Confederate force placed between them and Washington. Such a situation—similar to that at Fredericksburg—would be consistent with the strategically offensive and tactically defensive campaign that Longstreet thought had been agreed upon. Perhaps desperate for a convincing victory to justify his gamble of invading the North and concerned about his supplies in the medium-term, Lee declared, "If the enemy is there tomorrow, we must attack him." Longstreet apparently replied, "If he is there tomorrow, it will be because he wants you to attack—a good reason, in my judgment, for not doing so."[115]

In his report after the battle, Lee defended his cobbled-together offensives of July 2 and 3 on the grounds that retreat would have been difficult and awaiting attack was impracticable because of foraging difficulties.[116] General Alexander, however, found Lee's rationale less than persuasive:

> Now when it is remembered that we stayed for three days longer on that very ground, two of them days of desperate battle, ending in the discouragement of a bloody repulse, & then successfully withdrew all our trains & most of the wounded through the mountains; and, finding the Potomac too high to ford, protected them all & foraged successfully for over a week in a very restricted territory along the river, until we could build a bridge, it does not seem improbable that we could have faced Meade safely on the 2nd at Gettysburg without assaulting him in his wonderfully strong position. We had the prestige of victory with us, having chased him off the field & through the town. We had a fine defensive position on Seminary Ridge ready at our hand to occupy. It was not such a really *wonderful* position as the enemy happened to fall into, but it was no bad one, & it could never have been successfully assaulted.... *We could even have fallen back to Cashtown & held the mountain passes with all the prestige of victory, & popular sentiment would have forced Meade to take the aggressive.*[117]

Daniel Bauer has studied the food supplies that would have been available to Lee had he gone on the defensive in Pennsylvania and concludes that Lee seriously misjudged them.[118] One reason Lee did not go on the defensive was that he was on a roll. Having wrecked two Union corps the day before, he sensed an opportunity, as Allen Guelzo puts it, to "not only bag the remnants, but seize Cemetery Hill, the most advantageous ground in the entire region."[119]

If Lee's offensive strategy on July 2 was flawed, his execution proved disastrous. His failure, again, to give clear and forceful orders to Ewell's corps led to a crippling lack of coordination between the Confederates' left and right flanks. Lee's plan called for Ewell to demonstrate against the Union right and attack if an opportunity developed while Longstreet attacked the Union left. Even though Ewell had on the previous day demonstrated his reluctance to attack, Lee did not adequately oversee his efforts. There was no assault by the Confederate left wing on Day Two to divert attention from Longstreet's attack on the Confederate right, and Union troops that would have been needed on Ewell's front were free to reinforce their comrades fighting Longstreet.[120]

Likewise, Lee failed to oversee, personally or through staff, the execution of his orders on the right flank. No one, including Lee's early morning scouting party, had identified a secure route for Hood's and McLaws's divisions of Longstreet's corps (actually accompanied by "scout" Captain Johnston) to take to their attack positions. This lack of oversight compounded Longstreet's difficulties in proceeding unobserved to the southern Union flank. Alexander commented:

> That is just one illustration of how time may be lost in handling troops, and of the need of an abundance of competent staff officers by the generals in command. Scarcely any of our generals had half of what they needed to keep a *constant &* *close supervision on the execution of important orders.* An army is like a great machine, and in putting it into battle it is not enough for its commander to merely issue the necessary orders. He should have a staff ample to supervise the execution of each step, & to promptly report any difficulty or

misunderstanding. There is no telling the value of the hours which were lost by that division that morning.[121]

What about the allegation of Longstreet's critics that Lee had ordered him to attack at dawn? There is simply no credible evidence to support this contention. Alexander pointed out that Lee would have ordered Longstreet's troops into position during the night if he desired a dawn attack and that the enemy's position was not determined until morning (and then inaccurately).[122] Lee himself had delayed Longstreet's divisions on the Chambersburg Pike for ten hours the previous afternoon. McLaws's division did not approach Gettysburg until midnight, and Hood's division did not arrive until dawn. Lee was well aware of their inability to initiate an early morning assault on a position miles away from their bivouac.

Lee sent a scouting expedition out around dawn,[123] and he was not in a position to order an attack until he had specific information, based on daylight observations, on who should be attacked where. At about 11 a.m., Lee finally issued his only specific attack order of the day, directing Longstreet to proceed south and to get into position to attack,[124] and he consented to Longstreet's request that the attack be delayed until Brigadier General Evander Law's brigade of Hood's division could be brought up.[125] Law, another victim of the Chambersburg Pike bottleneck, had set out at about 3 a.m. and arrived at Gettysburg around noon. Lee could not have expected an attack before mid-afternoon. Even Douglas Southall Freeman, who severely criticized Longstreet for delaying the attack, contended that Lee had virtually surrendered control to Longstreet. "It is scarcely too much to say that on July 2 the Army of Northern Virginia was without a commander," Freeman writes.[126] As commanding general of that army and on-scene commander of the battle, Lee was responsible for where and when Longstreet attacked.

As Longstreet marched south toward the Union left, he received reliable scouting reports that the Union left flank was "hanging in the air" and could be rolled up. Twice he passed this information on to Lee and requested permission to launch a flanking attack. Lee declined, however, and repeated his order to attack—probably under the erroneous impression that he still was ordering a flanking attack of some sort. McLaws's and Hood's divisions had difficulty finding their way on unfamiliar roads to their designated attack positions and even had to retrace their steps when they discovered that a point on the line of march was visible from a Union signal station on Little Round Top. They were being guided by Captain Johnston of Lee's staff, and Lee himself rode part of the way south with Longstreet.[127] Lee oversaw and approved Longstreet's troop dispositions.[128]

Beginning their attack after 4 p.m., Longstreet's forces fought bravely in the Wheatfield, Peach Orchard, and Devil's Den and almost captured both Big Round Top and the critical Little Round Top. This near-success indicates what a brilliant victory they might have achieved if Lee had turned them loose for a flanking attack instead of squandering them in frontal assaults along the Union lines on Emmitsburg Road and Cemetery Ridge. The partnership between Lee and Jackson, which had worked magic at Second Manassas and Chancellorsville, had no replacement at Gettysburg. Nevertheless, Longstreet's attack might have succeeded had it been properly planned, executed, and supervised.

Union General Daniel Sickles had advanced his Third Corps, contrary to orders, into a vulnerable position in a peach orchard along Emmitsburg Road well in front of the intended Union line along Cemetery Ridge. Instead of simultaneously attacking the north-to-south Union line along its entire front, however, the Confederates attacked piecemeal. Hood's division launched an extended attack on the Union left flank before McLaws's division was ordered to attack Sickles's center and right. This staggered, or echelon, attack enabled the Union defenders to respond to each successive threat.

When Hood, McLaws, and their brigadiers had first taken up their positions, they had been surprised to find large Union troop concentrations where they had been informed there were no enemy forces. Both Hood and McLaws sought Longstreet's permission to avoid a desperate frontal assault, but Longstreet, having failed numerous times in the past twenty-four hours to change Lee's mind, carried out Lee's attack order.[129]

Lee, meanwhile, personally refused Hood's final request to send a brigade around the Union flank on the Round Tops.[130]

Each Confederate attack drove the enemy back and captured territory, but uncoordinated timing greatly reduced their collective effect. The attacks did not begin until about 4:30 p.m. First, Hood's men attacked on the far south of the battlefield, crossed and followed Plum Run, and captured Devil's Den below the Round Tops. They would have captured Little Round Top but for the courage of four Union regiments of Colonel Strong Vincent's brigade—the Eighty-third Pennsylvania, Twentieth Maine, Forty-fourth New York, and Sixteenth Michigan— and others who came to their aid. In fierce fighting, the Confederates drove Sickles's corps from the Peach Orchard, engaged in bitter combat for control of the adjoining Wheatfield, and finally drove the defenders back to the northern base of Little Round Top.

To their north, Dick Anderson's division of A. P. Hill's Third Corps participated ineffectively in the late stages of the attack. Brigadier General Carnot Posey's brigade advanced haphazardly, and Brigadier General William Mahone's brigade never moved off Seminary Ridge despite division orders to do so. Lee and Hill failed to reinforce the aggressive attacks by Brigadier General William Barksdale and Brigadier General Ambrose Wright.[131] Throughout the day, Hill's corps, including much of Anderson's division, acted as though they were unaware of Lee's plans or any role for them in the struggle. Lee apparently had intended for them to join in the sequential attacks beginning at the southern end of his line but took no actions to get them properly aligned or bring all of them into the fray as the afternoon turned to evening.[132]

On the Union side, Hancock took advantage of the disjointed Confederate attack and sent reinforcements to each successively attacked position. The Second Corps went to the Round Tops and to Sickles's left, and the Fifth Corps reinforced Sickles. The Sixth Corps, which arrived at 2 p.m. after marching thirty-four miles in seventeen hours, and the Twelfth Corps backed up the others and stopped the Confederates before they could puncture Cemetery Ridge. By the time Sickles's line finally was broken and the Wheatfield secured, darkness was beginning to fall and additional Union troops had moved into position to back up Sickles and hold the Cemetery Ridge line. At one critical juncture—when the rebels had broken the Union's Wheatfield lines and were about to advance onto Cemetery Ridge—Hancock sent in the 262 men of the First Minnesota Regiment to push them back at all costs, which they did with 82 percent casualties. The failed Confederate frontal attack in echelon cost them 6,500 casualties (to the Union's 6,000) and was reminiscent of similar failures by Lee's army during the Seven Days' Campaign.

Where was Lee while this major, uncoordinated, and costly attack was falling apart? He was overlooking the battle from the cupola and elsewhere at the Lutheran seminary on Seminary Ridge, part of the time with Generals Hill and Heth. He sent and received no more than a message or two and apparently sent only one order during the battle.[133] Having given his orders many hours before, when conditions were radically different, Lee stood by as the bloody assault faltered and failed. In a prelude to the more famous events of the next day, Lee allowed one third of his force to attack while the others remained in place.[134] In sharp contrast, George Meade moved his forces all over the battlefield to meet each new attack and took corrective actions when he discovered Sickles's disastrous abandonment of his assigned position. Meade's "hands-on" approach throughout the battle prevented a rebel breakthrough along his critical Cemetery Ridge line.[135]

Lee's uncoordinated assaults continued that night when Ewell's forces finally attacked Cemetery Hill—twenty-four hours too late for likely success and several hours too late to coordinate with Longstreet. The brave men of two brigades fought their way to the top of Cemetery Hill, but the failure of high command to provide support compelled them to retreat. Ewell failed in his efforts to commit his artillery to support the assault, while Early never committed the reserve brigade of Brigadier General John Brown Gordon to the battle. Once again, the attack on Cemetery Hill was planned in echelon—Johnson to attack first, followed by Early, and then Rodes. The reality was an ineffective assault by one brigade after another and the failure of many brigades to engage at all. In fact, Avery's and Hays's brigades had completed their successful attacks and been compelled to withdraw before Rodes launched his forces from the town itself. The strategy was poor and the execution was worse. The Confederates failed to secure and hold Cemetery Hill, which dominated the north end of the battlefield.[136] Early on the morning of July 2, Edward Johnson's division belatedly assaulted Culp's Hill with even less success.[137]

As Alexander points out, Lee wasted Ewell's Second Corps by leaving it in an isolated and harmless position northeast of the primary struggles on the second and third days of Gettysburg:

> Ewell's troops were all placed beyond, or N.E. of Gettysburg, bent around toward the point of the fish hook of the enemy's position. It was an awkward place, far from our line of retreat in case of disaster, & not convenient either for re-inforcing others or being reinforced. And...this part of the enemy's position was in itself the strongest & it was practically almost unassailable. On the night of the 1st Gen. Lee ordered him withdrawn & brought around to our right of the town. Gen. Ewell had seen some ground he thought he could take & asked permission to stay & to take it. Gen. Lee consented, but it turned out early next morning that the position could not be taken. Yet the orders to come out from the awkward place he was in—where there was no reasonable probability of his accomplishing any good on the enemy's line in his front & where his artillery was of no service—were never renewed & he stayed there till the last. The ground is there still for any military engineer to pronounce whether or not Ewell's corps & all its artillery was not practically paralysed & useless by its position during the last two days of the battle.[138]

The second day of Gettysburg, then, was another lost opportunity for which the commanding general of the Army of Northern Virginia must be held accountable. Over the objection of the corps and division commanders involved, Lee ordered Longstreet's First Corps to launch a frontal, echelon assault on strong Union positions. Lee stood by while Hill's Third Corps in the center of the Confederate lines and directly in front of Lee provided inadequate assistance to Longstreet.[139] Finally, Lee neither moved Ewell's Second Corps to an effective supporting attack position nor ensured that it attacked the Union right flank at the same time Longstreet was attacking the Union left. Lee had accomplished something: he put two more Union corps (Third and Fifth) and a division of the Second out of action. But the opportunity for even greater success had been missed.

Lee's performance the next day was even worse. Frustrated by two successive days of failure, he compounded his errors on the third and final day of Gettysburg.[140] His original plan for that day again involved simultaneous attacks by Ewell on the Confederate left and Longstreet on the right, but the plan was thwarted when Meade ordered an attack on Ewell's forces, which had occupied Union trenches the evening before. In a five-hour, very early morning battle on the north flank, Johnson's division of Ewell's corps tried again and again, without success, to capture Culp's Hill. The attack tied down the Twelfth and remnants of the First Union corps. Federal forces still held that critical position as dawn broke on the fateful third of July.[141]

With Ewell engaged, Lee changed his mind and decided to attack the center of the Union line. The evening before, Union Major General John Newton, Reynolds's replacement as commander of the First Corps, had told Meade that he should be concerned about a flanking movement by Lee, who would not be "fool enough" to frontally attack the Union army in the strong position into which the first two days' fighting had consolidated it.[142] Around midnight Meade told Brigadier General John Gibbon that if Lee went on the offensive the next day, he would attack Gibbon's Second Division of the Second Corps in the center of the Union line. Gibbon replied that if Lee did so, he would be defeated.[143]

Lee, however, saw things differently. Again ignoring the advice and pleas of Longstreet, Lee canceled Longstreet's early morning orders for a flank attack and instead ordered the suicidal assault known as Pickett's Charge.[144] After studying the ground over which the attack would occur,

Longstreet said to Lee, "The 15,000 men who could make a successful assault over that field had never been arrayed for battle."[145] Longstreet was not alone in his bleak assessment of the chances for success. Brigadier General Ambrose "Rans" Wright said there would be no difficulty reaching Cemetery Ridge but that staying there was another matter because the "whole Yankee army is there in a bunch."[146] On the morning of the third, Brigadier General Cadmus Wilcox told his fellow brigadier Richard Garnett that the Union position was twice as strong as Gaines's Mill at the Seven Days' Battles.[147]

Edward Porter Alexander shared the complete, almost blind, faith of the Confederate troops in Lee, later remarking, "... like all the rest of the army I believed that it would come out right, because Gen. Lee had planned it."[148] But historian Bevin Alexander has severely criticized Lee's order: "When his direct efforts to knock aside the Union forces failed, Lee compounded his error by destroying the last offensive power of the Army of Northern Virginia in Pickett's charge across nearly a mile of open, bullet-and-shell-torn ground. This frontal assault was doomed before it started."[149]

The famous attack was preceded by a massive artillery exchange— so violent and loud that it was heard 140 miles away. Just after one o'clock, Alexander unleashed his 170 rebel cannon against the Union forces on Cemetery Ridge. Two hundred Federal cannon responded. Across a mile of slightly rolling fields, the opposing cannons blasted away for ninety minutes. The Confederate goal was to soften up the Union line, particularly to weaken its defensive artillery capacity, prior to a massive assault on the center of that line. Some Federal batteries were hit, as were horses and caissons on the reverse slope near Meade's headquarters.

Alexander's cannonade continued until his supply of ammunition was dangerously low. A slowdown in the Union artillery response gave the false impression that the Confederate cannonade had inflicted serious damage. Although Alexander received some artillery assistance from Hill's guns to the north, Ewell's five artillery battalions northeast of the main Confederate line fired almost no rounds. Artillery fire was one thing that Ewell could have provided, but the commanding general and his chief of artillery also failed to coordinate this facet of the offensive.[150]

The time of decision and death was at hand for many of the fifty-five thousand Confederates and seventy-five thousand Yankees. The rebels were about to assault a position that Alexander described as "almost as badly chosen as it was possible to be." His rationale:

> Briefly described, the point we attacked is upon the long *shank* of the fishhook of the enemy's position, & our advance was exposed to the fire of the whole length of that shank some two miles. Not only that, that shank is not perfectly straight, but it bends forward at the Round Top end, so that rifled guns there, in secure position, could & did enfilade the assaulting lines. Now add that the advance must be over 1,400 yards of open ground, none of it sheltered from fire, & very little from view, & without a single position for artillery where a battery could get its horses & caissons under cover.
>
> I think any military engineer would, instead, select for attack the *bend* of the fishhook just west of Gettysburg. There, at least, the assaulting lines cannot be enfiladed, and, on the other hand the places selected for assault may be enfiladed, & upon shorter ranges than any other parts of the Federal lines. Again there the assaulting column will only be exposed to the fire of the front less than half, even if over one fourth, of the firing front upon the shank.[151]

Around 2:30, Alexander ordered a cease-fire and sent a hurried note to General Longstreet: "If you are coming at all, you must come at once or I cannot give you proper support, but the enemy's fire has not slackened at all. At least 18 guns are still firing from the cemetery itself."[152] Longstreet, convinced of the impending disaster, could not bring himself to give a verbal attack order to Major General George E. Pickett. Instead he merely nodded his permission to proceed after Pickett asked him, "General, shall I advance?"[153]

On the hidden western slopes of Seminary Ridge, nine brigades of thirteen thousand men began forming two mile-and-a-half-long lines for the assault on Cemetery Ridge. Their three division commanders were Pickett, Major General Isaac Trimble (in place of the wounded Dorsey Pender), and Brigadier General J. Johnston Pettigrew (in place of the wounded Henry Heth). Pickett gave the order, "Up men, and to your posts! Don't forget today that you are from old Virginia!"[154] With that, they moved out.

After sending his "come at once" message, Alexander noticed a distinct pause in the firing from the cemetery and then clearly observed the withdrawal of artillery from that planned point of attack. Ten minutes after his earlier message and while Longstreet was silently assenting to the attack, Alexander sent another urgent note: "For God's sake come quick. The 18 guns are gone. Come quick or I can't support you."[155] To Alexander's chagrin, however, the Union chief of artillery, Henry J. Hunt, moved five replacement batteries into the crucial center of the line. What Alexander did not yet know was that the Union firing had virtually ceased in order to save ammunition to repel the coming attack and to bring up fresh guns from the artillery reserve. Hunt had seventy-seven short-range guns in the position the rebels intended to attack, as well as numerous other guns, including long-range rifled artillery, along the line capable of raking an attacking army.

The rebel lines opened ranks to pass their now-quiet batteries and swept on into the shallow valley between the two famous ridges. A gasp arose from Cemetery Ridge as the two long gray lines, a hundred fifty yards apart, came into sight. It was three o'clock, the hottest time of a scorching day, and forty thousand Union soldiers were in position directly to contest the hopeless Confederate assault. Many defenders were sheltered by stone walls or wooden fences. Their awe at the impressive parade coming their way must have been mixed with an understandable fear of battle and a confidence in the strength of their numbers and position.

As the charging rebels approached the stronghold on Cemetery Ridge, their fear grew and their confidence waned with every step.[156] The forty-seven regiments (including nineteen from Virginia and fourteen from North Carolina) initially traversed the undulating landscape[157] in absolute silence except for the clunking of their wooden canteens. Although a couple of swales provided temporary shelter from most of the Union rifle fire, the Confederates were under constant observation from Little Round Top to the southeast. Long-range artillery fire began tearing holes in the Confederate lines. The attackers turned slightly left to cross the Emmitsburg Pike and found themselves in the middle of a Union semi-circle of rifles and cannon. They attempted to maintain their perfect parade order, but all hell broke loose when short-range round-shot from Federal cannon exploded along the entire ridge line—from Cemetery Hill on the north to Little Round Top on the south.

Minié balls and double loads of canister (pieces of iron) decimated the Confederate front ranks. The slaughter was indescribably horrible, but the courageous rebels closed ranks and marched on. Taking tremendous losses, they started up the final rise toward the copse that was their goal, all the while viciously assaulted from the front, from both flanks, and even from their rear. The rifle fire from Brigadier General George J. Stannard's advanced Vermont brigade, shot point-blank into the rebel right flank, was especially devastating. Soon the numbers of the attackers dwindled to insignificance. The survivors let loose their rebel yell and charged the trees near the center of Cemetery Ridge. With cries of "Fredericksburg," the men in blue cut down the remaining attackers with canister and Minié balls. General Lewis Armistead led 150 men in the final surge across the low stone wall, where he fell mortally wounded. The rest were killed, wounded, or captured within minutes.

Seventeen hundred yards away, Lee watched his gray and butternut troops disappear into the all-engulfing smoke on the ridge and then saw some of them emerge in retreat. Fewer than seven thousand of the original thirteen thousand returned to Seminary Ridge. There was no covering fire from Alexander's cannon because he was saving his precious ammunition to repel the expected counterattack. As the survivors returned to Confederate lines, Lee met them and sobbed, "It's all my fault this time."[158] It was.[159]

Lee and Longstreet tried to console Pickett, who was distraught over the slaughter of his men.[160] Lee told him that their gallantry had earned them a place in history, but Pickett responded: "All the glory in the world could never atone for the widows and orphans this day has made."[161] To his death, Pickett blamed Lee for the "massacre" of his division.[162]

The result of Lee's Day Three strategy was the worst single-charge slaughter of the whole bloody war,[163] with the possible exception of John Bell Hood's suicidal charge at Franklin, Tennessee, the following year. The Confederates suffered 7,500 casualties to the Union's 1,500. More than a thousand of those rebel casualties were killed—all in a thirty-minute bloodbath. Brigadier General Richard Garnett, whose five Virginia regiments led the assault, was killed, and 950 of his 1,450 men were killed or wounded. Three regiments—the Thirteenth and Forty-Seventh North Carolina and the Eighteenth Virginia—were virtually wiped out on Cemetery Ridge.[164]

That night Lee rode alone among his troops. At one point he met Brigadier General John D. Imboden, who remarked, "General, this has been a hard day on you." Lee responded, "Yes, it has been a sad, sad day to us." He went on to praise Pettigrew's and Pickett's men and then made this puzzling statement: "If they had been supported as they were to have been—but for some reason not fully explained to me were not—we would have held the position and the day would have been ours. Too bad. Too bad. Oh, too bad."[165] General Alexander found that comment inexplicable since Lee was the commanding general and had personally overseen the entire preparation for and execution of the disastrous charge.[166]

Even if Lee was nonplussed, his officers had little difficulty seeing the folly of Pickett's Charge and its similarity to the senseless Union charges at Fredericksburg the previous December. Having lost over half his own 10,500 men in the July 3 charge, Pickett submitted a battle report highly critical of that assault—and probably of the commander who ordered it. Lee declined to accept the report and ordered it rewritten.[167] It never was.

The only saving grace for Lee's battered army was that General Meade, believing his mission was to not lose rather than to win, failed to follow up his victory with an immediate infantry counterattack on the stunned and disorganized Confederates. To Lincoln's chagrin, Meade developed a case of the "slows" reminiscent of McClellan after Antietam and took nine days to pursue and catch Lee, who was burdened by a seventeen-mile ambulance train.[168] Unlike McClellan's army at Antietam, however, Meade's entire army had been engaged and battered in the fight at Gettysburg. After missing his chance for a quick and decisive strike, Meade wisely did not attack Lee's strongly entrenched position at Williamsport, Maryland, on the Potomac River after Meade had caught up with him. As the Confederates waited to cross, Confederate officers hoped for a Union assault: "Now we have Meade where we want him. If he attacks us here, we will pay him back for Gettysburg. But the Old Fox is too cunning."[169] Alexander recalled, ". . . oh! how we all did wish that the enemy would come out in the open & attack us, as we had done them at Gettysburg. But they had had their lesson, in that sort of game, at Fredbg. [Fredericksburg] & did not care for another."[170] Lee's army crossed the receding river and returned ignominiously to Virginia.[171]

Who had lost Gettysburg? Longstreet's role in the battle and campaign seems rather insignificant, and Lee consistently and mistakenly ignored his advice. Even before the campaign, Lee had convinced Davis to ignore Longstreet's recommendation that the bulk of Longstreet's troops be sent to another theater. Partially because Lee kept Longstreet from going west, the Gettysburg disaster was accompanied by defeats in two other theaters. Lee's decision made it more likely that Grant would defeat the Confederates in Mississippi and capture Vicksburg and Pemberton's army. And he kept Bragg so shorthanded that his army was maneuvered back into Georgia from Tennessee in the virtually bloodless Tullahoma Campaign.

Robert E. Lee, therefore, bore a great deal of responsibility for a demoralizing triple disaster in the summer of 1863—Gettysburg, Vicksburg, and Tullahoma. Confederate morale and prospects fell to a new low from which they never recovered. Longstreet had advised defensive tactics for the campaign and was against attacking on the last two days of the battle. He was not present on the first day, and his men fought bravely on the last two days. That evidence seems to indicate that Long-street was unfairly made a scapegoat for Gettysburg in order to remove blame from Lee, who protected his own reputation by suppressing Pick-ett's battle report.[172]

How about Lee's strategic and tactical performance? Early Confed-erate reaction was not favorable. The *Charleston Mercury* opined, "It is impossible for an invasion to have been more foolish and disastrous. It was opportune neither in time nor circumstance." Wade Hampton told Joseph Johnston that it was a "complete failure." In a July 26 diary entry, Robert G. H. Kean of the Confederate War Department called Gettys-burg "the worst disaster which has ever befallen our arms.... To fight an enemy superior in numbers at such terrible disadvantage of position in the heart of his own territory, when the freedom of movement gave him the advantage of selecting his own time and place for accepting battle, seems to have been a great military blunder.... Gettysburg has shaken my faith in Lee as a general."[173]

General Hampton concurred:

> To fight an enemy superior in numbers at such a terrible dis-advantage of position in the heart of his own territory, when freedom of movement gave him the advantage of accepting his own time and place for accepting battle, seems to have been a great military blunder...the position of the Yankees there was the strongest I ever saw...we let Meade choose the position and then we attacked.[174]

General Alexander shared the view that Lee had blundered: "Then perhaps in taking the aggressive at all at Gettysburg in 1863 & certainly in the place & dispositions for the assault on the 3rd day, I think, it will undoubtedly be held that [Lee] unnecessarily took the most desperate chances & the bloodiest road."[175] Historian William C. Davis, generally supportive of Lee's war effort, provides this insight into some specifics of Lee's performance at Gettysburg:

Confronted with a battle he did not want in ground not of his choosing, Lee exercised minimal control before he reached the field late on July 1. While struggling to concentrate the army, he could have sent staff to impose instructions on Hill and Ewell, but he did not, and left them to it. When he directed Ewell to take the key to the Union line on Cemetery Hill, he used the discretionary caveat "if practicable," an unproductive phrase with a mercurial general like Ewell. Once he established his headquarters on the field, Lee erratically communicated plans to his corps commanders.... Lee gave orders to his corps commanders but sent no staff with them to make certain his wishes were obeyed.[176]

Davis then offers an overall appraisal of Lee's performance at Gettysburg:

He forfeited any long- or midrange tactical reconnaissance Stuart might have provided, and as a result had no grasp of the overall battlescape. He learned of Union movements too late to react, and never identified Meade's center of gravity in order to direct his own efforts to best effect. He let Hill bring on a major engagement despite instructions not to do so, and then gave orders too imprecise and discretionary to be effective. Five years later Lee offered two reasons for defeat: Stuart's absence left him blind; and he could not deliver the "one determined and united blow" that he believed would have assured victory.... What he did not say was that he was ultimately responsible. He let Stuart go, and his own laissez-faire management helped bungle the attacks on July 1 and 2.... Every general has his worst battle. Gettysburg was Lee's.[177]

After the war, Lee provided his rationale for having attacked on the second and third days at Gettysburg:

It had not been intended to deliver a general battle so far from our base unless attacked, but coming unexpectedly upon the whole Federal army, to withdraw through the mountains with our extensive trains would have been difficult and dangerous. At the same time we were unable to await an attack, as the country was unfavorable for collecting supplies in the presence of the enemy who could restrain our foraging parties by holding the mountain passes with local and other troops. A battle had therefore become, in a measure, unavoidable, and the success already gained gave hope of a favorable issue.[178]

Lee, in fact, had *not* come upon "the whole Federal army." That whole army was not on the battlefield until late on the second day of the Gettysburg struggle. Later, even after suffering three days of terrible losses, Lee in fact *was* able to retreat safely through the mountains after the three-day battle. In addition, Lee's army managed to live off the country north of the Potomac for nine more days. Thus, Lee's rationale justifies neither his series of frontal attacks on the second day nor the suicidal charge on the third day.[179]

Furthermore, Lee's strategic campaign into the North, which almost certainly had to end in a retreat and thus the appearance of defeat, had resulted in actual defeat. Rhode Islander Elisha Hunt Rhodes's July 9 diary entry typified northern elation over Gettysburg: "I wonder what the South thinks of us Yankees now. I think Gettysburg will cure the Rebels of any desire to invade the North again."[180] Archer Jones writes that Lee "suffered a costly defeat in a three-day battle at Gettysburg. With Lee's loss of 28,000 men to the North's 23,000, the battle became a disaster of depletion for the Confederate army. His inevitable retreat to Virginia, seemingly the result of the battle rather than his inability to forage, made it a serious political defeat also."[181]

Considering the nearly equal number of combatants at Gettysburg, Lee's losses were staggering in both absolute and relative terms. Of the seventy-five thousand Confederates, 22,600 (30 percent) were killed or injured. The toll of general officers was appalling: six dead, eight wounded, and three captured. Just as significantly, the Southern field grade officers suffered high casualties, and their absence would be felt for the duration of the war. Of the 83,300 Union troops at Gettysburg, 17,700 (21 percent) were killed or wounded.[182] Although his losses were higher in absolute and proportional terms, Lee told Davis, "Our loss has been very heavy, that of the enemy's is proportionally so."[183]

Because the Richmond papers, and thus many others in the South, initially reported Gettysburg as a Confederate victory,[184] the South did not at first realize the extent of its losses in Pennsylvania. By July 31 Lee had deluded himself into calling the campaign a "general success."[185] A Virginia private who had fought at Gettysburg expressed a different view in a letter to his sister: "We got a bad whiping.... they are awhiping us...at every point.... I hope they would make peace so that we that is alive yet would get home agane...but I supose Jef Davis and lee dont care if all is killed."[186]

Regardless of what was known when, Lee's strategy and tactics at Gettysburg were the same that he had employed for the entire thirteen months he had commanded the Army of Northern Virginia. He attacked too often, and too often he initiated frontal attacks. Lee's approach had resulted in a terrible toll of death and injury. When he assumed command in June 1862, his army numbered about ninety-five thousand. From the Seven Days' through Cedar Mountain, Second Manassas, Chantilly, South Mountain, Antietam, Fredericksburg, Chancellorsville, and finally Gettysburg, Lee's little army had suffered about eighty thousand killed and wounded while inflicting about seventy-three thousand deaths and injuries on the enemy.

Not only had the outnumbered army of Lee suffered more casualties in absolute terms, its casualties as a percentage of its total strength were substantially higher than the Federals'. During the Seven Days' Battle, 21 percent of Lee's army was killed or wounded (to the enemy's 11 percent), at Second Manassas it lost 19 percent (to the Federals' 13 percent), at Antietam Lee lost an appalling 23 percent (to the "attacking" McClellan's 16 percent), at Fredericksburg Lee's generally entrenched forces lost only 6 percent (to Burnside's 11 percent), in his Chancellorsville "victory"

Lee lost 19 percent of his men (to Joe Hooker's 11 percent), and then at Gettysburg came the crushing three-day loss of 30 percent of Lee's remaining troops (to Meade's loss of 21 percent).[187] Lee's offensive strategy and tactics were bleeding his seriously undermanned army at an unsustainable rate. Lee's strategy and tactics were just what Union generals should have been doing, but they were totally inappropriate for a rebel general.

British Colonel Arthur Fremantle, an observer at Gettysburg and elsewhere, advised Lee concerning the flaws of Lee's aggressiveness: "Don't you see your system feeds upon itself? You cannot fill the places of these men. Your troops do wonders, but every time at a cost you cannot afford."[188] Later, Lee's own General D. H. Hill described the folly of the Army of Northern Virginia's penchant for the tactical offensive:

> We were very lavish of blood in those days, and it was thought to be a very great thing to charge a battery of artillery or an earth-work lined with infantry.... The attacks on the Beaver Dam intrenchments, on the heights of Malvern Hill, at Gettysburg, etc., were all grand, but of exactly the kind of grandeur which the South could not afford.[189]

All of the attacks mentioned by Hill had been personally ordered by Lee.

In a little over a year, therefore, Lee's army had lost as many men as it had when he took command and was losing its strength at a far faster rate than its manpower-rich foe. While the North, with its almost four-to-one manpower advantage, could afford its casualties and replace the men it lost, Lee's aggression had seriously depleted the supply of Confederate men of fighting age in the East, had drained men from the rest of the Confederacy, and had made his ultimate military defeat inevitable—unless Lincoln lost the war at the ballot box in 1864.

Allen Guelzo concludes his authoritative analysis of Gettysburg with a summary of Lee's role in the Confederate defeat: "It can be said, then, that Lee lost a battle he should have won, and lost it because (a) he began the battle without completely concentrating his forces, (b) he proved unable to coordinate the attacks of the forces he did have available, and (c) he failed to reckon with how tenaciously the Army of the Potomac... would hold its ground under direct infantry attack on July 3."[190]

In summary, Gettysburg demonstrated all of Lee's weaknesses. He initiated an unnecessary strategic offensive that, because of his army's inevitable return to Virginia, would be perceived as a retreat and thus a defeat. He rejected alternative deployments of Longstreet's corps that might have avoided or mitigated critical losses of the Mississippi River (including Vicksburg and then Port Hudson, Louisiana) or middle and southeastern Tennessee (including Chattanooga). His tactics were inexcusably and fatally aggressive on the second and third days at Gettysburg, he failed to take charge of the battlefield on any of the three days, his battle-plans were ineffective, and his orders (especially to Stuart and Ewell) were vague and too discretionary. Gettysburg indeed was Lee at his worst.

Not only would Lee's entire Army of Northern Virginia never again invade the North; it had been so damaged that it had become vulnerable to a war of attrition. Any remaining hope of foreign intervention ended as England halted the extension of credit and deliveries of ships to the Confederates.[191] The European powers reacted not only to Lee's Gettysburg Campaign itself but to the simultaneous losses in the Western and Middle Theaters. On July 28, the Confederate chief of ordnance, Josiah Gorgas, bemoaned the rapid change of rebel fortunes resulting from its defeats at Vicksburg, Port Hudson, and Gettysburg:

Lee failed at Gettysburg, and has recrossed the Potomac & resumed the position of two months ago, covering Richmond. Alas! he has lost fifteen thousand men and twenty-five thousand stands of arms. Vicksburgh [sic] and Port Hudson capitulated, surrendering thirty five thousand men and forty-five thousand arms. It seems incredible that human power could effect such a change in so brief a space. Yesterday we rode on the pinnacle of success—to-day absolute ruin seems to be our portion. The Confederacy totters to its destruction.[192]

Gettysburg indeed had been a Confederate disaster, and the record is clear that responsibility for it rests, for myriad reasons, with Robert E. Lee. Jeb Stuart, Richard Ewell, Jubal Early, Nelson Pendleton, and perhaps Longstreet played lesser roles in the defeat. The latter, however, who played a subordinate role in the battle and whose wise tactical counsel was rejected, has been unjustly blamed for his conduct at Gettysburg in an effort to deflect criticism away from Lee—the commanding officer who failed to command or command well in that campaign and battle.

# CHAPTER SEVEN

# DID ULYSSES S. GRANT WIN THE CIVIL WAR SIMPLY BY BRUTE FORCE AND SUPERIOR NUMBERS?

## THE MYTH

If rebel soldiers were invincible and their General Lee above reproach, reasons for the Confederacy's defeat had to be found elsewhere. How could Lee have lost to Ulysses S. Grant, of all people—a drunk and a butcher, according to the Myth, with barely any military talent? The answer must be the North's superior resources and its willingness to employ them with the necessary brutality.

In 1866, E. A. Pollard provided a classic version of the Myth's portrait of Grant:

> The new Federal commander in Virginia [Grant] was one of the most remarkable accidents of the war. That a man without

any marked ability, certainly without genius, without fortune, without influence, should attain the position of leader of all the Federal armies, and stand the most conspicuous person on that side of the war, is a phenomenon which would be inexplicable among any other people than the sensational and coarse mobs of admiration in the North. Gen. Grant's name was coupled with success; and this circumstance alone, without regard to merit of personal agency, without reference to any display of mental quality in the event, was sufficient to fix him in the admiration of the Northern public. It mattered not that Grant had illustrated no genius; it mattered not that he had smothered Fort Donelson by numbers; it mattered not that he had succeeded at Vicksburg through the glaring incompetency of a Confederate commander, and by the weight of eighty thousand men against twenty odd thousand; the North was prepared to worship him, without distinguishing between accident and achievement, and to entitle him the hero of the war.[1]

Pollard's inaccuracies, bias, overstatements, and strange criteria for success speak for themselves, but he did set the tone for a century of criticism of Grant.

Grant has been regarded as a "hammerer and a butcher who was often drunk, an unimaginative and ungifted clod who eventually triumphed because he had such overwhelming superiority in numbers that he could hardly avoid winning."[2] Grant "remains a clumsy butcher to many Americans, who look to a warped historical record that draws heavily on the efforts of Lost Cause writers."[3] He acquired the unfortunate and unfair label of "butcher" because of the high number of Union casualties associated with some of the campaigns and battles that won the American Civil War. He stands accused of unnecessarily slaughtering his own men in order to achieve victory.

Why has Grant so often been labeled a butcher? The accusations began during the war—particularly during his aggressive 1864 campaign against Lee to secure final victory for the Union. During that Overland Campaign, Mary Todd Lincoln complained, "[Grant] is a butcher and is not fit to be at the head of an army." On June 4, 1864, the Union's secretary of the navy, Gideon Welles, wrote in his diary, "Still there is heavy loss, but we are becoming accustomed to the sacrifice. Grant has not great regard for human life." One Southerner said at the time, "We have met a man this time, who either does not know when he is whipped, or who cares not if he loses his *whole* army."[4]

The "butcher" accusations continued in the early post-war period, and even Northern commentators joined in. In 1866, the *New York Times* war correspondent William Swinton wrote in his *Campaigns of the Army of the Potomac* that Grant relied "exclusively on the application of brute masses, in rapid and remorseless blows." John Codman Ropes told the Military Historical Society of Massachusetts that Grant suffered from a "burning, persistent desire to fight, to attack, in season and out of season, against intrenchments [sic], natural obstacles, what not."[5]

Beginning in the 1870s, the former Confederate officers who were constructing the Myth of the Lost Cause played a prominent role in criticizing Grant—especially in comparison with Lee. In his Lee's Birthday speech of 1872, Jubal A. Early said, "Shall I compare General Lee to his successful antagonist? As well compare the great pyramid which rears its majestic proportions in the Valley of the Nile, to a pygmy perched on Mount Atlas." In the 1880s, Lieutenant General Evander M. Law wrote, "What a part at least of his own men thought about General Grant's methods was shown by the fact that many of the prisoners taken during the [Overland] campaign complained bitterly of the 'useless butchery' to which they were subjected...."[6]

Writing in 1906 about the Overland Campaign, Lee's former adjutant, Walter H. Taylor, declared: "It is well to bear in mind the great inequality between the two contending armies, in order that one may have a proper appreciation of the difficulties which beset General Lee in the task of thwarting the designs of so formidable an adversary, and realize the extent to which his brilliant genius made amends for the paucity of numbers, and proved more than a match for brute force, as

illustrated in the hammering policy of General Grant." This last of the
Union commanders, Taylor contended, "put a lower estimate upon the
value of human life than any of his predecessors...."[7]

Sometimes the accusation has been more subtle. In his 1943 biography of Judah Benjamin, Robert D. Meade wrote: "In the spring of 1864
Grant took personal command of the Union Army in Virginia and, with
a heavily superior force, began his bludgeoning assaults on Lee's weakened but grimly determined troops." The nameless author of the jacket
copy for Bruce Catton's *Stillness at Dawn* (1953) described Grant (contrary to Catton's own view) as "a seedy little man who instilled no
enthusiasm in his followers and little respect in his enemies," a sentiment
echoed in the 1974 *Encyclopedia of American Biography*: "Grant in
1861 was a seedy failure who had resigned his commission years
before...."[8]

In 1965 the pro-Lee historian Clifford Dowdey wrote, "Absorbing
appalling casualties, [Grant] threw his men in wastefully as if their weight
was certain to overrun any Confederates in their path. In terms of generalship, the new man gave Lee nothing to fear," and he called Grant
"an opponent who took no count of his losses." A 1993 article in *Blue
& Gray* magazine referred to the "butcher's bill" of the first two weeks
of the Overland Campaign.[9] In 1999, the authoritative *Oxford Companion to American Military History* said that "Grant's popular reputation
as an impassive 'butcher' whose victories depended on luck and large
armies arose amidst strivings for sectional reconciliation."[10]

More recent examples abound. In 2001, a reporter wrote: "Despite
occasional flashes of brilliant strategy and admirable persistence, Grant
still comes off looking like a butcher in those final months." Another
reporter, writing in 2002 and regarding Grant as an intellectual light-
weight, referred to "last-in-class types, such as Ulysses S. Grant."[11]

Although concluding that "Grant was the greatest general of the
war," the great British military historian John Keegan nevertheless commented in 2009, "In the West, Grant won success by risk-taking and
unceasing aggressiveness, but his soldiers paid the price. Most of Grant's
battles were costly in casualties."[12]

The historian Gregory Mertz explained the problem with Grant's reputation: "Grant enjoyed little of the 'glory' for his contributions to the [Army of the Potomac's] ultimate success, and was the recipient of much of the blame for the 'disasters.' Despite moving continually forward from the Wilderness to Petersburg and Richmond, ultimately to Appomattox, and executing the campaign that ended the war in the East, Grant has received little credit, and is most remembered for the heavy losses of Cold Harbor, which tagged him with the reputation of a 'butcher.'"[13]

As often was the case, Edward Pollard led the way in myth-making. In 1866, he claimed that Lee's troops had suffered fewer than seven thousand casualties at the Wilderness while Grant's had incurred a whopping 27,310.[14] In our own day, the *Oxford Encyclopedia of the Civil War* (2011) erroneously charges that Grant's army suffered seventy-five thousand casualties in the six-week Overland Campaign and at Cold Harbor lost eight thousand men in ten minutes ("about 1,000 per minute").[15] Both numbers are exaggerated.

The "butcher" label has been tenacious. As the Associated Press reported in 2003, "Ask most schoolchildren and they will tell you that Robert E. Lee was a military genius while Ulysses S. Grant was a butcher who simply used the North's advantage in men and material to bludgeon the Confederates into submission."[16]

## THE OTHER SIDE

The persistent criticisms of Grant can be summarized as follows: (1) he was a butcher, (2) all he did in the war was bludgeon Lee's army in the Overland and Appomattox campaigns, (3) he attacked unnecessarily, (4) his armies suffered more casualties than Lee's, (5) he attacked Lee needlessly in the Overland Campaign, (6) the election of 1864 was such a landslide for Lincoln that Grant's aggressive series of nationwide campaigns was unnecessary, and (7) his high casualties in 1864–65 show that he was inferior to his predecessors in the Eastern Theater.

There are answers to each of these criticisms.

(1) Far from being a butcher, Grant fought with skill, audacity, swiftness, and aggressiveness. As a result, he imposed about thirty-seven thousand more casualties (killed, missing, wounded, captured) on his opponents than his own armies incurred.[17]

(2) Prior to coming to the East to defeat Lee, Grant had won a series of major campaigns and battles—including the Fort Henry–Fort Donelson Campaign, the brilliant Vicksburg campaign, and the Battle of Chattanooga—with swift and daring movements and a minimum of casualties.

(3) The strategic burden of winning the Civil War was on the North. The North had to defeat the South, and Grant was by far the most effective Union general in going on the offensive to win the war. On the other hand, the South needed only a deadlock or a tie, but Lee gambled by going on the offensive and thus decimated his own army at Seven Days' (especially Mechanicsville and Malvern Hill), Chancellorsville, Gettysburg (especially on Day Two and then Pickett's Charge on Day Three), the Wilderness, and Fort Stedman. Grant needed a win, went for it, and got it. Lee needed a tie, went for the win, and lost.

(4) In their authoritative study of the war's casualties, Grady McWhiney and Perry Jamieson find that Lee's army suffered about 121,000 killed and wounded while Grant's armies suffered about 94,000 killed and wounded. In those major battles, they concluded, Lee's army suffered an average of about 20 percent killed and wounded in each battle, while Grant's armies suffered about 18 percent killed and wounded.[18] An all-encompassing study of the war's casualties reveals that Lee's single losing army incurred about 209,000 casualties (killed, wounded, missing, captured), while Grant's several winning armies incurred a total of about 154,000 casualties—about 55,000 fewer than Lee's.[19]

(5) Lincoln brought Grant to the East as general in chief to pursue Confederate armies aggressively and perhaps win the war in time to ensure Lincoln's reelection in 1864. In the several months he had to accomplish that goal, Grant drove Lee's army into a virtual siege at Richmond and Petersburg, keeping Lee so occupied that he never considered aiding rebel

forces defending Atlanta. Sherman's capture of Atlanta in September, while Grant had Lee bottled up in Virginia, was decisive in Lincoln's reelection.

(6) Although Lincoln beat George McClellan by a margin of 55 to 45 percent in the November 1864 election, as late as the end of August virtually everyone (including Lincoln, Republican Party leaders and newspaper editors, and Confederate observers) thought Lincoln would lose. The fall of Atlanta changed Lincoln's prospects. Still, a switch in certain states of fewer than thirty thousand votes, out of the four million cast, would have given McClellan the electoral votes to defeat Lincoln— even after Atlanta, the Shenandoah Valley, and Mobile had been the scene of major Union victories within the ten weeks preceding the election.[20]

(7) Grant's Eastern predecessors—including McClellan, Burnside, Hooker, and Meade—incurred more casualties in the East (about 144,000) than Grant and had little to show for them.[21] They lacked Grant's perseverance. After their three years of strategic failure, Grant won the war in less than a year after launching the Overland Campaign.

Grant was about as aggressive as Lee, but his aggression was consistent with the Union's strategic and tactical need to take the war to the rebels, destroy their armies, and affirmatively win the war. With about fifty-five thousand fewer casualties than Lee, Grant won two theaters of the war, saved a Union army in a third, and proved to be the most successful general of the war. Yet in Gordon C. Rhea's words, "[t]he very nature of Grant's [offensive] assignment [especially in 1864] guaranteed severe casualties."[22]

In fact, an average of "only" 15 percent of Grant's Federal troops were killed or wounded in his battles over the course of the war—a total of slightly more than 94,000 men. In contrast, Lee had greater casualties both in percentages and real numbers: an average of 20 percent of his troops were killed or wounded in his battles—a total of more than 121,000 (far more than any other Civil War general). Lee had about 80,000 of his men killed or wounded in his first fourteen months in command (about the same number he started with). All of these casualties should be considered in the context of America's deadliest war. At least 620,000 military men died in the Civil War, 214,938 in battle and the rest from disease and other causes.[23] Perhaps another 130,000 civilians and soldiers (primarily Confederate) were unaccounted for.[24]

In their thought-provoking book *Attack and Die: Civil War Military Tactics and the Southern Heritage*, McWhiney and Jamieson provide some astounding numbers related to Grant's major battles and campaigns. First, they have determined that, in his five major campaigns and battles of 1862–63, he commanded a cumulative total of 220,970 soldiers, of whom 23,551 (10.7 percent) were killed or wounded. Second, they determined that, in his eight major campaigns and battles of 1864–65 (when he was determined to defeat or destroy Lee's army as quickly as possible), he commanded a cumulative total of 400,942 soldiers, of whom 70,620 (17.6 percent) were killed or wounded. Third, they determined that during the course of the war, therefore, he commanded a cumulative total of 621,912 soldiers in his major campaigns and battles, of whom a total of 94,171 (a militarily tolerable[25] 15.1 percent) were killed or wounded.[26] These loss percentages are remarkably low—especially considering that Grant was on the strategic and tactical offensive in most of these battles and campaigns.

We can put these numbers in perspective by comparing them with the casualty figures for the Army of Northern Virginia under Lee's command and with those for other Confederate commanders. During the course of the war, Lee, in his major campaigns and battles, commanded a cumulative total of 598,178 soldiers, of whom 121,042 were killed or wounded—a total loss of 20.2 percent, about one-third higher than Grant's. Other major Confederate commanders with higher percentages killed or wounded than Grant were Generals Braxton Bragg (19.5 percent), John Bell Hood (19.2 percent), and Pierre Gustave Tousant Beauregard (16.1 percent).[27]

McWhiney and Jamieson also tallied those Civil War battles in which either side incurred the heaviest percentage of losses suffered by one side during the entire war. Of the nineteen battles in which one side lost 19 percent or more of its troops (killed or wounded), only "one" involved such a loss by Grant's troops (and that was actually two battles—29.6 percent at Wilderness and Spotsylvania combined).[28] Given the number of battles his armies fought, this is a surprising but informative result.

Far from being the butcher of the battlefield, Grant determined what the North needed to do to win the war and did it. His record of unparalleled success—including Forts Henry and Donelson, Shiloh, Port Gibson, Raymond, Jackson, Champion's Hill, Vicksburg, Chattanooga, the Wilderness, Spotsylvania Court House, Petersburg, and Appomattox—establishes him as the greatest general of the Civil War.

John Keegan has studied the leading generals of the Civil War and concluded, "Grant was the greatest general of the war, one who would have excelled at any time in any army. He understood the war in its entirety and quickly grasped how modern methods of communication...had endowed the commander with the power to collect information more quickly and the means to disseminate appropriate orders in response."[29]

A brief examination of Grant's battles and campaigns will enable readers to draw their own conclusions about how successful Grant was and whether the casualties his armies incurred were reasonable.

## GRANT'S CAMPAIGNS AND BATTLES

Labeled a butcher by many historians, Grant has not received due credit for his successes. He accepted the surrender of three entire Confederate armies—at Fort Donelson in 1862, Vicksburg in 1863, and Appomattox Court House in 1865. No other general on either side accepted the surrender of even one army until Sherman, with Grant's blessing, accepted the capitulation of the remnants of the Confederate Army of Tennessee in North Carolina in late April 1865.

Overlooked by many are Grant's numerous successes in the West (Kentucky, Tennessee, and Mississippi) in 1862 and 1863. Acting on his own, he bloodlessly occupied Paducah and Smithfield, Kentucky, critical river junctures on the Ohio, as soon as Confederate Lieutenant General Leonidas Polk invaded neutral Kentucky in September 1861. Grant then moved on to quickly capture Forts Henry and Donelson and gain control of the Tennessee and Cumberland Rivers, putting a dagger in the left flank of the Confederacy. The capture of Forts Henry and Donelson, the Union's first major victory of the war, was accomplished with fewer than three thousand casualties (versus sixteen thousand for the rebels) and made Grant a national hero for the first time. Shortly thereafter, Grant recovered from a surprise Confederate attack at Shiloh, Tennessee (for which he was inexcusably unprepared), saved his army in a vicious two-day battle, and won a major strategic victory. His thirteen thousand casualties there (compared with the enemy's almost eleven thousand)— incurred, curiously enough, in a defensive battle—were his highest in any battle or campaign outside the East.

The next year, again without approval from above, Grant moved his army along the west bank of the Mississippi River to get below Vicksburg, where he completed a well-planned amphibious crossing of the Mississippi and took a daring gamble to feed his army off the countryside. He won a series of five battles in eighteen days against superior Confederate forces and accepted the surrender of Vicksburg and a nearly thirty-thousand-man army on July 4, 1863. This brilliant campaign split the Confederacy, opening the Mississippi to Union commerce and military movements and impeding the flow of supplies and foodstuffs from and through Mexico and the Trans-Mississippi to Confederate armies east of that river. Again, Grant was a national hero. He accomplished all of this with only about nine thousand casualties, while inflicting about forty-one thousand on the enemy. My detailed discussion of that important campaign below offers a fuller demonstration of Grant's talents.

In the fall of 1863, when the Union Army of the Cumberland was trapped in Chattanooga, Tennessee, after the Battle of Chickamauga, Grant was called to the rescue. While Lee vetoed possible rebel reinforcements from Virginia, Grant established a "cracker" (supply) line within five days of his arrival, organized reinforcements, captured Lookout Mountain, carried Missionary Ridge, and broke out of Chattanooga within a month. He sent Braxton Bragg's Army of Tennessee scurrying back to Georgia at a cost of almost six thousand Union casualties—to

the rebels' almost seven thousand. For a third time (after Fort Henry–
Fort Donelson and Vicksburg), Grant was a national hero. Although
compelled to attack a fortified enemy holding the high ground, he had
achieved another major offensive victory with a minimum of casualties.
His November 1863 victory at Chattanooga set the stage for Sherman's
1864 campaign toward Atlanta.

Keegan faults Grant with unceasing aggression in the West for which
his soldiers paid the price, but Grant actually won the Western (Mississippi Valley) and Middle theaters with a modicum of casualties. As the
Grant casualty chart in Chapter 5 shows, his armies suffered thirty-seven
thousand casualties (the largest number while on the defensive at Shiloh)
and inflicted eighty-four thousand casualties on the enemy.

Having ended Confederate control in the Mississippi Valley and
eastern Tennessee and having won Lincoln's confidence in his willingness
to fight and ability to win, Grant was summoned to the East in early
1864 to close out the war. There the Army of the Potomac had squandered opportunities to pursue the Army of Northern Virginia after the
Battles of Antietam (1862) and Gettysburg (1863), and it had recoiled
after the first major battle of each offensive campaign against Lee (Seven
Days', Fredericksburg, and Chancellorsville). That army had demonstrated, in the words of Gordon Rhea and others, that "superior numbers
and equipment alone did not win the war. Success was contingent upon
the outcome of battles and campaigns, and the Army of the Potomac
only became successful when it found someone who could use its
resources to the utmost."[30] Grant was that someone. The failure of his
predecessors, with the same superior resources, to win in the East demonstrates that superior resources alone were not sufficient for victory.

Grant's spectacular run of victories in the West gave Lincoln confidence that he would produce war-ending victories in the East by fully
exploiting all available resources. Divided sympathies in the North,
especially after the Emancipation Proclamation, made swift victory
imperative, writes the military historian Russell K. Weigley, and the
imminence of the presidential election of November 1864 added to the
urgency.[31] Grant was under pressure to produce early, positive results.

He organized a coordinated national strategy, kept pressure on the Confederates on all fronts, and drove Lee's army back to Richmond in a bloody campaign through the Wilderness, Spotsylvania Court House, the North Anna River, Cold Harbor, and Petersburg. At the beginning of the campaign to destroy Lee's army, Grant succinctly instructed Meade, "Lee's army will be your objective point. Wherever Lee goes there you will go also."[32]

Although this campaign proved costly to the Army of the Potomac, it was fatal for Lee's army. Taking advantage of Lee's having gravely weakened his outnumbered army in 1862 and 1863, Grant conducted a campaign of adhesion—sticking to the enemy—against the Army of Northern Virginia. As Rhea writes, Grant provided the backbone and leadership that the Army of the Potomac had been lacking:

> [I]t was a very good thing for the country that Grant came east. Had Meade exercised unfettered command over the Army of the Potomac, I doubt that he would have passed beyond the Wilderness. Lee would likely have stymied, or even defeated the Potomac army, and Lincoln would have faced a severe political crisis. It took someone like Grant to force the Army of the Potomac out of its defensive mode, and aggressively focus it on the task of destroying Lee's army.[33]

Grant's armies incurred the bulk of their casualties in 1864. His decisive Overland Campaign against Lee's army that year reflected his philosophy that "[t]he art of war is simple enough. Find out where your enemy is. Get at him as soon as you can. Strike him as hard as you can and as often as you can, and keep moving on."[34] The Overland Campaign was part of Grant's national effort to take advantage of Union strength and ensure the reelection of Lincoln. It resulted, however, in Grant's being accused of "butchery."

Although Meade's Army of the Potomac, under the personal direction of Grant, did suffer high casualties (41 percent) during its drive to the James River, it imposed even higher casualties on Lee's army (46 percent). In addition, that Federal army compelled Lee to retreat to a nearly besieged position at Richmond and Petersburg, a retreat that Lee had previously warned would be the death-knell of his own army. Rhea concludes, "A review of Grant's Overland Campaign reveals not the butcher of lore, but a thoughtful warrior every bit as talented as his Confederate opponent." As he advanced on Lee's army and Richmond, Grant was overseeing and facilitating a coordinated attack against Confederate forces all over the nation, particularly Sherman's campaign from the Tennessee border to Atlanta.

Ever the national general, Grant expressed his concerns in mid-1864 that Lee might send reinforcements to oppose Sherman as he maneuvered toward Atlanta, but as Grant hoped, Lee made no effort to send reinforcements to Georgia. Sherman's capture of Atlanta virtually ensured the reelection of Lincoln, and Sherman ultimately broke loose on a barely contested sweep through Georgia and the Carolinas that doomed the Confederacy. Grant's nationwide coordinated offensive of 1864–65 against the rebel armies not only won the war but demonstrated that he was a national general with a broad vision. Lee, by contrast, was shown to be a one-theater general suffering from Virginia myopia.

By the end of 1864, Grant's multi-front national campaign had succeeded in capturing Atlanta, Savannah, Mobile, and the Shenandoah Valley; reelecting Lincoln; virtually destroying the Army of Tennessee at Franklin and Nashville; and laying the groundwork for the final defeat of Lee and the Confederacy. Congress recognized Grant's achievements on December 17 by passing a joint resolution thanking him, his officers, and his soldiers and authorizing a gold medal to be struck and presented to him.

The following spring, Grant's troops cut off the last open railroad into Petersburg, broke through Lee's lines, outraced what was left of the fleeing Army of Northern Virginia, and compelled its surrender at Appomattox Court House on April 9, 1865. Executing Lincoln's conciliatory policies toward the South, Grant was gracious in his acceptance of Lee's surrender and extended generous terms to Lee's officers and soldiers.

Grant's victories at Vicksburg and Chattanooga, his aggressive Overland Campaign, and the companion Georgia and Carolina campaigns of Sherman that Grant oversaw all contributed, in the words of the authors of *Why the South Lost the Civil War,* to the "rapid diminution and ultimate death of [Confederate] morale, the will to win, during the last year or two of the war"[35]—and ultimately to Confederate defeat.

Unlike most Union generals, who were reluctant to take advantage of the North's numerical superiority and unwilling to persistently invade the Confederacy, Grant knew what had to be done and did it. He advanced aggressively and creatively, and he attacked with vigor. But he usually avoided suicidal frontal attacks.[36] He "made his best preparations and then went in without reserve or hesitation and with a simple faith in success."[37] In light of the large number of battles fought by his armies, the total of ninety-four thousand dead and wounded suffered by his commands was surprisingly small—especially when considered in light of the 121,000 dead and wounded among soldiers under the command of Robert E. Lee, who engaged in a similar number of battles and was not obliged to take the offensive. Rhea protests that Grant "has been painted into a corner of being a butcher, when in fact he was extremely thoughtful, very innovative and every bit the match of Lee."[38]

Just as Lee's disastrous Gettysburg campaign was the epitome of his unsuccessful Civil War generalship, Grant's brilliant Vicksburg campaign highlighted many of the traits that made him so successful throughout the war. An evaluation of Grant, therefore, must include a close look at that campaign.

## GRANT'S CLASSIC VICKSBURG CAMPAIGN

During the spring and early summer of 1863, Grant carried out what James M. McPherson has called "the most brilliant and innovative campaign of the Civil War" and T. Harry Williams has called "one of the classic campaigns of the Civil War and, indeed, of military history." In fact, the *U.S. Army Field Manual 100-5* (May 1986) describes the Vicksburg campaign as "the most brilliant campaign ever fought on

American soil," one which "exemplifies the qualities of a well-conceived, violently executed offensive plan."[39]

Vicksburg, the Gibraltar of the West, was the key to Union control of the Mississippi. Along with Port Hudson to the south, it was the only remaining Confederate stronghold on the river. Early in the war, Lincoln himself had stressed Vicksburg's importance when, pointing to a national map, he said, "See what a lot of land these fellows hold, of which Vicksburg is the key. The war can never be brought to a close until that key is in our pocket."[40]

Having been stymied in his earlier efforts to capture Vicksburg, Grant decided to march his army southward down the west bank of the Mississippi to get well below it. He planned to load his men on transports that would first have to be floated past the city's guns, transport his army to the Mississippi shore south of Vicksburg, strike inland against any Confederate forces they might meet, and eventually capture Vicksburg. He had spent months poring over maps and charts as he single-handedly devised this approach. His strong subordinate commanders—including Sherman, James B. McPherson, and John "Black Jack" Logan—opposed the plan as too risky.[41] Vicksburg was heavily fortified, but Grant's plan proved spectacularly effective. Surrounded by nine major forts or citadels, the city was protected by 172 guns commanding all approaches by water and land and a thirty-thousand-troop garrison. Grant had three options for attacking it: (1) return to Memphis for an overland approach from the north and east, (2) cross the river and directly assault the city, or (3) march his troops down the west bank of the Mississippi, cross it, and approach the city from the south and east. Grant rejected the first option because going back would be morale-deflating (Grant hated to retrace his steps). He rejected the second because it involved, he said, "immense sacrifice of life, if not defeat." "The third alternative was full of dangers and risks," the Vicksburg historian Edwin C. Bearss has said. "Failure in this venture would entail little less than total destruction. If it succeeded, however, the gains would be complete and decisive."[42]

Early April brought receding waters and the emergence of roads from Milliken's Bend northwest of Vicksburg to other points down-river on

208 THE MYTH OF THE LOST CAUSE

the west bank. Grant planned to march his troops over those roads to a location where he could ferry them to the east bank of the river. He enlisted the support of Admiral David Porter, who moved steamships and transport vessels from north of Vicksburg down to where Grant's troops would be awaiting transportation across the river.[43]

The cooperative Porter agreed to Grant's plan and eagerly set about organizing the vessels for a maritime parade past Vicksburg. He warned Grant that as the ironclad vessels did not have sufficient power to return upstream past Vicksburg's guns, this transit would be the point of no return. In preparation for the transit, Porter directed that boilers on the steamships be hidden and protected by barriers of cotton and hay bales, as well as bags of grain. The hay and cotton would also be useful later. Beginning at ten o'clock on the evening of April 16, Porter led the fleet of seven ironclad gunboats, four steamers, the tug *Ivy*, and an assortment of towed coal barges downstream. Coal barges and excess vessels were lashed to the sides of critical vessels to provide additional protection.[44] Confederate bonfires illuminated the Union vessels, which were under fire for two hours as they ran the gauntlet past the Vicksburg guns. Those guns fired 525 rounds and scored sixty-eight hits. Miraculously, only one vessel was lost, and no one on the vessels was killed.[45] Grant now had most of his marine transportation in place.[46]

Fortunately for Grant, the Confederate commander at Vicksburg, Lieutenant General John Pemberton, did not connect the passage of Porter's vessels with the possibility of a Union march down the west bank and an amphibious crossing. Back in Richmond, Lee told Davis that Grant "can derive no material benefit" from Porter's movement and predicted that the addition of artillery at Vicksburg would prevent Porter from repeating his performance. In contrast, a nineteen-year-old Vicksburg gunner perceptively wrote in his diary, "Their object, I think, in going below is to cross troops and try and get in the rear of Vicksburg."[47]

Beginning on March 31, Grant had started Major General John McClernand's four-division corps underway on the west bank route from Milliken's Bend by way of Richmond, Louisiana, to New Carthage, below Vicksburg. Construction of the narrow line of advance and supply required back-breaking canal digging, road building and repairing, and bridge building. After the transports had slipped by Vicksburg, Grant visited New Carthage on April 17 and approved an alternative and longer (forty-mile) west bank route to Perkins's Plantation, twelve miles south of New Carthage. Preparing the way for this march required building four bridges across two thousand feet of bayou.[48]

Grant returned to Milliken's Bend and on April 20 issued Special Orders No. 110 for the march by his entire army. McClernand's Thirteenth Corps was to be followed by Major General James McPherson's Seventeenth, and then Sherman's Fifteenth. On the critical issue of gathering supplies, Grant's order stated:

> Commanders are authorized and enjoined to collect all the beef cattle, corn and other necessary supplies on the line of march; but wanton destruction of property, taking of articles useless for military purposes, insulting citizens, going into and searching houses without proper orders from division commanders, are positively prohibited. All such irregularities must be summarily punished.

Realizing that the area of their intended operations and the single line of march were inadequate to supply his troops, Grant ordered a second collection of vessels to bring some additional supplies south past Vicksburg. Thus, on the night of April 22, six more protected steamers towing twelve barges loaded with rations steamed past Vicksburg under the command of Colonel Clark Lagow of Grant's staff. Despite General Lee's prediction, five of the steamers and half of the barges made it through the gauntlet of artillery batteries, which fired 391 rounds. Most of the vessels were commanded and manned by army volunteers from "Black Jack" Logan's division because the civilian vessel crews were afraid to run the Vicksburg gauntlet.[49]

Grant now had his transportation (seven transports and fifteen or sixteen barges), a modicum of supplies, and a gathering invasion force.

Sherman and Porter had serious doubts about the feasibility of transporting the supplies for Grant's army down a poor, swampy road on the west bank of the Mississippi River, across the water, and into Mississippi. Nevertheless, Grant pressed forward with his plan and started McPherson's corps south from New Carthage on April 25.[50]

Meanwhile Grant had created four diversions to the north and east of Vicksburg to deflect Confederate attention away from his planned campaign. First, he had sent Major General Frederick Steele's troops in transports one hundred miles northward up the Mississippi River toward Greenville, Mississippi. Concluding that Grant was retreating (to reinforce William Rosecrans in eastern Tennessee), Pemberton allowed about eight thousand rebel troops to be transferred from Mississippi back to Bragg in Tennessee.[51]

Second, Grant had initiated a cavalry raid from Tennessee to Louisiana through the length of central and eastern Mississippi. Incurring only a handful of casualties, Colonel Benjamin H. Grierson, a fellow Illinoisan, conducted the most successful Union cavalry raid of the entire war. Grant had devised this diversionary mission back on February 13, when he sent the following simple, flexible, and brilliant suggestion in a dispatch to General Hurlbut in Tennessee:

> It seems to me that Grierson with about 500 picked men might succeed in making his way South and cut the rail-road East of Jackson Miss. The undertaking would be a hazardous [sic] one but it would pay well if carried out. I do not direct that this shall be done but leave it for a volunteer enterprise.

On April 17, Grierson rode out of LaGrange, Tennessee, in command of 1,700 cavalrymen and a six-gun battery.[52] In the early days of the raid, he deftly split off part of his force, primarily to confuse the Confederates as to his location and intentions. First, on April 20, he sent 175 men determined to be incapable of completing the mission (the "Quinine Brigade") and a gun back to LaGrange with prisoners and captured property. The next day he sent a regiment and another gun east to break up the north-south Mobile & Ohio Railroad and to stir up even more confusion. To determine whether substantial enemy forces were present in the towns he intended to raid, Grierson assembled a group of nine hand-picked men, the "Butternut Guerillas," who scouted ahead dressed in Confederate uniforms and clothes.[53]

With still another thirty-five-man detached force drawing substantial Confederate infantry and cavalry away from his main force, Grierson continued to Newton on the east-west Southern Railroad (the eastern extension of the Vicksburg and Jackson Railroad) in the heart of Mississippi. There, on the 24th, he destroyed two trains (both filled with ammunition and commissary stores). He also tore up the railroad and tore down the telegraph line—both linking Meridian with Jackson and Vicksburg to the west. With the disruption of the key railroad to Vicksburg and the destruction of millions of dollars' worth of Confederate assets (including thirty-eight rail cars), Grierson's mission was complete—except for his final escape.[54]

Pemberton, who had sent troops to head off Grierson before he reached the railroad, now sent additional soldiers to try to cut off the escape of his raiders.[55] The raid's effect on Pemberton was precisely what Grant intended—on April 27 he sent seventeen messages to Mississippi commands about Grierson's raiders and not a single one about Grant's build-up on the west bank of the Mississippi. By the 29th, Pemberton had further played into Grant's hands by sending all his cavalry in pursuit of Grierson and advising his superiors, "The telegraph wires are down. The enemy has, therefore, either landed on this side of the Mississippi River, or they have been cut by Grierson's cavalry.... All the cavalry I can raise is close on their rear."[56]

Sixteen days and six hundred miles after starting their dangerous venture, Grierson's men reached the Union lines at Baton Rouge, Louisiana, on May 2—three days after Grant's amphibious landing at Bruinsburg on the Mississippi. They had survived several close calls, left havoc in their wake, and accomplished their primary mission of diverting attention from Grant's movements west and south of Vicksburg. They had inflicted one hundred casualties and captured over five hundred prisoners. Miraculously, all this had been accomplished with fewer than twenty-five casualties. There was good reason for Sherman to call it the "most brilliant expedition of the Civil War."[57]

Grant's third diversion involved another cavalry foray. While Grierson was traveling the length of Mississippi, other Union forces went on the offensive far to the east. Colonel Abel D. Streight led a "poorly mounted horse and mule brigade" from middle Tennessee into Alabama and drew the ever-dangerous cavalry of Nathan Bedford Forrest away from Grierson and his various detachments.[58]

To completely confuse Pemberton, Grant employed a fourth diversion. While he was moving south with McClernand and McPherson on the west (Louisiana) bank, Grant had Sherman's Fifteenth Corps threaten Vicksburg from the north. On April 27, Grant ordered Sherman to proceed up the Yazoo River and threaten Snyder's Bluff northeast of Vicksburg. On the 29th, Sherman debarked ten regiments of troops and appeared to be preparing an assault while eight naval gunboats bombarded the Confederate forts at Haines's Bluff. Having suffered no casualties, Sherman withdrew on May 1 and hastily followed McPherson down the west bank of the Mississippi. His troops were ferried across the river on May 6 and 7.[59]

Grant, meanwhile, had joined McClernand at New Carthage on the west bank on April 23. When Colonel James H. Wilson of Grant's staff and Admiral Porter determined that there were no suitable landing areas east of Perkins's Plantation, Grant on April 24 ordered the troops to proceed south another twenty-two miles to Hard Times, a west bank area sixty-three miles south of Milliken's Bend and directly across the river from Grand Gulf, Mississippi. According to Secretary of War Stanton's special observer, the former *New York Tribune* reporter and editor Charles A. Dana, McClernand moved his troops slowly and disobeyed Grant's orders to preserve ammunition and to leave all impediments behind. Instead, he had guns fired in a salute at a review and tried to bring his wife and servants along. Ten thousand soldiers were moved farther south by vessel, and the rest of the men bridged three bayous and completed their trek to Hard Times by April 27. On April 28, Confederate Brigadier General John

S. Bowen at Grand Gulf could see the Union armada gathering across the river and urgently requested reinforcements from Pemberton in Vicksburg. Focused on Grierson and Sherman, however, Pemberton refused to send reinforcements south toward Grand Gulf until late on April 29, when they were too late to halt the amphibious crossing.[60]

Two days later, with ten thousand of McClernand's troops embarked on vessels for a possible east bank landing, Porter's eight gunboats attacked the Confederate batteries on the high bluffs at Grand Gulf. After five and a half hours and the loss of eighteen killed and about fifty-seven wounded, the Union fleet had eliminated the guns of Fort Wade but not those of Fort Coburn, which stood forty feet above the river and was protected by a forty-foot-thick parapet. A disappointed Grant watched from a small tugboat, and Porter eventually halted the attack.[61]

Grant, however, did not give up; he simply moved south. That night, ten thousand troops left the vessels and marched across a peninsula while Porter slipped all of his vessels past the Confederate guns. Grant was planning to load his troops again and land them at Rodney, about nine miles south of Grand Gulf. He changed his mind, though, when a local black man told a landing party that Bruinsburg, a few miles closer, offered a good landing site and a good road inland to Port Gibson. Convinced of what he was going to do the next day, Grant sent orders that night to Sherman to head south immediately with two of his three divisions. On the morning of April 30, Grant moved down and across the Mississippi with McClernand's corps and one of McPherson's divisions from Disharoon's Plantation (near Hard Times), Louisiana. He then took them six miles south to Bruinsburg, Mississippi, and landed them without opposition.[62] In his memoirs, Grant explained the great relief he felt after the successful landing:

> When this was effected I felt a degree of relief scarcely ever equalled since. Vicksburg was not yet taken it is true, nor were its defenders demoralized by any of our previous moves. I was now in the enemy's country, with a vast river and the stronghold of Vicksburg between me and my base of supplies. But

I was on dry ground on the same side of the river with the enemy. All the campaigns, labors, hardships and exposures from the month of December previous to this time that had been made and endured, were for the accomplishment of this one object.[63]

Under the cover of several diversions, Grant had daringly marched his army through Louisiana bayous down the west bank of the Mississippi and launched a huge amphibious operation involving twenty-four thousand troops. The historian Terrence J. Winschel writes admiringly:

The movement from Milliken's Bend to Hard Times was boldly conceived and executed by a daring commander willing to take risks. The sheer audacity of the movement demonstrated Grant's firmness of purpose and revealed his many strengths as a commander. The bold and decisive manner in which he directed the movement set the tone for the campaign and inspired confidence in the army's ranks.[64]

## MOVING INLAND: PORT GIBSON AND RAYMOND

The first day ashore, Grant pushed McClernand two miles inland to high, dry ground and on toward the town of Port Gibson, where a bridge across Big Bayou Pierre led to Grand Gulf (which Grant coveted as a supply base on the Mississippi). Meanwhile, Grant oversaw the continuous transport of more of his troops across the Mississippi well into the night. Aided by the light of huge bonfires, McPherson's soldiers were transported until a collision between two transports at three o'clock in the morning stopped the operation until daylight.[65] Back upriver, Sherman was beginning to move south but remained worried about the long, vulnerable supply line. There was reason to be worried. As James R. Arnold observes, "Grant was at the end of an exceedingly precarious supply line, isolated in hostile territory, positioned between Port Hudson and Vicksburg—two well-fortified, enemy-held citadels—outnumbered by his enemy, and with an unfordable river to his rear. Few generals would have considered this anything but a trap. Grant judged it an opportunity."[66]

The next day, May 1, brought conflict and the first of Grant's five victories leading to the siege of Vicksburg—the Battle of Port Gibson.[67] Two Confederate brigades, which had belatedly marched as many as forty-four miles from near Vicksburg, and the garrison from Grand Gulf had crossed the bridge over the North Fork of Bayou Pierre at Port Gibson. They confronted McClernand's troops about three miles west of Port Gibson. McClernand split his forces along two parallel roads leading toward town and ran into strong opposition. General Bowen arrived from Grand Gulf to command the defenders.

The Confederate left fell back under intense attack from three of McClernand's divisions as Union sharpshooters picked off the brave and effective rebel gunners manning the defenders' artillery. Following the initial rebel retreat, McClernand and the visiting governor of Illinois, Richard Yates, delivered victory remarks and did some politicking with the troops. Grant put an end to those proceedings and ordered the advance to resume. Meanwhile, Grant had reinforced McClernand's left wing on the northern road with two of McPherson's brigades, and that wing, in the face of persistent enemy artillery, likewise drove the Confederates back toward Port Gibson. Victory was confirmed the next morning, May 2, when Grant's soldiers found Port Gibson abandoned by the Confederates, who had crossed and burned the bridges across Big Bayou Pierre (to Grand Gulf) and Little Bayou Pierre.[68]

Although Grant's troops were on the offensive all day at Port Gibson, the two sides' casualties were surprisingly comparable. Grant had 131 killed, 719 wounded, and twenty-five missing—a total of 875. Based on incomplete reports, the Confederate defenders had at least sixty-eight killed, 380 wounded, and 384 missing—a total of at least 892.[69]

Despite narrow roads, hilly terrain, and dense vegetation that aided the defenders, Grant's superior force had gained the inland foothold it needed and access to the interior. The battle set the tone for those that followed in the campaign and affected the morale of the winners and losers. Grant would consistently bring superior forces to each battlefield although his troops were outnumbered by the Confederates scattered around western Mississippi. From Vicksburg, Pemberton accurately and somewhat desperately telegraphed Richmond: "A furious battle has been going on since daylight just below Port Gibson.... Enemy's movement threatens Jackson, and, if successful, cuts off Vicksburg and Port Hudson from the east...." With minimal losses, Grant was moving inland. Meanwhile, a rattled Pemberton sent an urgent message to his field commanders directing them to proceed at once but neglecting to say to where.[70]

McClernand's mid-battle political speech was not the only evidence of his incompetence and problematic attitude. His men went ashore with no rations instead of the standard three days' worth. He rejected a brigadier's recommendation that he attack the enemy flank and instead ordered a frontal assault. When Grant ordered McClernand's artillery to conserve ammunition, an angry McClernand countermanded the order.[71] Having just crossed the Mississippi to initiate a challenging campaign of unknown duration, a subordinate military commander would be expected to honor the commanding general's concern about conserving ammunition for future contingencies. McClernand was setting himself up for a big fall. In fact, Stanton, aware of previous problems with McClernand, had sent Charles Dana a telegram on May 6 authorizing Grant "to remove any person who by ignorance in action or any cause interferes with or delays his operations."[72]

After his troops had quickly built a bridge across Little Bayou Pierre, Grant accompanied McPherson northeast to Grindstone Ford, the site of the next bridge across Big Bayou Pierre. They found the bridge still burning but only partially destroyed, and after rapid repairs they crossed Big Bayou Pierre. Because Grant was now in a position to cut off Grand Gulf, the Confederates abandoned that port town and retreated north toward Vicksburg. At Hankinson's Ferry, north of Grand Gulf, the Confederates retreated across a raft bridge over the Big Black River, the only remaining geographical barrier between Grant and Vicksburg.[73]

On May 3, Grant rode into the abandoned and ruined town of Grand Gulf, boarded the *Louisville*, took his first bath in a week, caught up on his correspondence, and rethought his mission. He had learned of the success of Grierson's diversionary mission[74] and also of the time-consuming campaign of the incompetent Union general Nathaniel P. Banks up the Red River. He decided to deviate radically from his orders from General Halleck, which called for McPherson's corps to move south to Port Hudson, await the return of Banks, and cooperate with him in the capture of that town—all before a decisive move on Vicksburg. Grant realized that he would lose about a month waiting to cooperate with Banks in taking Port Hudson and would gain only about twelve thousand troops from Banks. The intervening time, however, would give Confederates, under Department Commander Joseph E. Johnston, the opportunity to gather reinforcements from all over the South to save Vicksburg. So Grant decided instead to move inland with McPherson's and McClernand's corps, and he ordered Sherman to continue moving south to join him with two of his three divisions.[75]

Before leaving Grand Gulf at midnight on May 3, Grant wrote to Halleck:

> The country will supply all the forage required for anything like an active campaign and the necessary fresh beef. Other supplies will have to be drawn from Millikin's [sic] Bend. This is a long and precarious route but I have every confidance [sic] in succeeding in doing it.
>
> I shall not bring my troops into this place but immediately follow the enemy, and if all promises as favorably hereafter as it does now, not stop until Vicksburg is in our possession.[76]

Grant was going for Vicksburg—*now*. Until Sherman's troops arrived, Grant had only twenty-five thousand troops across the river to face fifty thousand Confederates in Mississippi with as many as another twenty thousand on the way.

When he moved inland to Hankinson's Ferry at daybreak on May 4, Grant learned that McPherson's men had captured intact the bridge across the Big Black River and established a bridgehead on the opposite shore. While awaiting the arrival of Sherman's corps, Grant ordered McPherson and McClernand to probe the countryside, giving the enemy the impression that Grant would directly attack Vicksburg from the south. McPherson's patrols discovered that the Confederates were fortifying a defensive line south of Vicksburg. With the arrival of Sherman and the bulk of his corps on May 6 and 7 (after a sixty-three-mile march from Milliken's Bend to Hard Times and ferrying across to Grand Gulf), Grant was ready to move in force.[77]

Realizing that Vicksburg by now was well defended on the south and that its defenders could flee to the northeast if he attacked from the south, Grant decided on a more promising but riskier course of action. As T. Harry Williams puts it, "the general called dull and unimaginative and a mere hammerer executed one of the fastest and boldest moves in the records of war."[78] He cut loose from his base at Grand Gulf, withdrew McPherson from north of the Big Black River, and ordered all three of his army's corps to head northeast between the Big Black on the left and Big Bayou Pierre on the right. His goal was to follow the Big Black, cut the east-west Southern Railroad between Vicksburg and Jackson, the state capital, around the town of Edwards Station, and then move west along the railroad to Vicksburg. In what Thomas Buell calls "the most brilliant decision of his career," Grant "would attack first Johnston and then Pemberton before they could unite and thereby outnumber him, the classic example of defeating an enemy army in detail."[79] Given the poor condition of the dirt roads, the tenuous supply situation, and the threat of Confederate interference from many directions, this plan, in the words of Ed Bearss, "was boldness personified and Napoleonic in its concept."[80] William B. Feis admires Grant's craftiness: "From the outset, Grant designed his movements to sow uncertainty in Pemberton's mind as to the true Federal objective. The key to success, especially deep in Confederate territory, was to maintain the initiative and make the enemy guess at his objectives."[81] Grant was determined not only to occupy Vicksburg but to trap Pemberton's army rather than allow it to escape to fight again. As he would do later in Virginia, Grant stayed focused on defeating, capturing, or destroying the opposing army, not simply occupying geographic positions. This approach was critical to ultimate Union victory in the war.

General Fuller pointed out that not only was Grant's plan daring and contrary to his instructions from Halleck, but that, just as importantly, he insisted that his commanders move with haste to execute it. His orders to them in those early days of May were filled with words urging them to implement his orders expeditiously. He clearly wanted to move quickly inland to negate any forces other than Pemberton's, destroy Vicksburg's supply line, and then quickly turn on Vicksburg with his own rear protected.[82]

As Grant moved inland, he planned to live off the previously unmolested countryside. His troops slaughtered livestock and harvested crops and gardens to obtain food and fodder. They also gathered an eclectic collection of buggies and carriages to assemble a crude and heavily guarded wagon train that would carry salt, sugar, hard bread, ammunition, and other crucial supplies from Grand Gulf to Grant's army. Grant would depend on those intermittent and vulnerable wagon trains to meet some of his needs for two weeks until a supply line was opened on the Yazoo River north of Vicksburg on May 21.[83] From May 8 to 12, Grant's army moved out of its Grand Gulf beachhead and up this corridor, with McClernand hugging the Big Black on the left and guarding all the ferries, Sherman in the center, and McPherson on the right. They gradually swung in a more northerly direction (pivoting on the Big Black) and moved within a few miles of the critical railroad without serious opposition. Then, on May 12, McPherson ran into stiff opposition south of the town of Raymond.[84] Aggressive assaults ordered by Confederate Brigadier General John Gregg, who believed he was facing a single brigade, threw McPherson's soldiers into disarray. Strong counterattacks led by Logan drove the outnumbered Confederates back into and through Raymond. Gregg's aggressiveness cost him one hundred dead, 305 wounded and 415 missing, for a total of 820 casualties. McPherson reported his casualties as sixty-six killed, 339 wounded, and thirty-seven missing, for a total of 442. Grant's campaign of maneuver and his concentration of force were resulting in progress at the cost of moderate casualties.[85]

Even more importantly, Grant's daring crossing of the Mississippi and inland thrust were sowing confusion at the highest levels of the Confederacy. Pemberton, in command at Vicksburg, was caught between conflicting orders from President Jefferson Davis and his department commander, General Joseph Johnston. Davis told Pemberton that holding Vicksburg and Port Hudson was critical to connecting the eastern Confederacy to the Trans-Mississippi. The Northern-born Pemberton, who had been eased out of his Charleston, South Carolina, command for suggesting evacuation of that city, decided to obey the president and defend Vicksburg at all costs. He did this despite orders on May 1 and 2 from Johnston that, if Grant crossed the Mississippi, Pemberton should unite all his troops to defeat him. Grant was the beneficiary of Pemberton's decision, because Pemberton kept his fifteen brigades in scattered defensive positions behind the Big Black River while Grant moved away from them toward Jackson. Meanwhile Johnston, sitting in Tullahoma, Tennessee, with little to do, moved to oppose Grant only when belatedly ordered to do so by Davis and Secretary of War James A. Seddon on May 9—and he did so with only three thousand troops at first.[86]

## CAPTURING JACKSON, THE STATE CAPITAL

The battle at Raymond caused Grant to realize the seriousness of the Confederate threat to his right flank—and then to his rear—if he simply continued north to the railroad and then turned west toward Vicksburg. He had received reports that General Johnston had arrived in Jackson and that reinforcements from the east and south were headed for that town. Jackson was the obvious rail junction for Confederate troops and supplies headed for Vicksburg. Thus, Grant decided to attack the capital, eliminating the troops there as a threat to his Vicksburg campaign. On the evening of May 12, therefore, he issued orders for McPherson to move on Clinton (on the railroad ten miles west of Jackson) and then on to Jackson and for Sherman to move on Jackson from the southwest through Raymond. They carried out their orders on the 13th and threatened Jackson by nightfall.[87]

In accordance with orders from Seddon that Johnston had initially protested on grounds of illness, Johnston arrived at Jackson that evening. Advised by Gregg that Union troops were astride the railroad to Vicksburg, that only six thousand Confederate troops were in the vicinity of Jackson, and that Confederate reinforcements were on the way (which he already knew), Johnston hoped to assemble twelve thousand troops at Jackson within a day and trap Grant between Pemberton's force and his. To accomplish this, he sent three couriers with messages directing Pemberton to organize a converging attack and, if practicable, to attack the Federal troops at Clinton. "Time is all important," he stressed. Johnston concluded a concurrent telegram to Seddon, "I am too late." In light of Grant's initiative and Pemberton's hesitance to carry out Johnston's order or abandon Vicksburg, Johnston was indeed too late.[88] Partly because Grant's spy network had advised him of Johnston's arrival and plans for reinforcement, Grant did not hesitate to continue his expedited offensive.[89]

Because of Grant's concentration of force at Jackson and despite torrential downpours, his troops were able to drive the Confederates from Jackson in less than a day of battle on May 14.[90] McPherson fought his way in from the west and Sherman from the southwest, occupying the city by mid-afternoon. Jackson cost the Union forty-two killed, 251 wounded, and seven missing (a total of 299 casualties), while the Confederates suffered an estimated five hundred casualties and the loss of seventeen cannon. Confederate industrial losses in Jackson were substantial. Johnston himself burned all the city's cotton and five million dollars in railroad rolling stock. Sherman followed up by burning an arsenal, foundries, machine shops, and cotton factories and warehouses. During the assault, Grant had used McClernand to protect his western exposure against an attack by Pemberton that never came. Pemberton spent the day probing southeast of Vicksburg for Grant's almost non-existent line of communication with Grand Gulf, and Johnston retreated from Jackson to the north away from Pemberton's movement. Even worse for the rebels, Johnston turned back reinforcements that were moving toward Jackson by rail.[91]

Learning from McPherson that one of Johnston's three couriers carrying his May 12 "attack" message to Pemberton was a Union spy, Grant immediately turned his army westward to deal with Pemberton. He ordered McClernand to Bolton Station, about twenty miles west of Jackson and the point on the railroad nearest to Jackson where Johnston might merge his and Pemberton's forces. He also ordered McPherson to move swiftly west along the railroad and ordered Sherman to destroy the railroads[92] and enemy property in and around Jackson. These actions were all accomplished without delay on May 15, and Grant at last was prepared to march directly toward Vicksburg.[93]

## CHAMPION'S HILL AND THE BIG BLACK RIVER

At five in the morning on May 16, Grant learned from two railroad workers that Pemberton was moving toward him with about twenty-five thousand troops. The actual number was twenty-three thousand. Grant immediately sent Sherman orders to cease his destructive work at Jackson and move hastily west to join him, McClernand, and McPherson. Pemberton, meanwhile, having wasted his time on the southward movement to cut off Grant from his Grand Gulf base, had finally decided to obey his orders from Johnston and move east toward Jackson to confront Grant. Pemberton occupied a strong defensive position at Champion's Hill, astride the Vicksburg and Jackson Railroad, the main road between the two towns, and two parallel roads. Pemberton's men, however, were exhausted from their confused handling on the 15th, while Grant's troops had been efficiently moved into a threatening position.[94]

At the May 16 Battle of Champion's Hill, the thirty-two thousand troops in McPherson's and McClernand's corps moved against twenty-three thousand Confederate defenders. Pushing his Thirteenth Corps ahead on the Raymond Road and the Middle Road, a parallel road to the north, McClernand encountered Confederate troops who were linked by a connecting road. Uncertainty dogged the Confederate troops as word spread of General Pemberton's belated decision, made that morning, to attempt to disengage from the enemy and move northeast to join Johnston. This decision (his third different strategic decision in three days as he tried to figure out what Grant was doing) came too late, and the armies were soon locked in battle.[95]

After the initial blocking action on the Raymond and Middle Roads, Pemberton gave orders for some infantry to follow his wagon train back toward Vicksburg, away from the conflict, and eventually to turn northeast and link up with Johnston. He soon discovered a new Federal threat, however, which caused him to cancel that order. Coming in from the east farther north on the Jackson Road and angling toward Champion's Hill and a crucial crossroads intersection with the Middle Road was McPherson's Seventeenth Corps. Pemberton had no choice but to attempt to block their march as well as McClernand's.[96]

Under Grant's oversight and McPherson's control, Union soldiers launched a late morning assault on the north side of the battlefield. By early afternoon, they had taken Champion's Hill and gained control of Jackson Road west of the crossroads, cutting off one of Pemberton's two escape routes back toward Vicksburg. They had shattered one Confederate division and captured sixteen precious guns.[97] Seeing the north end of his line collapsing, Pemberton ordered reinforcements from his right. Despite their reluctance, Generals Bowen and William Wing Loring, who faced McClernand on the south end of the lines, at last ordered two of their brigades to march north toward the crossroads. At 2:30 that afternoon, those veteran Arkansas and Missouri brigades launched a furious assault on the Union soldiers who only recently had taken control at the crossroads. The two rebel brigades drove the Yankees out of the crossroads and beyond the crest of Champion's Hill.[98]

Grant and McPherson organized yet another attack to regain the lost ground. As at Belmont, Donelson, and Shiloh, Grant took charge at a critical moment and turned adversity into victory. He said, "[Brigadier General Alvin P.] Hovey's division and [Colonel George] Boomer's brigade are good troops. If the enemy has driven them he is not in good plight himself. If we can go in here and make a little showing, I think he will give way." Led by a newly arrived division of McPherson's corps, the Federals made that "little showing" and drove the stubborn rebels off Champion's Hill and out of the crossroads. To ensure the success of this counterattack, Grant even recalled the advance troops that blocked the Jackson Road toward Vicksburg. The success of the Union counterattack was aided by Loring's additional delay in reinforcing Pemberton with troops from the right wing—apparently due to an ongoing dispute between Pemberton and Loring.[99]

With Union forces pressing them all along the front and only one retreat route open (the Raymond Road that McClernand still had not blocked), Bowen's and Major General Carter L. Stevenson's divisions fled southwest to the Raymond Road and then westward across the Big Black River. Loring's division, covering the retreat, was cut off by an Indiana battery (part of McClernand's corps) that had pursued fleeing rebels west on the Jackson Road and then had cut across the countryside to get to the Raymond Road. Unable to get his seven thousand men across Bakers Creek and back to Pemberton, Loring abandoned his twelve guns (which Union soldiers retrieved the next day) and headed toward Jackson. By the time he joined Johnston at Jackson, Loring's force had melted to four thousand.[100] The Battle of Champion's Hill involved about three hours of skirmishing and four hours of fierce fighting on Grant's center and right. Aggressive assaults by McPherson's corps had compelled a Confederate retreat, but McClernand's failure to advance aggressively on the left first allowed Confederate reinforcements to be sent against McPherson and later permitted many of the hard-pressed rebels to flee back to the Big Black River. Instead of pushing forward on his front, McClernand sought reinforcements from the already engaged Union forces on the center and right of the battlefield—a request Grant vetoed. Although Grant was on the offensive throughout the battle and attained his goal of pushing the enemy back toward Vicksburg, the numbers of his dead and wounded were remarkably similar to his enemy's: both sides had about four hundred killed and 1,800 wounded, but Grant's two hundred missing paled alongside the Confederates' 1,700 missing. In addition, Grant captured thirty pieces of artillery and cut off Loring's division from the rest of Pemberton's army.[101]

This battle, which James R. Arnold says was "arguably the decisive encounter of the war," eliminated the possibility of escape by Pemberton's army and cleared the way for the siege of Vicksburg. While Pemberton had kept 40 percent of his troops behind the Big Black River, Grant had pressed forward with all available troops, gaining a decisive three-to-two advantage in manpower. Grant later described the military significance of the victory: "We were now assured of our position between Johnston and Pemberton, without a possibility of a junction of their forces."[102]

The demoralized Confederates having moved back to the Big Black River, Grant sent word to the trailing Sherman to take his Fifteenth Corps northwest and cross that river at Bridgeport, flanking Pemberton's troops. But before Sherman could arrive on their flank, the Confederates had been beaten again. At the Big Black River in front of Grant, the Confederates again had a respectable defensive position from which to confront Grant's assault. Inexplicably, however, they built a parapet of cotton bales and dirt on the east side of the river instead of on the higher ground west of the river, failing to take full advantage of the river's defensive potential during the brief battle that ensued. Pemberton kept his men east of the river, hoping that Loring was going to show up and need protection crossing. In his over-commitment to the east bank, Pemberton withdrew all the artillery horses to the west bank, making withdrawal of those guns east of the river difficult or impossible.[103]

On the morning of May 17, Grant's troops arrived near the river and came under fire as the Battle of the Big Black River began.[104] A brigade of Iowa and Wisconsin troops scurried under fire to an old river meander scar near the center of the battlefield, from which they launched a dramatic three-minute charge through a swamp and abatis (an obstacle of cut trees with sharp points aimed at attackers) and broke the Confederate lines—to the shock of everyone on the field. They captured many startled defenders while the rest of the rebels east of the deep river started a major "skedaddle." A few tried to swim across the river, while most scrambled back across two "bridges" (one being a converted steamboat), which the Confederates then burned behind them as they fled to Vicksburg. Although the bridge-burning prevented Grant's immediate pursuit across the high river, fast-moving Union troops trapped at least a thousand Confederates on the east side of the river. Grant captured those soldiers, eighteen guns, and the last obstacle between his army and Vicksburg—at the small cost of thirty-nine killed, 237 wounded, and three missing.[105]

Just before the battle began, an officer from General Banks's staff had arrived with a letter to Grant from General in Chief Halleck, dated May 11, ordering Grant to return to Grand Gulf and cooperate with General Banks in capturing Port Hudson. Grant told the startled officer he was too late and that Halleck would not have given the order if he had known Grant's current position. The next day, May 18, Grant crossed the Big Black and met Sherman, who had crossed miles above as planned. They rode together hastily toward their long-sought position on the Yazoo River northeast of Vicksburg, where they could establish a base for supplies moved upriver from the Mississippi.[106] In his memoirs, Grant remembered the moment of elation he shared with Sherman:

> In a few minutes Sherman had the pleasure of looking down from the spot coveted so much by him the December before on the ground where his command had lain so helpless for offensive action. He turned to me, saying that up to this minute he had felt no positive assurance of success. This, however, he said was the end of one of the greatest campaigns in history and I ought to make a report of it at once. Vicksburg was not yet captured, and there was no telling what might happen before it was taken; but whether captured or not, this was a complete and successful campaign.[107]

As Grant approached Vicksburg, he could look back on the past eighteen successful days with satisfaction. He had entered enemy territory against a superior force and with no secure supply-line, fought and won five battles, severely damaged the Mississippi capital, driven away Johnston's relief force, driven Pemberton's army back into Vicksburg, inflicted over seven thousand casualties (killed, wounded, and missing) on the enemy, separated Loring's seven thousand troops from the main enemy army, and reduced Pemberton's army by fourteen thousand troops. Grant's own casualties were between 3,500 and 4,500. Ed Bearss summarizes the greatness of Grant's campaign to that point:

> During these 17 days, Grant's army had maneuvered and fought while dependent upon a dangerously exposed and tenuous supply line, and the men lived in part off the country. Union losses during this period had been about 3,500 officers and men. Students of history up to that time had to go back to the campaigns of Napoleon to find equally brilliant results accomplished in the same space of time *with such corresponding small losses.*[108]

## ASSAULTING AND BESIEGING VICKSBURG

Wasting no time, Grant immediately moved on Vicksburg with all three of his corps and ordered the first assault at 2 p.m. on the 19th. Riding the momentum of his string of successes, Grant wanted to catch the defenders before they had an opportunity to fully organize. Although that assault tightened the noose around the town and gave Grant's troops covered and advanced positions, the Union's nine hundred casualties (to the rebels' two hundred) indicated that capture of the town by assault would be difficult. Nevertheless, Grant decided on a second assault. Johnston's army threatened in his rear, and Grant wanted to avoid bringing in reinforcements. His soldiers, moreover, believed they could carry the town's fortifications, and he wanted to give them an opportunity to try. On May 22, all three corps launched simultaneous attacks but were repulsed. In response to dubious claims of success by McClernand, Grant sent him reinforcements and continued attacks elsewhere. These assaults failed, however, and left Grant with 3,200 casualties to the defenders' five hundred. So Grant settled in for a siege.[109]

In his memoirs, Grant expressed his regrets for the May 22 assault but explained his reasons for doing so:

> We were in a Southern climate, at the beginning of the hot season. The Army of the Tennessee had won five successive victories over the garrison of Vicksburg in the three preceding weeks.... The Army of the Tennessee had come to believe that they could beat their antagonist under any circumstances. There was no telling how long a regular siege might last. As I have stated, it was the beginning of the hot season in a Southern climate. There was no telling what the casualties might be among Northern troops working and living in trenches, drinking surface water filtered through rich vegetation, under a tropical sun. If Vicksburg would have been carried in May, it would not only have saved the army the risk it ran of a greater danger than from the bullets of the enemy, but it would have given us a splendid army, well equipped and officered, to operate elsewhere with.[110]

General Fuller pointed out that Grant had seven reasons to attack rather than simply besiege Vicksburg: (1) Johnston was gathering an army in his rear, (2) a quick victory would allow Grant to attack Johnston, (3) Union reinforcements would be required to perfect the siege, (4) the troops were impatient to take Vicksburg, (5) the weather was getting hotter, (6) water was scarce, and (7) the men were not anxious to dig entrenchments. Although he has been criticized in hindsight for initiating the May 22 assault, Grant had sufficient reasons to justify his attempt to take the town by assault. Even though his casualties that day were five hundred killed and 2,550 wounded, Grant's casualties in the three prior weeks of fighting had been a mere seven hundred killed and 3,400 wounded. Cumulatively, these casualties were a fair price to pay for having struck at the heart of the Western Confederacy and trapping a thirty-thousand-man army in the citadel on the Mississippi, the capture of which would culminate in an extraordinarily significant Union victory.[111]

From afar, Robert E. Lee gave President Davis some belated advice on the Vicksburg situation and paid a tribute to Grant's speedy execution of his campaign. On May 28, barely more than a week after downplaying Grant's chances for success in Mississippi, Lee revealed a fresh-found concern. He wrote, "I am glad to hear that the accounts from Vicksburg continue encouraging—I pray & trust that Genl Johnston may be able to destroy Grant's army—I fear if he cannot attack soon, he will become too strong in his position—No time should ever be given them to fortify. *They work so fast.*"[112]

After the May 22 attack on Vicksburg, Grant had his troops dig in for a sustained siege. They dug trenches and protected them with sandbags and logs while Union sharpshooters kept the besieged defenders from interfering with the construction. With only four engineering officers in his army, Grant directed every West Point graduate to supervise the siege line construction. With Johnston assembling an "Army of Relief," consisting of thirty-one thousand troops from all over the South, to trap him, Grant received reinforcements of his own from Missouri, Tennessee, and Kentucky. His army grew from fifty-one thousand to seventy-seven thousand. As reinforcements arrived, Grant used them to cut off all communication out of Vicksburg south along the Mississippi, secure the countryside back to the Big Black River, and destroy bridges across that river, protecting his army from attack by Johnston's force from the east.[113]

Grant's gambling campaign left him somewhat vulnerable to a Confederate counterattack between May 22 and June 8, when the first division of Union reinforcements arrived. During that interval, Grant had about fifty-one thousand troops sandwiched between Pemberton's 29,500 and Johnston's 22,000 (30,000 by June 3). But between Johnston's temerity and the lack of Confederate coordination, Grant was spared an attack.

In Virginia, Lee learned that Grant had reached the Yazoo and optimistically speculated, "The enemy may be drawing to the Yazoo for the purpose of reaching their transports and retiring from the contest, which I hope is the case." As Kenneth P. Williams notes, "Grant's persistence during the winter and his brilliant campaign behind Vicksburg had taught Lee nothing about the character of the soldier he would a year later have to face."[114] More importantly to Grant, his president recognized the greatness of what he had accomplished. On May 26 Lincoln wrote, "Whether Gen. Grant shall or shall not consummate the capture of Vicksburg, his campaign from the beginning of this month up to the twenty second day of it, is one of the most brilliant in the world."[115]

As Grant's troops advanced their lines, particularly on the eight roads into Vicksburg, he at last found a means of ridding himself of the conniving McClernand. McPherson and Sherman read in Northern newspapers that McClernand had issued a congratulatory order to his troops that effectively disparaged their troops. The offended generals complained to Grant, who relieved McClernand of command on June 18 for publishing unapproved orders. When McClernand received the relief order, he exclaimed "Well, sir, I am relieved," and then, noting a hint of satisfaction on the delivering officer's face, he added, "By God, sir, we are both relieved!" Major General Edward Ord replaced McClernand as corps commander.[116]

On June 22, Grant learned that some of Johnston's cavalry had crossed the Big Black River and now threatened his rear. Grant immediately put Sherman in charge of the half of his army protecting against such an attack and readied other forces to reinforce Sherman if needed. With thirty thousand men and seventy-two guns, Sherman's "Army of Observation" guarded all of the Big Black River crossings. Johnston backed off. He may have been reluctant to attack Grant because Union scout and double-agent Charles Bell had personally told Johnston that Grant had eighty-five thousand troops (an exaggeration of more than twenty thousand at the time). Bell also had reported more accurately to Grant on Johnston's own strength and disposition.[117]

On June 25 and July 1, Union troops exploded mines in tunnels they had dug under the Confederate lines. Although these explosions did not afford the besiegers an opportunity to enter the city, they did force the defenders to further constrict their lines. For forty-seven days, the Confederate forces and Vicksburg residents were subjected to continuous Union fire from ships and shore that may have totaled eighty-eight thousand shells and killed perhaps twenty civilians. With deserters reporting that morale and food supplies were running low in Vicksburg and with his trenches having been advanced as far as possible, Grant planned an all-out assault for July 6. Ironically, Johnston had chosen that same date for his own long-delayed assault on Grant.[118]

For six weeks, Grant's soldiers dug day and night in order to advance their lines, set off explosions beneath the rebel defenses, and improve their prospects for a final assault. Grant rejected some officers' views that another assault should have been launched before the one planned for July 6. After May 22, the siege of Vicksburg was a relatively bloodless one for Grant's army, even though a siege is usually costlier for the besiegers than the defenders. Between May 23 and July 3, 104 of Grant's men were killed, 419 wounded, with seven missing, while they killed more than 805 and wounded more than 1,938 of the enemy, of whom at least 129 were missing.[119]

## CONFEDERATE SURRENDER

With the noose tightening and food running low, Pemberton finally relented. On the morning of July 3, he raised white flags and sent out a pair of officers to arrange an armistice during which capitulation terms could be negotiated. Rejecting that proposal, "Unconditional Surrender" Grant wrote to Pemberton, "The useless effusion of blood you propose stopping by this course can be ended at any time you may choose, by the unconditional surrender of the city and garrison."[120]

That afternoon Grant and Pemberton met to discuss the possibility of the latter's surrender. Although they could not agree on terms, Grant promised to send a letter that night giving final terms. In that letter he proposed paroling, instead of imprisoning, Pemberton's soldiers. Grant apparently made that concession, which Pemberton had requested, to save Union transportation resources and to encourage desertions by the freed and demoralized rebel troops. In fact, Pemberton's signalmen had decoded Porter's signals to Grant that he lacked adequate vessels to transport almost thirty thousand prisoners to the North, so Pemberton held out for parole rather than imprisonment. Grant had little choice in the matter. Pemberton accepted Grant's offer of parole, and his July 4 surrender of his 29,500-man army (along with 172 guns and sixty thousand rifles)[121] made the national holiday a memorable one for the North—especially in conjunction with Lee's defeat at Gettysburg on July 1–3. As a result of Vicksburg's fall, the Confederate commander at Port Hudson surrendered his six thousand soldiers to Banks on July 9, thereby relinquishing the last Confederate position on the Mississippi.[122]

Grant's decision to parole Pemberton's men placed a burden on the South to support them—even though hundreds of Confederates declined to be paroled and elected Union prison camp rather than face the possibility of fighting again. Thousands were ill and hardly able to move. Thousands of others spoke with their feet and headed home never to fight again. Faced with a disaster and having no weapons to enforce his orders, Pemberton gave his entire army a thirty-day furlough, which President Davis countermanded. Pemberton switched to staggered furloughs—after which most of his soldiers did not reappear to be exchanged for Union prisoners captured elsewhere. The deserting troops became a public safety hazard throughout Mississippi, and Pemberton ordered railroad depot guards to shoot them if they did not leave trains on which they had swarmed to return home.[123] Unfortunately for the Union, several thousand Confederates violated their paroles and later resumed fighting even though they had not been exchanged under the terms of their paroles.

After the fall of Vicksburg, Grant sent Sherman back to Jackson to drive out Johnston and his troops and complete its destruction. As early as July 3, Grant had wired Sherman of the anticipated surrender and told him to "make your calculations to attack Johnston; destroy the railroad north of Jackson." The first of Sherman's fifty-thousand-man force left their lines east of Vicksburg on July 5, approaching Jackson in three prongs by July 9. Besieged and bombarded, Johnston evacuated Jackson on July 16 and retreated to middle Alabama. By July 19 Sherman had advanced twelve miles east of Jackson to Brandon. Sherman's first successful independent command completed its mission by destroying all railroads within fifty miles of Jackson as well as what little of value remained in that unfortunate town.[124] From May 1 at Port Gibson through the mid-July return to Jackson, the Union offensive of Grant and Banks resulted in the fall of Vicksburg, Port Hudson, and Jackson, as well as the capture of 241 guns in Grant's campaign and another fifty-one at Port Hudson—all at a cost of one-third the losses suffered by the Confederates. Grant's and Banks's battlefield casualties (killed, wounded, missing, or captured) totaled 14,846 while the Confederate casualties were 47,625. Of the 2,153 captured Confederate officers, fifteen were generals.[125]

The casualty ratio for Grant's Vicksburg campaign alone is even more impressive. His troops suffered 9,400 casualties while inflicting more than 40,000 on the enemy. At Vicksburg they captured an astounding sixty thousand rifles, mostly excellent British Enfields the rebels had imported.[126] Considering that Grant was on the offensive, that he achieved his strategic goals, and that the defenders should have had a tactical advantage, his 1:4 casualty ratio is an amazing tribute to his generalship.

## LEGACY OF THE VICKSBURG CAMPAIGN

Thus ended the greatest campaign of the war. As Hattaway and Jones write, "Grant succeeded because his superb campaign had embodied all of the elements that had made for Napoleon's victories—distraction, a penetration to threaten communications and turn the enemy, and the use of interior lines."[127] One third of the Confederacy had been severed, and its main armies and population centers were denied horses and food from Texas and elsewhere west of the Mississippi. The river was free for the transport of Union troops and resumed its role as a highway for transporting crops from the Midwest. The Union controlled the Mississippi Valley, and the states of Louisiana, Texas, Arkansas, Mississippi, and Alabama were no longer major arenas in the war.[128]

Grant's plan for the Vicksburg campaign was daring. He had to proceed rapidly to avoid being crushed between two Confederate forces, abandoning his supply line and living off the land until he had a secure position on the Mississippi near Vicksburg. He was directly involved all the way as his army crossed the river, fought and won five battles in eighteen days, twice drove the rebels from Jackson, trapped a thirty-thousand-man army in Vicksburg, and accepted the surrender of the besieged city and army.

"The country had at last the military hero for which it had longed, and Grant's name was on every lip," writes Allan Nevins.[129] The hero of Vicksburg was promoted to major general in the regular army, the nation's highest military rank at that time.[130] (Previously he had been a major general of volunteers, a wartime-only position.) Lincoln, who obviously had been following Grant's activities closely, sent him one of the most memorable letters of congratulation ever written by an American president to one of his commanders:

> Executive Mansion
> Major General Grant
> Washington, July 13, 1863
>
> My Dear General:
> I do not remember that you and I ever met personally. I write this now as a grateful acknowledgment for the almost inestimable service you have done the country. I wish to say a word further. When you first reached the vicinity of Vicksburg, I thought you should do, what you finally did—march the troops across the neck, run the batteries with the transports, and thus go below; and I never had any faith, except in a general hope that you knew better than I, that the Yazoo Pass expedition, and the like, could succeed. When you got below and took Port Gibson, Grand Gulf and vicinity, I

thought you should go down the river and join Ge. Banks; and when you turned Northward East of the Big Black, I feared it was a mistake. I now wish to make the personal acknowledgment that you were right, and I was wrong.

Yours very truly
A. Lincoln[131]

While Lee's army of seventy-five thousand was losing twenty-three thousand of its men to death or injury (30 percent of his troops) in his disastrous Gettysburg campaign, Grant carried out his brilliant Vicksburg campaign with the loss of a mere 2,254 of his 29,373 troops (8 percent of his troops) killed or wounded at Champion's Hill and 3,052 of his 45,556 troops (7 percent of his troops) killed or wounded at Vicksburg itself.[132] For the entire campaign, Grant lost a total of only 9,362 (1,514 killed, 7,393 wounded, and 453 missing or captured). The Confederates opposing Grant lost almost forty-one thousand men (two thousand killed, five thousand wounded, and 33,718 captured.)[133]

The impact of the two campaigns on Confederate morale was crushing. In Richmond, the War Department clerk J. B. Jones wrote on July 8, "But, alas! we have sad tidings from the West. Gen. Johnston telegraphs from Jackson, Miss., that Vicksburg capitulated on the 4th inst. This is a terrible blow, and has produced much despondency." Absorbing the blows of Vicksburg, Port Hudson, and Gettysburg on July 28, the Confederate chief of ordnance, Josiah Gorgas, wrote in his diary, "Yesterday we rode on the pinnacle of success—today absolute ruin seems to be our portion. The Confederacy totters to its destruction."[134]

Although Brigadier General Grenville M. Dodge had obtained intelligence for Grant on the pre-campaign situation in Vicksburg itself and on the mid-campaign position and strength of Johnston,[135] Grant often moved without the full intelligence he would have liked. "During the campaign," writes Feis, "Grant showed that success was possible even without adequate intelligence as long as a commander maintained the offensive and refused to let inevitable uncertainty lead to paralysis. But he also demonstrated at times that there was no substitute for competent collection and use of information."[136]

Perhaps the keys to the campaign's success were, in Noah Andre Trudeau's words, Grant's "bold leadership and shrewd risk-taking" and that he "knew his objective and never lost sight of it."[137] Grant's campaign was noteworthy for its focus, deception, celerity, flexibility, maneuver, and cunning.[138] As Edwin C. Bearss, the master historian of Vicksburg, concludes, "The oft told story that Grant was a heedless, conscienceless butcherer, devoid of the skills associated with history's great captains is shown by the Vicksburg Campaign to be a shallow canard."[139]

## GRANT'S WINNING CHARACTERISTICS

Ulysses Grant won the Civil War. He was responsible for a large percentage of all major Union victories in the Western, Middle, and Eastern theaters.

What made him such a successful general? As T. Harry Williams writes, "The qualities of Grant's generalship deserve more analysis than those of Lee, partly because they have not been sufficiently emphasized but largely because Grant was a more modern soldier than his rival."[140] Here is a look at Grant's winning characteristics.

### MODESTY

Grant's modesty was a distinguishing trait. One of his acquaintances described him as "a man who could remain silent in several languages." Adam Badeau, his military secretary, discussed Grant's mix of humility and decisiveness:

> Not a sign about him suggested rank or reputation or power. He discussed the most ordinary themes with apparent interest, and turned from them in the same quiet tones, and without a shade of difference in his manner, to decisions that involved the fate of armies, as if great things and small were to him of equal moment. In battle, the sphinx awoke. The

outward calm was even then not entirely broken; but the utterance was prompt, the ideas were rapid, the judgment was decisive, the words were those of command. The whole man became intense, as it were, with a white heat.[141]

## LUCID ORDERS

Unlike Lee[142] and many other generals on both sides, Grant wrote orders that were lucid and unambiguous—even when issued in the heat of battle.[143] General Meade's chief of staff commented that "there is one striking feature of Grant's orders; no matter how hurriedly he may write them on the field, no one ever has the slightest doubt as to their meaning, or even has to read them over a second time to understand them."[144] Horace Porter described Grant's drafting a flurry of orders after his arrival at Chattanooga: "His work was performed swiftly and uninter-ruptedly, but without any marked display of nervous energy. His thoughts flowed as freely from his mind as the ink from his pen; he was never at a loss for an expression, and seldom interlined a word or made a material correction."[145] "Historians have always regarded Grant's orders as some of the clearest in the war, rarely leaving room for misunderstanding or misinterpretation," writes R. Steven Jones, citing evidence that Grant often wrote his own orders because that was quicker than explaining to someone else what he wanted to say.[146]

Grant's orders were lucid because they were simple. His oral and written orders set goals, leaving the means to the discretion of his sub-ordinates. "Better than any Civil War general, Grant recognized the battlefield was in flux," writes Jean Edward Smith. "By not specifying movements in detail, he left his subordinate commanders free to exploit whatever opportunities developed."[147] That approach reflected Grant's willingness to delegate discretionary authority to Sherman, Sheridan, Meade, and other subordinates.

## TOPOGRAPHICAL MEMORY

James McPherson attributes to Grant a "topographical memory." He "could remember every feature of the terrain over which he traveled, and find his way over it again; he could also look at a map and visualize the features of terrain he had never seen.... Grant could see in his mind the disposition of troops over thousands of square miles, visualize their relationship to roads and terrain, and know how and where to move them to take advantage of topography."[148]

Grant's subordinate Horace Porter recalled that "it was always noticeable in a campaign how seldom he consulted [maps], compared with the constant examination of them by most other prominent commanders. The explanation of it is that he had an extraordinary memory as to anything that was presented to him graphically. After looking critically at a map of a locality, it seemed to become photographed indelibly upon his brain, and he could follow its features without referring to it again."[149]

## USE OF STAFF

Grant made excellent use of his staff. While the members of Lee's staff, mainly lieutenant colonels, were not much more than glorified clerks, Grant's staff, which ultimately included some generals, "was an organization of experts in the various phases of strategic planning."[150] A prime example of an excellent staff officer is Horace Porter, Grant's aide-de-camp beginning in the spring of 1864, who served as his personal emissary to Sherman in Georgia in late 1864 and advised him in selecting the commander for the successful assault on Fort Fisher, North Carolina. Porter, who served Grant until 1872, described his commander as "direct, open, intelligent, offensiveminded, dedicated, and having 'singular mental powers which are rare military qualities.'"[151] Porter also pointed out that Grant "studiously avoided performing any duty which some one else could do as well or better than he, and in this respect demonstrated his rare powers of administration and executive methods."[152]

R. Steven Jones's exhaustive analysis of Civil War generals' use of personal staffs shows that Porter was just one of several military professionals Grant used effectively on his personal staff—particularly in the second half of the war. By the time of the Overland Campaign, Grant's staff had progressed from a "civilian staff" to an "accidental staff" to a "professional staff." As early as Shiloh, one of Grant's aides was positioning artillery, another herding troops to the right area, and two others trying to get Lew Wallace's division into the fight. Throughout the Overland Campaign, Grant frequently sent members of his personal staff as his emissaries and even as his alter egos to far sectors of the battlefield and to other theaters, such as Georgia. Jones concludes that only Grant among Civil War generals took the lead in expanding the duties of personal staff and that he developed something close to the Prussian system of delegation of responsibility.[153] Summarizing Grant's role as a commonsense innovator in the use of staff, Jones writes:

> In Grant, all of the factors compatible with staff advancement came together: large armies, cooperative operations, and a willingness to experiment with staff improvements. Grant was not a staff reformer; he was a competent, intelligent general looking for more efficient ways to fight a complicated war. As such, he spent no time talking or writing about staff work. He did not promote his innovations as a model for the whole United States Army. He simply found a creative way to use an organizational element available to all Civil War generals—the personal staff—and made it his right hand of command.[154]

## PERSEVERANCE

Perseverance, including a disinclination to retrace his steps, was an important aspect of Grant's character. He displayed it at Vicksburg when he launched his daring campaign across the Mississippi south of Vicksburg instead of returning to Memphis to start another overland campaign from the north. During that campaign, James R. Arnold observes, Grant "accepted war's uncertainty by flexibly adjusting to new circumstances while maintaining a determined focus on the main chance."[155]

Again, in 1864–65, Grant demonstrated his perseverance (Gordon Rhea calls it "persistence") as he carried out his campaign of adhesion against Lee's Army of Northern Virginia, achieving all his goals within a year.[156] As he explained in his official reports, "The battles of the Wilderness, Spotsylvania, North Anna, and Cold Harbor, bloody and terrible as they were on our side, were even more damaging to the enemy, and so crippled him as to make him wary ever after of taking the offensive."[157] That comment was typical of Grant's "refusal to treat reverses as defeats."[158] Arnold sums up Grant's determination and focus throughout the war: "Grant was a simple man who dealt with the facts as he found them. While his contemporaries saw war in all its complexities and too often took counsel of their fears, from Belmont to Appomattox Grant saw the main chance, stuck to it, and thus led his armies to victory."[159]

## FULL USE OF SUPERIOR UNION RESOURCES

Grant's effective recognition and deployment of the North's superior resources distinguished him from McClellan and Halleck and most other Union generals. Gary Gallagher writes, "The North always enjoyed a substantial edge in manpower and almost every manufacturing category, but none of Grant's predecessors proved equal to the task of harnessing and directing that latent strength. Grant's ability to do so stands as one of his greatest achievements."[160] Arnold adds, "When he massed for battle he brought every available soldier to the field, sublimating those secondary considerations that so often consumed the attention and resources of weaker generals."[161]

By brilliantly concentrating his forces in each battle of the Vicksburg campaign, he negated the Confederates' overall numerical superiority in that theater. In fact, Grant was remarkable for fighting uncomplainingly with the soldiers he had on hand. "He rarely complained, never asked for reinforcements, and went ahead and did the job with whatever resources were available."[162] Unlike McClellan, Grant did not grossly exaggerate the strength of his opponents in an effort to secure reinforcements, excuse inaction, or justify a potential defeat.[163] Lincoln told his third secretary, "[Grant] doesn't ask me to do impossibilities for him, and he's the first general I've had that didn't."[164] When Grant did ask for more troops, he did so subtly, as when he wrote, "The greater number of men we have, the shorter and less sanguinary will be the war. I give this entirely as my views and not in any spirit of dictation—always holding myself in readiness to use the material given me to the best advantage I know how."[165]

## MINIMIZING SUPPORT PERSONNEL

The more successful Grant was in advancing into Confederate territory, consistent with the Union's strategic goals, the more manpower he needed to establish garrisons and provide logistical support for his front-line troops.[166] By late 1863 and in 1864, he decided to deal with this problem by conducting army-size raids with little or no logistical support, destroying the Confederate infrastructure, and reducing the need for garrisons and supply lines in his rear.[167] His efficiently moving against Vicksburg, sending Sherman on his Meridian campaign, approving Sherman's March to the Sea, and reducing the Washington, D.C., garrisons in 1864 all were consistent with this approach.

## FULLY USING ASSIGNED GENERALS

Although Grant became frustrated with generals he perceived as lacking timely aggressiveness and with incompetent political generals, he rehabilitated several Eastern generals who had been shipped west after less than glowing careers. Among these generals who served at least somewhat successfully under Grant were Joe Hooker, O. O. Howard, and Ambrose Burnside. In his powers of rehabilitation, Grant was superior to Lee, who "dumped" his less successful generals onto other theaters.[168]

## DECISIVENESS

Grant was decisive. Colonel James F. Rusling of the quartermaster general's staff recalled that in the winter of 1863–64, a quartermaster officer approached Grant for approval of millions of dollars of expenditures for the coming Atlanta campaign, and Grant approved the expenditure after briefly examining the papers involved. Questioning Grant's swift decision, the officer asked him if he was sure he was right. Grant replied, "No, I am not, but in war anything is better than indecision. *We must decide.* If I am wrong we shall soon find it out and can do the other thing. But *not to decide* wastes both time and money and may ruin everything."

In discussing Grant's influence on the usually victorious Army of the Tennessee, Steven E. Woodworth points to his prompt and decisive counterattack at Shiloh: "Perhaps in part at least it was not so much that Grant infused confidence into his army as that he refrained from destroying—by timid campaigning—the confidence of men who knew they had survived the worst the enemy had to throw at them."[169]

Grant's decisiveness paid off especially in the heat of battle. He learned as early as Belmont and Fort Donelson that in every battle there is a critical point when both armies are exhausted and "the one which can nerve itself for one more attack at such a time is very likely to win." Grant applied that lesson again at Shiloh, Champion's Hill, and Chattanooga.[170]

## MORAL COURAGE

Grant displayed what he himself called "moral courage." His friend William T. Sherman remarked, "But I tell you where he beats me, and where he beats the world. He don't care a damn for what the enemy does out of his sight.... He uses such information as he has, according to his best judgment. He issues his orders and does his level best to carry them out without much reference to what is going on about him."[171]

David Donald quotes an early analysis of Grant, written in 1908 by C. F. Atkinson: "Grant's distinguishing feature as a general...was his character, which was controlled by tremendous will; with Grant action was translated from thought to deed by all the force of a tremendous personality. This moral strength of Grant's may be news to some present-day historians, but it was overpoweringly apparent to all who were thrown into close association with him."[172]

As James McPherson points out, moral courage went beyond the physical courage that Grant and others had demonstrated while carrying out attacks in the Mexican War under the command of others:

This was a quality different from and rarer than physical courage.... Moral courage involved a willingness to make decisions and give the orders. Some officers who were physically brave shrank from this responsibility because decision risked error and initiative risked failure. This was George B. McClellan's defect as a commander; he was afraid to risk his army in an offensive because he might be defeated. He lacked the moral courage to act, to confront that terrible moment of truth, to decide and to risk.[173]

General Fuller said, "In the Vicksburg campaign Grant's moral courage has seldom been equaled, certainly seldom surpassed."[174] A subordinate, Major General Jacob D. Cox, said, "[Grant's] quality of greatness was that he handled great affairs as he would little ones, without betraying any consciousness that this was a great thing to do."[175] T. Harry Williams notes that Grant's approach was to "seek out the enemy and strike him until he is destroyed"—an approach that required "a tremendous will and a dominant personality."[176] Grant had both; he had character.

## POLITICAL COMMON SENSE

Unlike McClellan, Beauregard, Joseph Johnston, and many other Civil War generals, Grant made it his business to get along with his president. That cooperation included tolerating political generals—men like McClernand, Sigel, Banks, and Butler—until Grant had given them enough rope to hang themselves. T. Harry Williams cites Grant's handling of McClernand, a friend of Lincoln, as a prime example: "In this whole affair Grant showed that he realized the vital relation between politics and modern war."[177]

Grant's political instincts also kept him from "retreating" back up the Mississippi River to begin a fresh campaign against Vicksburg or moving back toward Washington after "setbacks" in the Overland Campaign. Such regressive moves, he knew, would provoke an unfavorable public reaction and damage the morale of his soldiers and the public.[178]

## FOCUS ON ENEMY ARMIES

Grant's recognition early in the war that he needed to defeat, capture, or destroy opposing armies, not simply occupy geographic positions, was critical to his success. At Fort Donelson, Vicksburg, and Richmond, Grant maneuvered his troops to capture enemy armies as well as to occupy important locations. He stood in stark contrast to McClellan, Hooker, Rosecrans, and Meade, who ignored Lincoln's admonitions to pursue and destroy enemy armies, as well as with Halleck, who was satisfied with his hollow capture of Corinth.[179]

## MANEUVERABILITY

Although he was consistently on the strategic offensive, Grant practiced the art of maneuver as much as possible. In his Vicksburg campaign, which Thomas Buell calls "the equivalent of a Second World War blitzkreig,"[180] he caught his adversaries completely off-guard, proving that he could be, in the words of Edwin Bearss, "daring and innovative."[181] At Chattanooga, he maneuvered on both of Bragg's flanks before the central attack on Missionary Ridge broke through. During his Overland Campaign, he maneuvered around Lee's right flank until he forced Lee back into the lethal partial siege at Richmond and Petersburg. As Jean Edward Smith writes,

> Grant's detaching a 115,000-man army from his foe and secretly crossing the James River was a perilous maneuver and an incredible tactical accomplishment, and it in no way diminishes Patton's accomplishment [in changing fronts during the Battle of the Bulge in 1944] to say that it pales alongside Grant's withdrawal from Cold Harbor and his crossing of the James in June 1864.[182]

The final word on this subject should go to General Fuller:

> Grant has gone down to history as a bludgeon general, a general who eschewed manoeuvre and who with head down,

seeing red, charged his enemy again and again like a bull: indeed an extraordinary conclusion, for no general, not excepting Lee, and few generals in any other war, made greater use of manoeuvre in the winning of his campaigns, if not of his battles. Without fear of contradiction, it may be said that Grant's object was consistent; strategically it was to threaten his enemy's base of operations, and tactically to strike at the rear, or, failing the rear, at a flank of his enemy's army.[183]

## INTELLIGENT AGGRESSIVENESS

Unlike most Union generals, Grant knew what had to be done—take advantage of the North's numerical superiority and invade and conquer the Confederacy—and he did it. "Better than any other Northern soldier," writes Bruce Catton, "better than any other man save Lincoln himself, [Grant] understood the necessity for bringing the infinite power of the growing nation to bear on the desperate weakness of the brave, romantic, and tragically archaic little nation that opposed it...."[184]

General Cox said, "[Grant] reminds one of Wellington in the combination of lucid and practical common-sense with aggressive bulldog courage."[185] Grant advanced aggressively and creatively, attacking with vigor but usually avoiding suicidal frontal attacks. In light of the large number of battles fought by his five winning armies, the total of ninety-four thousand killed and wounded (154,000 total casualties) suffered by his commands was surprisingly small—especially when compared to the 121,000 killed and wounded (209,000 total casualties) among the soldiers in one losing army commanded by Robert E. Lee.

In his study of Grant's use of military intelligence, William Feis disagrees with Sherman's conclusion that Grant did not "care a damn for what the enemy does out of his sight." After analyzing Grant's increasing use of intelligence throughout the war, Feis concludes, "In reality, he cared a great deal about what the enemy did on the 'other side of the hill,' but unlike Henry Halleck, George McClellan, or William Rosecrans, he refused to allow that concern to become an obsession in which the search for 'perfect' information became an end in itself, effectively stifling intuitive risk taking."[186]

## SUMMARY

Grant's modesty, lucid orders, topographical memory, full use of his staff, perseverance, full use of Union resources, minimizing support personnel, full use of assigned generals, decisiveness, moral courage, political common sense, focus on enemy armies, maneuverability, and intelligent aggressiveness all combined to make him the best general of the Civil War and to demolish the myth of "Grant the Butcher." Grant was one of the greatest generals in American history.

# CHAPTER EIGHT

# DID THE NORTH WIN BY WAGING "TOTAL WAR"?

## THE MYTH

The contention of some historians that the Civil War was the first modern "total war," setting the precedent for the murderous wars of the twentieth century, appears to be a new twist on the Myth of the Lost Cause. It implies that the Union prevailed by waging war of unethical scope and severity. "It was Lincoln, Grant, and the Civil War that incorporated total war into modern experience," asserts Charles Strozier. He adds that "the totality of the modern state seems to require unconditional surrender as a necessary correlative of its total wars. The American Civil War brought that into focus."[1]

The accusation of brutality in the Union armies' conquest of the South began right after the war. In 1866, Pollard contrasted the Yankees' behavior with that of Lee's army, which, he maintained, abided by its commander's order to protect the property that lay in the path of its Gettysburg campaign. "No house was entered without authority; no granary was pillaged; no property was taken without payment on the spot; and vast fields of grains were actually protected by Confederate guards...."[2] In fact, however, the rebels in Pennsylvania foraged extensively and confiscated livestock, transportation vehicles, and thousands of wagonloads of grains and produce—sufficient to constitute a fifteen-, twenty- or fifty-mile reserve train of wagons.[3] Confederate "payments" for property were made in essentially worthless Confederate currency, and as many as several hundred blacks were kidnapped and sent South into slavery.

By mid-1863, Pollard continued, Southerners were exasperated by "what they had experienced of the enemy's barbarities in their own homes," and some urged a due measure of retaliation by Lee's army in Pennsylvania. "[I]t was not advised that houses should be burned, or robbed, jewelry stolen, and women raped in Pennsylvania, in exact imitation of the acts of Northern troops in Virginia and Mississippi," but that "a devastation of the enemy's country" should be inflicted "to teach the enemy a lesson." Lee ignored such calls for vengeance, writes Pollard, who provided no evidence of or specifics about the alleged barbarity of the Union forces.[4]

Jefferson Davis leveled the charge of unconscionable brutality fifteen years later in his description of Colonel Benjamin Grierson's diversionary "raid from the northern border of Mississippi through the interior of the state." "Among the expeditions for pillage and arson," Davis charged, "this stands prominent for savage outrages against defenseless women and children, constituting a record alike unworthy [of] a soldier and gentleman."[5] Grierson's three cavalry regiments kept Mississippians on edge for perhaps seventeen days, caused General Pemberton to send thousands of troops to find and intercept them, diverted rebel attention away from Grant's movements (their main mission), and destroyed railroad tracks, stations, and rolling stock, but there is no record of "pillaging," and certainly not of attacking or molesting any civilians, let alone women and children. Nevertheless, Davis's little lie took root.

It is only fairly recently that the twentieth-century concept of "total war" has been applied to the Civil War. According to Mark E. Neely Jr., the term was first used in 1948 by John B. Walters in an article about Sherman for the *Journal of Southern History* and was quickly adopted by the famed Civil War historian T. Harry Williams. His masterly *Lincoln and His Generals* begins with the assertion: "The Civil War was the first of the modern total wars...."

Other prominent Civil War historians followed Williams down that path.[6] For example, in 1996 James M. McPherson commented that "by 1864 a group of generals including Grant, Sherman, and Sheridan had emerged to top commands in the North with a firm grasp on the need for coordinated offensives in all theaters, a concept of the 'total war' strategy necessary to win this conflict, the skill to carry out the strategy, and the relentless, even ruthless determination to keep pressing it despite a high cost of casualties until the South surrendered unconditionally."[7]

McPherson explains, "The kind of conflict the Civil War had become merits the label of total war. To be sure, Union soldiers did not set out to kill Southern civilians. Sherman's bummers destroyed property; Allied bombers in World War II destroyed hundreds of thousands of lives as well. But the strategic purpose of both was the same: to eliminate the resources and break the will of the people to sustain war."

## THE REALITY

The reality is that the North won by "hard war," not total war. Total war—defined by the wanton killing of massive numbers of civilians—has a long and brutal history. It was waged by Genghis Khan, Tamerlane, the Romans against the Carthaginians, Catholics and Protestants in Germany's Thirty Years War, Germans in the First and Second World Wars, and the Russians and Japanese in World War II. The Civil War simply does not belong in this category.

The methods, not the "strategic purpose," make a conflict a "total war." Unlimited, large-scale attacks on civilians—like those on London, Coventry, Dresden, Berlin, Tokyo, Hiroshima, Nagasaki, and countless other cities in World War II—are absent from the Civil War. If Sherman's bummers, on their March to the Sea, had executed large numbers of civilians, they could be accused of total warfare. But the intentions of eliminating enemy resources and breaking the will of its people, logical goals of virtually any war, do not make a war "total."

Most of the killings of civilians during the Civil War occurred in Missouri, Kansas, the Appalachian sections of many Confederate states, and Texas. They were generally carried out by civilians engaged in local guerilla warfare and not by organized military units. The worst was the execution of about 150 men and boys in Lawrence, Kansas, in 1863 by William Quantrill's pro-Confederate Raiders. Not long afterward, in 1864, Bloody Bill Anderson executed twenty-four unarmed Union soldiers pulled from a train, and he slaughtered 127 men in a pursuing militia posse, including the captured and wounded.[8]

Perhaps the most common killings of innocents by military units were the executions of surrendering or surrendered black Union troops and their officers in many places, including Fort Pillow,[9] Olustee (Florida), Milliken's Bend, Saltville (Virginia), the Crater, and Poison Springs (Arkansas).[10] Neither Confederate nor Union regular armies, however, engaged in large-scale campaigns that included the deliberate killing of innocent civilians. Civil War armies engaged in hard war—but not total war. The evidence deserves more detailed examination.

What did Sherman's army really do in Mississippi, Georgia, and the Carolinas in 1864–65? In early 1864, his army lived off the countryside in his Meridian Campaign, a "dress rehearsal" for the March to the Sea.[11] As they stormed through Georgia later that year, "sixty thousand Union troops destroyed railroads, torched cotton bales, emptied corncribs and smokehouses, and seized hogs, horses, and mules. Most significantly, [they] freed thousands and thousands of enslaved laborers along their path."[12] Sherman's large army was able to live off the country between Atlanta and Savannah because Sherman had studied an 1860 census report on the population, livestock, and agricultural production of each Georgia county he passed through. He later said, "No military expedition was ever based on sounder or surer data."[13]

His March to the Sea is described in the *Oxford Encyclopedia of the Civil War*:

Sherman's men were under orders to "forage liberally on the country during the march"—that is, to seize the food, fodder, and horses needed to sustain the army. Foraging parties organized daily in each regiment performed their tasks with a vengeance. Self-appointed or especially ruthless foragers, known as "bummers," were little more than ransacking thieves as they plundered the possessions of rich and poor, of slaves as well as their masters.... At a cost of just 2,000 casualties, Sherman's march across Georgia crippled much of the war-making potential and morale of the Confederacy. His army accounted for some $100 million in property damage as it brought the war home with frightening reality to Confederate civilians.[14]

The Lost Causer Pollard had to stretch the evidence to speculate that civilians were killed in the March to the Sea. He described massive damage to, or theft of, barns, crops, furniture, pianos, jewelry, beehives, sorghum barrels, and other property. Labeling Sherman's property destruction "savage warfare," Pollard continued, "If [a property owner] escaped, and was hiding in a thicket, this was *prima facie* evidence that he was a skulking rebel; and most likely some ruffian, in his zeal to get rid of such vipers, gave him a dose of lead, which cured him of his Secesh tendencies."[15] Not much there to support allegations of total war.

Sherman's army continued its destructive progress through the Carolinas in early 1865. His men particularly hated South Carolina, the birthplace of secession, and they probably destroyed more property there than anywhere else. The notorious burning of one-third of the capital city, Columbia,[16] was the combined work of evacuating Confederates burning large quantities of cotton in the streets, high winds blowing up, and drunken Union soldiers (before Sherman had them stopped). All these actions were consistent with Sherman's statements that "we are not only fighting hostile armies, but a hostile people" and must make them "feel the hard hand of war."

There are few reports of rapes or killings of civilians perpetrated by Sherman's army. A recent study by Lisa Frank of the relationship between his soldiers and Southern women excoriates the soldiers for entering bedrooms and parlors, as well as seizing personal treasures and letters, in an effort to humiliate and demoralize elite white women along their route. There is no mention of rape or murder.[17] Being caught in the path of Sherman's army was harrowing, but it was not total war.

What did Sheridan's troops do in the Shenandoah Valley in 1864–65? They burned barns, silos, crops, and some houses; they stripped the valley of livestock and foodstuffs that had been used to support Confederate troops throughout the war. There was no program to kill civilians, and, at most, only a few of them died. Two years later, Pollard harshly described Sheridan's destruction of agriculture: "Of this and other like atrocities of the enemy, there has been attempted a very weak excuse, to the effect that if the private property of the inhabitants of the Confederacy had not been destroyed, it might have been converted to the uses of the belligerent Government, and have helped to sustain it. Once for all, it may be said that this excuse excludes every sentiment of humanity in war, and may be logically carried to the last extremity of savage warfare."[18] Understatement was not a characteristic of Pollard's work; overstatement became a basis for myths.

Sherman's and Sheridan's destructive sweeps through the South occurred late in the conflict, when the North realized that it would have to wage "hard war" to win. Grant had realized after "Bloody Shiloh" in April 1862 that a decisive Union victory would not bring down the Confederate government without "complete conquest." In his memoirs he wrote, "Up to that time it had been the policy of our army, certainly of that portion commanded by me, to protect the property of the citizens whose territory was invaded.... After this, however, I regarded it as humane to both sides to protect the persons of those found at their homes, but to consume everything that could be used to support or supply armies.... [S]uch supplies within the reach of Confederate armies I regarded as much contraband as arms or ordnance stores. Their destruction was accomplished without bloodshed and tended to the same result as the destruction of armies.... Promiscuous pillaging, however, was discouraged and punished."[19] This policy—hard war, not total war—was followed with few exceptions for the balance of the war.

The North's approach to slavery exemplifies the movement toward hard war. Lincoln rejected appeals for emancipation for more than a year into the war. He made several offers of compensated emancipation to the Border States—Delaware, Kentucky, Maryland, and Missouri—to secure their continued allegiance to the Union. When the need for more Union soldiers and the need to deplete the labor force of the South outweighed the Border State concerns, the president issued his Preliminary Emancipation Proclamation in September 1862 and his final proclamation on January 1, 1863.

Even though Lincoln's emancipation of Southern slaves fulfilled his dual goals and was clearly intended "to eliminate the resources and break the will of the [Southern] people to sustain war," it was not an act of total war. It did result in an increasingly overwhelming loss of "property" by the Southern people and culminated in the Thirteenth Amendment, which Congress passed and sent to the states for ratification in January 1865. In tandem with Lincoln's anti-slavery moves, Congress passed two confiscation acts to deprive the enemy of property; the Confederate Congress passed similar legislation.

The Civil War was a "mighty scourge," as Lincoln called it, but despite the best efforts of the Myth-makers, it was not America's introduction to "total war." The mass killings of civilians that did take place were the work of Confederate sympathizers. War is not pretty, but claims that the Union waged total war are far from the mark.

# CHAPTER NINE

# CONCLUSION

T he Myth of the Lost Cause may have been the most successful propaganda campaign in American history. For almost 150 years it has shaped our view of the causation and fighting of the Civil War. As discussed in detail in prior chapters, the Myth was just that—a false concoction intended to justify the Civil War and the South's expending so much energy and blood in defense of slavery.

Contrary to the Myth, slavery was not a benign institution that benefitted whites and blacks alike. It was a cruel institution maintained by force, torture, and murder. It thrived on the exploitation of black labor and on the profits made from sales of surplus slaves. The latter practice resulted in the breaking up of black families and the absence of any contract of marriage between slaves. Masters' rapes of slaves resulted in additional profits, a whitening of the slave population, and white marital discord, which was "remedied" by idolization of white Southern womanhood.

Despite the stories of slaves' happiness and contentment, whites maintained militias because they were in constant fear of slave revolts and slave escapes. They also hired slave-catchers to capture and return runaway slaves—and also to snatch free blacks off the streets both North and South. The tens of thousands of prewar runaway slaves and the hundreds of thousands of slaves who fled to Union lines during the Civil War were a testament to slaves' dissatisfaction with their lives under the peculiar institution and their desire for freedom.

Many of the same people who argued that slavery was a prosperous and benevolent practice rather inconsistently contended that the Civil War was unnecessary because slavery was a dying institution, a proposition that became a classic component of the Myth. The historical record, however, belies this notion. The booming cotton-based economy, the rise in slave prices to an all-time high in 1860, the amount of undeveloped land in the South, and the expanding use of slaves in manufacturing and other agriculture-related industries all indicated that slavery was thriving and not about to expire. Southerners had only begun to make maximum use of their four- to six-billion-dollar slave property and were not about to relinquish voluntarily the most valuable property they owned. If slavery was a dying institution, why did Southern states complain about the possible loss of billions of dollars invested in slaves, fight for the expansion of slavery into the territories, cite the preservation of slavery as the reason for secession, claim that slavery was necessary to maintain white supremacy, and conduct the war in a manner that placed greater value on slavery and white supremacy than on Confederate victory?

In addition to the economic value of slavery, there was the social value to consider. The institution was based on white supremacy and provided the elite planter class with a means of mollifying the large majority of whites who were not slave-owners. In addition to aspiring to become slave-owners, these other whites could at least endure their low economic and social status by embracing their superiority to blacks in Southern society.

As of 1860, therefore, slavery was a thriving enterprise. It benefitted only whites, treated blacks in a sub-human manner, and promised to return great profits and social benefits for whites for years to come.

A primary tenet of the Myth is that slavery was not a primary cause of the Civil War—that war instead was brought about by a desire and clamor for states' rights. Late-war and postwar apologists for the Confederacy have consistently maintained that slavery had little or nothing to do with secession. Nothing could be further from the truth.

The United States had been embroiled in disputes over slavery ever since the Declaration of Independence and the U.S. Constitution were modified, at Southerners' insistence, to protect and preserve slavery. The Missouri Compromise of 1820, with its focus on slavery in the territories, was the first major indication that the North-South split on the issue was widening. During the 1830s, with the rise of abolitionism in the North, slave revolts (and perceived slave revolts) in the South, and the growth of the Underground Railroad to aid runaway slaves, sectional differences became more heated.

In the 1850s the pot boiled over. The multi-part Compromise of 1850 contained a strengthened fugitive slave provision that caused consternation and defiance in the North and then anger in the South when many Northerners flaunted it. Stephen Douglas's Kansas-Nebraska Act of 1854 voided the Missouri Compromise and opened all territories to the possibility of slavery. Northern reaction to that "popular sovereignty" law was so strong that a new Republican Party was formed to oppose any extension of slavery to the territories.

Guerilla warfare between pro- and anti-slavery settlers broke out in Missouri and Kansas. When President James Buchanan in 1857 supported a fraudulent pro-slavery Kansas territorial constitution, Douglas opposed him and split the Democratic party into Northern and Southern wings. Just days after Buchanan's 1857 inauguration, the Supreme Court issued its notorious *Dred Scott* decision. The Southern-dominated court said Congress could not prohibit slavery in any territories (as it had done in 1787, 1789, 1820, 1850, and 1854) and that blacks were not U.S. or state citizens and thus had no legal rights.

All these developments, along with the Lincoln-Douglas debates of 1858,[1] set the stage for the presidential election of 1860. Slavery in the territories was virtually the only issue in the race. Republican Lincoln wanted slavery in none of them, Southern Democrat John Breckinridge wanted slavery in all of them, Northern Democrat Douglas wanted the issue decided in each territory by popular sovereignty, and Unionist John Bell ducked the issue. Lincoln, of course, won. Despite his assurances that he would take no action against slavery where it existed, Lincoln was labeled an "abolitionist" by many Southern leaders. The seven states of the Deep South seceded before Lincoln took office.

The seceding states made their motives clear in many ways. The Southern press, congressmen, and state leaders railed against Lincoln's election because they believed they were going to lose the control of the federal government that they had held since 1789. The presidency had been dominated by Southern and Southern-sympathizing presidents (including Buchanan and Franklin Pierce in the 1850s), presidents had nominated Supreme Court justices sympathetic to slavery, and Southerners had consistently dominated Congress through seniority, the Constitution's "three-fifths" clause, and other means. Southerners were disturbed that a Republican central government would not aggressively support slavery, that Northern states would be better able to undermine the fugitive slave law, and that "free" states would eventually end slavery by amending the Constitution. It was not the concept of states' rights that was driving them to secession but the fear of losing control of the federal government and thus the ability to support slavery and compel Northern states to do so as well.

One clue that slavery was a cause of secession is found in the 1860 census, which shows that the seven states that seceded before Lincoln's inauguration had the highest numbers of slaves per capita and the highest percentage of family slave ownership of all the states. The four states of the Upper South that seceded after the firing on Fort Sumter had the next-highest numbers. Finally, the four border slave states that did not

secede had the lowest numbers of slaves per capita and the lowest percentage of family slave ownership of all slave states.

But the best evidence that slavery was the driving force behind secession is the statements made by the states and their leaders themselves at
the time, including the official state secession convention records, secession resolutions, and secession-related declarations. They railed against
"Black Republicans," the supposedly abolitionist Lincoln, the failure to
enforce the Constitution's fugitive slave clause and federal fugitive slave
acts, the threat to the South's multi-billion-dollar investment in slaves,
abolitionism, racial equality, and the threat blacks posed to Southern
womanhood. These documents make it clear that slavery was not only
the primary cause of secession but virtually the only cause.

As the states of the Deep South were in the process of seceding,
moderates in Washington—especially Border State representatives—
launched negotiations. The primary "compromise" proposals were
those of Kentucky's Senator John Crittenden. All of them related to
one issue: slavery. In fact, they were all aimed at enhancing protections for slavery and alleviating slave states' fears about threats to it.
There could be no question about what was causing secession and
driving the nation toward war. Republicans, urged by Lincoln not to
reverse the results of the presidential election, defeated Crittenden's
pro-slavery proposals.

Pro-slavery and pro–white supremacy arguments were made by
commissioners sent by the Deep South states to urge each other, the
Upper South, and border states to secede. The commissioners first advocated for quick secession so the earliest seceding states were not alone;
they also pushed for an early convention to form a confederacy. Their
letters and speeches contained the same pro-slavery and pro–white
supremacy arguments as their states' secession documents, and they often
were embellished with emotional appeals about the horrors the South
would suffer if slavery was abolished.

Confederate leaders made similar statements in defense of slavery in
the early days of the Confederacy. President Jefferson Davis described
the formation of an anti-slavery political party in the North, praised the

benefits of slavery, and concluded that the threat to slavery left the South with no choice but to secede.

Vice President Alexander Stephens said that slavery was the cornerstone of the Confederacy, Thomas Jefferson had erred in stating that all men are created equal, and the Confederacy was based on equality of whites and subservience of blacks. After Lincoln issued his Emancipation Proclamation, Robert E. Lee described it as a "savage and brutal policy."

The Constitution of the Confederacy was similar to that of the United States but added provisions for the protection of slavery. Tellingly, it even contained a supremacy clause conferring final legal authority on the central government, not the states. That provision and the extra protections for slavery reveal the seceding states' priorities.

After the Confederacy's formation and the firing on Fort Sumter, four Upper South states (North Carolina, Virginia, Tennessee, and Arkansas) joined the Confederacy, having been entreated to do so by the Deep South on the basis of slavery. Statements of their leaders demonstrate the major role that slavery played in their leaving the Union.

One of the more fascinating indications of the Confederates' motivation was their failure to deploy virtually any of their three and a half million slaves as soldiers. Adherents of the Myth, in order to minimize the role of slavery in secession and the formation of the Confederacy, have alleged that thousands of black soldiers fought for the Confederacy. That did not happen. The evidence reveals instead that although Confederates used blacks as laborers and officers' "servants," they could not countenance the arming and related emancipation of slaves.

It was clear to certain Southern military leaders that the outmanned Confederacy needed to resort to slaves as soldiers if they hoped to have a chance of success. Just after the First Battle of Bull Run in July 1861, General Richard Ewell recommended to President Davis the arming of slaves. Davis, having just proclaimed that secession and the Confederacy were all about slavery, rejected the idea.

The need for such an approach became more obvious as a result of the huge rebel casualty counts in 1862 and 1863. Thus, on January 2, 1864, Major General Patrick Cleburne submitted to General Joseph

Johnston a well-considered proposal to arm and free slaves. The reaction from Davis, Alexander Stephens, General Braxton Bragg, and most other senior Confederates was extremely hostile. The word "traitor" was bandied about. Cleburne, one of the rebels' best generals, was never promoted to lieutenant general or corps command.

By late 1864, the Confederates had suffered irreplaceable casualties in Virginia and Georgia, lost Atlanta, lost Mobile Bay and then Mobile, and lost the Shenandoah Valley. Their fate had been sealed by the November reelection of Lincoln, the steel backbone of the Union. That event was followed by the loss of Savannah, as well as the twin disasters at Franklin and Nashville, Tennessee. Therefore, Davis and Lee belatedly began to see that without using slave soldiers the Confederacy was certainly doomed.

Nevertheless, their moderate proposals to arm and free slaves were fiercely resisted by politicians, the press, soldiers, and the people of the South. The opponents made it quite clear that the proposals were inconsistent with the reason for the Confederacy's existence and the supremacy of the white race. They feared such an approach would lead to black political, economic, and social equality and invoked the ever-reliable doctrine of protecting Southern womanhood.

In early 1865, Sherman marched virtually unimpeded through the Carolinas, Grant tightened his grip on Richmond and Petersburg, and tens of thousands of Union troops were transferred into the Eastern Theater. Despite the increasingly desperate situation, Davis and Lee's weak proposal to arm slaves was barely passed by the Confederate Congress. Since it did not provide emancipation for slaves and required consent from states and slaves' owners, the measure was next to worthless. Its implementation was laughable—two companies of black medics were assembled in the Richmond area. The Confederate Congress and people had made it clear that they would rather lose the war than give up slavery.

Slavery hampered Confederate diplomacy and cost the South critical support from Great Britain and France, even though these powers, dependent on Southern cotton and happy to see the American colossus split in half, had good economic and political reasons to support the rebels. When the reality of the slavery problem on the international front finally sank in, last-minute, half-hearted, blundering efforts to trade emancipation for diplomatic recognition failed.

Slavery and white supremacy similarly hampered Confederate efforts to swap prisoners of war with the Union. Since the rebels were greatly outnumbered, they should have been eager to engage in one-for-one prisoner swaps. When blacks began fighting for the Union, however, Davis and Lee refused to exchange any black prisoners on the grounds that they were Southern property. Blacks lucky enough to survive after capture (many did not) were returned to their owners or imprisoned as criminals. Lincoln and Grant insisted that black prisoners had to be treated and exchanged the same as whites. Because the North benefitted militarily, it did not hesitate to stop all prisoner exchanges when Davis and Lee would not back down.

The evidence, then, is overwhelming that, contrary to the Myth of the Lost Cause, the preservation of slavery and its concomitant white supremacy were the primary causes of the Southern states' secession and their creation of the Confederacy.

Adherents of the Myth contend that the South could not have won the Civil War because of the North's superior industrial, transportation, and manpower resources. Although the Union did have those advantages, its strategic burden was far heavier than the South's. The Confederacy occupied an enormous territory (equivalent to most of western Europe) that had to be conquered in order for the North to claim victory and compel the rebellious states to return to the Union. A tie or a stalemate would amount to a Southern victory because the Confederacy and slavery would be preserved. The Union, therefore, had to go on the strategic and tactical offensive, for every day of inaction was a minor victory for the Confederates (a fact that too many Union generals failed to comprehend). Offensive warfare consumes more resources than defensive warfare. In addition, widespread use of new weaponry—rifles, rifled artillery, repeating weapons, deadly Minié balls, and breechloaders instead of muzzleloaders—gave the tactical advantage to the defense in the Civil War.

The Confederacy's scarcity of manpower also militated in favor of staying on the strategic and tactical defensive. Had the South done so, making the North pay a heavy price for going on the offensive, it might have undermined Northern morale and ultimately Lincoln himself. Davis, Lee, and other rebel leaders always knew that the 1864 presidential election in the North would be critical to their success, but they pursued a costly offensive strategy that had ended the South's prospects for military victory (or even stalemate) by the time Lincoln faced the voters.

If Lincoln had lost the 1864 election to a Democrat, especially George McClellan, the Confederacy likely could have obtained a truce, the preservation of slavery, and perhaps even independence, at least for portions of the South. McClellan had demonstrated his extreme reluctance to engage in the offensive warfare necessary for a Union victory and had shown great concern for Southerners' property rights in their slaves. The possibility of a Democratic victory in 1864 was by no means far-fetched. Until the end of that summer, Lincoln, like nearly everyone else, thought he was going to lose. Had the South fought more wisely, it might have so demoralized the voters of the North—who were already divided over controversial issues like emancipation, the draft, and civil liberties—that they would have given up on the war and Lincoln.

The primary author of the South's imprudently aggressive approach to the war was, of course, Robert E. Lee. Though the Myth-makers insist he was one of the greatest generals of all time, Lee's actual record left much to be desired. First, he was a one-theater general apparently more concerned with the outcome in Virginia than in the Confederacy as a whole. He consistently refused to send reinforcements to other theaters and harmfully delayed them on the one occasion when he was ordered to relinquish some troops. Again and again, his actions indicated that he did not know or care what was happening outside his theater. For example, when he initiated the Maryland (Antietam) campaign of 1862, he advised Davis to protect Richmond with reinforcements from the Middle Theater, where rebels at the time were outnumbered three to one.

Second, Lee was too aggressive—both strategically and tactically. His Antietam and Gettysburg campaigns resulted in about forty thousand casualties the South could not afford, including the loss of experienced and talented veterans. Gettysburg also represented lost opportunities in other theaters because Lee kept his whole army intact in the East to invade Pennsylvania. Again and again, Lee launched frontal assaults that decimated his troops—Mechanicsville, Malvern Hill, Antietam (counterattacks), Chancellorsville (after Jackson's flanking assault), the second and third days at Gettysburg, the Wilderness, and Fort Stedman at the end of the war. Lee's losing, one-theater army incurred an astounding 209,000 casualties—more than the South could afford and fifty-five thousand more than Grant's five winning armies suffered in three theaters. Lee's other weaknesses included poor orders, failure to control the battlefield, and a deliberately inadequate staff.

Realizing that Lee was in need of exculpation, his advocates decided to make James Longstreet their scapegoat. They argued that Gettysburg cost Lee the war and that Longstreet was responsible for that loss. Gettysburg alone did not cost the war, and Longstreet played a relatively minor role in Lee's defeat there. Lee should have sought a defensive battle instead of attacking an entrenched foe. Lee's major errors in the Gettysburg campaign were his vague orders allowing Jeb Stuart to roam the countryside when Lee needed his scouting and screening abilities, his failure to mandate taking the high ground when he had the numerical advantage on the first day of the battle, his frontal assaults (against Longstreet's advice) on the second and third days, his failure on all three days to exercise battlefield control, and his failure to coordinate actions of his army's three corps, which made three uncoordinated attacks over the last twenty-four hours of the battle. Longstreet's supposedly delayed attack on Day Two (when Lee personally failed to adequately reinforce the attack) pales alongside Lee's performance as the cause for Confederate defeat at Gettysburg.

Since Grant ultimately defeated Lee, adherents of the Myth had to denigrate Grant in order to exalt Lee. They attacked the Union commander as a drunk and a butcher who won only by brute force. There is little evidence that Grant did much drinking in the Civil War and none that it affected his performance. The "butcher" epithet implied that he heedlessly sacrificed his own men in irresponsible attacks on the enemy. As the earlier casualty tables show, Grant's armies incurred a total of 154,000 casualties in three theaters while imposing 191,000 casualties on their opponents. Recent historians who have closely examined both Lee's and Grant's records and casualties have concluded that if there was a Civil War butcher, it was not Grant.

Anyone contending that Grant won solely by brute force has failed to study his victories at Forts Henry and Donelson, Shiloh, Vicksburg, and Chattanooga. His brilliant Vicksburg campaign continues to be studied around the world because of the deception, celerity, and concentration of force with which he baffled and defeated his opponents. The only three armies that surrendered between Sumter and Appomattox all surrendered to Grant. He was clearly the best general of the Civil War and one of the greatest in American history.

The last aspect of the Myth is that the North won by waging "total war." This allegation fails to distinguish between "hard war," which involves destruction of enemy armies and enemy property of all sorts, and "total war," which additionally involves the deliberate and systematic killing and rape of civilians. Total war was often waged long before the Civil War and was waged again in the twentieth century. The Civil War, however, which saw some localized and vicious guerilla warfare, was not a "total war" on the part of anyone—certainly not the Union.

The Myth of the Lost Cause, then, is a tangle of falsehoods. It should no longer play a significant role in the historiography and Americans' understanding of the Civil War.

# ACKNOWLEDGMENTS

M y book completion process always includes manuscript reviews by trusted friends and associates to minimize the number of errors and oversights in the text. I received valuable input from about a dozen people.

Two of them, Gettysburg and Lincoln expert Allen Guelzo and attorney and Civil War fount of information Mike Harrington, went way beyond the call of duty and spent many hours providing me with expert criticism that has greatly improved this book.

Others who were quite helpful are Kentucky Theater expert Charles Bogart, Larry Clowers (a.k.a. Ulysses S. Grant), "Middle" Theater expert Steve Davis, unparalleled wordsmith Steve Farbman, editor par excellence Elaine Joost, rising Civil War superstar Brian Matthew Jordan, Grant Papers editor and Sherman expert John Marszalek, Shenandoah Valley expert Jonathan Noyalas, military intelligence expert Ed Powell, Eastern Theater expert Jeffry Wert, and another rising star, Jonathan White. I do not use the word "expert" lightly, and all of these folks qualify as such. Their expertise goes beyond the subject areas I have mentioned, and their help was indispensable.

I also want to thank Regnery History publisher Alex Novak for his confidence in me and my Regnery editor Tom Spence for his exhaustive review of my final manuscript and his transformation of that document into a lucid and literate publication.

Despite all of the fine input from these reviewers and editors, some errors must be lurking in this book. For any and all of those, I take full responsibility.

# NOTES

## CHAPTER ONE: THE MYTH OF THE LOST CAUSE

1.  These terms come from Charles B. Dew, who discussed the lobbying efforts by early-seceded states to convince other Southern states to secede. A native Southerner, Dew had learned as a youth that the one and only cause of secession had been states' rights (except in the minds of Yankees or deranged people) but was astonished when he discovered evidence of racist lobbying, albeit unsuccessful, by Alabama commissioner Stephen F. Hale to encourage secession by Kentucky. Charles B. Dew, *Apostles of Disunion: Southern Secession Commissioners and the Causes of the Civil War* (Charlottesville: University Press of Virginia, 2001), 1–2, 75. This type of lobbying by state commissioners is discussed in detail below.

2.  William C. Davis points out why the Civil War occasioned such myth-making by ex-Confederates: "Out of any conflict, the losers create more myths than the winners. It is hardly a surprise. After all, winners have little to explain to themselves. They won. For the loser, however, coping

with defeat, dealing with it personally and explaining it to others, places enormous strains on the ego, self-respect, and sense of self-worth of the defeated." William C. Davis, *The Cause Lost: Myths and Realities of the Confederacy* (Lawrence: University Press of Kansas, 1996), 175.

3.  Gary W. Gallagher, "Introduction," in Gary W. Gallagher and Alan T. Nolan, *The Myth of the Lost Cause and Civil War History* (Bloomington: University of Indiana Press, 2000, 2010), 1–9 at 1.

4.  David Moltke-Hansen, "Turn Signals: Shifts in Values in Southern Life Writing," in Raymond Arsenault and Orville Vernon Burton, *Dixie Redux: Essays in Honor of Sheldon Hackney* (Montgomery, AL: New South Books, 2013), 166–97 at 181.

5.  Nolan, "Anatomy" in Gallagher and Nolan, *Myth*, 14.

6.  Gallagher, "Introduction" in Gallagher and Nolan, *Myth*, 2.

7.  Joshua Zeitz, *Lincoln's Boys: John Hay, John Nicolay, and the War for Lincoln's Image* (New York: Penguin Books, 2014), 262.

8.  Gallagher, "Introduction" in Gallagher and Nolan, *Myth*, 2, 8.

9.  W. J. Cash, *The Mind of the South* (New York: Doubleday, 1954), 136 (emphasis added).

10.  Gallagher, "Introduction," in Gallagher and Nolan, *Myth*, 1.

11.  Mark Perry, *Conceived in Liberty: Joshua Chamberlain, William Oates, and the American Civil War* (New York: Viking, 1997), 368.

12.  Alan T. Nolan, *Lee Considered: General Robert E. Lee and Civil War History* (Chapel Hill: University of North Carolina Press, 1991), 154–55.

13.  Edward L. Ayers and Carolyn R. Martin (eds.), *America on the Eve of the Civil War* (Charlottesville: University of Virginia Press, 2010), 123.

14.  Gordon Rhea, "Fellow Southerners!", *North & South* 13, no. 5 (Jan. 2012): 12–17 at 17.

15.  Michael Eric Dyson, "Foote and the Problem of Race," in Jon Meacham (ed.), *American Homer: Reflections on Shelby Foote and His Classic The Civil War: A Narrative* (New York: Random House, 2011), 67–72 at 67.

16.  Zeitz, *Lincoln's Boys*, 268. Reconstruction itself is beyond the scope of this book.

17.  Ibid., 270.

18.  Ibid., 308–10.

19.  Ibid., 312–13.

20.  Nolan, "Anatomy" in Gallagher and Nolan, *Myth*, 27.

## CHAPTER TWO: WHAT WAS THE NATURE OF SLAVERY IN 1861 AND WAS IT A DYING INSTITUTION?

1. Nolan, "Anatomy" in Gary W. Gallagher and Alan T. Nolan, *The Myth of the Lost Cause and Civil War History* (Bloomington: University of Indiana Press, 2000, 2010) 14, quoting Michael C. C. Adams, *Our Masters the Rebels* (Cambridge: Harvard University Press, 1978), 3.

2. James Oliver Horton and Lois E. Horton, *Slavery and the Making of America* (Oxford: Oxford University Press, 2005), 142–43; quote at 142.

3. Bruce Levine, *Confederate Emancipation: Southern Plans to Free and Arm Slaves During the Civil War* (Oxford: Oxford University Press, 2006), 7.

4. *Atlanta Southern Confederacy*, Jan. 20, 1865, quoted in Levine, *Confederate Emancipation*, 7.

5. E. A. Pollard, *Southern History of the War* (New York: C. B. Richardson, 1866), 562.

6. "Memories of the War," *DeBow's Review* 3 (Mar. 1867), 225–33 at 226–27, quoted in Levine, *Confederate Emancipation*, 9.

7. Horton and Horton, *Slavery*, 175.

8. Levine, *Confederate Emancipation*, 78. Almost eighty thousand blacks enlisted in the Mississippi Valley alone. Michael T. Meier, "Lorenzo Thomas and the Recruitment of Blacks in the Mississippi Valley, 1863–1865" in John David Smith (ed.), *Black Soldiers in Blue: African American Troops in the Civil War Era* (Chapel Hill: University of North Carolina Press, 2002), 248–75 at 268.

9. The total number of slaves who defected to Union forces is estimated between five hundred thousand and seven hundred thousand. Joseph T. Glatthaar, "Black Glory: The African-American Role in Union Victory" in Gabor S. Boritt (ed.), *Why the Confederacy Lost* (New York and Oxford: Oxford University Press, 1992), 133–62 at 142.

10. Levine, *Confederate Emancipation*, 71.

11. Nolan, "Anatomy," in Gallagher and Nolan, *Myth*, 16.

12. Jefferson Davis, *The Rise and Fall of the Confederate Government*, vol. I (New York: Da Capo Press, Inc., 1990) (Reprint of 1881 edition), 161–62 (emphasis added).

13. Nolan, "Anatomy" in Gallagher and Nolan, *Myth*, 16.

14.  Levine, *Confederate Emancipation*, 73–74.

15.  W. J. Cash, *The Mind of the South* (New York: Doubleday, 1954), 73.

16.  Alan T. Nolan, *Lee Considered: General Robert E. Lee and Civil War History* (Chapel Hill: University of North Carolina Press, 1991), Nolan, *Lee Considered*, 165.

17.  Gordon Rhea, "Fellow Southerners!", *North & South* 13, no. 5 (Jan. 2012): 12–17 at 14.

18.  Horton and Horton, *Slavery*, 8–9, quote at 9.

19.  Ibid., 9.

20.  Kenneth M. Stampp, *The Peculiar Institution: Slavery in the Ante-Bellum South* (New York: Vintage Books, 1956, 1989), 32–33.

21.  Horton and Horton, *Slavery*, 43.

22.  Frederick Law Olmsted, *The Cotton Kingdom: The Classic Firsthand Account of the South in the Years Preceding the Civil War* (New York: Alfred A. Knopf, 1953, 1970) (reprint of New York: Mason Brothers, 1861), 452.

23.  Stampp, *Peculiar Institution*, 85.

24.  Ibid., 87–140.

25.  Ibid., 144–47.

26.  Ibid., 206–9.

27.  Sally Jenkins, and John Stauffer, *The State of Jones: The Small Southern County That Seceded from the Confederacy* (New York: Anchor Books, 2010), 63–64.

28.  Cash, *Mind of the South*, 94.

29.  Eugene D. Genovese, *Roll, Jordan, Roll: The World the Slaves Made* (New York: Pantheon Books, 1974), 595.

30.  Horton and Horton, *Slavery*, 112–16; quoted on 113. See Edward H. Bonekemper III, "Negroes' Freedom of Contract in Antebellum Virginia, 1620–1860," unpublished M.A. dissertation, Old Dominion University (1971).

31.  Stampp, *Peculiar Institution*, 139–40.

32.  Horton and Horton, *Slavery*, 120.

33.  Sylvia R. Frey, *Water from the Rock: Black Resistance in a Revolutionary Age* (Princeton: Princeton University Press, 1991), 236.

34. Stampp, *Peculiar Institution*, 191.

35. Ibid., 237.

36. Horton and Horton, *Slavery*, 123.

37. Thomas Nelson Page, *Robert E. Lee: The Southerner* (New York: Charles Scribner's Sons, 1908), 69–70.

38. Cash, *Mind of the South*, 97.

39. Harriett Jacobs, *Incidents in the Life of a Slave Girl: Written by Herself*, edited by Jean Fagan Yellin (Cambridge: Harvard University Press, 1987), 28, quoted in Horton and Horton, *Slavery*, 123.

40. Gilbert Osofsky, *Puttin' on Ole Massa: The Slave Narratives of Henry Bibb, William Wells Brown, and Solomon Northup* (New York: Harper & Row, 1969), 169.

41. Levine, *Confederate Emancipation*, 54–55.

42. Cash, *Mind of the South*, 97–98.

43. Genovese, *Roll, Jordan, Roll*, 458.

44. Cash, *Mind of the South*, 100–1.

45. Nolan, "Anatomy," in Gallagher and Nolan, *Myth*, 21.

46. Allan Nevins, *Ordeal of the Union*, vol. IV (New York: Charles Scribner's Sons, 1947–50), 468.

47. Horton and Horton, *Slavery*, 159.

48. Edward L. Ayers and Carolyn R. Martin (eds.), *America on the Eve of the Civil War* (Charlottesville: University of Virginia Press, 2010), 5–6.

49. Ibid., 18.

50. Ibid., 39–42.

51. Stampp, *Peculiar Institution*, 63–64, quote at 64.

52. Charles B. Dew, "Apostles of Secession," *North & South* 4, no. 4 (April 2001): 42. Article I, Section 9, of the U.S. Constitution prohibited Congress from ending the importation of slaves before 1808. Henry Steele Commager, *Documents of American* History (New York: Appleton-Century-Crofts, 1958), 141.

53. Christopher Dickey, *Our Man in Charleston: Britain's Secret Agent in the Civil War South* (New York: Crown Publishers, 2015), 78, 83, 94–102, 216–19, 310–12, and *passim*.

54. Rhea, "Fellow Southerners!", 16.

55. Harold D. Woodman, *Slavery and the Southern Economy: Sources and Readings* (New York: Harcourt, Brace & World, Inc., 1966), 71, citing U. B. Phillips, "The Economic Cost of Slaveholding in the Cotton Belt," *Political Science Quarterly* XX, no. 2 (1905): 267.

56. Woodman, *Slavery*, 89.

57. Ibid., 91–92.

58. Ibid., 40.

59. In fact, an economic analysis of what slave prices would have been without the Civil War estimates that prime field hands would have sold for 52 percent more in 1890 than in 1860. Robert William Fogel and Stanley L. Engerman, *Time on the Cross: The Economics of American Negro Slavery* (Boston: Little, Brown and Company, 1974), 94–97. Those economists also conclude that increased urbanization, despite contrary claims, was not a threat to slavery but rather that "slaves were shifted from the cities to the countryside not because the cities didn't want slaves, but because as slave prices rose, it was easier for the cities than the countryside to find acceptable, lower-cost alternatives to slave labor." Ibid., 97–102.

60. Charles S. Sydnor, *Slavery in Mississippi* (Baton Rouge: Louisiana State University Press, 1933, 1966), 200.

61. Woodman, *Slavery*, 83.

62. Ibid., 83.

63. Sydnor, *Slavery in Mississippi*, 202.

64. Woodman, *Slavery*, 107.

65. James L. Huston, *The British Gentry, the Southern Planter, and the Northern Family Farmer: Agriculture and Sectional Antagonism in North America* (Baton Rouge: Louisiana State University Press, 2015), 244.

66. Fogel and Engerman, *Time on the Cross*, 97.

67. Woodman, *Slavery*, 109.

68. Stampp, *Peculiar Institution*, 417–18.

69. Fogel and Engerman, *Time on the Cross*, 103–6.

70. Ibid., 89–94.

71. Woodman, *Slavery*, 232–33.

72. Nolan, "Anatomy," in Gallagher and Nolan, *Myth*, 21.

73. Address of John Townsend to Edisto Island Vigilant Association, Oct. 29, 1860, on University of Michigan's *Making of America* website: http://name.umdl.umich.edu/ABT7252.0001.001.

74. Winthrop D. Jordan, *White Over Black: American Attitudes Toward the Negro, 1550–1812* (Chapel Hill: University of North Carolina Press, 1968), 542, 569.

75. Ayers and Martin, *America*, 51–52.

76. Hinton Rowan Helper, *The Impending Crisis of the South: How to Meet It* (New York: Burdick Brothers, 1857), 65–67, quoted in Woodman, *Slavery*, 206.

77. Cash, *Mind of the South*, 78.

# CHAPTER THREE: WAS SLAVERY THE PRIMARY CAUSE OF SECESSION AND THE CIVIL WAR?

1. It was important for Southern leaders to justify a war that had destroyed two-thirds of the assessed value of the South's property, 40 percent of its livestock, half its farm machinery, and one-fourth of its white men between twenty and forty—not to mention the severe damage to its industries and railroads. Its wealth decreased by 60 percent. James McPherson, *Ordeal by Fire* (New York: Knopf, 1982), 476. "Leaders of such a catastrophe must account for themselves. Justification is necessary." Nolan, "Anatomy" in Gary Gallagher and Alan T. Nolan, *The Myth of the Lost Cause and Civil War History* (Bloomington: University of Indiana Press, 2000, 2010), 13.

2. Edward A. Pollard, *Life of Jefferson Davis with a Secret History of the Southern Confederacy* (Atlanta: National Publishing Co., 1869), 453, quoted in Bruce Levine, *Confederate Emancipation: Southern Plans To Free and Arm Slaves During the Civil War* (Oxford: Oxford University Press, 2006), 11.

3. John Leyburn, "An Interview with Gen. Robert E. Lee," *Century Magazine* 30 (May 1885): 166–67, quoted in Levine, *Confederate Emancipation*, 11.

4. Jefferson Davis, *The Rise and Fall of the Confederate Government*, vol. I (New York: Da Capo Press, Inc., 1990), 66–67.

5.   Alexander Stephens, Constitution Society, Constitution.org, http://www.
     constitution.org/cmt/ahs/consview00.htm.

6.   Nolan, "Anatomy" in Gallagher and Nolan, *Myth*, 15.

7.   Ibid., 20.

8.   Edward A. Pollard, *The Lost Cause: A New Southern History of the War
     of the Confederates* (New York: Gramercy Books, 1994; reprint of New
     York: E. B. Treat & Company, 1866 [mistakenly identified in reprint as
     1886]), xxxi.

9.   Gordon C. Rhea, "Fellow Southerners!", *North & South* 13, no. 5 (Jan.
     2012): 13.

10.  Ibid., 14–15.

11.  Edward L. Ayers and Carolyn R. Martin (eds.), *America on the Eve of
     the Civil War* (Charlottesville: University of Virginia Press, 2010), 127.

12.  Ibid., 21.

13.  John Nicolay and John Hay, *Abraham Lincoln: A History*, vol. I (New
     York: The Century Company, 1886, 1890, 1914), 312.

14.  Pollard, *Lost Cause*, 80–81.

15.  Eric Foner, *Gateway to Freedom: The Hidden History of the Under-
     ground Railroad* (New York: W. W. Norton, 2015), 4.

16.  The Northwest Ordinance, July 13, 1787, Art. 6, in Henry Steele Com-
     mager, *Documents of American History* (New York: Appleton-Century-
     Crofts, 1958), 128–32 at 132.

17.  James Oliver Horton and Lois E. Horton, *Slavery and the Making of
     America* (Oxford: Oxford University Press, 2005), 149–56.

18.  Foner, *Gateway to Freedom*, 217.

19.  Michael C. C. Adams, *Living Hell: The Dark Side of the Civil War* (Bal-
     timore: Johns Hopkins University Press, 2014), 6.

20.  Dwight T. Pitcaithley, "Secession of the Upper South: States Rights and
     Slavery," *North & South* 12, no. 1 (Feb. 2010): 14–19 at 18.

21.  Edward L. Ayers, "What Caused the Civil War?" *North & South* 8, no.
     5 (Sept. 2005): 12–18 at 17.

22.  Even in the non-seceding border slave states, slavery was the issue that
     posed the greatest threat of subsequent secession. Lincoln had his hands
     full defusing the slavery issue to keep them in the Union. See William C.

Harris, *Lincoln and the Border States: Preserving the Union* (Lawrence: University Press of Kansas, 2011). In the first seventeen months of the war, he three times overruled subordinates who had attempted to emancipate slaves.

23.  Joseph T. Glatthaar, *Soldiering in the Army of Northern Virginia: A Statistical Portrait of the Troops Who Served under Robert E. Lee* (Chapel Hill: University of North Carolina Press, 2011), 161, 164–65.

24.  Tellingly, Pollard only stated that seven states had left the Union before Lincoln's inauguration and provided no quotations from the secession or related documents explaining why the seceding states said they were seceding. Pollard, *Lost Cause*, 98.

25.  South Carolina Declaration, Dec. 24, 1860, David S. Heidler and Jeanne T. Heidler (eds.), *Encyclopedia of the American Civil War: A Political, Social, and Military History* (New York and London: W. W. Norton & Company, 2002), 2240–43.

26.  Timothy B. Smith, *The Mississippi Secession Convention: Delegates and Deliberations in Politics and War, 1861–1865* (Jackson: University Press of Mississippi, 2014), 15–16.

27.  Ibid., 17–20.

28.  Ibid., 227–28; Heidler and Heidler, *Encyclopedia*, 2243.

29.  Smith, *Mississippi Secession*, 77–78.

30.  *State of Mississippi's Declaration of the Immediate Causes which Induce and Justify the Secession of the State of Mississippi from the Federal Union*, Jan. 9, 1861, Ibid., 229; Heidler and Heidler, *Encyclopedia*, 2243–44 at 2243.

31.  Smith, *Mississippi Secession*, 230; Heidler and Heidler, *Encyclopedia*, 2243–44.

32.  Smith, *Mississippi Secession*, 146–47, 151.

33.  Florida's Secession Ordinance, Jan. 10, 1861, Heidler and Heidler, *Encyclopedia*, 2244; OR, Ser. IV, I.

34.  Alabama's Secession Ordinance, Jan. 11, 1861, Heidler and Heidler, *Encyclopedia*, 2244–45 at 2244; OR, Ser. IV, I.

35.  At the Alabama secession convention, John T. Morgan stated that Alabama's "ordinance of Secession rests, in a great measure, upon our assertion

278 NOTES TO PAGES 43–47

of a right to enslave the African race." A colleague, G. T. Yelverton, added: "The question of Slavery is the rock upon which the Old Government split; it is the cause of secession." Pitcaithley, "Secession," 15, citing Smith, *The History and Debates of the Convention of the People of Alabama*, 196, 229.

36. Georgia's Secession Resolution, Jan. 19, 1861, Heidler and Heidler, *Encyclopedia*, 2246; OR, Ser. IV, I.

37. Georgia's Declaration of Causes of Seceding, Jan. 29, 1861, Heidler and Heidler, *Encyclopedia*, 2246–49.

38. Louisiana's Secession Ordnance, Jan. 26, 1861, Heidler and Heidler, *Encyclopedia*, 2249–50.

39. "A Declaration of the Causes which Impel the State of Texas to Secede from the Federal Union," Feb. 2, 1861, Heidler and Heidler, *Encyclopedia*, 2250–52 at 2251.

40. Ibid., 2251–52.

41. U.S. Congress, *Congressional Globe* (Appendix), 36th Cong., 2d sess., Dec. 4, 1860, 1.

42. Ibid., 4. cited in Pitcaithley, "Secession," 15.

43. For the full text of Crittenden's proposed constitutional amendments, see Heidler and Heidler, *Encyclopedia*, 2252–54.

44. Remarks of Senator John J. Crittenden in the U.S. Senate, Dec. 18, 1860, in Brooks D. Simpson, Stephen W. Sears, and Aaron Sheehan-Dean (eds.), *The Civil War: The First Year Told by Those Who Lived It* (New York: Literary Classics of the United States, 2011), 128–42 at 128–29.

45. Ibid., 139–41; Amendments Proposed by Senator Crittenden, Dec. 18, 1860, Heidler and Heidler, *Encyclopedia*, 2252–54 at 2252–53.

46. Heidler and Heidler, *Encyclopedia*, 2253–54.

47. Louis P. Masur, *The Civil War: A Concise History* (Oxford: Oxford University Press, 2011), 21.

48. Chester G. Hearn, *Lincoln, the Cabinet and the Generals* (Baton Rouge: Louisiana State University Press, 2010), 53.

49. Ibid., 53–54.

50. Address of Louisiana Commissioner George Williamson to Texas Secession Convention, Jan. 11, 1861, http://www.civilwarcauses.org/gwill.htm,

quoting E. W. Winkler (ed.), *Journal of the Secession Convention of Texas*, 120–23.

51.  Charles B. Dew, *Apostles of Disunion: Southern Secession Commissioners and the Causes of the Civil War* (Charlottesville: University Press of Virginia, 2001). Many of the commissioner-related documents are reproduced in one of the final volumes of *The War of the Rebellion: A Compilation of the Official Records of the Union and Confederate Armies* (128 vols.) (Washington: Government Printing Office, 1880–1901) (hereafter OR), Series IV, I, 1–84.

52.  Charles B. Dew, "Apostles of Secession," *North & South* 4, no. 4 (April 2001): 24–38 at 27.

53.  Dew, *Apostles*, 18–19; Dew, "Apostles," 26–31.

54.  Dew, "Apostles," 24.

55.  Dew, *Apostles*, 18–19.

56.  Ibid., 74–81.

57.  Adams, *Living Hell*, 7.

58.  Dew, "Apostles," 27. Most state commissioners, as well as other advocates of secession, usually referred to the "Black Republican Party"—with obvious racial connotations.

59.  William L. Harris's address to Georgia General Assembly, Dec. 17, 1860, in Dew, *Apostles*, 83–89 (hereafter Harris Address) at 85.

60.  Harris Address, 86–87.

61.  Ibid., 89.

62.  Dew, "Apostles," 30.

63.  Ibid. 24.

64.  Dew, *Apostles*, 39–41.

65.  Ibid., 41–42.

66.  Ibid., 43.

67.  Ibid., 42–44.

68.  Ibid., 45–47.

69.  Ibid., 47–49.

70.  See, e.g., Moore's appointment of John G. Shorter as commissioner to Georgia, Dec. 21, 1860, OR, Series IV, I, 55.

71.  Moore to State Convention, January 8, 1861, OR, Ser. IV, I, 30.

72.  Winston to A. B. Moore, Jan. 2, 1861, OR, Series IV, I, 1–2.
73.  Shorter to Brown, Jan. 3, 1861, OR, Series IV, I, 16–17 (emphases added).
      The phrase "homogeneous people" [i.e., "all us whites"] also appeared
      in fellow Alabama Commissioner Edward C. Bullock's January 11, 1861,
      letter to Florida convention president J. C. McGehee. Bullock to McGe-
      hee, OR, Series IV, I, 46.
74.  Brown to Shorter, Jan. 5, 1861, OR, Series IV, I, 18-19 (emphasis added).
75.  Elmore to Moore, Jan. 5, 1861, OR, Series IV, I, 19–22.
76.  The convention's decision was subject to a popular vote. In early March
      the people of Texas voted three-to-one in favor of secession.
77.  Williamson Address, 1–2.
78.  Ibid., 2–3.
79.  Dew, *Apostles*, 32–33.
80.  Ibid., 34–35.
81.  Ibid., 35–36.
82.  Hubbard to A. B. Moore, Jan. 3, 1860, OR, Series IV, I, 3.
83.  Dew, *Apostles*, 59–61.
84.  Ibid., 62–63.
85.  Ibid., 63–66.
86.  Ibid., 66–67.
87.  Ibid., 70.
88.  Ibid., 71–72, 75.
89.  Dew, "Apostles," 33.
90.  Dew, *Apostles*, 51–52.
91.  Hale to A. B. Moore, Jan. 3 (?), 1861, OR, Series IV, I, 4; Hale to Magof-
      fin, Dec. 27, 1860, Ibid., 4–11 at 5.
92.  Hale to Magoffin, Ibid., 5.
93.  Ibid., 6–8.
94.  Ibid., 7–8.
95.  Ibid., 8–9.
96.  Ibid., 9.
97.  Ibid., 10.
98.  Ibid.

99.  Ibid. Governor Magoffin replied to Hale's letter in a non-committal response that expressed hope for a multi-state convention that would resolve the divisive issues and stated a concern that some of the seceding states were planning to pass laws prohibiting the purchase of slaves from border slave states (like Kentucky). Magoffin to Hale, Dec. 28, 1860, Ibid., 11–15.

100. Dew, *Apostles*, 55.

101. Curry to Hicks, Dec. 28, 1860, OR, Series IV, I, 39-42 at 39–41.

102. Ibid., 42.

103. Curry to Moore, Jan. 8, 1861, OR, Series IV, I, 38.

104. Dew, *Apostles*, 32–33.

105. Ibid., 33–34.

106. Cooper to Stewart, Dec. 26, 1860, OR, Series IV, I, 23-25; Stewart to Moore, Dec. 30. 1860, Ibid., 25–28.

107. Dew, *Apostles*, 57; Dew, "Apostles," 33.

108. Clopton to Burton, Jan. 1, 1861, OR, Series IV, I, 34-38 at 35–36.

109. Ibid., 37.

110. Clopton to Moore, Jan. 8, 1861, OR, Series IV, I, 33.

111. Dew, *Apostles*, 58; Dew, "Apostles," 33.

112. Dew, *Apostles*, 76–80.

113. Dew, "Apostles," 33. All but the last sentence also appears in Dew, *Apostles*, 81.

114. Inaugural Address of Jefferson Davis, August 18, 1861, in Thomas C. Mackey (ed.), *A Documentary History of the American Civil War Era, Vol. II, Political Arguments* (Knoxville: University of Tennessee Press, 2013), 89–92 at 91.

115. See Dew, *Apostles*, 13–14.

116. Jefferson Davis' Message to Confederate Congress, Apr. 29, 1861, Commager, *Documents*, 389–391 at 390.

117. Ibid., 390–91.

118. Ibid., 391.

119. Ibid.

120. Ibid., see Dew, *Apostles*, 14–15.

121. Lee to James Seddon, Jan. 10, 1863, Clifford Dowdey and Louis H. Manarin (eds.), *The Wartime Papers of R. E. Lee* (New York: Bramhall House, 1961), 388–90 at 390 (emphasis added).

122. Dew, *Apostles*, 15–16.

123. Ibid., 16.

124. Davis, *Rise and Fall*, I: xix, 78–80, 83, II: 763.

125. Gary W. Gallagher, "'Flaggers' on the Fringe: Serious students of the war should ignore such irrelevant distraction," *Civil War Times* 54, no. 2 (April 2015): 19–21 at 20.

126. Provisional Constitution of the Confederate States of America, Feb. 8, 1861, OR, Series IV, I, 92–99.

127. This language would be cited in 1864–1865 by opponents of the suggested arming and freeing of slaves. Levine, *Confederate Emancipation*, 46.

128. Constitution of the Confederate States of America, March 11, 1861, OR, Series IV, I, 136–147; Commager, *Documents*, 376–384 (full text) at 379, 383; Heidler and Heidler. *Encyclopedia*, 488–90, 2254–61 (full text).

129. Commager, *Documents*, 379.

130. Ibid., 383.

131. The Confederate Constitution's Supremacy Clause read: "The Constitution and the laws of the Confederate States, made in pursuance thereof, and all treaties made, or which shall be made, under the authority of the Confederate States, shall be the supreme law of the land; and the judges in every State shall be bound thereby, anything in the Constitution or laws of any State to the contrary." Commager, *Documents*, 384.

132. As of 2011.

133. Rhea, "Fellow Southerners!", 13.

134. Lawrence M. Denton, *Unionists in Virginia: Politics, Secession and Their Plan To Prevent Civil War* (Charleston, SC: History Press, 2014), 73.

135. Pitcaithley, "Secession, 14–19.

136. Ibid. 18.

137. Pitcaithley, "Secession," 16.

138. Ibid.

139. Ibid.

140. Jay Gillespie, "Slavery and States' Rights in the Old North State," *North & South* 11, no. 5 (Oct. 2009): 68–75 at 74.

141. Pitcaithley, "Secession," 16–17.

142. William W. Freehling and Craig M. Simpson (eds.), *Showdown in Virginia* (Charlottesville: University of Virginia Press, 2010), 6, 59.

143. Ibid., 129.

144. DeBow, "Memories of the War," 226–27, quoted in Levine, *Confederate Emancipation*, 9.

145. See Levine, *Confederate Emancipation*, 13 and notes for examples.

146. Horton and Horton, *Slavery*, 61–62; quote at 62. Even George Washington of Virginia opposed the use of free blacks as soldiers in his Continental Army until he realized he needed all the manpower he could get.

147. See Kevin M. Levin, "Confederate Like Me: Rebels Who Brought Their Slaves to War Assumed a Shared Loyalty to the Confederate Cause—as Do Some History Revisionists Today," *The Civil War Monitor* 3, no. 1 (Spring 2013): 60–67, 78–79 at 66. The internet is full of unsupported stories of black Confederate soldiers. Even worse, a 2010 Virginia textbook, *Our Virginia: Past and Present*, asserted that "thousands of Southern blacks fought in the Confederate ranks, including two battalions under the command of Stonewall Jackson." When challenged, the author claimed she had read this information on the internet. Ibid., 79.

148. Ibid., 66, citing Kenneth W. Noe, *Reluctant Rebels: The Confederates Who Joined the Army after 1861* (Chapel Hill: UNC, 2010), 43–44; Andrew Ward, *The Slaves' War: The Civil War in the Words of Former Slaves* (Boston: Mariner Books, 2008), 93.

149. Donald C. Pfanz, *Richard S. Ewell: A Soldier's Life* (Chapel Hill: University of North Carolina Press, 1998), 139. Years after the war Davis claimed that the notion of arming slaves was unheard of in 1861 and denied Ewell's version of their conversation. Ewell's story is supported by a July 1862 letter he wrote to his niece stating, "It is astonishing to me that our people do not pass laws to form Regiments of blacks. The Yankees are fighting low foreignors [sic] against the best of our people, whereas were we to fight our negroes they would be a fair offset & we would not be fighting kings against men to use a comparison from

chequers." Ibid. Daniel Mallock, "Cleburne's Proposal," *North & South* 11, no. 2 (Dec. 2008): 64–72, 66–67; Levine, *Confederate Emancipation*, 18.

150. Ibid.

151. Mallock, "Cleburne's Proposal," 68–69.

152. Cleburne et al. to Joseph Johnston et al., Jan. 2, 1864, OR, Series I, LII, Part II, 586–92 (full text) at 586–87.

153. OR, Series I, LII, Part II, 588–89.

154. Ibid., 589–91; Don H. Doyle, *The Cause of All Nations: An International History of the American Civil War* (New York: Basic Books, 2015), 270–71. See discussion below of "Confederate Foreign Diplomacy."

155. OR, Series. I, LII, Part II, 590 (emphasis added).

156. Ibid., 590–91.

157. Ibid., 592.

158. As early as March 7, 1864, the *New York Times* was lauding the use of black Union troops. Its referral to a "prodigious revolution" reflected growing Northern "acceptance of the Negro as a soldier capable of fighting for the preservation of the Union and for the freedom of the slave." Dudley Taylor Cornish, *The Sable Arm: Black Troops in the Union Army, 1861–1865* (Lawrence: University Press of Kansas, 1956, 1987), xi–xii.

159. Benjamin Quarles, *The Negro in the Civil War* (Boston: Little, Brown and Co., 1953), 278.

160. Horton and Horton, *Slavery*, 182–83.

161. Charles Jones Jr., "Negro Slaves During the Civil War: Their Relations to the Confederate Government," *The Magazine of American History with Notes and Queries* 16, 175 (1886), quoted in Mallock, "Cleburne's Proposal" at 70.

162. Mallock, "Cleburne's Proposal," 68–69.

163. Ibid.," 69 (emphasis added).

164. Walker to Davis, Jan. 12, 1864, OR, Series I, LII, Part II, 595.

165. Davis to Walker, Ibid., 596.

166. Seddon to Johnston, Jan. 24, 1864, OR, Series I, LII, Part II, 606–7.

167. Johnston Circular to Division Commanders, Jan. 31, 1864; ibid., 608.

168. Mallock, "Cleburne's Proposal," 71.

169. Under the "Peter Principle" (in this case, the "Double Peter Principle" since he previously had been promoted beyond his abilities), the incompetent Bragg had been elevated to this influential position after he resigned as Army of Tennessee commander following the collapse of his army at Chattanooga in November 1863.

170. Mallock, "Cleburne's Proposal," 71.

171. Ibid., 67. Taking this line of thought a step further was Stephen Davis, who writes, "Many have thought since then that had Cleburne taken his staff's advice and not presented his controversial paper at Dalton, he would likely have won promotion to corps commander sometime later. The history of the Georgia campaign, and of the Army of Tennessee, might thus have been dramatically different." Stephen Davis, "Pat Cleburne's Emancipation Proposal," *Blue & Gray Magazine* VI, no. 4 (Apr. 1989): 19.

172. Levine, *Confederate Emancipation*, 38.

173. Doyle, *The Cause*, 272–73. "But one can hardly help thinking about how [Cleburne's "brilliant but impolitic" proposal's] harsh truths and radical recommendations played on the Confederate president's mind between January...and November 1864 when, facing the failure of impressment policy and an even more desperate manpower situation, he made his own proposal for the radical modification of slavery, as he put it." William A. Blair and Karen Fisher Younger, *Lincoln's Proclamation: Emancipation Reconsidered* (Chapel Hill: University of North Carolina Press, 2009), 141.

174. Leonne M. Hudson, "Robert E. Lee and the Arming of Black Men," in Clayton E. Jewett (ed.), *The Battlefield and Beyond: Essays on the American Civil War* (Baton Rouge: Louisiana State University Press, 2012), 28–48, at 33–34.

175. Seddon to Johnston, Jan. 21, 1864, OR, Series I, LII, Part II, 606–7 at 606.

176. Lee to Andrew Hunter, Jan. 11, 1865, OR, Ser. IV, III, 1012–13. Although Lee's January 11, 1865, letter is also reproduced in Alan T. Nolan, *Lee Considered: General Robert E. Lee and Civil War History* (Chapel Hill: University of North Carolina Press, 1991), 175–77, it unsurprisingly does

not appear at all in the pro-Lee Clifford Dowdey and Louis H. Manarin, *The Wartime Papers of R. E. Lee* (New York: Bramhall House, 1961).

177. Ibid., 1013.

178. Lee to Ethelbert Barksdale, *Richmond Sentinel*, Feb. 23, 1864, quoted in Mallock, "Cleburne's Proposal," 72.

179. *Macon Telegraph and* Confederate, March 30, 1865, quoted in Levine, *Confederate Emancipation*, 55; *Memphis Appeal*, Oct. 31, 1864, quoted in Ibid.; Richmond *Examiner*, Feb. 25, 1865, quoted in Ibid., 4.

180. *Charleston Mercury*, Nov. 3, 1864, quoted in Levine, *Confederate Emancipation*, 4–5.

181. *Richmond Whig*, Nov. 9, 1864, quoted in Levine, *Confederate Emancipation*, 50.

182. Doyle, *The Cause*, 275; Levine, *Confederate Emancipation*, 4–5.

183. See John David Smith (ed.), *Black Soldiers in Blue: African American Troops in the Civil War Era* (Chapel Hill: University of North Carolina Press, 2002).

184. OR, Series IV, III, 1009–10.

185. Levine, *Confederate Emancipation*, 43–44, 50.

186. Levine, *Confederate Emancipation*, 46.

187. Levin, "Confederate Like Me," 66–67.

188. Levine, *Confederate Emancipation*, 40–59, quotation at 59.

189. Hudson, "Lee," in Jewett, *Battlefield and Beyond*, 42.

190. Pollard, *Lost Cause*, 660.

191. Blair and Younger, *Lincoln's Proclamation*, 142.

192. Quarles, *Negro in Civil War*, 280–81; Michael Fellman, *The Making of Robert E. Lee* (Baltimore: Johns Hopkins University Press, 2003) (reprint of New York: Random House, 2000), 217.

193. Levine, *Confederate Emancipation*, 125.

194. Bruce Levine, "Black Confederates," *North & South* 10, no. 2 (July 2007): 40–45, at 44–45 (emphasis added by Levine).

195. "Perhaps the deeper meaning of this project [of arming the slaves] was that honor-bound gentlemen such as Lee found it hard to accept, as their republic crumbled, that they had really fought and suffered and died for slavery as opposed to nationhood." Fellman, *Making of Lee*, 218.

196. Joseph T. Glatthaar, "Black Glory: the African-American Role in Union Victory" in Boritt, *Why the Confederacy Lost*, 133–36 at 137, 158.

197. Levine, *Confederate Emancipation*, 157.

198. "By successful diplomacy, by winning the support of Great Britain or France, the South most likely could have canceled out all the economic advantages of the North." French recognition and military and naval support had been critical, probably indispensable, to the seceding colonists in the American Revolution.

199. Richard N. Current, "God and the Strongest Battalions" in Donald et al., *Why the North Won*, 21–37, at 32. Norman A. Graebner, "Northern Diplomacy and European Neutrality" in Donald et al., *Why the North Won*, 58–80, at 59–60.

200. See chapter, "The Unspeakable Dilemma" in Doyle, *The Cause*, 257–80. Norman Graebner downplays the influence of the slavery issue: "Lincoln's Emancipation Proclamation, although designed, at least partially, to influence European attitudes toward the Union cause, had little effect on European sentiment and none on European action." Graebner, "Northern Diplomacy" in Donald et al., *Why the North Won*, 68.

201. Doyle, *The Cause*, 257–58.

202. Christopher Dickey, *Our Man in Charleston* (New York: Crown Publishers, 2015), 306–12, long quotation at 311–12.

203. Ibid., 258–69 (emphasis added). In late 1864 Charleston's Bishop Patrick Lynch wrote an 83-page booklet defending slavery in a failed effort to obtain papal recognition. "Bishop Lynch's reply to the pope's concerns about slavery was revealing of the fixed mind of the Confederate South. For Lynch and the entire Confederate leadership, slavery was beyond debate. It was the cornerstone of the Southern nation, the foundation of King Cotton's prosperous realm, and the guarantor of white racial supremacy." Ibid., 269–70.

204. Lee to Davis, July 6, 1864, in Douglas Southall Freeman (ed.), *Lee's Dispatches: Unpublished Letters of General Robert E. Lee, C.S.A., to Jefferson Davis and the War Department of the Confederate States of America 1862–65* (Baton Rouge: Louisiana State University Press, 1957) (revision of 1914 edition), 367–68.

205. Fellman, *Making of Lee*, 202–3.

206. Doyle, *The Cause*, 273–79.

207. Ibid., 280.

208. James M. McPherson, *Battle Cry of Freedom: The Civil War Era* (New York: Ballantine Books, 1988), 800. To accusations that Grant's no-exchange policy was the cause of many prison-camp deaths, Professor James Gillispie retorted that retaining Southern prisoners was the only security against a widespread Confederate policy of executing black prisoners and their white officers and that it also was intended to shorten the war by reducing the number of combatants—especially on the Rebel side. James Gillispie, "Letter to Editor," *North & South 5*, no. 7 (Oct. 2002): 6.

209. Nolan, "Anatomy," in Gallagher and Nolan, *Myth*, 20.

## CHAPTER FOUR: COULD THE SOUTH HAVE WON THE CIVIL WAR?

1.   Lee's farewell to his Army, April 10, 1865, in Henry Steele Commager, *Documents of American History* (New York: Appleton-Century-Crofts, 1948, 1949, 1958), 447.

2.   David Herbert Donald, ed., *Why the North Won the Civil War* (New York: Simon & Schuster, 1962, 1996), 7.

3.   Richard N. Current, "God and the Strongest Battalions" in Donald, *Why the North Won the Civil War*, 32.

4.   Nolan, "Anatomy" in Gary Gallagher and Alan T. Nolan, *The Myth of the Lost Cause and Civil War History* (Bloomington: University of Indiana Press, 2000, 2010), 17.

5.   John Cook, "Could the South Have Won the War?", Conference Keynote Address, http://www.americancivilwar.asn.au/conf/2003/2003conf_could_sth_win.pdf (July 2003), 2.

6.   James M. McPherson, *Drawn with the Sword: Reflections on the American Civil War* (New York: Oxford University Press, 1966), 134.

7.   James M. McPherson, *Battle Cry of Freedom: The Civil War Era* (New York: Ballantine Books, 1988), 336. Other historians making the same point include Bell Irvin Wiley, *The Road to Appomattox* (Baton Rouge:

Louisiana State University Press, 1994) (reprint of Memphis: Memphis State College Press, 1956), 77, and Charles P. Roland, *An American Iliad: The Story of the Civil War* (Lexington: University Press of Kentucky, 1991), 41.

8.  Alan T. Nolan, "Demolishing the Myth: Evaluating Lee's Generalship," *North & South* 3, no. 5 (June 2000): 29–36 at 18, 35.

9.  G. F. R. Henderson, *Stonewall Jackson and the American Civil War* (New York: Da Capo Press, 1988; reprint of New York: Grossett & Dunlap, 1943), 82.

10.  McPherson, *Battle Cry of Freedom*, 336; Alan T. Nolan, *Lee Considered: General Robert E. Lee and Civil War History* (Chapel Hill: University of North Carolina Press, 1991), 65. Both quoting *The Times* of London, Aug. 29, 1862.

11.  Herman Hattaway and Archer Jones, *How the North Won: A Military History of the Civil War* (Urbana: University of Illinois Press, 1991, reprint of 1983 edition), 18.

12.  William W. Freehling and Craig M. Simpson (eds.), *Showdown in Virginia* (Charlottesville: University of Virginia Press, 2010), 105–6.

13.  Joseph E. Johnston, *Narrative of Military Operations During the Civil War* (New York: Appleton, 1874), 421.

14.  P. G. T. Beauregard, "The First Battle of Bull Run," in Robert Underwood Johnson and Clarence Clough Buel, eds., *Battles and Leaders of the Civil War* (4 vols.) (New York: Thomas Yoseloff, 1956, reprint of Secaucus, N.J.: Castle, 1887–88), 222.

15.  Edward Porter Alexander, *Fighting for the Confederacy: The Personal Recollections of General Edward Porter Alexander*, Gary W. Gallagher, ed. (Chapel Hill: University of North Carolina Press, 1989), 415.

16.  James M. McPherson, *The War that Forged a Nation: Why the Civil War Still Matters* (Oxford: Oxford University Press, 2015), 147.

17.  "The point is that the South could still have won, save only for the rapid diminution and ultimate death of morale, the will to win, during the last year or two of the war." Richard Beringer et al., *Why the South Lost the Civil War* (Athens: University of Georgia Press, 1986), 31.

18.  As in the Revolutionary War, the underdog could greatly benefit from European intervention. The South failed to achieve this significant action because of its refusal to end slavery (abhorred in Europe) and Lee's strategic defeat at Antietam at the very time England (and thus France) was contemplating involvement.

19.  Cook, "Could the South?", 3.

20.  Freehling and Simpson, *Showdown*, 10.

21.  Freehling et al, "Could the Confederacy Have Won the Civil War?", 16.

22.  See Sylvia R. Frey, *Water from the Rock: Black Resistance in a Revolutionary Age*, (Princeton: Princeton University Press, 1991).

23.  David Eicher, Joe Harsh, Richard McMurry, Robert Tanner, Russell Weigley, and Steve Woodworth, "Confederate Strategy Considered," *North & South* 4, no. 7 (Sept. 2001): 12–22 at 19.

24.  Ibid., 21–22.

25.  Hattaway et al, *How the North Won*, ix.

26.  Beringer et al, *Why the South Lost*, 16.

27.  Allan Nevins, *Ordeal of the Union*, vol. VIII (New York and London: Charles Scribner's Sons, 1947–50), 92–96.

28.  Freehling et al, "Could the Confederacy?", 17.

29.  Edward A. Pollard, *The Lost Cause: A New Southern History of the War of the Confederates* (New York: Gramercy Books, 1994; reprint of New York: E. B. Treat & Company, 1866 [mistakenly identified in reprint as 1886]), 508.

30.  Nevins, *Ordeal*, VIII, 92–96.

31.  William C. Davis, *Crucible of Command: Ulysses S. Grant and Robert E. Lee—The War They Fought, the Peace They Forged* (New York: Da Capo, 2015), 241.

32.  Lee to his wife, Apr. 19, 1863, Dowdey and Manarin, *Papers*, 437–38 at 438.

33.  See Edward H. Bonekemper III, *McClellan and Failure: A Study of Civil War Fear, Incompetence and Worse* (Jefferson, NC: McFarland & Company, 2007, 2010).

34.  Pollard, *Lost Cause*, 571–72.

35.  Ibid., 574–75.

36.  CQ, *Elections*, 94; Bonekemper, "Lincoln's 1864 Victory." See more detailed analysis in Edward H. Bonekemper III, *A Victor, Not a Butcher: Ulysses S. Grant's Overlooked Military Genius* (Washington: Regnery, 2004) (reprinted as *Ulysses S. Grant: A Victor, Not a Butcher: The Military Genius of the Man Who Won the Civil War*), Appendix III ("How Close Was the Election of 1864?"), 325–32.

37.  See Edward H. Bonekemper III, "Lincoln's 1864 Victory Was Closer than It Looked," *Washington Times*, July 15, 2000, B3.

38.  McPherson, *Battle Cry*, 804.

39.  But see Jonathan W. White, *Emancipation, the Union Army and the Reelection of Abraham Lincoln* (Baton Rouge: Louisiana State University Press, 2014), in which the author describes various types of coercion that were used to obtain soldiers' Lincoln votes and discourage them from voting for McClellan.

40.  Hearn, *Lincoln, Cabinet, Generals*, 260.

41.  Grant to Stanton, Nov. 10, 1864, John Y. Simon, John F. Marszalek, et al., eds., *The Papers of Ulysses S. Grant*. 32 vols. (Carbondale: Southern Illinois University Press, 1967–2012), 12, 398.

42.  John Hay, *Inside Lincoln's White House: The Complete Civil War Diary of John Hay*, Michael Burlingame and John R. Turner Ettlinger, eds. (Carbondale: Southern Illinois University Press, 1997), Nov. 16, 1864, 251.

43.  William C. Davis, *The Cause Lost: Myths and Realities of the Confederacy* (Lawrence: University Press of Kansas, 1996), 142–47.

44.  See Bonekemper, *McClellan and Failure*.

45.  David Herbert Donald, Jean Harvey Baker, and Michael F. Holt, *The Civil War and Reconstruction* (New York: W. W. Norton & Co., 2001), 427.

# CHAPTER FIVE: WAS ROBERT E. LEE ONE OF THE GREATEST GENERALS IN HISTORY?

1.  Michael Fellman, *The Making of Robert E. Lee* (Baltimore: Johns Hopkins University Press, 2000), 191–93. See below for Lost Causers' elevation of Lee to a Christ-like figure.

2. John Keegan, *The Face of Battle* (New York: Dorset Press, 1986) (originally New York: Viking, 1976), 55.

3. Jackson has had his own share of Lost Cause worshippers. For example, his primary biographer, James I. Robertson Jr., describes him as a "spiritual prince" "standing alone on a high pedestal" and concludes that Jackson's devotion to God, duty, and country "remain treasured legacies of the American people just as they are inspirations to people everywhere." Nolan, "Anatomy," in Gary W. Gallagher and Alan T. Nolan, *The Myth of the Lost Cause and Civil War History* (Bloomington: University of Indiana Press, 2000, 2010), 18.

4. Early histories of the Civil War included James Dabney McCabe Jr.'s *Life and Campaigns of Gen. Robert E. Lee* (1866), William Swinton's *The Twelve Decisive Battles of the War* (1867) and *Campaigns of the Army of the Potomac* (1882), John Esten Cooke's *A Life of Gen. Robert E. Lee* (1871), and Edward A. Pollard's *Lee and His Lieutenants* (1867).

5. Thomas Lawrence Connelly, *The Marble Man: Robert E. Lee and His Image in American Society* (New York: Alfred A. Knopf, 1977), 47–61; Gary W. Gallagher, ed., *Lee the Soldier* (Lincoln: University of Nebraska Press, 1996), xviii.

6. Bruce, "Lee and Strategy" in Gary W. Gallagher, *Lee the Soldier* (Lincoln: University of Nebraska Press, 1996), 133.

7. Nolan, "Anatomy," in Gallagher and Nolan, *Myth*, 18.

8. Douglas Southall Freeman, *R.E. Lee*, vol. IV (New York and London: Charles Scribner's Sons, 1934–35), 505 (emphases added).

9. John A. Garrity, ed., *Encyclopedia of American Biography* (New York: Harper & Row, 1974), 653–54 (emphases added).

10. John Whiteclay Chambers II, ed., *The Oxford Companion to American Military History* (Oxford: Oxford University Press, 1999), 388–89 (emphasis added).

11. Piston, "Cross Purposes" in Gary W. Gallagher, ed., *The Third Day at Gettysburg & Beyond* (Chapel Hill: University of North Carolina Press, 1994), 47–51. "When the Civil War ended, Early and Pendleton were generally viewed as failures…. For Early and Pendleton, the worship of Lee seems to have given meaning to otherwise empty lives." Ibid., 48, 50.

12. Ibid., 43–84; Gallagher, "Generals" in Gabor S. Boritt, *Why the Confederacy Lost* (New York: Oxford University Press, 1992), 90–91; Douglas Southall Freeman, *Lee's Lieutenants: A Study in Command*, vol. III (New York: Charles Scribner's Sons, 1942–44) (1972 reprint), 770.

13. Pendleton must have been grateful that Lee had retained him as his chief of artillery despite his woeful performance. The religious Lee may have done so because Pendleton was a clergyman. "Lee's commitment to Christian faith may well solve the puzzle of his reliance upon William Nelson Pendleton as his chief of artillery long after it should have become apparent that he was in over his head." Richard Rollins, "Robert E. Lee and the Hand of God," *North & South* 6, no. 2 (Feb. 2003): 13–25 at 21. Pendleton indeed may have been Lee's 'spiritual friend' whom Lee never intended 'to exercise serious battlefield command.'"

14. J. William Jones, *Personal Reminiscences of General Robert E. Lee* (Richmond: United States Historical Society Press, 1874, 1989).

15. Connelly, *Marble Man*, 39–42, 73–90, 110; William Garrett Piston, *Lee's Tarnished Lieutenant: James Longstreet and His Place in Southern History* (Athens: University of Georgia Press, 1987), 130.

16. Connelly, *Marble Man*, 107–10.

17. Fitzhugh Lee, *General Lee: A Biography of Robert E. Lee* (New York: Da Capo Press, 1994; reprint of Wilmington, NC: Broadfoot Publishing Co., 1989; original published in 1894 by D. Appleton and Co.), 418.

18. Douglas Southall Freeman, *R. E. Lee* (New York and London: Charles Scribner's Sons, 1934–35).

19. Douglas Southall Freeman, *Lee's Lieutenants: A Study in Command* (New York: Charles Scribner's Sons, 1972).

20. Douglas Savage, *The Court Martial of Robert E. Lee: A Historical Novel* (Conshohocken, PA: Combined Books, 1993).

21. "Since the political definition of losing is retreat, Lee had lost the battle [of Antietam]. Since he would have had to withdraw after any battle, his decision to fight assured a negative political result in the South and a positive one in the North." Jones, "Military Means" in Boritt, *Why the Confederacy Lost*, 60.

22. Douglas Southall Freeman and Grady McWhiney, eds., *Lee's Dispatches: Unpublished Letters of General Robert E. Lee, C.S.A., to Jefferson Davis and the War Department of the Confederate States of America 1862–65* (Baton Rouge: Louisiana State University Press, 1957, 1994) (update of Freeman's original 1914 edition), xxxiv, xl. As late as 1941, Freeman was compiling a Civil War bibliography, looking for books that "have made new protagonists for the South," and admitting that he wanted to identify books "that have brought a new generation of Americans to understanding the Southern point of view." Nolan, "Anatomy" in Gallagher and Nolan, *Myth*, 15.

23. Piston, *Lee's Tarnished Lieutenant*, 174–76.

24. Gallagher, *Lee the Soldier*, xix–xx.

25. Piston, *Lee's Tarnished Lieutenant*, 183.

26. Emory M. Thomas, *Robert E. Lee: A Biography* (New York: W. W. Norton & Co., 1995).

27. Thomas Nelson Page, *Robert E. Lee: The Southerner* (New York: Charles Scribner's Sons, 1908); idem, *Robert E. Lee: Man and Soldier* (New York: Charles Scribner's Sons, 1911).

28. Page, *Lee the Southerner*, xiii.

29. Ibid., 5.

30. Ibid., 289.

31. Ibid., 52.

32. Page, *Lee the Southerner*, 257.

33. Alan T. Nolan, *Lee Considered: General Robert E. Lee and Civil War History* (Chapel Hill: University of North Carolina Press, 1991), 5.

34. Ibid., 59.

35. Mark Mayo Boatner III, *The Civil War Dictionary* (New York: David McKay Co., 1959, 1988), "Lee, Robert Edward."

36. Nolan, *Lee Considered*, 59.

37. Edward Porter Alexander, *The Military Memoirs of a Confederate* (New York: Charles Scribner's Sons, 1907).

38. Edward Porter Alexander, *Fighting for the Confederacy: The Personal Recollections of General Edward Porter Alexander* (Chapel Hill: University of North Carolina Press, 1989).

39. J. F. C. Fuller, *Grant and Lee: A Study in Personality and Generalship* (Bloomington: Indiana University Press, 1957) (reprint of 1933 edition), 8.

40. Gallagher, "Generals," in Boritt, *Why the Confederacy Lost*, 90, 95.

41. J. F. C. Fuller, *The Generalship of Ulysses S. Grant* (Bloomington: Indiana University Press, 1958) (Reprint of 1929 edition), 375.

42. B. H. Liddell Hart, "Lee: A Psychological Problem," *Saturday Review* XI (December 15, 1934): 365 ff.

43. Idem, "Why Lee Lost Gettysburg," *Saturday Review*, XI (March 23, 1935), 561 ff.

44. T. Harry Williams, "Freeman: Historian of the Civil War: An Appraisal," *Journal of Southern History* XXI (Feb. 1955): 91, 96, 98–100.

45. Thomas Lawrence Connelly, "Robert E. Lee and the Western Confederacy: A Criticism of Lee's Strategic Ability," *Civil War History* 15 (June 1969): 116–32.

46. Idem, "The Image and the General: Robert E. Lee in American Historiography," *Civil War History*, 19 (March 1973), 50–64.

47. Gallagher, "Generals" in Boritt, *Why the Confederacy Lost*, 95–96.

48. Connelly, *Marble Man*, 87–89.

49. Piston, *Lee's Tarnished Lieutenant*.

50. Nolan, *Lee Considered*; Gallagher, "Generals" in Boritt, *Why the Confederacy Lost*, 97; Gallagher, *Lee the Soldier*, xxiii.

51. Savage, *Court Martial*.

52. John D. McKenzie, *Uncertain Glory: Lee's Generalship Re-Examined* (New York: Hippocrene Books, 1997).

53. McWhiney and Jamieson, *Attack & Die, supra*.

54. Fuller, *Generalship of Grant*, 375.

55. I am not contending that some other Confederate general would have done better than Lee; the Confederacy, like the Union, had few experienced and competent generals. My contention is that Lee himself, especially after his experiences early in the war (for example, the disasters at Mechanicsville and Malvern Hill), should have realized he needed to do things differently: be less aggressive and more defensive, recognize the

importance of other theaters, enhance his staff, and take other steps to make better use of his army, himself, and the Confederacy.

56. See Lee Casualty Table.

57. Jackson was foolishly reconnoitering between the lines as dusk approached when he was shot by friendly North Carolina troops.

58. Lee's admirers often point to his supposedly predicting the point of the Army of the Potomac's river crossings the day before this campaign started (for example, Dowdey, *Lee's Last Campaign*, 32). If Lee was so sure of that, it is difficult to understand why he left Longstreet's corps so far from the rest of his army that it did not engage at the Wilderness until midmorning of the second day of the two-day battle.

59. Lee suffered an irreplaceable 50 percent casualty rate, while Grant, compelled to attack to fulfill his strategic goals, suffered a tolerable and replaceable 45 percent casualty rate. Gordon C. Rhea, "'Butcher' Grant and the Overland Campaign," *North & South* 4, no. 1 (Nov. 2000): 44–55 at 55. See Grant and Lee casualty tables below.

60. Nolan, *Lee Considered*, 260.

61. Grady McWhiney, "Who Whipped Whom: Confederate Defeat Reexamined," in John T. Hubbell, ed., *Conflict and Command* (Kent, OH: Kent State University Press, 2012), 325–47 at 346.

62. Rollins, "Lee and God," 23–24.

63. See text below for "killed and wounded" casualties incurred by Grant's and Lee's armies.

64. For documentation of these statistics, see Edward H. Bonekemper III, *Grant and Lee: Victorious American and Vanquished Virginian* (Westport, CT: Praeger/Greenwood, 2008) (Washington: Regnery, 2012), 267–69, 302–22.

65. For documentation of these statistics, see Bonekemper, *Grant and Lee*, 267–301, and Bonekemper, *Victor*, 283–323.

66. McWhiney, "Who Whipped Whom?", 345.

67. Fuller, *Grant and Lee*, 267.

68. Bevin Alexander, *Lost Victories: The Military Genius of Stonewall Jackson* (New York: Henry Holt, 1992), 221.

69. Alexander, *Great Generals*, 25–26.

70. Russell F. Weigley, *The American Way of War: A History of United States Military Strategy and Policy* (New York: Macmillan, 1973), 127.

71. Fellman, *Making of Lee*, 131.

72. "Perhaps the best way to illustrate the advantage defenders enjoyed over attackers is by a comparison of casualties. In half the twenty-two major battles of the Civil War the Federals attacked. They lost 119,000 men [casualties] when they assaulted and 88,000 when they defended—a difference of 31,000 men. The Confederates lost 117,000 when they attacked, but only 61,000 when they defended—a difference of 56,000 men, or enough to have given the South another large army." McWhiney, "Who Whipped Whom?" in Hubbell, *Conflict and Command*, 346.

73. Gallagher, "Generals" in Boritt, *Why the Confederacy Lost*, 98–108; Gallagher, "Another Look at the Generalship of R. E. Lee," 275–89, in Gallagher, *Lee the Soldier*.

74. William C. Davis, *Crucible of Command: Ulysses S. Grant and Robert E. Lee—The War They Fought, the Peace They Forged* (New York: Da Capo, 2015), 234–35. Support for this position is found in Rollins, "Lee and God," 18–21.

75. Davis, *Crucible*, 320.

76. Fuller, *Grant and Lee*, 261.

77. Archer Jones, "What Should We Think About Lee's Thinking?" *Columbiad* 1, no. 2 (Summer 1997): 73–85 at 84–85.

78. McWhiney and Jameson, *Attack and Die*, 19–22.

79. Justice Schiebert, *Seven Months in the Rebel States During the North American War, 1863* (Tuscaloosa, AL: Confederate Publishing Co., 1958), 75n, cited in Davis, *Crucible*, 328.

80. See Rollins, "Lee and God," 18–20.

81. Davis, *Crucible*, 329.

82. Lafayette McLaws to B. F. Johnson Publishing Co., July 13, 1895, reprinted in *North & South* I, no. 1 (Nov. 1997): 38, 40.

83. T. Harry Williams, "The Military Leadership of North and South" in David Herbert Donald, *Why the North Won the Civil War* (New York: Simon and Schuster, 1960, 1966, 2005), 38–57 at 52.

84. Archer Jones, *Confederate Strategy from Shiloh to Vicksburg* (Baton Rouge: Louisiana State University Press, 1991), 29.

85. Connelly, "Lee and the Western Confederacy", 118.

86. Philip Katcher, *The Army of Robert E. Lee* (London: Arms and Armour Press, 1994), 27.

87. Fuller, *Grant and Lee*, 255.

88. Connelly, *Marble Man*, 202–3.

89. Bonekemper, *Grant and Lee*, 159–63. After advising Davis that Longstreet should be moved to Knoxville "& thence rejoin me," Lee urged, "No time ought now to be lost or wasted. Everything should be done that can be done at once, so that the troops may be speedily returned to this department." Lee to Davis, September 23, 1863, *Papers of Lee*, 602–4 at 602–3.

90. Pollard, *Lost Cause*, 455–56.

91. Thomas Lawrence Connelly and Archer Jones, *The Politics of Command: Factions and Ideas in Confederate Strategy* (Baton Rouge: Louisiana State University Press, 1973), 180–81.

92. William Tecumseh Sherman, *Memoirs of General W. T. Sherman* (New York: Literary Classics of the United States, 1990), 752.

93. Fellman, *Making of Lee*, 187.

94. Williams, "Military Leadership" in Donald, *Why the North Won*, 52.

95. Alexander, *How Great Generals Win*, 164–65, quoting Liddell Hart, *Sherman: Soldier, Realist, American*, 356, and Sherman, *Memoirs*, 271.

96. McPherson, *Drawn with the Sword*, 130.

97. Pollard, *Lost Cause*, 655.

98. Davis, *Crucible*, 315.

99. Williams, "Military Leadership" in Donald, *Why the North Won*, 52.

100. T. Harry Williams, *Lincoln and His Generals* (New York: Alfred A. Knopf, 1952), 313; Wiley, *Road to Appomattox*, 115–16.

101. Paddy Griffith, *Battle Tactics of the Civil War* (New Haven: Yale University Press, 1996), 56.

102. Freeman, *R. E. Lee*, III, 230. For details on various members of Lee's staff through the war, see ibid., I, 638–43.

103. Allen C. Guelzo to author, April 7, 2015.

104. Williams, *Lincoln and His Generals*, 313.

105. Davis, *Crucible*, 317.

106. Wiley, *Road to Appomattox*, 115.

107. Thomas, *Lee*, 303.

108. Between March 29 and April 9, 1865, the Appomattox Campaign, about 6,266 Confederate troops were killed or wounded. Thomas L. Livermore, *Numbers & Losses in the Civil War in America: 1861–1865* (Millwood, NY: Kraus Reprint Co., 1977) (reprint of Bloomington: Indiana University Press, 1957), 137, 141.

109. Dowdey, *Lee*, 520.

110. Dowdey and Manarin, *Papers of Lee*, 897–98.

111. Williams, "Military Leadership" in Donald, *Why the North Won*, 53.

# CHAPTER SIX: DID JAMES LONGSTREET LOSE THE BATTLE OF GETTYSBURG AND THUS THE WAR?

1. William C. Davis, *Crucible of Command: Ulysses S. Grant and Robert E. Lee—The War They Fought, the Peace They Forged* (New York: Da Capo, 2015), 471.

2. Allen C. Guelzo, *Gettysburg: The Last Invasion* (New York: Alfred A. Knopf, 2013), 456–57.

3. Michael Fellman, *The Making of Robert E. Lee* (Baltimore: Johns Hopkins University Press, 2000), 159–61.

4. Thomas Nelson Page, *Robert E. Lee: The Southerner* (New York: Charles Scribner's Sons, 1908), 152.

5. Even adherents of much of the Lost Cause Myth did not focus on Longstreet until Jubal Early attacked him in the early 1870s. For example, Richmond editor Edward Pollard said the following in 1866 about Longstreet on Day Two at Gettysburg: "Longstreet...attacked with great fury.... Longstreet, with hat in hand, seemed to court the death which avoided him." He said nothing about delays, pouting, or petulance on Longstreet's part. Edward A. Pollard, *The Lost Cause: A New Southern History of the War of the Confederates* (New York: Gramercy Books, 1994; reprint of New York: E. B. Treat & Company, 1866 [mistakenly identified in reprint as 1886]), 407–8.

6.    Stewart Sifakis, *Who Was Who in the Civil War: A Comprehensive, Illustrated Biographical Reference to More Than 2,500 of the Principal Union and Confederate Participants in the War Between the States* (Berwyn Heights, MD: Heritage Books, 2014), 394.

7.    John Whiteclay Chambers II (ed.), *The Oxford Companion to American Military History* (Oxford: Oxford University Press, 1999), 402.

8.    Douglas Southall Freeman, *Lee's Lieutenants: A Study in Command* (New York: Charles Scribner's Sons, 1972); Freeman, *R. E. Lee* (New York and London: Charles Scribner's Sons, 1934–35).

9.    The speech is reprinted in Gary W. Gallagher, *Lee the Soldier* (Lincoln: University of Nebraska Press, 1996), 37–73.

10.   William Garrett Piston, *Lee's Tarnished Lieutenant: James Longstreet and His Place in Southern History* (Athens: University of Georgia Press, 1987), 118; Mark Perry, *Conceived in Liberty: Joshua Chamberlain, William Oates, and the American Civil War* (New York: Viking, 1997), 367. Longstreet had made himself a target by criticizing Lee. "The story of the 'lateness' on July 2nd is, nevertheless, pure cock-and-bull." Allen C. Guelzo to author, April 7, 2015.

11.   Piston, *Lee's Tarnished Lieutenant*, 37–45, 84–85, 121–22; Perry, *Conceived in Liberty*, 367.

12.   Jefferson Davis, *The Rise and Fall of the Confederate Government*, II (New York: Da Capo Press, Inc., 1990), 377–78.

13.   Perry, *Conceived in Liberty*, 367–68.

14.   Thomas Lawrence Connelly, *The Marble Man: Robert E. Lee and His Image in American Society* (New York: Alfred A. Knopf, 1977), 84–85.

15.   Perry, *Conceived in Liberty*, 368–69.

16.   J. William Jones, "Within a Stone's Throw of Independence at Gettysburg," *Southern Historical Society Papers* 12 (March 1884): 111–12, quoted in Nolan, *Lee Examined*, 169.

17.   Perry, *Conceived in Liberty*, 370–71.

18.   Ibid., 370.

19.   Freeman, *R. E. Lee*, III, 149. A few years later, Freeman appeared to back off somewhat; he continued to allege that Longstreet sulked, delayed, and did not fully use his forces, but he concluded, "To Longstreet's credit was

the belief that Cemetery Ridge, on July 2–3, was too strong to be stormed successfully. If, when the balance of Longstreet's account is struck, it still is adverse to him, it does not warrant the traditional accusation that he was the villain of the piece. The mistakes of Lee and of Ewell and the long absence of Stuart were personal factors of failure as serious as Longstreet's." Freeman, *Lee's Lieutenants*, 3, 188–89.

20.  Freeman, *R. E. Lee*, III, 149–50.

21.  Emory M. Thomas, *Robert E. Lee: A Biography* (New York: W. W. Norton & Company, 1995), 302.

22.  A possible criticism of Longstreet is that he failed to advise Lee that the actual situation on the rebel right flank was radically different than Lee had supposed. The Emmitsburg Pike was no longer open when he ordered an attack on it. Lee's supporters may have been reluctant to criticize Longstreet for that omission because it made Lee's initial order look wrong and because consultations with Lee would have delayed Longstreet and been inconsistent with the simplistic and inaccurate criticism of Longstreet based on his alleged delay in attacking.

23.  Davis, *Crucible*, 328.

24.  See Phillip Thomas Tucker, *Barksdale's Charge: The True High Tide of the Confederacy at Gettysburg, July 2, 1863* (Havertown, PA: Casemate, 2013).

25.  Thomas, *Lee*, 301–2, quotation on 302.

26.  Connelly, *Marble Man*, 87–89.

27.  John Keegan, *The American Civil War: A Military History* (New York: Alfred A. Knopf, 2009), 328; idem, "A Brit Rates Our Generals," *Civil War Times* XLVIII, no. 6 (Dec. 2009): 54–59 at 58. Unfortunately, Keegan's book is filled with errors. See Edward H. Bonekemper III, "Flawed Treatise by an Iconic Historian" (review of Keegan's *The American Civil War*), *Civil War Times* XLIX, no. 2 (April 2010).

28.  William L. Barney, *The Oxford Encyclopedia of the Civil War* (New York: Oxford University Press, 2001, 2011), 198.

29.  Nolan, "Anatomy," in Gary W. Gallagher and Alan T. Nolan, *The Myth of the Lost Cause and Civil War History* (Bloomington: University of Indiana Press, 2000, 2010), 23–24.

30.  Kenneth Nivison, "Gettysburg and the Americanization of the Civil War," in Clayton E. Jewett, ed., *The Battlefield and Beyond: Essays on the American Civil War* (Baton Rouge: Louisiana State University Press, 2012), 291–309, at 292–93.

31.  Perry, *Conceived in Liberty*, 365–66, 370.

32.  Allen C. Guelzo, however, argues that Lee may have been correct in keeping his army intact because "if Lee had managed to take Washington, the war would have been over in an afternoon." Guelzo also believes the Union did not focus on the real line of operations in the "West," Chattanooga-Atlanta-Savannah, until late 1863. Guelzo to author, April 7, 2015.

33.  Guelzo asserts this was a huge mistake because Civil War armies "were mass armies, heavily dependent on depots of supply, and these were only available through large cities with rail connections. Concentrating on Lee's army merely resulted in a series of bloody and inconsequential head-buttings. It was when Grant abandoned the head-butting and laid siege to Richmond that the game was over...." Guelzo to the author, April 7, 2015.

34.  Freeman, *R. E. Lee*, II, 483; Allan, "Conversations," February 19, 1870, in Gallagher, *Lee the Soldier*, 17.

35.  Thomas Lawrence Connelly, *Autumn of Glory: The Army of Tennessee, 1862–1865* (Baton Rouge: Louisiana State University Press, 1971, 1991), 94.

36.  Herman Hattaway and Archer Jones, *How the North Won: A Military History of the Civil War* (Urbana: University of Illinois Press, 1991), 362.

37.  Ibid., 503–4; Connelly, *Autumn of Glory*, 104; Steven E. Woodworth, *Davis and Lee at War* (Lawrence: University of Kansas Press, 1995), 219–21.

38.  Hattaway and Jones, *How the North Won*, 362.

39.  Ibid.

40.  Lee to James A. Seddon, April 9, 1863; Lee to Jefferson Davis, April 16, 1863: Dowdey and Manarin, *Papers*, 429–30, 435. "[Lee's] new theories were rationalizations. Like his emphatic reaction, these were subconsciously designed to forestall the diminution of his army and prevent the

derangement of his own plans for the spring campaign." Hattaway and Jones, *How the North Won*, 363.

41. Lee to General Samuel Cooper, Adjutant and Inspector General, April 16, 1863, Dowdey and Manarin, *Papers*, 434.

42. Woodworth, *Davis and Lee*, 220–21.

43. Ibid., 433–34.

44. Lee to his wife, April 19, 1863, Dowdey and Manarin, *Papers*, 437–38.

45. Connelly, *Autumn of Glory*, 114.

46. For details concerning Chancellorsville, see Stephen W. Sears, *Chancellorsville* (Boston and New York: Houghton Mifflin Company, 1996) (hereafter Sears, *Chancellorsville*); Ernest B. Furgurson, *Chancellorsville 1863: The Souls of the Brave* (New York: Alfred A. Knopf, 1992) (hereafter Furgurson, *Chancellorsville*); Freeman, *R. E. Lee*, II, 507–63.

47. Edward Porter Alexander, *Fighting for the Confederacy: The Personal Recollections of General Edward Porter Alexander* (Chapel Hill: University of North Carolina Press, 1989), 213.

48. Ibid., 92.

49. Hattaway and Jones, *How the North Won*, 385.

50. Ernest B. Furgurson, *Chancellorsville 1863: The Souls of the Brave* (New York: Alfred A. Knopf, 1992), 318.

51. Lee's later attempt to have Longstreet launch a flanking attack at Gettysburg was another in a series. "Lee's habit was, once he found a winning formula to keep repeating it. It had worked at 2nd Bull Run and at Chancellorsville, so back to the pump he went." Allen C. Guelzo to author, April 7, 2015.

52. On several occasions, Jackson had recommended flanking offensive campaigns into the North, but Lee and Davis rejected his recommendations. Bevin Alexander, *How Great Generals Win* (New York: W. W. Norton & Co., 1993), 123–42; Allan, "Conversations," December 17, 1868, in Gallagher, *Lee the Soldier*, 15.

53. "[Chancellorsville] looked to be a great Confederate victory, but the appearance was deceiving." Bevin Alexander, *Lost Victories: The Military Genius of Stonewall Jackson* (New York: Henry Holt and Company, 1992), 322.

54.  Livermore, *Numbers & Losses in the Civil War in America: 1861–1865* (Millwood, NY: Kraus Reprint Co., 1977), 98–99. Stephen Sears states that the Confederates had thirty more soldiers killed than the Union and only 439 fewer wounded. Sears, *Chancellorsville*, 442.

55.  General Order No. 63, May 14, 1863, William F. Fox, *Regimental Losses in the American Civil War, 1861–1865: A Treatise on the Extent and Nature of the Mortuary Losses in the Union Regiments, with Full and Exhaustive Statistics Compiled from the Official Records on File in the State Military Bureaus and at Washington* (Dayton: Morningside House, 1985), 559.

56.  Lee to James A. Seddon, May 10, 1863, Dowdey and Manarin, *Papers*, 482.

57.  Lee to Jefferson Davis, May 11, 1863, Dowdey and Manarin, *Papers*, 483–4.

58.  McPherson, *Battle Cry of Freedom*, 645; Steven E. Woodworth, *Davis and Lee at War* (Lawrence: University of Kansas Press, 1995), 230.

59.  Lee to John B. Hood, May 21, 1863, Dowdey and Manarin, *Papers*, 490.

60.  Harry W. Pfanz, *Gettysburg: The Second Day* (Chapel Hill and London: University of North Carolina Press, 1987), 4.

61.  Alexander, *Fighting for the Confederacy*, 222.

62.  James M. McPherson, *Battle Cry of Freedom: The Civil War Era* (New York: Ballantine Books, 1988), 646–47.

63.  Lee's arguments are reflected in his letters of April and May 1863. Lee to James A. Seddon, April 9, 1863; Lee to Samuel Cooper, April 16, 1863; Lee to Jefferson Davis, April 16, 1863; Lee to James A. Seddon, May 10, 1863; Lee to Jefferson Davis, May 11, 1863; Dowdey and Manarin, *Papers*, 430–31, 433–34, 434–35, 482, 483–84. See Thomas Lawrence Connelly and Archer Jones, *The Politics of Command: Factions and Ideas in Confederate Strategy* (Baton Rouge: Louisiana State University Press, 1973), 126–8.

64.  Lee to Jefferson Davis, June 23, 1863, Dowdey and Manarin, *Papers*, 527–8; Hattaway and Jones, *How the North Won*, 401–2, 404. Steven Woodworth notes, "Calling for Beauregard a month earlier, when the northern invasion itself was still being debated by the cabinet, would have

made fatally obvious to the cautious president that what Lee had in mind was an all-out end-the-war gamble." Woodworth, *Davis and Lee*, 238–39.

65.  Hattaway and Jones, *How the North Won*, 414.

66.  Lee to Jefferson Davis, June 25, 1863, Dowdey and Manarin, *Papers*, 530, 531.

67.  Lee to Jefferson Davis, June 25, 1863, Dowdey and Manarin, *Papers*, 532. Bruce criticizes Lee's post-battle explanation that he wanted to draw Hooker away from the Rappahannock and maneuver to gain a battlefield victory: "This discloses a piece of strategy with no definite objective, but one resting on a contingency. There is certainly something quixotic in the idea of moving an army two hundred miles for the purpose of finding a battlefield, leaving his base of supplies one hundred miles or more at the end of the railroad at Winchester [the railroad actually ended at Staunton, Virginia], when able to carry along only ammunition enough for a single battle, as was necessarily the case." Bruce, "Lee and Strategy," in Gallagher, *Lee the Soldier*, 117.

68.  Alexander, *Fighting for the Confederacy*, 219–20.

69.  Jones, "Military Means," in Gabor S. Boritt, *Why the Confederacy Lost*, (New York: Oxford University Press, 1992), 67.

70.  Connelly, *Autumn of Glory*, 114.

71.  Connelly, "Lee and the Western Confederacy," 124.

72.  Ibid. "Lee's Pennsylvania campaign demanded that the Confederacy not use eastern reserves to attempt to lift the Vicksburg siege; Bragg, weakened to aid Johnston [near Vicksburg], was driven from Middle Tennessee by Rosecrans's brilliant Tullahoma campaign; and Johnston's fragment was too small to operate effectively against the heavily reinforced Grant." Hattaway and Jones, *How the North Won*, 415.

73.  Beringer et al., *Why the South Lost*, 264, 300; Archer Jones, *Civil War Command & Strategy* (New York: Free Press, 1992), 168; "If on the other hand [Lee] fought a battle in Pennsylvania, he could choose his position and compel the Union army to fight another battle of Fredericksburg [what Longstreet recommended and Lee did not do]. But again Lee overlooked the political effect of fighting. Even a victorious defensive battle

would look like a defeat because of the inevitable retreat of a raiding army forced to concentrate and unable to forage." Jones, "Military Means," in Boritt, *Why The Confederacy Lost*, 68.

74.  Alexander, *Fighting for the Confederacy*, 110, 222. Often overlooked is the fact that Meade's nearest supply railhead was inconveniently located at Westminster, Maryland. Allen C. Guelzo to author, April 7, 2015.

75.  "Rather than a menace, Lincoln perceived Lee's raid, like the previous advance to Antietam, as an opportunity to strike the enemy when vulnerable and far from his base, 'the best opportunity' he said, 'we have had since the war began.'" Hattaway and Jones, *How the North Won*, 400.

76.  In 1868 Lee allegedly told William Allan that his intentions in moving north were defensive: "First [Lee] did not intend to give general battle in Pa. if he could avoid it—the South was too weak to carry on a *war of invasion*, and his offensive movements against the North were never intended except as parts of a defensive system." Allan, "Conversations" in Gallagher, *Lee the Soldier*, 13. Lee's actions in 1862 and 1863 seem inconsistent with that description.

77.  Perhaps the two best studies of Lee's Gettysburg campaign are Edwin B. Coddington, *The Gettysburg Campaign: A Study in Command* (New York: Charles Scribner's Sons, 1984) (hereafter Coddington, *Gettysburg Campaign*), and Allen C. Guelzo, *Gettysburg: The Last Invasion* (New York: Alfred A. Knopf, 2013).

78.  Weigley, *American Way of War*, 116.

79.  Gary W. Gallagher, "Brandy Station: The Civil War's Bloodiest Arena of Mounted Combat, *Blue & Gray* VIII, issue 1 (Oct. 1990): 8–22, 44–53 at 13.

80.  William Willis Blackford, *War Years with Jeb Stuart* (Baton Rouge: Louisiana State University Press, 1945, 1993), 211–12.

81.  Ibid., 212–13.

82.  Lee to his wife, June 9, 1863, Dowdey and Manarin, *Papers*, 506, 507.

83.  Allen C. Guelzo to author, April 7, 2015.

84.  Guelzo, *Gettysburg*, 129, 459. Guelzo's view: "It cannot be repeated too often: Lee did not lack for intelligence—for *strategic* information about the location, strength, and movement of the enemy; what he lacked was

screening—*tactical* concealment of his own movements from observation and contact by the enemy." Ibid., 459.

85. In addition, Lee had skilled cavalry with him, including the Sixth, Seventh, Eleventh, and Thirty-fifth Virginia cavalry regiments (heroes of Fleetwood Hill at Brandy Station), that he could have used, but did not, for scouting purposes. Nevertheless, after the war, Lee blamed Stuart for disobeying orders, keeping Lee uninformed and thereby forcing the fighting at Gettysburg. Allan, "Conversations," April 15, 1868, and February 19, 1870, in Gallagher, *Lee the Soldier*, 13–14, 17.

86. Josiah Gorgas, *The Civil War Diary of General Josiah Gorgas*, Frank E. Vandiver and Sarah Woolfolk Wiggins, eds. (Birmingham: University of Alabama Press, 1947, 1955), 70.

87. Lee to Jefferson Davis, June 23 and 25, 1863, Dowdey and Manarin, *Papers*, 527–28, 530–31, 532–33.

88. Lee to Jefferson Davis, June 25, 1863, Dowdey and Manarin, *Papers*, 531.

89. Lee to Jefferson Davis, June 25, 1863 (second letter), Dowdey and Manarin, *Papers*, 531.

90. For details of Day One, see Guelzo, *Gettysburg*, 137–231, and Coddington, *Gettysburg*, 260–322.

91. Harry w. Pfanz, *Gettysburg: The Second Day*. Chapel Hill: University of North Carolina Press, 1987), 20.

92. Jay Luvaas and Harold W. Nelson, eds., *The U.S. Army War College Guide to the Battle of Gettysburg* (Carlisle, PA: South Mountain Press, 1986), 5; Marshall D. Krolick, "Gettysburg: The First Day, July 1, 1863," *Blue & Gray* V, issue 2 (Nov. 1987): 8–20 at 14–15. On Buford's critical role on June 30 and July 1 at Gettysburg, see Edward Longacre, *General John Buford: A Military Biography* (Conshohocken, PA: Combined Books, 1995), 179–203; Krolick, "The First Day."

93. Krolick, "The First Day," 15.

94. Coddington, *Gettysburg Campaign*, 281.

95. Gary Kross, "That One Error Fills Him with Faults: Gen. Alfred Iverson and His Brigade at Gettysburg," *Blue & Gray* XII, issue 3 (February 1995): 22, 52–53. July 1 was the day Lee expected his army to concentrate at Gettysburg-Cashtown. "But he did expect a general engagement thereafter

with isolated portions of the AOP [Army of the Potomac]. Lee's ideal scenario would have been for Reynolds' left wing to have rushed pell-mell into the waiting arms of the entire ANV [Army of Northern Virginia] at Gettysburg, and been crushed; Lee could then have waited cheerfully to see if Meade would attack him with the rest of the reduced AOP, or allow him to spend the balance of the summer running rampant through central Pennsylvania." Allen C. Guelzo to author, April 7, 2015.

96. Pfanz, *The Second Day*, 22.

97. Ibid., 23.

98. Pfanz made this Lee-Meade comparison and also concluded, "Obviously [Lee] did not expect a battle that would limit his army's ability to maneuver as early as 1 July or he would not have given hundreds of wagons precedence over much needed infantry." Ibid., 22.

99. Jeffrey D. Wert, *General James Longstreet: The Confederacy's Most Controversial Soldier—A Biography* (New York: Simon & Schuster, 1993), 255.

100. Ibid., 72; Coddington, *Gettysburg Campaign*, 315.

101. Allen C. Guelzo presents a contrary view. He says that Lee viewed a general engagement as one involving all three of his corps. "Lee wished to hold off until Longstreet's corps was up; and he had every reason to believe that there was no hurry, and that the attack on Cemetery Hill could wait for the morning. He did not need another Malvern Hill." Allen C. Guelzo to author, April 7, 2015.

102. Wert, *Lee's Tarnished Lieutenant*, 49.

103. Freeman, *Lee's Lieutenants*, III, 94–95.

104. Coddington, *Gettysburg Campaign*, 316–17; Guelzo, *Gettysburg*, 213; Gallagher, "'If the Enemy Is There, We Must Attack Him': R. E. Lee and the Second Day at Gettysburg," 497–521, in Gallagher, *Lee the Soldier*, 508.

105. Coddington, *Gettysburg Campaign*, 320. William Garrett Piston concluded likewise. Piston, *Lee's Tarnished Lieutenant*, 49.

106. Guelzo, *Gettysburg*, 215–16.

107. Chris Mackowski and Kristopher D. White, "Second-Guessing Dick Ewell: Why Didn't the Confederate General Take Cemetery Hill on July 1, 1863?" *Civil War Times* 49, no. 4 (Aug. 2010): 34–41 at 41.

108. Freeman, *R. E. Lee*, III, 91; Pfanz, *The Second Day*, 111. Lee was uncomfortable enough about the extent of Union occupation that he sent Captain Johnson of his staff—with disastrous results—to reconnoiter to the south of Cemetery Hill. See below.

109. Hattaway and Jones, *How the North Won*, 406.

110. For details of Day Two (July 2), see Guelzo, *Gettysburg*, 233–370 and Coddington, *Gettysburg Campaign*, 323–441.

111. Coddington, *Gettysburg Campaign*, 372–74.

112. Guelzo, *Gettysburg*, 238–43. "The gentlest conclusion to draw is that Johnston climbed *some other hill*, and thought it was the Round Tops (which, in turn, may account for his surprise at leading [Lafayette] McLaws and [Thomas] Moncure [Longstreet subordinates] along a road and up a rise which, without warning, revealed them to Federal signalmen), and thus completely overlooking the mass of Union troops between Cemetery Hill and the Round Tops that morning." Ibid., 243.

113. Ibid.

114. Ibid., 324.

115. Ibid., 361; Pfanz, *The Second Day*, 26. Pfanz states that the exact dialogue will never be known. Pfanz, *The Second Day*, 26–27.

116. Lee to Samuel Cooper, Battle Report of Gettysburg Campaign, January 20, 1864, Dowdey and Manarin, *Papers*, 376.

117. Alexander, *Fighting for the Confederacy*, 233–34 (emphasis added). The italicized passage suggests an intriguing, perhaps compelling, option that Longstreet did not recommend and Lee did not exercise.

118. Daniel Bauer, "Did a Food Shortage Force Lee to Fight?: An Investigation into Lee's Claim that He Had to Attack at Gettysburg Because His Army Lacked Sufficient Rations to Do Anything Else," *Columbiad: A Quarterly Review of the War Between the States* I, no. 4 (Winter 1998): 57–74.

119. Allen C. Guelzo to author, April 7, 2015.

120. Lee to Samuel Cooper, Battle Report of Gettysburg Campaign, January 20, 1864, Dowdey and Manarin, *Papers*, 577.

121. Alexander, *Fighting for the Confederacy*, 236.

122. Ibid., 237.

123. Pfanz, *The Second Day*, 106. Pfanz also says there were other early morning probes of the Union left by Colonel Armistead H. Long and, of all people, General Pendleton. Ibid., 105–6.

124. Coddington, *Gettysburg Campaign*, 378; Freeman, *R. E. Lee*, III, 93; Freeman, *Lee's Lieutenants*, III, 115.

125. Alexander, *Fighting for the Confederacy*, 278; Coddington, *Gettysburg Campaign*, 378.

126. Freeman, *R. E. Lee*, III, 150.

127. Coddington, *Gettysburg Campaign*, 378–81; Freeman, *R.E. Lee*, III, 95–97.

128. Piston, *Lee's Tarnished Lieutenant*, 55–58.

129. Coddington, *Gettysburg Campaign*, 382.

130. Ibid., 55–58.

131. Guelzo, *Gettysburg*, 328–34.

132. Freeman, *R. E. Lee*, III, 100–101. For details and a unique perspective, see Phillip Thomas Tucker, *Barksdale's Charge: The True High Tide of the Confederacy at Gettysburg, July 2, 1863* (Havertown, PA: Casemate Publishers, 2013).

133. Lee's inaction prompted Arthur J. L. Fremantle, a British military observer at Gettysburg, to comment, "It is evidently his system to arrange the plan thoroughly with the three corps commanders, and then leave to them the duty of modifying and carrying it out to the best of their abilities." Piston, "Cross Purposes" in Gallagher, *Third Day*, 31, 43.

134. Piston, *Lee's Tarnished Lieutenant*, 58. Lee's uncoordinated attacks at Gettysburg were similar to those of McClellan at Antietam the prior summer.

135. Bruce points to Lee's failure, on both July 2 and 3, to launch properly coordinated attacks: "For two days, Gettysburg presents the spectacle of two desperately fought and bloody battles by less than one third of [Lee's] army on each occasion, the other two thirds looking on, for the conflict was visible from nearly every point on the Confederate lines. Does not all this present another question to solve [than] whether a corps commander

was quick or slow? Was the commander-in-chief justified in assigning such a task to such a force?" Bruce, "Lee and Strategy" in Gallagher, *Lee the Soldier*, 122.

136. Freeman, *R. E. Lee*, III, 101–2; Harry W. Pfanz, *Gettysburg—Culp's Hill & Cemetery Hill* (Chapel Hill: University of North Carolina Press, 1993), 235–83.

137. Pfanz, *Culp's and Cemetery Hills*, 284–327.

138. Alexander, *Fighting for the Confederacy*, 234–35. Similarly, Gary Pfanz criticized Lee for leaving Ewell, with one-third of Lee's outnumbered infantry, in an isolated position unsuited to offensive operations. Pfanz, *Second Day*, 426.

139. Pfanz faulted Lee for his hands-off supervision of Longstreet, whom Lee "... seems not to have hurried ... along," and Hill ("He did not rectify Hill's faulty deployment of Anderson's division or his inadequate measures to sustain Anderson's attack...."). Pfanz, *Second Day*, 426–27. For details on Hill's inadequate performance, see Ibid., 99, 114, 386–87.

140. For details of Day Three, see Gallagher, *Third Day*, 1–160; Coddington, *Gettysburg Campaign*, 442–534; Guelzo, Gettysburg, 371–446.

141. Coddington, *Gettysburg Campaign*, 465–76; Pfanz, *Culp's Hill & Cemetery Hill*, 284-309; Pfanz, *Second Day*, 438.

142. Coddington, *Gettysburg Campaign*, 450.

143. Shelby Foote, *The Civil War: A Narrative*, vol. II (New York: Random House, 1958–74), 525.

144. On this particular Lee-Longstreet dispute, see Piston, "Cross Purposes" in Gallagher, *Third Day*, 31–55.

145. Coddington, *Gettysburg Campaign*, 460. Longstreet later stated that Lee had written to him in the 1863–64 winter that, "If I only had taken your counsel even on the 3d [July 3], and had moved around the Federal left, how different all might have been." James Longstreet, "Lee's Right Wing at Gettysburg," 339–53, in Robert Underwood Johnson and Clarence Clough Buel, eds., *Battles and Leaders of the Civil War*, vol. III (New York: Thomas Yoseloff, 1956), 349.

146. Coddington, *Gettysburg Campaign*, 488.

147. Wert, *Longstreet*, 287.

148. Alexander, *Fighting for the Confederacy*, 254.

149. Alexander, *Great Generals*, 26.

150. Alexander, *Fighting for the Confederacy*, 251.

151. Ibid., 252.

152. Ibid., 258.

153. Ibid., 260; Coddington, *Gettysburg Campaign*, 500.

154. Freeman, *Lee's Lieutenants*, III, 157. Many of the attacking soldiers were not from Virginia.

155. Coddington, *Gettysburg Campaign*, 501.

156. Confederate Captain Joseph Graham, of the Charlotte Artillery, wrote in late July 1863 of Pettigrew's infantry "mov[ing] right through my Battery, and I feared then I could see a want of resolution in our men. And I heard many say, 'that is worse than Malvern Hill,' and 'I don't hardly think that position can be carried,' etc., etc., enough to make me apprehensive about the result...." Gallagher, "Lee's Army" in Gallagher, *Third Day*, 23.

157. The swales were deeper then than they are today; early twentieth-century plowing for crops reduced their depth by making the field more level.

158. Alexander, *Fighting for the Confederacy*, 266; Coddington, *Gettysburg Campaign*, 526; Wert, *Longstreet*, 292.

159. Bruce, "Lee and Strategy" in Gallagher, *Lee the Soldier*, 123–24.

160. John C. Waugh, *The Class of 1846: From West Point to Appomattox: Stonewall Jackson, George McClellan and Their Brothers* (New York: Warner Books, 1994), 487.

161. Piston, *Lee's Tarnished Lieutenant*, 62.

162. Wert, *Longstreet*, 292.

163. "Properly led on the decisive afternoon at Gettysburg, George Pickett's Virginians and Johnston Pettigrew's Carolinians would not have been sent across the killing fields from Seminary to Cemetery Ridge, against the massed Union army. But their bravery at Chancellorsville had persuaded their general that they were invincible, and so he sent them. And so Gettysburg was lost, and so the war." Furgurson, *Chancellorsville*, 350.

164. Coddington, *Gettysburg Campaign*, 525–26.

165. Freeman, *R. E. Lee*, III, 133–34.

166. Alexander, *Fighting for the Confederacy*, 278–80.

167. Fuller, *Grant and Lee*, 118.

168. Lee to Jefferson Davis, July 29, 1863, Dowdey and Manarin, *Papers*, 563.

169. Richard F. Welch, "Gettysburg Finale," *America's Civil War* (July 1993): 50–57.

170. Alexander, *Fighting for the Confederacy*, 271. But Lincoln and much of the Union army were greatly disappointed about the lack of an attack, which ensured Lee's escape. For details of the post-Gettysburg chase, see Ted Alexander, "Ten Days in July: The Pursuit to the Potomac," *North & South* 2, no. 6 (Aug. 1999): 10–34.

171. Coddington, *Gettysburg Campaign*, 535–74.

172. Longstreet, however, was in many ways his own enemy. He lashed out at critics with his own inaccurate and impolitic version of events, especially in James Longstreet, *From Manassas to Appomattox: Memoirs of the Civil War in America* (New York: Smithmark, 1994. Reprint of Philadelphia: Lipincott, 1896).

173. Fellman, *Making of Lee*, 149–50.

174. McKenzie, *Uncertain Glory*, 169–70.

175. Ibid., 92.

176. Davis, *Crucible*, 327–28.

177. Ibid., 330.

178. Lee to Samuel Cooper, Battle Report of Gettysburg Campaign, January 20, 1864, Dowdey and Manarin, *Papers*, 576.

179. Lee's attacks at Gettysburg "were an unhappy caricature of the most unfortunate aspects of his tactics." Woodworth, *Davis and Lee*, 245. On the plentitude of food available for Lee's army, see Bauer, "Food Supplies?"

180. Robert Hunt Rhodes, ed., *All for the Union: The Civil War Diary and Letters of Elisha Hunt Rhodes* (New York: Orion Books, 1991), 117.

181. Jones, "Military Means," in Boritt, *Why the Confederacy Lost*, 68.

182. Livermore, *Numbers & Losses*, 102–3.

183. Lee to Jefferson Davis, July 31, 1863, Dowdey and Manarin, *Papers*, 565.

184. Because of the misleadingly positive newspaper reports, Lee had cautioned his wife, "You will have learned before this reaches you that our success at Gettysburg was not as great as reported." Gary W. Gallagher, "Lee's Army Has Not Lost Any of Its Prestige: The Impact of Gettysburg on the Army of Northern Virginia and the Confederate Home Front," 1–30, in Gallagher, *Third Day*, 18. Lee to his wife, July 12, 1863, Dowdey and Manarin, *Papers*, 547.

185. Lee to Jefferson Davis, July 31, 1863, Dowdey and Manarin, *Papers*, 565.

186. Wiley, *Road to Appomattox*, 64–65.

187. "Principally, [Gettysburg] cost the Confederacy an immense number of killed and wounded, far greater in proportion to Lee's resources than the battle losses suffered by the Union. As President Davis later wrote, stressing the casualties: 'Theirs could be repaired, ours could not.'" Hattaway and Jones, *How the North Won*, 415.

188. Winston Groom, *Shrouds of Glory: From Atlanta to Nashville: The Last Great Campaign of the Civil War* (New York: Atlantic Monthly Press, 1995), 42.

189. Wert, *Longstreet*, 151.

190. Guelzo, *Gettysburg*, 461.

191. Joseph T. Glatthaar, "Black Glory: The African-American Role in Union Victory," 133–62 (hereafter Glatthaar, "Black Glory") in Boritt, *Why the Confederacy Lost*, 149–50.

192. Gorgas, *Journals*, 75.

# CHAPTER SEVEN: DID ULYSSES S. GRANT WIN THE CIVIL WAR SIMPLY BY BRUTE FORCE AND SUPERIOR NUMBERS?

1. Edward A. Pollard, *The Lost Cause: A New Southern History of the War of the Confederates* (New York: Gramercy Books, 1994; reprint of New York: E. B. Treat & Company, 1866 [mistakenly identified in reprint as 1886]), 509.

2. T. Harry Williams, *McClellan, Sherman and Grant* (New Brunswick: Rutgers University Press, 1962), 81. Williams was simply stating the views of others—not his own.

3.  Gallagher, "Introduction" in Gary W. Gallagher and Alan T. Nolan, *The Myth of the Lost Cause and Civil War History* (Bloomington: University of Indiana Press, 2000, 2010), 7.

4.  David Herbert Donald, *Lincoln* (New York: Simon & Schuster, 1995), 515; Gideon Welles, *Diary of Gideon Welles*, vol. II (Boston and New York: Houghton Mifflin, 1911), 45; Herman Hattaway, "The Changing Face of Battle," *North & South* 4, no. 6 (Aug. 2001): 34–43 at 42.

5.  Pollard, *Lost Cause*, 669; William Swinton, *Campaigns of the Army of the Potomac* (New York: Richardson, 1866), 440; John C. Ropes, "Grant's Campaign in Virginia in 1864," *Papers of the Military Historical Society of Massachusetts*, vol. 4, 495, quoted in Gordon C. Rhea, *Cold Harbor: Grant and Lee May 23–June 6, 1864* (Baton Rouge: Louisiana State University Press, 2002), xii.

6.  Gary W. Gallagher, "'Upon Their Success Hang Momentous Interests': Generals," in Gabor S. Boritt, *Why the Confederacy Lost*, (New York: Oxford University Press, 1992), 79–108 at 90–91, quoting Jubal A. Early, *The Campaigns of Gen. Robert E. Lee. An Address by Lieut. General Jubal A. Early, before Washington and Lee University, January 19, 1872* (Baltimore: Murphy, 1872), 44; E. M. Law, "From the Wilderness to Cold Harbor" in Johnson and Underwood, *Battles and Leaders*, IV, 118–44 at 143.

7.  Walter H. Taylor, *General Lee: His Campaigns in Virginia 1861–1865 with Personal Reminiscences* (Lincoln: University of Nebraska Press, 1994), 231, 241.

8.  Robert Douthat Meade, *Judah P. Benjamin: Confederate Statesman* (Baton Rouge: Louisiana State University Press, 1943, 2001), 284–85; Bruce Catton, *The Army of the Potomac: A Stillness at Appomattox* (Garden City: Doubleday & Company, 1953) dust jacket; Garraty, *Encyclopedia*, 653.

9.  Clifford Dowdey, *Lee* (Gettysburg: Stan Clark Military Books, 1991), 433; J. Michael Miller, "Strike Them a Blow: Lee and Grant at the North Anna River," *Blue & Gray Magazine*, issue 4 (April 1993): 12–22, 44–55. Elsewhere Dowdey describes Grant as a "boring-in type of attacker, who usually scorned finesse." Clifford Dowdey, *Lee's Last Campaign: The*

*Story of Lee and His Men Against Grant—1864* (Wilmington, NC: Broadfoot Publishing Company, 1988), 93.

10.  John Whiteclay Chambers II (ed.), *The Oxford Companion to American Military History* (Oxford: Oxford University Press, 1999), 302.

11.  Larry McGehee, "U. S. Grant Had a Career of Many Hills and Valleys," *Potomac News & Manassas Journal & Messenger* (Woodbridge, VA): September 8, 2001, A6; David Von Drehle, "Welcome to the Democrats' Misreading: How the Liberal Elite Keep Losing Big Elections to the 'Regular' Guys Like Bush and Reagan,." *Washington Post*, November 10, 2002, A4. Grant actually graduated twenty-first in his 1843 class of thirty-nine.

12.  John Keegan, *The American Civil War: A Military History* (New York: Alfred A. Knopf, 2009), 329; John Keegan, "A Brit Rates Our Generals," *Civil War Times* XLVIII, no. 6 (Dec. 2009): 58. See Grant Casualty Table in Chapter 5.

13.  Gregory A. Mertz, "No Turning Back: The Battle of the Wilderness," *Blue & Gray Magazine* XII, no. 5 (June 1995): 8–20, 48–50 at 50.

14.  Pollard, *Lost Cause*, 516. As shown in the casualty tables in Chapter 5, Lee's Wilderness casualties were about 11,125 and Grant's were about 17,666.

15.  William L. Barney, *The Oxford Encyclopedia of the Civil War* (New York: Oxford University Press, 2001, 2011), 152–53. Grant's casualties in the Overland Campaign were about fifty-five thousand. During the brief, disastrous charge at Cold Harbor, Grant probably incurred about 3,500 casualties. His total casualties for entire day were about six thousand. See the exhaustive study of these casualties in Gordon Rhea, "Cold Harbor: Anatomy of a Battle," *North & South* 5, no. 2 (Feb. 2002): 40–62 at 59–61.

16.  Don Lowry, *No Turning Back: The Beginning of the End of the Civil War: March–June 1864* (New York: Hippocrene Books, 1962), 519; Rhea, *Cold Harbor*, xi; E. B. Long, "Ulysses S. Grant for Today," in David L. Wilson and John Y. Simon (eds.), *Ulysses S. Grant: Essays and Documents* (Carbondale: University of Illinois Press, 1981), 22; "Reconsidering Grant and Lee: Reputations of Civil War Generals Shifting," Associated

Press, Jan. 8, 2003, http://www.cnn.com/2003/SHOWBIZ/books/01/08/ wkd.Grant.vs.lee.ap/index.html. Denigrating Grant in comparison to, and often to deify, Lee has a long history.

17. See Grant Casualty Table in Chapter 5.

18. Grady McWhiney and Perry D. Jamieson, *Attack and Die: Civil War Military Tactics and the Southern Heritage* (Tuscaloosa: University of Alabama Press, 1982), 19, 24, 25, 158.

19. See Grant and Lee casualty tables in Chapter 5.

20. See Bonekemper, *Victor*, Appendix III, "The Critical Election of 1864: How Close Was It?" 325–32; Edward H. Bonekemper III, "Lincoln's 1864 Victory Was Closer Than It Looked," *Washington Times*, July 15, 2000, B3.

21. Charles A. Dana, *Recollections of the Civil War* (New York: Collier Books, 1893, 1963), 187–89.

22. Rhea, *Cold Harbor*, xii.

23. McWhiney and Jamieson, *Attack and Die*, 19–24, 158; Grant Casualty Table in Chapter 5; *Washington Post*, May 28, 2001, A21. The 214,938 known American and Confederate battle deaths ranked behind the 291,557 in World War II, but ahead of 53,402 in World War I, 47,410 in the Vietnam War, 33,686 in the Korean War, 4,435 in the American Revolution, 2,260 in the War of 1812, 1,733 in the Mexican War, 1,000 in the Indian Wars, 385 in the Spanish-American War, and 148 in the Gulf War. *Washington Post*, May 28, 2001, A21.

24. David Hacker, "A Census-Based Count of the Civil War Dead," *Civil War History* LVII, no. 4 (Dec. 2011): 307–48.

25. See the casualty rates that follow in the text for other Civil War generals.

26. McWhiney and Jamieson, *Attack and Die*, 158.

27. Ibid., 19–21.

28. Ibid., 10–11.

29. Keegan, *American Civil War*, 328; Keegan, "Brit Rates," 58.

30. Gordon Rhea, Richard Rollins, Stephen Sears, and John Y. Simon, "What Was Wrong with the Army of the Potomac?" *North & South* 4, no. 3 (March 2001): 12–18 at 18.

31.    Russell F. Weigley, *The American Way of War: A History of United States Military Strategy and Policy* (New York: Macmillan Publishing Co., Inc., 1973), 128–29.

32.    Simon, Marszalek et al, *Papers of Grant*, I, xv; X, 273–75 at 274.

33.    Rhea et al., "What Was Wrong?" 15.

34.    Brooks D. Simpson, *Ulysses Grant: Triumph Over Adversity, 1822–1865* (New York: Houghton Mifflin, 2000), 458.

35.    Beringer et al, *Why the South Lost*, 31.

36.    "No Civil War general—not even Lee—was more aggressive than Grant. He assumed the offensive in nearly every campaign or battle he directed." McWhiney and Jamieson, *Attack and Die*, 157.

37.    Williams, *McClellan, Sherman and Grant*, 77.

38.    "Reconsidering Grant and Lee."

39.    James M. McPherson, "The Unheroic Hero," *The New York Review of Books* XLVI, no. 2 (February 4, 1999): 16–19 at 18; Williams, *McClellan, Sherman and Grant*, 95; Al W. Goodman Jr., "Grant's Mississippi Gamble," *America's Civil War* 7, no. 3 (July 1994): 50–56 at 54; Terrence J. Winschel, "Vicksburg: 'Thank God. The Father of Waters again goes unvexed to the sea,'" *America's Civil War* 16, no. 3 (July 2003): 18–19 at 19. Grant's version of the Vicksburg Campaign is in Ulysses S. Grant, "The Vicksburg Campaign" in *Battles and Leaders*, III, 493–539 and in Grant, *Memoirs*, 303–83.

40.    Terrence J. Winschel, "Grant's March Through Louisiana: 'The Highest Examples of Military Energy and Perseverance,'" *Blue & Gray* XIII, no. 5 (June 1996): 8–22 at 9.

41.    J. F. C. Fuller, *The Generalship of Ulysses S. Grant* (Bloomington: Indiana University Press, 1958), 137.

42.    Winschel, "Grant's March," 13–15.

43.    Grant, *Memoirs*, 305–6.

44.    Grant, *Memoirs*, 306–8; Bruce Catton, *Grant Moves South* (Boston: Little, Brown and Company, 1960), 411–15; Winschel, "Grant's March," 17; Keith Poulter, "Decision in the West: The Vicksburg Campaign, Part II: Running the Batteries," *North & South* 1, no. 3 (Feb. 1998): 68–75 at 69.

45.  Edwin Cole Bearss, *Unvexed to the Sea: The Campaign for Vicksburg*, vol. II (Dayton: Morningside House, Inc., 1991), 53–74; James R. Arnold, *Grant Wins the War: Decision at Vicksburg* (New York: John Wiley & Sons, Inc., 1997), 78.

46.  Grant, *Memoirs*, 306–8; Catton, *Grant Moves South*, 411–15; Winschel, "Grant's March," 17; Poulter, "Decision Part II," 69.

47.  Smith, *Grant*, 236–37; Arnold, *Grant Wins*, 78–79.

48.  Grant, *Memoirs*, 309; 16–19; Nevins, *Ordeal of the Union*, VI, 415. Ever innovative, Grant had tried building a canal (the Duckport Canal) to assist in the movement from Hard Times to New Carthage, but the effort was unsuccessful. Winschel, "Grant's March," 14–15.

49.  Bearss, *Vicksburg*, II, 74–82; Grant, *Memoirs*, 310-14; Smith, *Grant*, 237; Arnold, *Grant Wins*, 79–81.

50.  Arnold, *Grant Wins*, 81–82.

51.  William B. Feis, *Grant's Secret Service: The Intelligence War from Belmont to Appomattox* (Lincoln: University of Nebraska Press, 2002), 144–45.

52.  Kenneth P. Williams, *Grant Rises in the West*, vol II (Lincoln: University of Nebraska Press, 1997), 339; Dave Roth, "Grierson's Raid: A Cavalry Raid at Its Best, April 17–May 2, 1863," *Blue & Gray* X, no. 5 (June 1993): 12–24, 48–65 at 13; Grant to Hurlbut, Feb. 13, 1863, Simon, Marszalek et al, *Papers of Grant*, VII, 316–17 at 317. For more details on Grierson's raid, see Bearss, *Vicksburg*, II, 187–236.

53.  Roth, "Grierson's Raid," 21–24.

54.  Ibid., 48–51.

55.  Ibid., 58–61.

56.  Arnold, *Grant Wins*, 87; Williams, *Grant Rises in the West*, II, 345.

57.  Russell F. Weigley, *A Great Civil War: A Military and Political History, 1861–1865* (Bloomington and Indianapolis: Indiana University Press, 2000), 265; Roth, "Grierson's Raid," 13, 64–65; Foote, *Civil War*, II, 334; Smith, *Grant*, 239; Arnold, *Grant Wins*, 87.

58.  Feis, *Grant's Secret Service*, 146; Roth, "Grierson's Raid," 48–49.

59.  Grant, *Memoirs*, 318; Weigley, *Great Civil War*, 265; Catton, *Grant Moves South*, 422–24; Winschel, "Grant's March," 19.

60. Feis, *Grant's Secret Service*, 158; Winschel, "Grant's March," 19; Dana, *Recollections*, 56–58; Arnold, *Grant Wins*, 87–89.

61. Grant, *Memoirs*, 315–17; Winschel, "Grant's March," 19–20.

62. Grant, *Memoirs*, 317–21; Poulter, "Decision Part II," 75.

63. Grant, *Memoirs*, 321.

64. Winschel, "Grant's March," 22.

65. Terrence J. Winschel, "Grant's Beachhead for the Vicksburg Campaign: The Battle of Port Gibson, May 1, 1863," *Blue & Gray* XI, no. 3 (Feb. 1994): 8–22, 48–56 at 15–19.

66. Arnold, *Grant Wins*, 98.

67. For details and battle maps of the Battle of Port Gibson, see Winschel, "Grant's Beachhead"; Arnold, *Grant Wins*, 101–18; and Bearss, *Vicksburg*, II, 353–407. For battle maps of the battles of Port Gibson, Raymond, and Jackson, see Keith Poulter, "Decision in the West: The Vicksburg Campaign, Part III," *North & South* 1, no. 4 (April 1998): 77–83.

68. Grant, *Memoirs*, 321–24; Winschel, "Grant's Beachhead," 20–22, 48–55. Bearss, Ed, "The Vicksburg Campaign: Grant Moves Inland," *Blue & Gray* XVIII, no. 1 (October 2000): 6–22, 46–52, 65 at 6; Goodman, "Grant's Gamble," 52–56. Even after the fall of Port Gibson, General Pemberton in Vicksburg had no idea what Grant was doing. He telegraphed his local commander, "Is it not probable that the enemy will himself retire tonight?" Goodman, "Grant's Gamble," 56.

69. Winschel, "Grant's Beachhead," 56.

70. Ibid.; Arnold, *Grant Wins*, 116–17; Michael B. Ballard, "Misused Merit: The Tragedy of John C. Pemberton," in Steven E. Woodworth (ed.), *Civil War Generals in Defeat* (Lawrence: University of Kansas Press, 1999), 141–60 at 157.

71. Poulter, "Decision Part III," 77.

72. E. M. Stanton to C. M. Dana, May 6, 1863, in Dana, *Recollections*, 66.

73. Grant, *Memoirs*, 324–27; Bearss, "Grant Moves Inland," 6; Weigley, *Great Civil War*, 265.

74. On May 3, Grant wrote to Halleck of Grierson's raid and concluded: "He has spread excitement throughout the State, destroyed railroads, trestle

works, bridges, burning locomotives & rolling stock taking prisoners destroying stores of all kinds [sic]. To use the expression of my informant 'Grierson has knocked the heart out of the State.'" Grant to Halleck, May 3, 1863, Simon, Marszalek et al, *Papers of Grant*, VIII, 144.

75.  Grant, *Memoirs*, 326–28; Bearss, "Grant Moves Inland," 6–7; Weigley, *Great Civil War*, 266.

76.  Grant to Halleck, May 3, 1863, Simon, Marszalek et al, *Papers of Grant*, VIII, 145–48 at 147–48.

77.  Poulter, "Decision III," 78.

78.  Grant, *Memoirs*, 328–29; Bearss, "Grant Moves Inland," 7–8.

79.  Williams, *McClellan, Sherman and Grant*, 95.

80.  Thomas B. Buell, *The Warrior Generals: Combat Leadership in the Civil War* (New York: Crown Publishers, Inc., 1997), 247.

81.  Feis, *Grant's Secret Service*, 160.

82.  Fuller, *Generalship of Grant*, 140–46.

83.  Noah Andre Trudeau, "Climax at Vicksburg," *North & South* 1, no. 5 (June 1998): 80–89 at 83.

84.  For details on the Battle of Raymond, see Bearss, *Vicksburg*, II, 483–517.

85.  Grant, *Memoirs*, 330–31; Bearss, "Grant Moves Inland," 8–21; Arnold, *Grant Wins*, 129–36; William F. Fox, *Regimental Losses in the American Civil War, 1861–1865* (Dayton: Morningside House, Inc., 1985), 544, 550.

86.  Bearss, "Grant Moves Inland," 10; Smith, *Grant*, 245; William C. Davis, *Jefferson Davis: The Man and His Hour* (Baton Rouge: Louisiana State University Press, 1962), 501–4. For General Johnston's critique of Davis's involvement in the defense of Vicksburg, and particularly his refusal to provide reinforcements from west of the Mississippi, see Joseph E. Johnston, "Jefferson Davis and the Mississippi," in *Battles and Leaders*, III, 472–82. Johnston was responding to Davis's criticism of Johnston's conduct of the campaign in Davis, *Rise and Fall*, II, 333–55. There Davis found no fault with Pemberton's conduct but stated that Johnston failed to act at all, let alone promptly, to come to Pemberton's and Vicksburg's relief.

87.  Grant, *Memoirs*, 332; Bearss, "Grant Moves Inland," 21–22; William B.
     Feis, "Charles S. Bell: Union Scout," *North & South* 4, no. 5 (June 2001):
     26–37, 28–29; Grant to McClernand, McPherson, and Sherman (three
     dispatches), May 12, 1863, Simon, Marszalek et al, *Papers of Grant*, VIII,
     204–8; Grant to McClernand (two dispatches), May 13, 1863, Ibid.,
     208–9. Grant's entire order to Sherman after the battle at Raymond
     reflects Grant's decision to take Jackson and his characteristic pithiness—
     especially in dealing with Sherman: "After the severe fight of today at
     Raymond and repulse of the enenemy [sic] towards Clinton and Jackson,
     I have determined to move on the latter place by way of Clinton, and take
     the Capitol of the state and work from there westward. McPherson is
     ordered to march at day light to Clinton. You will march at 4. A. M. in
     the morning and follow McPherson. McClernand will follow you with
     three Divisions, and send his fourth back to old Auburn, to await the
     arrival of trains now on the road (from Grand Gulf), and Blairs Division
     to conduct them after the Enemy." Grant to Sherman, May 12, 1863,
     Ibid., 207–8.
88.  Grant, *Memoirs*, 333; Bearss, "Grant Moves Inland," 46–47.
89.  Feis, *Grant's Secret Service*, 161.
90.  For details on the Battle of Jackson, see Bearss, *Vicksburg*, II, 519–58.
91.  Grant, *Memoirs*, 334–38; Bearss, "Grant Moves Inland," 47–51, 65;
     "The Opposing Forces in the Vicksburg Campaign," in *Battles and Lead-
     ers*, III, 546–50 at 549; Weigley, *Great Civil War*, 267; Harold S. Wilson,
     *Confederate Industry: Manufacturers and Quartermasters in the Civil
     War* (Jackson: University of Mississippi Press, 2002), 192–93.
92.  Feis, "Charles S. Bell," 29. Sherman's men tore up railroad ties and rails,
     set the ties on fire, heated the rails on those fires, and then bent the rails
     around trees and telegraph poles in what became known as "Sherman
     necklaces." Bearss, "Grant Moves Inland," 52.
93.  Grant, *Memoirs*, 338–40; Bearss, "Grant Moves Inland," 51–52; Feis,
     *Grant's Secret Service*, 162.
94.  Grant, *Memoirs*, 340–41; Feis, *Grant's Secret Service*, 163; Ed Bearss,
     "The Vicksburg Campaign. Grant Marches West: The Battles of Cham-
     pion Hill and Big Black Bridge," *Blue & Gray* XVIII, no. 5 (June 2001):

6–24, 44–52 (hereafter Bearss, "Grant Marches West) at 8–9. The Bearss article contains excellent maps of both those battles. For more details and battle maps on the Battle of Champion's Hill, see Arnold, *Grant Wins*, 147–99, and Bearss, *Vicksburg*, II, 559–651.

95. Bearss, "Grant Marches West," 9–11.

96. Ibid., 16.

97. Ibid., 12, 16–19; Arnold, *Grant Wins*, 158–69.

98. Bearss, "Grant Marches West," 13, 20–21; Arnold, *Grant Wins*, 170–78.

99. Bearss, "Grant Marches West," 14, 21–24; Arnold, *Grant Wins*, 178–92; Foote, *Civil War*, II, 372–73.

100. Bearss, "Grant Marches West," 15, 44–45.

101. Grant, *Memoirs*, 342–48; Livermore, *Numbers & Losses*, 99–100; Bearss, "Grant Marches West," 45.

102. Arnold, *Grant Wins*, 197–99; Foote, *Civil War*, II, 375; Grant, *Memoirs*, 349.

103. Grant, *Memoirs*, 349–50; Bearss, "Grant Marches West," 45; Kirk Freeman, "Big Black River," *Military Heritage* 2, no. 3 (Dec. 2000): 76–85 at 78–80; Al W. Goodman Jr., "Decision in the West (Part IV): Between Hell and the Deep Sea: Pemberton's Debacle at Big Black River Bridge," *North & South* 1, no. 5 (June 1998): 74–79 at 74–77.

104. For details and battle maps of the Battle of the Big Black River, see Freeman, "Big Black River"; Goodman, "Decision"; Arnold, Grant Wins, 225–32; and Bearss, Vicksburg, II, 653–89.

105. Grant, *Memoirs*, 350–53; Bearss, "Grant Marches West," 45–46; Freeman, "Big Black River," 81–85; Goodman, "Decision," 77–79; Dick Barton, "Charge at Big Black River," *America's Civil War* 12, no. 4 (Sept. 1999): 54–61.

106. Grant, *Memoirs*, 350–54; Bearss, "Grant Marches West," 49.

107. Grant, *Memoirs*, 354. In fact, Sherman had verbally and by letter urged Grant before the crossing of the Mississippi not to undertake the risky campaign with no base or line of supply. Grant was more concerned about the impact in the North if he appeared to be retreating by returning to Memphis to restart a presumably safer overland campaign against Vicksburg. As soon as Vicksburg was besieged, Sherman himself revealed his

earlier opposition. But Grant was fully forgiving: "(Sherman's) untiring energy and great efficiency during the campaign entitle him to a full share of all the credit due for its success. He could not have done more if the plan had been his own." Grant, *Memoirs*, 364.

108. Weigley, *American Way of War*, 139–40; Bearss, "Grant Marches West," 52 (emphasis added).

109. Grant, *Memoirs*, 354–56; Bearss, *Vicksburg*, III, 753–873. *Chicago Times* reporter Sylvanus Cadwallader observed McClernand's May 22 attack and wrote: "McClernand had commenced his attack. He expected to succeed. But that he ever carried any part of the fortifications on his front, as he signaled Grant he had already done, was absolutely false." Sylvanus Cadwallader, *Three Years with Grant* (New York: Alfred A. Knopf, 1956), 92. Sherman agreed that McClernand had lied and thereby caused many additional casualties. Sherman, *Memoirs*, 352–53.

110. Grant, *Memoirs*, 588–89.

111. Fuller, *Generalship of Grant*, 154; Livermore, *Numbers & Losses*, 100; Grant, *Memoirs*, 358.

112. Lee to Davis, May 28, 1863, Freeman, *Lee's Dispatches*, 96–99 at 98 (emphasis added).

113. Grant, *Memoirs*, 359–60, 1134; Arnold *Armies of Grant*, 127; E. Chris Evans, "Return to Jackson: Finishing Stroke to the Vicksburg Campaign, July 5–25, 1863," *Blue & Gray* XII, no. 6 (Aug. 1995): 8–22, 50–63 at 12; Trudeau, "Climax at Vicksburg," 86.

114. David M. Smith, "Too Little Too Late at Vicksburg," *America's Civil War*, Vol. 13, No. 2 (May 2000), 38–44; Williams, *Grant Rises in the West*, II, 452–53.

115. Lincoln to I. N. Arnold, May 26, 1863, Basler, *Works of Lincoln*, vol. VI, 30–31 at 30.

116. Grant, *Memoirs*, 359–60, 1134; Evans, "Return to Jackson," 12; Trudeau, "Climax at Vicksburg," 87; and Bearss, *Vicksburg*, III, 875–81. McClernand's termination was due to "a rather long list of vexatious shortcomings which had been constantly accumulating against him for months, and his uncontrollable itching for newspaper notoriety"—as well

as his costly and dubious claims of initial success during the May 22 assault on Vicksburg's fortifications. Cadwallader, *Three Years*, 92.

117. Grant, *Memoirs*, 368; Evans, "Return to Jackson," 12.

118. Grant, *Memoirs*, 369–70; Phillip A. B. Leonard, "Forty-seven Days. Constant bombardment, life in bomb shelters, scarce food and water, and rapidly accumulating filth were the price of resistance for the resolute Confederate citizens of besieged Vicksburg, Mississippi," *Civil War Times Illustrated* XXXIX, no. 4 (August 2000): 40–49, 68–69; Evans, "Return to Jackson," 14; Smith, "Too Little," 44; Andrew Hickenlooper, "The Vicksburg Mine" in *Battles and Leaders* III, 539–42. Vicksburg residents' primary meats were mules and rats. Anonymous, "Daily Life during the Siege of Vicksburg," in William E. Gienapp (ed.), *The Civil War and Reconstruction: A Documentary Collection* (New York and London: W. W. Norton and Company, 2001), 159–62.

119. Michael Morgan, "Digging to Victory," *America's Civil War* 16, no. 3 (July 2003): 22–29; Arnold, *Grant Wins*, 298.

120. Grant, *Memoirs*, 374–75.

121. Grant, *Memoirs*, 384; S. H. Lockett, "The Defense of Vicksburg," in *Battles and Leaders*, III, 482–92 at 492. Lockett was the Confederate chief engineer at Vicksburg.

122. Grant, *Memoirs*, 375–82.

123. Bearss, *Vicksburg*, III, 1301–10; Bruce Catton, *This Hallowed Ground: The Story of the Union Side of the Civil War* (Garden City, NY: Doubleday, 1956, 1962), 122; Arnold, *Grant Wins*, 298–99; Davis, *Jefferson Davis*, 508–9.

124. Evans, "Return to Jackson"; Feis, "Charles S. Bell," 30–31.

125. Arnold, *Grant Wins*, 301; Fuller, *Generalship of Grant*, 158.

126. Grant, *Memoirs*, I, 572.

127. Hattaway and Jones, *How the North Won*, 415.

128. Evans, "Return to Jackson," 63.

129. Nevins, *Ordeal of the Union*, VI, 425.

130. Smith, *Grant*, 256.

131. Basler, *Works of Lincoln*, VI, 326.

132. McWhiney and Jamieson, *Attack and Die*, 8, 19–21, 158.

133. "Opposing Forces" at 549–50; Weigley, *American Way of War*, 140.

134. J. B. Jones, *A Rebel War Clerk's Diary at the Confederate States Capital* (2 vols.) (Philadelphia: J. B. Lippincott & Co., 1866) (1982 reprint), I, 374; Gorgas, *Diary*, 55.

135. Fuller, *Generalship of Grant*, 154; Livermore, *Numbers & Losses*, 100; Grant, *Memoirs*, 358.

136. Feis, *Grant's Secret Service*, 173–74.

137. Trudeau, "Climax at Vicksburg," 88.

138. Steven Woodworth commented, "Twenty years later [President] Davis still did not understand that Grant had no supply lines for the Confederates to cut or that Pemberton, in allowing himself to be bottled up in Vicksburg, had made the worst possible move." Steven E. Woodworth, *Jefferson Davis and His Generals: The Failure of Confederate Command in the West* (Lawrence: University Press of Kansas, 1990), 310.

139. Bearss, *Vicksburg*, III, 1311.

140. T. Harry Williams, "The Military Leadership of North and South" in Donald, *Why the North*, 53.

141. Adam Badeau, , *Military History of Ulysses S. Grant, from April, 1861, to April, 1865*, vol. II (New York: D. Appleton and Company, 1868), 21.

142. Edward H. Bonekemper III, *How Robert E. Lee Lost the Civil War* (Fredericksburg, VA: Sergeant Kirkland's Press, 1998), 203.

143. McPherson, "Unheroic Hero."

144. Keegan, *Mask of Command*, 200. Grant probably modeled his orders on those of Zachary Taylor, of whom Grant wrote: "Taylor was not a conversationalist, but on paper he could put his meaning so plainly that there could be no mistaking it. He knew how to express what he wanted to say in the fewest well-chosen words." Grant, *Memoirs*, 95.

145. Horace Porter, *Campaigning with Grant* (New York: Smithmark Publishers, 1994), 7.

146. R. Steven Jones, *The Right Hand of Command: Use & Disuse of Personal Staffs in the Civil War*. (Mechanicsburg, PA: Stackpole Books, 2000), 111–12.

147. Smith, *Grant*, 202.

148. James M. McPherson, *Drawn with the Sword: Reflections on the American Civil War* (New York: Oxford University Press, 1966), 165.

149. Porter, *Campaigning with Grant*, 66.

150. Williams, *Lincoln and His Generals*, 313.

151. Richard H. Owens, "An Astonishing Career," *Military Heritage* 3, no. 2 (Oct. 2001): 64–73.

152. Porter, *Campaigning with Grant*, 250.

153. Jones, *Right Hand*, 86–122, 176–219.

154. Ibid., 219.

155. Arnold, *Grant Wins*, 4.

156. McPherson, "Unheroic Hero"; Rhea, *Cold Harbor*, 388.

157. OR, Ser. I, XLVI, I, 22.

158. Rhea, *Cold Harbor*, 388.

159. Arnold, *Armies of Grant*, 275.

160. Gallagher, "'Upon Their Success'" in Boritt, *Why the Confederacy Lost*, 91.

161. Arnold, *Grant Wins*, 4.

162. Smith, *Grant*, 138; Fuller, *Grant and Lee*, 81.

163. Williams, *Lincoln and His Generals*, 271.

164. William O. Stoddard Jr., *William O. Stoddard: Lincoln's Third Secretary* (New York: Exposition Press, 1955), 197–98.

165. Williams, *McClellan, Sherman and Grant*, 97.

166. Weigley, *American Way of War*, 130.

167. Hattaway and Jones, *How the North Won*, xvi.

168. Catton, *Grant Takes Command*, 105.

169. Steven E. Woodworth, "The Army of the Tennessee and the Element of Military Success," *North & South* 6, no. 4 (May 2003): 44–55 at 52.

170. Catton, *Grant Moves South*, 217; Arnold, *Armies of Grant*, 108.

171. Williams, *McClellan, Sherman and Grant*, 59.

172. Donald, "Military Leadership," 53–54.

173. McPherson, "Unheroic Hero."

174. Fuller, *Generalship of Grant*, 190.

175. Jacob Dolson Cox, *Military Reminiscences of the Civil War*, vol. II (New York: Charles Scribner's Sons, 1900), 41.

176. Williams, *McClelland, Sherman and Grant*, 105–6.

177. Williams, T. Harry, "The Military Leadership of North and South," in Donald, *Why the North Won the Civil War*, 54–55.

178. Williams, T. Harry, "The Military Leadership of North and South," in Donald, *Why the North*, 50–52.

179. McPherson, James M., "Lincoln and the Strategy of Unconditional Surrender," in Boritt, Gabor S. (ed.), *Lincoln, the War President: The Gettysburg Lectures* (New York: Oxford University Press, 1992), 45.

180. Buell, *Warrior Generals*, 247.

181. Bearss, *Vicksburg*, III, 1311.

182. Smith, *Grant*, 369.

183. Fuller, *Generalship of Grant*, 195.

184. Catton, *Grant Moves South*, 489.

185. Cox, *Reminiscences*, II, 41.

186. Feis, *Grant's Secret Service*, 267.

# CHAPTER EIGHT: DID THE NORTH WIN BY WAGING "TOTAL WAR"?

1.   Charles Strozier, "The Tragedy of Unconditional Surrender," *Military History Quarterly*, 2 (Spring 1990), 12, 14.

2.   Edward A. Pollard, *The Lost Cause: A New Southern History of the War of the Confederates* (New York: Gramercy Books, 1994; reprint of New York: E. B. Treat & Company, 1866 [mistakenly identified in reprint as 1886]), 404.

3.   Kent Masterson Brown, *Lee, Logistics, and the Pennsylvania Campaign* (Chapel Hill: University of North Carolina Press, 2005), 48–49.

4.   Pollard, *Lost Cause*, 404–5.

5.   Jefferson Davis, *The Rise and Fall of the Confederate Government*, vol. II, (New York: Da Capo Press, Inc., 1990), 335.

6.   Mark E. Neely Jr., "Was the Civil War a Total War?" in John T. Hubbell (ed.), *Conflict and Command* (Kent, Ohio: Kent State University Press, 2012), 17–42 at 20–21.

7.   James M. McPherson, *Drawn with the Sword: Reflections on the American Civil War* (New York: Oxford University Press, 1966), 130.

8.   Ibid., 74–75.

9.   "The North was still in an uproar over the slaughter of 231 of the Mississippi River fort's 571 troops, most of them black, after its capture April 12 [1864]. Union officers said the Rebels massacred the black troops after the garrison surrendered; the Rebels claimed the defenders died during the fighting. The Confederate commander, Nathan Bedford Forrest, boasted that 'the river was dyed with the blood of slaughter for two hundred yards.... Negro soldiers cannot cope with Southerners.'" Joseph Wheelan, *Bloody Spring: Forty Days That Sealed the Confederacy's Fate* (New York: Da Capo, 2014), 28–29.

10.  John David Smith (ed.), *Black Soldiers in Blue: African American Troops in the Civil War Era* (Chapel Hill: University of North Carolina Press, 2002), 125–26, 144–45, 150–68, 185–87, 200–26. These were not isolated incidents. In early 1863, a Southern newspaper correspondent in Tennessee wrote, "All 'contrabands' captured by the rebels on the Federal wagon-trains are immediately shot. Twenty thus killed are lying on the Murfreesboro pike." *Harpers Weekly*, Feb. 7, 1863, quoted in Horton and Horton, *Slavery*, 179–180.

11.  For details, see Herman Hattaway, "Dress Rehearsal for Hell: In early 1864, Mississippi was a proving ground for the 'total war' that would make Sherman infamous—and victorious," *Civil War Times Illustrated* XXXVII, no. 5 (Oct. 1998): 32–39, 74–75. Note the use again of "total war" terminology.

12.  Timothy Johnson, "Reconstructing the Soil: Emancipation and the Roots of Chemical-Dependent Agriculture in America," in Brian Allen Drake (ed.), *The Blue, the Gray, and the Green: Toward an Environmental History of the Civil War* (Athens: University of Georgia Press, 2015), 191–208 at 191.

13.  Charles Royster, *The Destructive War: William Tecumseh Sherman, Stonewall Jackson, and the Americans* (New York: Vintage Books, 1993), 329.

14.  William L. Barney, *Oxford Encyclopedia, The Oxford Encyclopedia of the Civil War* (New York: Oxford University Press, 2001, 2011), 266–87.

15.  Pollard, *Lost Cause*, 612. Similar reports of property damage in Georgia and the Carolinas appeared in Dowdey, *Lee's Last Campaign*, 366–67.

After presenting a litany of Sherman's alleged depredations in Georgia, Pollard made a back-door admission when comparing them to the later Carolinas march: "In Georgia, not many dwelling-houses were burned; in South Carolina the rule was the other way...." Pollard, *Lost Cause*, 663.

16. Not, as many allege, the entire city. For a strong anti-Sherman view of the Columbia fire and destruction, see Pollard, *Lost Cause*, 665–70.

17. Lisa Tendrich Frank, *The Civilian War: Confederate Women and Union soldiers during Sherman's March* (Baton Rouge: Louisiana State University Press, 2015).

18. Pollard, *Lost Cause*, 597.

19. Grant, *Memoirs,* I, 368–69.

# CHAPTER NINE: CONCLUSION

1. See Fergus M. Bordewich, "Face the Nation: Abraham Lincoln's debates with Stephen A. Douglas for the U.S. Senate in 1858 turned the back-woods rail-splitter into presidential timber," *Smithsonian* (Sept. 2008), 61–69.

# BIBLIOGRAPHY

## MEMOIRS, LETTERS, PAPERS, AND OTHER PRIMARY DOCUMENTS

Alexander, Edward Porter. *Fighting for the Confederacy: The Personal Recollections of General Edward Porter Alexander.* Edited by Gary W. Gallagher. Chapel Hill: University of North Carolina Press, 1989.

———. *The Military Memoirs of a Confederate.* New York: Charles Scribner's Sons, 1907.

Badeau, Adam. *Military History of Ulysses S. Grant, from April, 1861, to April, 1865.* 3 vols. New York: D. Appleton and Company, 1868.

Basler, Roy P., ed. *The Collected Works of Abraham Lincoln.* 8 vols. New Brunswick: Rutgers University Press, 1953.

Blackford, William Willis. *War Years with Jeb Stuart.* Baton Rouge: Louisiana State University Press, 1945. 1993 Reprint.

Cadwallader, Sylvanus. *Three Years with Grant.* New York: Alfred A. Knopf, 1956. Published version of 1896 manuscript entitled inaccurately *Four Years with Grant.*

Commager, Henry Steele. *Documents of American History.* New York: Appleton-Century-Crofts, 1948, 1949, 1958.

Cox, Jacob Dolson. *Military Reminiscences of the Civil War.* 2 vols. New York: Charles Scribner's Sons, 1900.

Dana, Charles A. *Recollections of the Civil War.* New York: Collier Books, 1893, 1963.

Davis, Jefferson. *The Rise and Fall of the Confederate Government.* 2 vols. New York: Da Capo Press, Inc., 1990. Reprint of 1881 edition.

Dowdey, Clifford, and Manarin, Louis H., eds. *The Wartime Papers of R.E. Lee.* New York: Bramhall House, 1961. Since this volume contains *edited* versions of Lee's correspondence (perhaps to make him look better?), try checking other sources for the exact language of those documents.

Freeman, Douglas Southall, and Grady McWhiney, eds. *Lee's Dispatches: Unpublished Letters of General Robert E. Lee, C.S.A., to Jefferson Davis and the War Department of the Confederate States of America 1862–65.* Baton Rouge: Louisiana State University Press, 1957, 1994. Update of Freeman's original 1914 edition.

Gaff, Alan D. *On Many a Bloody Field: Four Years in the Iron Brigade.* Bloomington: Indiana University Press, 1996.

Gienapp, William E., ed. *The Civil War and Reconstruction: A Documentary Collection.* New York: W.W. Norton & Company, 2001.

Gordon, John B. *Reminiscences of the Civil War.* Baton Rouge: Louisiana State University Press, 1993. Reprint of New York: Charles Scribner's Sons, 1903.

Gorgas, Josiah. *The Civil War Diary of General Josiah Gorgas.* Edited by Frank E. Vandiver and Sarah Woolfolk Wiggins. Birmingham: University of Alabama Press, 1947, 1955.

Grant, Ulysses S. *Memoirs and Selected Letters: Personal Memoirs of U. S. Grant, Selected Letters 1839–1865.* Reprint. New York: Literary Classics of the United States, Inc., 1990.

Hay, John. *Inside Lincoln's White House: The Complete Civil War Diary of John Hay.* Edited by Michael Burlingame, and John R. Turner Ettlinger. Carbondale: Southern University Press, 1997.

Johnson, Robert Underwood, and Buel, Clarence Clough, eds. *Battles and Leaders of the Civil War.* 4 vols. New York: Thomas Yoseloff, Inc., 1956. Reprint of Secaucus, New Jersey: Castle, 1887–88.

Johnston, Joseph E. *Narrative of Military Operations During the Civil War.* New York: Appleton, 1874.

Jones, J. B. *A Rebel War Clerk's Diary at the Confederate States Capital.* 2 vols. Philadelphia: J. B. Lippincott & Co., 1866, 1982 reprint.

Longstreet, James. *From Manassas to Appomattox: Memoirs of the Civil War in America.* New York: Smithmark Publishers, Inc., 1994. Reprint of 1896 edition.

Mackey, Thomas C., ed. *A Documentary History of the American Civil War Era, Vol. II, Political Arguments.* Knoxville: University of Tennessee Press, 2013.

Nicolay, John G. *The Outbreak of Rebellion.* New York: Charles Scribner's Sons, 1992. Reprint of Harrisburg: The Archive Society, 1881.

Osofsky, Gilbert. *Puttin' on Ole Massah: The Slave Narratives of Henry Bibb, William Wells Brown, and Solomon Northup.* New York: Harper & Row, 1969.

Porter, Horace. *Campaigning with Grant.* New York: Smithmark Publishers, Inc., 1994. Reprint.

Rhodes, Robert Hunt, ed. *All for the Union: The Civil War Diary and Letters of Elisha Hunt Rhodes.* New York: Orion Books, 1991. Originally published by Andrew Mowbray Incorporated in 1985.

Sherman, William Tecumseh. *Memoirs of General W. T. Sherman.* New York: Literary Classics of the United States, Inc., 1990. Reprint of 1885 second edition.

Simon, John Y., and John F. Marszalek, et al., eds. *The Papers of Ulysses S. Grant.* 32 vols. Carbondale: Southern Illinois University Press, 1967–2012.

Simpson, Brooks D., Stephen W. Sears, and Aaron Sheehan-Dean, eds. *The Civil War: The First Year Told by Those Who Lived It.* New York: Literary Classics of the United States, 2011.

Stoddard, William O., Jr. *William O. Stoddard: Lincoln's Third Secretary.* New York: Exposition Press, 1955.

Taylor, Walter H. *General Lee: His Campaigns in Virginia 1861–1865 with Personal Reminiscences.* Lincoln: University of Nebraska Press, 1994. Reprint of Norfolk: Nusbaum Books, 1906.

Tower, R. Lockwood, ed. *Lee's Adjutant: The Wartime Letters of Colonel Walter Herron Taylor, 1862–1865.* Columbia: University of South Carolina Press, 1995.

*The War of the Rebellion: A Compilation of the Official Records of the Union and Confederate Armies.* 128 vols. Washington, DC: Government Printing Office, 1880–1901.

Watkins, Sam R. *"Co. Aytch," Maury Grays, First Tennessee Regiment; or, A Side Show of the Big Show.* Wilmington, NC: Broadfoot Publishing Company, 1987. Reprint of 1952 edition and of Nashville: Cumberland Presbyterian Publishing House, 1882.

Welles, Gideon. *Diary of Gideon Welles.* 3 vols. Boston and New York: Houghton Mifflin Company, 1911.

Williamson, George. Address to Texas Secession Convention, Jan. 11, 1861, http://www.civilwarcauses.org/gwill.htm, quoting E. W. Winkler, ed., *Journal of the Secession Convention of Texas,* 120–23.

# STATISTICAL ANALYSES

Fox, William F. *Regimental Losses in the American Civil War, 1861–1865: A Treatise on the Extent and Nature of the Mortuary Losses in the Union Regiments, with Full and Exhaustive Statistics Compiled from the Official Records on File in the State Military Bureaus and at Washington.* Dayton, Morningside House, Inc., 1985. Reprint of Albany: Brandow Printing Company, 1898.

Livermore, Thomas L. *Numbers & Losses in the Civil War in America: 1861–1865.* Millwood, NY: Kraus Reprint Co., 1977. Reprint of Bloomington: Indiana University Press, 1957.

Phisterer, Frederick. *Statistical Record: A Treasury of Information about the U.S. Civil War.* Carlisle, PA: John Kallmann Publishers, 1996. Reprint of *Statistical Record of the Armies of the United States* (1883), a supplementary volume to Scribner's Campaigns of the Civil War series.

———. *Statistical Record of the Armies of the United States.* Edison, New Jersey: Castle Books, 2002. Reprint of 1883 book.


# ENCYCLOPEDIAS

Barney, William L. *The Oxford Encyclopedia of the Civil War.* New York: Oxford University Press, 2001, 2011.

Boatner, Mark Mayo III. *The Civil War Dictionary.* New York: David McKay Company, Inc., 1959, 1988.

Chambers, John Whiteclay II, ed. *The Oxford Companion to American Military History.* Oxford: Oxford University Press, 1999.

Current, Richard N., ed. *Encyclopedia of the Confederacy.* 4 vols. New York: Simon & Schuster, 1993.

Garrity, John A., ed. *Encyclopedia of American Biography.* New York: Harper & Row, 1974.

Heidler, David S., and Heidler, Jeanne T., ed. *Encyclopedia of the American Civil War: A Political, Social, and Military History.* New York: W. W. Norton & Company, 2002.

Jones, Terry L. *Historical Dictionary of the Civil War.* Second edition. 2 vols. Lanham, MD: Scarecrow Press, 2011.

*The Library of Congress Civil War Desk Reference.* Washington: Library of Congress, 2002.

Sifakis, Stewart. *Who Was Who in the Civil War: A Comprehensive, Illustrated Biographical Reference to More Than 2,500 of the Principal Union and*

*Confederate Participants in the War Between the States.* Berwyn Heights, MD: Heritage Books, Inc., 2014.

Wagner, Margaret E., Gary W. Gallagher, and Paul Finkelman, ed. *The Library of Congress Civil War Desk Reference.* New York: Simon & Schuster, 2002.

# OTHER BOOKS AND MANUSCRIPTS

Abbazia, Patrick. *The Chickamauga Campaign, December 1862-November 1863.* New York: Wieser & Wieser, Inc., 1988.

Adams, Michael C.C. *Living Hell: The Dark Side of the Civil War.* Baltimore: Johns Hopkins University Press, 2014.

Alexander, Bevin. *How Great Generals Win.* New York: W. W. Norton & Co., 1993.

———. *Lost Victories: The Military Genius of Stonewall Jackson.* New York: Henry Holt and Company, 1992.

Ambrose, Stephen E. *Halleck: Lincoln's Chief of Staff.* Baton Rouge: Louisiana State University Press, 1962, 1990.

Arnold, James R. *The Armies of U.S. Grant.* London: Arms and Armour Press, 1995.

———. *Grant Wins the War: Decision at Vicksburg.* New York: John Wiley & Sons, Inc., 1997.

Arsenault, Raymond, and Orville Vernon Burton. *Dixie Redux: Essays in Honor of Sheldon Hackney.* Montgomery: New South Books, 2013.

Atkinson, Charles Francis. *Grant's Campaigns of 1864 and 1865: The Wilderness and Cold Harbor (May 3–June 3, 1864).* London: Hugh Rees, Ltd., 1908. University of Michigan Library reprint.

Ayers, Edward L., and Carolyn R. Martin, eds. *America on the Eve of the Civil War.* Charlottesville: University of Virginia Press, 2010.

Bearss, Edwin Cole. *Unvexed to the Sea: The Campaign for Vicksburg.* 3 vols. Dayton: Morningside House, Inc., 1991. Reprint of 1986 edition.

Beringer, Richard E., Herman Hattaway, Archer Jones, and William N. Still Jr. *Why the South Lost the Civil War.* Athens: University of Georgia Press, 1986.

Blair, William A., and Karen Fisher Younger. *Lincoln's Proclamation: Emancipation Reconsidered.* Chapel Hill: University of North Carolina Press, 2009.

Bonekemper, Edward H., III. *Grant and Lee: Victorious American and Vanquished Virginian.* Washington, DC: Regnery Publishing, 2012.

———. *How Robert E. Lee Lost the Civil War.* Fredericksburg, VA: Sergeant Kirkland's Press, 1998.

———. *Lincoln and Grant: The Westerners Who Won the Civil War.* Washington, DC: Regnery Publishing, 2015.

———. *McClellan and Failure: A Study of Civil War Fear, Incompetence, and Worse.* Jefferson, NC: McFarland & Company, 2007, 2010.

———. "Negroes' Freedom of Contract in Antebellum Virginia, 1620–1860," unpublished M.A. dissertation, Old Dominion University (1971).

———. *Ulysses S. Grant: A Victor, Not a Butcher: The Military Genius of the Man Who Won the Civil War.* Washington, DC: Regnery Publishing, 2004.

Boritt, Gabor S., ed. *Lincoln's Generals.* New York: Oxford University Press, 1994.

———. *Lincoln, the War President.* New York: Oxford University Press, 1992.

———, ed. *Why the Confederacy Lost.* New York: Oxford University Press, 1992.

Bowers, John. *Stonewall Jackson: Portrait of a Soldier.* New York: William Morrow and Company, Inc., 1989.

Brown, Kent Masterson. *Lee, Logistics, and the Pennsylvania Campaign.* Chapel Hill: University of North Carolina Press, 2005.

Buell, Thomas B. *The Warrior Generals: Combat Leadership in the Civil War.* New York: Crown Publishers, Inc., 1997.

Bushong, Millard Kessler. *Old Jube: A Biography of General Jubal A. Early.* Shippensburg, PA: White Mane Publishing Company, Inc., 1955, 1990.

Cannan, John, ed. *War in the East: Chancellorsville to Gettysburg, 1863.* New York: Gallery Books, 1990.

Carhart, Tom. *Lost Triumph: Lee's Real Plan at Gettysburg and Why It Failed.* New York: G.P. Putnam's Sons, 2005.

Casdorph, Paul D. *Lee and Jackson: Confederate Chieftains.* New York: Paragon House, 1992.

Cash, W. J. *The Mind of the South.* New York: Doubleday, 1954.

Castel, Albert E. *Decision in the West: The Atlanta Campaign of 1864.* Lawrence: University Press of Kansas, 1992.

Catton, Bruce. *The Army of the Potomac: Glory Road.* Garden City, NY: Doubleday & Company, Inc., 1952.

———. *The Army of the Potomac: Mr. Lincoln's Army.* Garden City, NY: Doubleday & Company, Inc., 1951, 1962.

———. *The Army of the Potomac: A Stillness at Appomattox.* Garden City, NY: Doubleday & Company, Inc., 1953.

———. *Grant Moves South.* Boston: Little, Brown and Company, 1960.

———. *Grant Takes Command.* Boston: Little, Brown and Company, 1969.

———. *Terrible Swift Sword.* Garden City, NY: Doubleday & Company, Inc., 1963.

———. *This Hallowed Ground: The Story of the Union Side of the Civil War.* Garden City, NY: Doubleday & Company, Inc., 1956, 1962.

————. *U.S. Grant and the American Military Tradition.* Boston: Little, Brown and Company, 1954.

Clark, Champ, ed. *Gettysburg: The Confederate High Tide.* Alexandria, VA: Time-Life Books, Inc., 1985.

Coburn, Mark. *Terrible Innocence: General Sherman at War.* New York: Hippocrene Books, 1993.

Coddington, Edwin B. *The Gettysburg Campaign: A Study in Command.* New York: Charles Scribner's Sons, 1968, 1979.

Commager, Henry Steele. ed. *The Blue and the Gray: Two Volumes in One: The Story of the Civil War as Told by Participants.* New York: The Fairfax Press, 1982. Reprint of Indianapolis: Bobbs-Merrill, 1950.

Conger, Arthur L. *The Rise of U.S. Grant.* New York: Da Capo, 1996. Reprint of New York: Century Co., 1931.

Congressional Quarterly, Inc. *Presidential Elections, 1789–1996.* Washington, DC: Congressional Quarterly, Inc., 1997.

Connelly, Thomas Lawrence. *Army of the Heartland: The Army of Tennessee, 1861–1862.* Baton Rouge: Louisiana State University Press, 1967.

————. *Autumn of Glory: The Army of Tennessee, 1862–1865.* Baton Rouge: Louisiana State University Press, 1971, 1991.

————. *The Marble Man: Robert E. Lee and His Image in American Society.* New York: Alfred A. Knopf, 1977.

————and Archer Jones. *The Politics of Command: Factions and Ideas in Confederate Strategy.* Baton Rouge: Louisiana State University Press, 1973.

————and Barbara R. Bellows. *God and General Longstreet: The Lost Cause and the Southern Mind.* Baton Rouge: Louisiana State University Press, 1982.

Cooling, Benjamin Franklin. *Forts Henry and Donelson: The Key to the Confederate Heartland.* Knoxville: University of Tennessee Press, 1987.

Cornish, Dudley Taylor. *The Sable Arm: Black Troops in the Union Army, 1861–1865.* Lawrence: University Press of Kansas, 1956, 1987.

Cozzens, Peter. *The Shipwreck of Their Hopes: The Battles for Chattanooga.* Urbana: University of Illinois Press, 1994.

Davis, Burke. *The Long Surrender.* New York: Vintage Books, 1985.

Davis, William C. *The Cause Lost: Myths and Realities of the Confederacy.* Lawrence: University Press of Kansas, 1996.

————. *Crucible of Command: Ulysses S. Grant and Robert E. Lee—The War They Fought, the Peace They Forged.* New York: Da Capo, 2015.

————. *Jefferson Davis: The Man and His Hour.* Baton Rouge, Louisiana State University Press, 1991, 1996.

Denton, Lawrence M. *Unionists in Virginia: Politics, Secession and Their Plan To Prevent Civil War.* Charleston, SC: History Press, 2014.

Dew, Charles B. *Apostles of Disunion: Southern Secession Commissioners and the Causes of the Civil War.* Charlottesville: University Press of Virginia, 2001.

Donald, David Herbert, ed. *Lincoln.* New York: Simon & Schuster, 1995.

———.*Why the North Won the Civil War.* New York: Simon & Schuster, 1962, 1996.

———, Jean Harvey Baker, and Michael F. Holt. *The Civil War and Reconstruction.* New York: W.W. Norton & Company, 2001.

Dowdey, Clifford. *Lee.* Gettysburg: Stan Clark Military Books, 1991. Reprint of 1965 edition.

———. *Lee's Last Campaign: The Story of Lee and His Men Against Grant—1864.* Wilmington, NC: Broadfoot Publishing Company, 1988. Reprint of New York: Little, Brown and Company, 1960.

Doyle, Don H. *The Cause of All Nations: An International History of the American Civil War.* New York: Basic Books, 2015.

Drake, Brian Allen, ed. *The Blue, the Gray, and the Green: Toward an Environmental History of the Civil War.* Athens: University of Georgia Press, 2015.

Feis, William B. *Grant's Secret Service: The Intelligence War from Belmont to Appomattox.* Lincoln: University of Nebraska Press, 2002.

Fellman, Michael. *Citizen Sherman: A Life of William Tecumseh Sherman.* New York: Random House, 1995.

———. *The Making of Robert E. Lee.* Baltimore: Johns Hopkins University Press, 2000.

Fishel, Edwin C. *The Secret War for the Union: The Untold Story of Military Intelligence in the Civil War.* Boston: Houghton Mifflin, 1996.

Fleming, Thomas. *A Disease in the Public Mind: A New Understanding of Why We Fought the Civil War.* New York: Da Capo Press, 2013.

Flood, Charles Bracelen. *Grant and Sherman: The Friendship That Won the Civil War.* New York: Farrar, Straus and Giroux, 2005.

Fogel, Robert William, and Stanley L. Engerman. *Time on the Cross: The Economics of American Negro Slavery.* Boston: Little, Brown and Company, 1974.

Foner, Eric. *Gateway to Freedom: The Hidden History of the Underground Railroad.* New York: W. W. Norton, 2015.

Foote, Shelby, ed. *The Civil War: A Narrative.* 3 vols. New York: Random House, 1958–1974.

Frank, Lisa Tendrich. *The Civilian War: Confederate Women and Union Soldiers During Sherman's March.* Baton Rouge: Louisiana State University Press, 2015.

Freehling, William W. *The Road to Disunion: Secessionists at Bay, 1776–1854*. New York: Oxford University Press, 1990.

———. *The Road to Disunion: Secessionists Triumphant, 1854–1861*. New York: Oxford University Press, 2007.

———and Craig M. Simpson, eds. *Showdown in Virginia*. Charlottesville: University of Virginia Press, 2010.

Freeman, Douglas Southall. *Lee's Lieutenants: A Study in Command*. 3 vols. New York: Charles Scribner's Sons, 1942–44 (1972 reprint).

———. *R. E. Lee*. 4 vols. New York and London: Charles Scribner's Sons, 1934–35.

Frey, Sylvia R. *Water from the Rock: Black Resistance in a Revolutionary Age*. Princeton: Princeton University Press, 1991.

Fuller, J. F. C. *The Generalship of Ulysses S. Grant*. Bloomington: Indiana University Press, 1958. Reprint of 1929 edition.

———. *Grant and Lee: A Study in Personality and Generalship*. Bloomington: Indiana University Press, 1957. Reprint of 1933 edition.

Furgurson, Ernest B. *Chancellorsville 1863: The Souls of the Brave*. New York: Alfred A. Knopf, 1992.

Gallagher, Gary W. *Lee and His Generals in War and Memory*. Baton Rouge: Louisiana State University, 1998.

———, ed. *Lee the Soldier*. Lincoln: University of Nebraska Press, 1996.

———, ed. *The Third Day at Gettysburg & Beyond*. Chapel Hill: University of North Carolina Press, 1994.

———, ed., and Alan T. Nolan. *The Myth of the Lost Cause and Civil War History*. Bloomington: University of Indiana Press, 2000, 2010.

Genovese, Eugene D. *Roll, Jordan, Roll: The World the Slaves Made*. New York: Pantheon Books, 1974.

Glatthaar, Joseph T. *Partners in Command: The Relationships Between Leaders in the Civil War*. New York: Macmillan, Inc., 1994.

———. *Soldiering in the Army of Northern Virginia: A Statistical Portrait of the Troops Who Served under Robert E. Lee*. Chapel Hill: University of North Carolina Press, 2011.

Goodwin, Doris Kearns. *Team of Rivals: The Political Genius of Abraham Lincoln*. New York: Simon & Schuster, 2005.

Gott, Kendall D. *Where the South Lost the War: An Analysis of the Fort Henry-Fort Donelson Campaign, February 1862*. Mechanicsburg, PA: Stackpole Books, 2003.

Grant, Susan-Mary, and Peter J. Parish, eds. *Legacy of Disunion: The Enduring Significance of the American Civil War*. Baton Rouge: Louisiana State University Press, 2003.

Griffith, Paddy. *Battle Tactics of the Civil War*. New Haven: Yale University Press, 1996.

Groom, Winston. *Shrouds of Glory: From Atlanta to Nashville: The Last Great Campaign of the Civil War*. New York: The Atlantic Monthly Press, 1995.

Guelzo, Allen C. *Gettysburg: The Last Invasion*. New York: Alfred A. Knopf, 2013.

Hagerman, Edward. *The American Civil War and the Origins of Modern Warfare: Ideas, Organization, and Field Command*. Bloomington: Indiana University Press, 1992.

Harris, William C. *Lincoln and the Border States: Preserving the Union*. Lawrence: University Press of Kansas, 2011.

Harsh, Joseph L. *Confederate Tide Rising: Robert E. Lee and the Making of Southern Strategy, 1861–1862*. Kent: Kent State University Press, 1998.

Hassler, Warren W., Jr. *Commanders of the Army of the Potomac*. Baton Rouge: Louisiana State University Press, 1962.

Hattaway, Herman, and Jones, Archer. *How the North Won: A Military History of the Civil War*. Urbana: University of Illinois Press, 1991. Reprint of 1983 edition.

Hearn, Chester G. *Lincoln, the Cabinet and the Generals*. Baton Rouge: Louisiana State University Press, 2010.

Heleniak, Roman J., and Hewitt, Lawrence L., ed. *The Confederate High Command & Related Topics: The 1988 Deep Delta Civil War Symposium*. Shippensburg, PA: White Mane Publishing Co., Inc., 1990.

Henderson, G. F. R. *Stonewall Jackson and the American Civil War*. New York: Da Capo Press, Inc., 1988; reprint of New York: Grossett & Dunlap, 1943.

Holt, Michael F. *The Fate of their Country*. New York: Hill and Wang, 2004.

Horton, James Oliver and Lois E. Horton. *Slavery and the Making of America*. Oxford: Oxford University Press, 2005.

Hubbell, John T., ed. *Conflict and Command*. Kent, Ohio: Kent State University Press, 2012.

Huston, James L. *The British Gentry, the Southern Planter, and the Northern Family Farmer: Agriculture and Sectional Antagonism in North America*. Baton Rouge: Louisiana State University Press, 2015.

Jenkins, Sally, and John Stauffer. *The State of Jones: The Small Southern County That Seceded from the Confederacy*. New York: Anchor Books, 2010.

Jewett, Clayton E., ed. *The Battlefield and Beyond: Essays on the American Civil War*. Baton Rouge: Louisiana State University Press, 2012.

Johnson, Clint. *Civil War Blunders*. Winston-Salem: John F. Blair, 1997.

Jones, Archer. *Civil War Command & Strategy: The Process of Victory and Defeat*. New York: The Free Press, 1992.

———. *Confederate Strategy from Shiloh to Vicksburg*. Baton Rouge: Louisiana State University Press, 1991.

Jones, J. William. *Personal Reminiscences of General Robert E. Lee*. Richmond, United States Historical Society Press, 1874, 1989.

Jones, R. Steven. *The Right Hand of Command: Use & Disuse of Personal Staffs in the Civil War*. Mechanicsburg, PA: Stackpole Books, 2000.

Jones, Terry L. *Lee's Tigers: The Louisiana Infantry in the Army of Northern Virginia*. Baton Rouge: Louisiana State University Press, 1987.

Jordan, David M. *Winfield Scott Hancock: A Soldier's Life*. Bloomington: Indiana University Press, 1996.

Jordan, Winthrop D. *White Over Black: American Attitudes Toward the Negro, 1550–1812*. Chapel Hill: University of North Carolina Press, 1968.

Katcher, Philip. *The Army of Robert E. Lee*. London: Arms and Armour Press, 1994.

Keegan, John. *The American Civil War: A Military History*. New York: Alfred A. Knopf, 2009.

———. *The Face of Battle*. New York: Dorset Press, 1986.

———. *The Mask of Command*. New York: Viking, 1987.

Kennett, Lee. *Marching Through Georgia: The Story of Soldiers and Civilians During Sherman's Campaign*. New York: HarperCollins, 1995.

Kiper, Richard L. *Major General John Alexander McClernand: Politician in Uniform*. Kent: Kent State University Press, 1999.

Lawson, Melinda. *Patriot Fires: Forging a New American Nationalism in the Civil War North*. Lawrence: University Press of Kansas, 2002.

Lee, Fitzhugh. *General Lee: A Biography of Robert E. Lee*. New York: Da Capo Press, 1994. Reprint of Wilmington, North Carolina: Broadfoot Publishing Company, 1989 and New York: D. Appleton and Company, 1894.

Levine, Bruce. *Confederate Emancipation: Southern Plans To Free and Arm Slaves During the Civil War*. Oxford: Oxford University Press, 2006.

Long, David E. *The Jewel of Liberty: Abraham Lincoln's Re-election and the End of Slavery*. New York: Da Capo Press, 1997. Reprint of Mechanicsburg, PA: Stackpole Books, 1994.

Longacre, Edward G. *General John Buford: A Military Biography*. Conshohocken, PA: Combined Books, Inc., 1995.

Lossing, Benson. *A History of the Civil War, 1861–65, and the Causes That Led up to the Great Conflict*. New York: The War Memorial Association, 1912.

Lowry, Don. *Fate of the Country: The Civil War from June–September 1864*. New York: Hippocrene Books, 1992.

———. No Turning Back: The Beginning of the End of the Civil War: March–June, 1864. New York: Hippocrene Books, 1992.

Luvaas, Jay, and Harold W. Nelson, ed. The U.S. Army War College Guide to the Battle of Gettysburg. Carlisle, PA: South Mountain Press, Inc., 1986.

Marszalek, John F. Sherman: A Soldier's Passion for Order. New York: Macmillan, Inc., 1993.

———. The Shiloh Campaign, March–April 1862. New York: Wieser & Wieser, Inc., 1987.

———. The Vicksburg Campaign, April, 1862–July, 1863. New York: Wieser & Wieser, Inc., 1990.

Marvel, William. Lee's Last Retreat: The Flight to Appomattox. Chapel Hill: University of North Carolina Press, 2002.

Masur, Louis P. The Civil War: A Concise History. Oxford: Oxford University Press, 2011.

Matloff, Maurice, ed. American Military History. 2 vols. Washington, DC: U.S. Army Center of Military History, 1985.

McDonough, James Lee. Chattanooga: A Death Grip on the Confederacy. Knoxville: University of Tennessee Press, 1984.

McFeely, William. Grant: A Biography. New York: W.W. Norton & Company, 1981.

McKenzie, John D. Uncertain Glory: Lee's Generalship Re-Examined. New York: Hippocrene Books, 1997.

McMurry, Richard M. Two Great Rebel Armies: An Essay in Confederate Military History. Chapel Hill: University of North Carolina Press, 1989.

McPherson, James M. Battle Cry of Freedom: The Civil War Era. New York: Ballantine Books, 1988.

———. Drawn with the Sword: Reflections on the American Civil War. New York: Oxford University Press, 1966.

———. Ordeal by Fire. New York: Knopf, 1982.

———. The War that Forged a Nation: Why the Civil War Still Matters. Oxford: Oxford University Press, 2015.

McWhiney, Grady, and Perry D. Jamieson. Attack and Die: Civil War Military Tactics and the Southern Heritage. Tuscaloosa: University of Alabama Press, 1982.

Meacham, Jon, ed. American Homer: Reflections on Shelby Foote and His Classic The Civil War: A Narrative. New York: Random House, 2011.

Meade, Robert Douthat. Judah P. Benjamin: Confederate Statesman. Baton Rouge: Louisiana State University Press, 1943, 2001.

Miers, Earl Schenck. *The Web of Victory: Grant at Vicksburg.* Baton Rouge: Louisiana State University Press, 1984. Reprint of New York: Alfred Knopf, 1955.

———. *The Last Campaign: Grant Saves the Union.* Philadelphia: J. B. Lippincott Company, 1972.

Morris, Roy, Jr. *Sheridan: The Life and Wars of General Phil Sheridan.* New York: Crown Publishers, Inc., 1992.

Murphin, James V. *The Gleam of Bayonets: The Battle of Antietam and the Maryland Campaign of 1862.* Baton Rouge: Louisiana State University Press, 1965.

Nevins, Allan. *Ordeal of the Union.* 8 vols. New York and London: Charles Scribner's Sons, 1947–50.

Nofi, Albert A. *The Gettysburg Campaign, June and July, 1863.* New York: Wieser & Wieser, Inc., 1986.

Nolan, Alan T. *Lee Considered: General Robert E. Lee and Civil War History.* Chapel Hill: University of North Carolina Press, 1991.

Olmsted, Frederick Law. *The Cotton Kingdom: A Traveller's Observations on Cotton and Slavery in the American Slave States.* Edited by Arthur M. Schlesinger. New York: Alfred A. Knopf, 1953, 1970.

Osborne, Charles C. *Jubal: The Life and Times of General Jubal A. Early, CSA, Defender of the Lost Cause.* Baton Rouge: Louisiana State University Press, 1992.

Page, Thomas Nelson. *Robert E. Lee: Man and Soldier.* New York: Charles Scribner's Sons, 1911.

———. *Robert E. Lee: The Southerner.* New York: Charles Scribner's Sons, 1908.

Perret, Geoffrey. *A Country Made by War: From the Revolution to Vietnam—the Story of America's Rise to Power.* New York: Random House, 1989.

———. *Ulysses S. Grant: Soldier & President.* New York: Random House, 1997.

Perry, Mark. *Conceived in Liberty: Joshua Chamberlain, William Oates, and the American Civil War.* New York: Viking, 1997.

Pfanz, Donald C. *Richard S. Ewell: A Soldier's Life.* Chapel Hill: University of North Carolina Press, 1998.

Pfanz, Harry W. *Gettysburg—Culp's Hill & Cemetery Hill.* Chapel Hill: University of North Carolina Press, 1993.

———. *Gettysburg: The Second Day.* Chapel Hill: University of North Carolina Press, 1987.

Piston, William Garrett. *Lee's Tarnished Lieutenant: James Longstreet and His Place in Southern History.* Athens: University of Georgia Press, 1987.

Pollard, Edward A. *The Lost Cause. A New Southern History of the War of the Confederates.* New York: Gramercy Books, 1994. Reprint of New York: E.B. Treat & Company, 1866 (mistakenly identified in reprint as 1886).

Potter, David M. *The Impending Crisis 1848–1861.* New York: Harper & Row, 1976.

Priest, John M. *Antietam: The Soldiers' Battle.* Shippensburg, PA: White Mane Publishing Co., Inc., 1989.

Quarles, Benjamin. *The Negro in the Civil War.* Boston: Little, Brown and Co., 1953.

Rhea, Gordon C. *The Battle of the Wilderness May 5–6, 1864.* Baton Rouge: Louisiana State University Press, 1994.

———. *The Battles for Spotsylvania Court House and the Road to Yellow Tavern, May 7–12, 1864.* Baton Rouge: Louisiana State University Press, 1997.

———. *Cold Harbor: Grant and Lee May 26–June 3, 1864.* Baton Rouge: Louisiana State University Press, 2002.

———. *To the North Anna River: Lee and Grant May 13–25, 1864.* Baton Rouge: Louisiana State University Press, 2000.

Robertson, James I., Jr. *General A. P. Hill: The Story of a Confederate Warrior.* New York: Random House, 1987.

———. *The Stonewall Brigade.* Baton Rouge: Louisiana State University Press, 1963 [1991 Reprint].

———. *Stonewall Jackson: the Man, the Soldier, the Legend.* New York: Macmillan Publishing USA, 1997.

Roland, Charles P. *An American Iliad: The Story of the Civil War.* Lexington: University Press of Kentucky, 1991.

Rowland, Thomas J. *George B. McClellan and Civil War History in the Shadow of Grant and Sherman.* Kent: Kent State University Press, 1998.

Royster, Charles. *The Destructive War: William Tecumseh Sherman, Stonewall Jackson, and the Americans.* New York: Vintage Books, 1993.

Savage, Douglas. *The Court Martial of Robert E. Lee: A Historical Novel.* Conshohocken, PA: Combined Books, Inc., 1993.

Scott, Robert Garth. *Into the Wilderness with the Army of the Potomac.* Bloomington: Indiana University Press, 1985.

Sears, Stephen W. *Chancellorsville.* Boston: Houghton Mifflin Company, 1996.

———. *Controversies & Commanders: Dispatches from the Army of the Potomac.* Boston: Houghton Mifflin Company, 1999.

———. *George B. McClellan: The Young Napoleon.* New York: Ticknor & Fields, 1988.

————. *To the Gates of Richmond: The Peninsula Campaign.* New York: Ticknor & Fields, 1992.

Shaara, Michael. *The Killer Angels.* New York: Ballantine Books, 1974.

Simpson, Brooks D. *Ulysses S. Grant: Triumph Over Adversity, 1822–1865.* Boston: Houghton Mifflin Company, 2000.

Simpson, Harold B. *Hood's Texas Brigade: Lee's Grenadier Guard.* Fort Worth: Landmark Publishing, Inc., 1970. Vol. 2 of four-volume set of *Hood's Texas Brigade.*

Smith, Gene. *Lee and Grant: A Dual Biography.* New York: Promontory Press, 1984.

Smith, Jean Edward. *Grant.* New York: Simon & Schuster, 2001.

Smith, John David, ed. *Black Soldiers in Blue: African American Troops in the Civil War Era.* Chapel Hill: University of North Carolina Press, 2002.

Smith, Timothy B. *The Mississippi Secession Convention: Delegates and Deliberations in Politics and War, 1861–1865.* Jackson: University Press of Mississippi, 2014.

Stackpole, Edward J. *They Met at Gettysburg.* New York: Bonanza Books, 1956.

Stampp, Kenneth M. *The Peculiar Institution: Slavery in the Ante-Bellum South.* New York: Vintage Books, 1956, 1989.

Stern, Philip Van Doren. *Robert E. Lee: The Man and the Soldier.* New York: Bonanza Books, 1963.

Stewart, George R. *Pickett's Charge: A Microhistory of the Final Attack at Gettysburg, July 3, 1863.* Boston: Houghton Mifflin Co., 1959.

Swinton, William. *Campaigns of the Army of the Potomac.* New York: Richardson, 1866.

Sydnor, Charles S. *Slavery in Mississippi.* Baton Rouge, Louisiana State University Press, 1933, 1966.

Thomas, Emory M. *Robert E. Lee: A Biography.* New York: W. W. Norton & Company, 1995.

Trudeau, Noah Andre. *Bloody Roads South: The Wilderness to Cold Harbor, May–June 1864.* Boston: Little, Brown and Co., 1989.

————. *The Last Citadel: Petersburg, Virginia June 1864–April 1865.* Baton Rouge: Louisiana State University Press, 1991.

————. *Out of the Storm: The End of the Civil War, April–June 1865.* Boston: Little, Brown and Co., 1994.

Tucker, Phillip Thomas. *Barksdale's Charge: The True High Tide of the Confederacy at Gettysburg, July 2, 1863.* Havertown, PA: Casemate Publishers, 2013.

Vandiver, Frank E. *Mighty Stonewall.* College Station: Texas A&M University Press, 1989. Reprint of 1957 edition.

Ward, Geoffrey C., Ric Burns, and Ken Burns. *The Civil War: An Illustrated History*. New York: Alfred A. Knopf, Inc., 1990.

Warner, Ezra J. *Generals in Blue: Lives of the Union Commanders*. Baton Rouge: Louisiana State University Press, 1964.

———. *Generals in Gray: Lives of the Confederate Commanders*. Baton Rouge: Louisiana State University Press, 1959.

Waugh, John C. *The Class of 1846: From West Point to Appomattox: Stonewall Jackson, George McClellan and Their Brothers*. New York: Warner Books, Inc., 1994.

———. *Reelecting Lincoln: The Battle for the 1864 Presidency*. New York: Crown Publishers, Inc., 1997.

Weigley, Russell F. *The American Way of War: A History of United States Military Strategy and Policy*. New York: Macmillan Publishing Co., Inc., 1973.

———. *A Great Civil War: A Military and Political History, 1861–1865*. Bloomington: Indiana University Press, 2000.

Weir, William. *Fatal Victories*. Hamden, Connecticut: Archon Books, 1993.

Werstein, Irving. *Abraham Lincoln Versus Jefferson Davis*. New York: Thomas Y. Crowell Company, 1959.

Wert, Jeffrey D. *A Brotherhood of Valor: The Common Soldiers of the Stonewall Brigade, C.S.A., and the Iron Brigade, U.S.A.* New York: Simon & Schuster, 1999.

———. *General James Longstreet: The Confederacy's Most Controversial Soldier—A Biography*. New York: Simon & Schuster, 1993.

Wheelan, Joseph. *Bloody Spring: Forty Days That Sealed the Confederacy's Fate*. New York: Da Capo, 2014.

Wheeler, Richard. *Lee's Terrible Swift Sword: From Antietam to Chancellorsville, An Eyewitness History*. New York: HarperCollins Publishers, Inc., 1992.

———. *On Fields of Fury: From the Wilderness to the Crater: An Eyewitness History*. New York: HarperCollins Publishers, 1991.

White, Jonathan W. *Emancipation, the Union Army and the Reelection of Abraham Lincoln*. Baton Rouge: Louisiana State University Press, 2014.

Wiley, Bell Irvin. *The Road to Appomattox*. Baton Rouge: Louisiana State University Press, 1994. Reprint of Memphis: Memphis State College Press, 1956.

Wilkinson, Warren. *Mother, May You Never See the Sights I Have Seen: The Fifty-seventh Massachusetts Veteran Volunteers in the Army of the Potomac, 1864–1865*. New York: Harper & Row, 1990.

Williams, Kenneth P. *Grant Rises in the West*. 2 vols. Lincoln: University of Nebraska Press, 1997. Originally vols. 3 and 4 of *Lincoln Finds a General: A Military Study of the Civil War*, New York: Macmillan, 1952.

——. *Lincoln Finds a General: A Military Study of the Civil War.* Vol. 1. Bloomington: Indiana University Press, 1985. Reprint of 1949 edition.

——. *Lincoln Finds a General: A Military Study of the Civil War.* Vols. 2 and 5. New York: The Macmillan Company, 1959. Reprint of 1949 edition.

Williams, T. Harry. *Lincoln and His Generals.* New York: Alfred A. Knopf, Inc., 1952.

——. *McClellan, Sherman and Grant.* New Brunswick: Rutgers University Press, 1962.

Wilson, David L., and John Y. Simon, eds. *Ulysses S. Grant: Essays and Documents.* Carbondale: University of Illinois Press, 1981.

Wilson, Harold S. *Confederate Industry: Manufacturers and Quartermasters in the Civil War.* Jackson: University of Mississippi Press, 2002.

Woodman, Harold D. *Slavery and the Southern Economy: Sources and Readings.* New York: Harcourt, Brace & World, Inc., 1966.

Woodworth, Steven E., ed. *Civil War Generals in Defeat.* Lawrence: University of Kansas Press, 1999.

——, ed. *Davis and Lee at War.* Lawrence: University of Kansas Press, 1995.

——, ed. *Grant's Lieutenants from Cairo to Vicksburg.* Lawrence: University of Kansas Press, 2001.

——. *Jefferson Davis and His Generals: The Failure of Confederate Command in the West.* Lawrence: University Press of Kansas, 1990.

——. *Nothing But Victory: The Army of the Tennessee, 1861–1865.* New York: Alfred A. Knopf, 2005.

Zeitz, Joshua. *Lincoln's Boys: John Hay, John Nicolay, and the War for Lincoln's Image.* New York: Penguin Books, 2014.

# PERIODICAL ARTICLES

Alexander, Ted. "Ten Days in July: The Pursuit to the Potomac," *North & South* 2, no. 6 (Aug. 1999): 10–34.

Anderson, Kevin. "Grant's Lifelong Struggle with Alcohol: Examining the Controversy Surrounding Grant and Alcohol," *Columbiad: A Quarterly Review of the War Between the States* 2, no. 4 (Winter 1999): 16–26.

Arnold, James R. "Grant Earns a License To Win," *Columbiad: A Quarterly Review of the War Between the States* 1, no. 2 (Summer 1997): 31–41.

Ayers, Edward L. "What Caused the Civil War?", *North & South* 8, no. 5 (Sept. 2005): 12–18.

Barton, Dick. "Charge at Big Black River," *America's Civil War* 12, no. 4 (Sept. 1999): 54–61.

"The Battles at Spotsylvania Court House, Virginia May 8–21, 1864," *Blue & Gray Magazine* I, no. 6 (June–July 1984): 35–48.

Bauer, Daniel. "Did a Food Shortage Force Lee To Fight?: An Investigation into Lee's Claim That He Had To Attack at Gettysburg Because His Army Lacked Sufficient Rations To Do Anything Else," *Columbiad: A Quarterly Review of the War Between the States* I, no. 4 (Winter 1998): 57–74.

Bearss, Ed. "The Vicksburg Campaign: Grant Marches West: The Battles of Champion Hill and Big Black Bridge," *Blue & Gray Magazine* XVIII, no. 5 (June 2001): 6–24, 44–52.

———. "The Vicksburg Campaign: Grant Moves Inland," *Blue & Gray Magazine* XVIII, no. 1 (October 2000): 6–22, 46–52, 65.

Bonekemper, Edward H., III. "Lincoln's 1864 Victory Was Closer Than It Looked," *Washington Times*, July 15, 2000, B3.

———. "Slavery, Not States' Rights, Inspired Secession," *Washington Times*, Aug. 23, 2003, B3.

Bordewich, Fergus M. "Face the Nation: Abraham Lincoln's debates with Stephen A. Douglas for the U.S. Senate in 1858 turned the backwoods rail-splitter into presidential timber," *Smithsonian* (Sept. 2008): 61–69.

Bruce, George A. "Strategy of the Civil War," *Papers of the Military Historical Society of Massachusetts* 13, (1913): 392–483.

Castle, Albert. "The Fort Pillow Massacre: A Fresh Examination of the Evidence," *Civil War History* 4 (March 1958): 37–50.

Connelly, Thomas Lawrence. "The Image and the General: Robert E. Lee in American Historiography," *Civil War History* 19 (March 1973): 50–64.

———. "Robert E. Lee and the Western Confederacy: A Criticism of Lee's Strategic Ability," *Civil War History* 15 (June 1969): 116–32.

Cooling, Benjamin Franklin. "Forts Henry & Donelson: Union Victory on the Twin Rivers," *Blue & Gray Magazine* IX, no. 3 (Feb. 1992): 10–20, 45–53.

Davis, Stephen. "Atlanta Campaign. Hood Fights Desperately. The Battles for Atlanta: Events from July 10 to September 2, 1864," *Blue & Gray Magazine* VI, no. 6 (Aug. 1989): 8–39, 45–62.

———. "Pat Cleburne's Emancipation Proposal," *Blue & Gray Magazine* VI, no. 4 (Apr. 1989): 19.

Dew, Charles B. "Apostles of Secession," *North & South* 4, no. 4 (April 2001): 24–38.

Eicher, David, Joe Harsh, Richard McMurry, Robert Tanner, Russell Weigley, and Steve Woodworth. "Confederate Strategy Considered," *North & South* 4, no. 7 (Sept. 2001): 12–22.

Evans, E. Chris. "'I Almost Tremble at Her Fate': When Sherman came to Columbia, South Carolina, secession's hotbed became a bed of coals," *Civil War Times Illustrated* XXXVII, no. 5 (Oct. 1998): 46–51, 60–67.

———. "Return to Jackson: Finishing Stroke to the Vicksburg Campaign, July 5–25, 1863," *Blue & Gray Magazine* XII, no. 6 (Aug. 1995): 8–22, 50–63.

Feis, William B. "Charles S. Bell: Union Scout," *North & South* 4, no. 5 (June 2001): 26–37.

———. "'He Don't Care a Damn for What the Enemy Does out of His Sight': A Perspective on U. S. Grant and Military Intelligence," *North & South* 1, no. 2 (Jan. 1998): 68–81.

Fleming, Martin K. "The Northwestern Virginia Campaign of 1861: McClellan's Rising Star— Lee's Dismal Debut," *Blue & Gray Magazine* X, no. 6 (August 1993): 10–17, 48–54, 59–65.

Freeman, Kirk. "Big Black River," *Military Heritage* 2, no. 3 (Dec. 2000): 76–85.

Gallagher, Gary W. "Brandy Station: The Civil War's Bloodiest Arena of Mounted Combat," *Blue & Gray Magazine* VIII, no. 1 (October 1990): 8–22, 44–53.

———. "'Flaggers' on the Fringe: Serious students of the war should ignore such irrelevant distraction," *Civil War Times* 54, no. 2 (April 2015): 19–21.

Garavaglia, Louis A. "Sherman's March and the Georgia Arsenals," *North & South* 6, no. 1 (Dec. 2002): 12–22.

Gillespie, Jay, "Slavery and States' Rights in the Old North State," *North & South* 11, no. 5 (Oct. 2009): 68–75.

Goodman, Al W., Jr. "Decision in the West (Part IV): Between Hell and the Deep Sea: Pemberton's Debacle at Big Black River Bridge," *North & South* 1, no. 5 (June 1998): 74–79.

———. "Grant's Mississippi Gamble," *America's Civil War* 7, no. 3 (July 1994): 50–56.

"Grant and Lee, 1864: From the North Anna to the Crossing of the James," *Blue & Gray Magazine* XI, no. 4 (April 1994): 11–22, 44–58.

Hacker, David. "A Census-Based Count of the Civil War Dead," *Civil War History* LVII, no. 4 (Dec. 2011): 307–48.

Handlin, Oscar, "Why Lee Attacked," *The Atlantic Monthly* CXCV (March 1955): 65–66.

Hattaway, Herman. "The Changing Face of Battle," *North & South* 4, no. 6 (Aug. 2001): 34–43.

———. "Dress Rehearsal for Hell: In early 1864, Mississippi was a proving ground for the 'total war' that would make Sherman infamous—and victorious," *Civil War Times Illustrated* XXXVII, no. 5 (Oct. 1998): 32–39, 74–75.

Jones, Archer. "What Should We Think About Lee's Thinking?," *Columbiad* 1, no. 2 (Summer 1997): 73–85.

Keegan, John. "A Brit Rates Our Generals," *Civil War Times* XLVIII, no. 6 (Dec. 2009): 54–59.

Kelly, Dennis. "Atlanta Campaign. Mountains to Pass, A River to Cross: The Battle of Kennesaw Mountain and Related Actions from June 10 to July 9, 1864," *Blue & Gray Magazine* VI, no. 5 (June 1989): 8–30, 46–58.

Kendall, Drew J. "'Murder' at Malvern Hill," *Military History* 19, no. 3 (Aug. 2002): 42–48.

Krolick, Marshall D. "Gettysburg: The First Day, July 1, 1863," *Blue & Gray Magazine* V, no. 2 (November 1987): 8–20.

Leonard, Phillip A. B. "Forty-seven Days. Constant bombardment, life in bomb shelters, scarce food and water, and rapidly accumulating filth were the price of resistance for the resolute Confederate citizens of besieged Vicksburg, Mississippi," *Civil War Times Illustrated* XXXIV, no. 4 (Aug. 2000): 40–49, 68–69.

Levin, Kevin M., "Confederate Like Me: Rebels Who Brought Their Slaves to War Assumed a Shared Loyalty to the Confederate Cause—as Do Some History Revisionists Today," *The Civil War Monitor* 3, no. 1 (Spring 2013): 60–67, 78–79.

Liddell Hart, B. H. "Lee: A Psychological Problem," *Saturday Review* XI (December 15, 1934): 365ff.

———. "Why Lee Lost Gettysburg," *Saturday Review* XI (March 23, 1935): 561ff.

Lowe, David W. "Field Fortifications in the Civil War," *North & South* 4, no. 6 (Aug. 2001): 58–73.

Mackowski, Chris, and Kristopher D. White, "Second-Guessing Dick Ewell: Why Didn't the Confederate General Take Cemetery Hill on July 1, 1863?", *Civil War Times* 49, no. 4 (Aug. 2010): 34–41.

Mallock, Daniel, "Cleburne's Proposal," *North & South* 11, no 2 (Dec. 2008): 64–72.

McMurry, Richard M. "Atlanta Campaign. Rocky Face to the Dallas Line: The Battles of May 1864," *Blue & Gray Magazine* VI, no. 4 (April 1989): 10–23, 46–62.

McPherson, James M. "The Unheroic Hero," *The New York Review of Books* XLVI, no. 2 (February 4, 1999): 16–19.

Meyers, Christopher C. "'Two Generals Cannot Command This Army': John A. McClernand and the Politics of Command in Grant's Army of the Tennessee," *Columbiad: A Quarterly Review of the War Between the States* 2, no. 1 (Spring 1998): 27–41.

Miller, J. Michael. "Strike Them a Blow: Lee and Grant at the North Anna River," *Blue & Gray Magazine*, no. 4 (April 1993).

Mitchell, Joseph B. "Confederate Losses at Gettysburg: Debunking Livermore," *Blue & Gray Magazine* VI, no. 4 (April 1989): 38–40.

Morgan, Michael. "Digging to Victory," *America's Civil War* 16, no. 3 (July 2003): 22–29.

Nofi, Albert A. "Calculating Combatants," *North & South* 4, no. 2 (January 2001): 68–69.

Nolan, Alan T. "Demolishing the Myth: Evaluating Lee's Generalship," *North & South* 3, no. 5 (June 2000), 29–36.

Owens, Richard H. "An Astonishing Career," *Military Heritage* 3, no. 2 (Oct. 2001): 64–73.

Pitcaithley, Dwight T. "Secession of the Upper South: States Rights and Slavery," *North & South* 12, no. 1 (Feb. 2010): 14–19.

Popowski, Howard J. "'We've Met Once Before ... in Mexico'," *Blue & Gray Magazine* I, no. 6 (June–July 1984): 9–13.

Poulter, Keith. "Decision in the West: The Vicksburg Campaign, Part 1: The Entering Wedge," *North & South* 1, no. 2 (Jan. 1998): 18–25.

———. "Decision in the West: The Vicksburg Campaign, Part II: Running the Batteries," *North & South* 1, no. 3 (Feb. 1998): 68–75.

———. "Decision in the West: The Vicksburg Campaign, Part III," *North & South* 1, no. 4 (April 1998): 77–83.

———. "Stop Insulting Robert E. Lee!," *North & South* 1, no. 5 (1998): 6.

Rhea, Gordon C. "'Butcher' Grant and the Overland Campaign," *North & South* 4, no. 1 (Nov. 2000): 44–55.

———. "Cold Harbor: Anatomy of a Battle, "*North & South* 5, no. 2 (Feb. 2002): 40–62.

———. "Fellow Southerners!", *North & South* 13, no. 5 (Jan. 2012): 12–17.

———, Richard Rollins, Stephen Sears, and John Y. Simon. "What Was Wrong with the Army of the Potomac?," *North & South* 4, no. 3 (March 2001): 12–18.

Riggs, Derald T. "Commander in Chief Abe Lincoln," *America's Civil War* 13, no. 3 (July 2000): 34–40.

Rollins, Richard. "Robert E. Lee and the Hand of God," *North & South* 6, no. 2 (Feb. 2003): 13–25.

Roth, Dave. "Grierson's Raid: A Cavalry Raid at Its Best, April 17–May 2, 1863," *Blue & Gray Magazine* X, no. 5 (June 1993): 12–24, 48–65.

Smith, David M. "Too Little Too Late at Vicksburg," *America's Civil War* 13, no. 2 (May 2000): 38–44.

Strozier, Charles. "The Tragedy of Unconditional Surrender," *Military History Quarterly*, 2 (Spring 1990), 505–10.

Trudeau, Noah Andre. "Climax at Vicksburg," *North & South* 1, no. 5 (June 1998): 80–89.

———. "'A Frightful and Frightening Place'," *Civil War Times Illustrated* XXXVIII, no. 2, 42–56.

Ward, Andrew. "No Choice: You're a slave, the Yankees are coming, and your fate is 'refugeeing' with your master to god-knows-where," *America's Civil War* 21, no. 2 (May 2008).

Williams, T. Harry. "Freeman: Historian of the Civil War: An Appraisal," *Journal of Southern History* XXI (February 1955): 91–100.

Winschel, Terrence. "Grant's Beachhead for the Vicksburg Campaign: The Battle of Port Gibson, May 1, 1863," *Blue & Gray Magazine* XI, no. 3 (Feb. 1994): 8–22, 48–56.

———. "Grant's March Through Louisiana: 'The Highest Examples of Military Energy and Perseverance'," *Blue & Gray Magazine* XIII, no. 5 (June 1996): 8–22.

———. "The Siege of Vicksburg," *Blue & Gray Magazine* XX, no. 4 (Spring 2003): 6–24, 47–50.

———. "Vicksburg: 'Thank God. The Father of Waters again goes unvexed to the sea.'," *America's Civil War* 16, no. 3 (July 2003): 18–19.

Woodworth, Steven E. "The Army of the Tennessee and the Element of Military Success," *North & South* 6, no. 4 (May 2003): 44–55.

———. "Shiloh's Harsh Training Ground," *America's Civil War* 15, no. 2 (May 2002): 34–40.

Young, Alfred C., "Numbers and Losses in the Army of Northern Virginia," *North & South* 3, no. 3 (March 2000): 14–29.

Zentner, Joe, and Syrett, Mary. "Confederate Gibraltar," *Military History* 19, no. 6 (February 2003): 26–32, 73.

# INDEX